Race, Sex, and Social Order
in Early New Orleans

Early America: History, Context, Culture

Joyce E. Chaplin and Philip D. Morgan, Series Editors

Race, Sex, and Social Order in Early New Orleans

JENNIFER M. SPEAR

The Johns Hopkins University Press

Baltimore

© 2009 The Johns Hopkins University Press
All rights reserved. Published 2008
Printed in the United States of America on acid-free paper
2 4 6 8 9 7 5 3 1

The Johns Hopkins University Press
2715 North Charles Street
Baltimore, Maryland 21218-4363
www.press.jhu.edu

Library of Congress Cataloging-in-Publication Data

Spear, Jennifer M., 1967–
Race, sex, and social order in early New Orleans / Jennifer M. Spear.
p. cm.
Includes bibliographical references and index.
ISBN-13: 978-0-8018-8680-5 (hardcover : alk. paper)
ISBN-10: 0-8018-8680-5 (hardcover : alk. paper)
1. New Orleans (La.)—Social conditions. 2. New Orleans (La.)—
Race relations. 3. New Orleans (La.)—Social life and customs.
4. Racially mixed people—Louisiana—New Orleans—Social
conditions. 5. Racially mixed people—Louisiana—
New Orleans—History. I. Title.
HN80.N45.S64 2009
306.7089009763'35—dc22   2008027263

A catalog record for this book is available from the British Library.

*Special discounts are available for bulk purchases of this book. For more
information, please contact Special Sales at 410-516-6936 or
specialsales@press.jhu.edu.*

The Johns Hopkins University Press uses environmentally friendly
book materials, including recycled text paper that is composed of at
least 30 percent post-consumer waste, whenever possible. All of our
book papers are acid-free, and our jackets and covers are printed on
paper with recycled content.

To Thomas Spear and Joan Fiator

CONTENTS

ON GOOD FRIDAY, 1788, a devastating fire spread through New Orleans, eventually destroying three-quarters of the city's buildings. As the fire threatened his house, notary Pierre Pedesclaux ordered his children to save the notary registries in his possession. Pedesclaux's actions saved the records while his house burned to the ground. Without Pedesclaux's heroic efforts, and those of the parish priests who saved the sacramental records, as well as the continuing efforts of all the archivists since then, this book never could have been written. Hurricane Katrina underscored that without their efforts, we historians would have no histories to study. For their role in preserving New Orleans' early history, and facilitating my research, my foremost thanks goes to the staffs of the Archives of the Archdiocese of New Orleans (especially Dr. Charles Nolan and Dorenda Dupont), the New Orleans Notarial Archives (especially Howard Margot, who first told me the story of Pedesclaux and the fire), the Louisiana Division of the New Orleans Public Library (especially Greg Osborn), the Historic New Orleans Collection (particularly Mark Cave), the Manuscripts Department and the Louisiana Collection of the Howard-Tilton Memorial Library at Tulane University, Marie E. Windell at the Louisiana and Special Collections Department at the Earl K. Long Library, University of New Orleans, Katherine Nachod at the Tulane Law Library, the Archives of the Ursuline Nuns of New Orleans, and the Louisiana Historical Center at the Louisiana State Museum. Beyond the Crescent City, my thanks to the staffs at the Bancroft, Huntington, and John Carter Brown Libraries and the Mississippi Department of Archives and History in Jackson, Mississippi.

Research and a much needed sabbatical was financed by the Hellman Family Faculty Fund, the University of California at Berkeley's Faculty Development Program and the Committee on Research, the American Historical Association, the John Carter Brown Library, and the Huntington Library. My special thanks to Norman Fiering, former director of the John Carter Brown Library, for supporting my work since its early days as a dissertation. My research was greatly facilitated by the assistance provided by Clint Bruce, Nadia Lour, Kristenn Templeman, Bill Wagner, and especially Jacqueline Shine. For a place to live during my frequent and lengthy stays in New Orleans, I am indebted to Suzanne B. Dietzel and David Rae Morris who opened their home to me and, even more enjoyably, introduced me to the city's culinary and musical delights.

It has become commonplace to confess that one's work is not a solitary venture. Anyone who knows how I work knows how true this is for me. From my dissertation study group and committee to commentators and audiences at conferences and workshops to those who have had the patience to read through multiple versions as the book kept taking new form, I hope you will see some of your influences reflected in the following pages. Thanks to Robert Frame, Rachel Barrett Martin, Brett Mizelle, and Matt Mulcahy; Jean O'Brien-Kehoe (whose passion for colonial history first attracted me to this subject), David Roediger, Elaine Tyler May, Lisa Norling, and the late Susan Geiger; everyone from the University of Minnesota Early American History Workshop; all of the commentators and audiences who have sat through readings of my work, but especially Vaughan Baker, Ira Berlin, Patricia Cleary, Patricia Cooper, Judith Fossett, Franklin Knight, María-Elena Martinez, Simon Middleton, Mary Beth Norton, Sharon Salinger, Nancy Shoemaker, and Justin Wolfe. To the students in my seminars on colonialism, race, gender, and sexuality and readings in racial formation, my gratitude for allowing me to hash out some of my ideas and vent some of my bugaboos. Special thanks to Robin Einhorn, Linda Lewin, Mark Brilliant, Joyce Chaplin, Emily Clark, Sylvia Frey, and Jean O'Brien who read the entire manuscript at least once and always had encouraging words, as well as to Tarak Barkawi, Juliana Barr, Sharon Block and Kathy Brown, Margaret Chowning, Kirsten Fischer and Jennifer Morgan, Chris Grasso, Mark Healey, David Henkin, Martha Hodes, Kerwin Lee Klein, Laz Lima, Janet Moore Lindman and Michel Lise Tarter, Sue Peabody, Dan Richter, Peter Sahlins, John Wood Sweet, Tyler Stovall, Bill Taylor, and Richard Waller. Joyce Chaplin and Philip Morgan, the series editors of Early America: History, Context, Culture, and Robert J. Brugger at the Johns Hopkins University Press took on this project at a most auspicious moment, for which I am truly thankful. When revising finally became copy editing, Tom Spear, Robert Frame, and M.J. Devaney had the patience to cull extraneous examples and correct my dangling participles, thats and whichs, and awkward sentences. My work has benefited greatly from all these readings, but, as always, the blame for all remaining cumbersome and unpolished passages lies, of course, with me.

I especially want to thank the small but growing community of scholars working on early Louisiana. In 1992, Gwendolyn Midlo Hall and Dan Usner paved the way, insisting that the colonial history of the lower Mississippi River Valley was important in its own right and for what light it could shed on the rest of North America. I have benefited from conversations with Dan (whose comments on a very early draft of chapter 6 persuaded me to ground myself much more firmly in the practices of everyday life), Warren Billings, Virginia Meacham Gould, and the late Kimberly Hanger. Fellow members of the "Louisiana Mafia"—Ken Aslakson, Juliana Barr (honorary member, Texas branch), Emily Clark, Alecia Long, Sophie White, Diana Williams, and Mary Williams—generously shared their own research and findings with me and enlivened my own journey into old New Orleans.

And to those who did their best to distract me from that journey into the past, my deepest appreciation. Trips to old and New Mexico with Heather Spear and Juliana Barr, darts at the Albatross with Mark Brilliant and Robin Einhorn, and just sitting around the backyard with Madison and Rachel Barrett Martin forced me into the twenty-first century. To Sheila Spear, there are no words to express how much I owe her; she has encouraged and supported me in all I have done. I dedicate this book to Tom Spear, my father, for his editorial skills and, perhaps more importantly, his nervous anxiety, without which I never would have finished, and to Joan Fiator, my aunt, who died without having a chance to read this book, but not before she taught me that interracial families were about more than just race.

Race, Sex, and Social Order
in Early New Orleans

Introduction

In 1700, Pierre Le Moyne, sieur d'Iberville, sailed up the Mississippi River, gathering information about the territory he had just claimed as the French colony of Louisiana. When the expedition approached a Bayougoulas settlement, the villagers, according to André Pénicaut, "fled into the depths of the woods with their women and children." They were enticed back when a Biloxi Indian, a member of Iberville's troupe, convinced them that the Frenchmen "were good people." Returning with a calumet, the Bayougoulas welcomed the visitors, offering them the pipe and inviting them to eat. After ascertaining that their guests had had sufficient sustenance, the hosts asked Iberville "whether we would require as many women as there were men in our party," a gesture of hospitality among many southeastern Indians that was often misread by Europeans. Iberville politely refused this offer of female companionship, making "them understand that their skin—red and tanned [rouge et bazanée]—should not come close to that of the French, which was white [blanche]."[1]

Despite his rejection of Bayougoulas women, however, Iberville realized the benefits, with respect to the practical matter of establishing a colony, of encouraging "the French who will settle in this country to marry Indian girls." Before setting out for Louisiana, he had requested and received permission from Louis XIV to implement just such a policy.[2] Iberville's use of skin color to oppose nonmarital sex between French men and Indian women at the same time that he advocated intercultural marriage as state policy encapsulates the major themes of this book: the tensions between ideology and practice that bedeviled Europeans as they set out to colonize North America, the centrality of sex in the establishment of those colonies, and the justificatory role that racial ideologies played in everything.

By the time the first colonizers arrived in Louisiana at the turn of the eighteenth century, Europeans had been thinking and writing about Indians and Africans for over two hundred years. In a rich and well-developed literature, scholars have analyzed how, as Europeans found themselves increasingly involved in trans-Atlantic ventures that depended on the exploitation of Africans and Indians, European ideas about differences between themselves and those who would become colonized others developed. As Europeans hungered for Indian lands and African labor, they transformed their ethnocentric notions of cultural difference into ideas of immutable, inheritable, racial difference.[3] These ideas—what Europeans thought they knew about Africans and Indians—formed what one historian has called an "image archive," textual and visual representations that circulated throughout Europe from the fifteenth century on, crossing national and linguistic boundaries with ease.[4]

Yet, as Iberville's contradictory positions exemplify, European ideas about Africans and Indians did not necessarily determine colonial policies involving actual Africans and Indians. Rather, as Europeans conceptualized how these groups would fit, or not, into new colonial societies, they drew selectively on the image archive in order to identify and signify differences that were then used to organize and justify social hierarchies and determine access to economic, political, and social rights.[5] It was this process—the politics of race, or its codification into law and social order, rather than images and descriptions that floated through the pages of Christopher Columbus's letters, Richard Hakluyt's collections of travel narratives, or Diderot's *Encyclopédie*—that gave form to the world within which colonial North Americans, indigenous and immigrant, lived.[6] But even though focusing on the politics of race grounds disembodied, floating discourses in historical and geographic specificity and reveals how tangible circumstances and needs shaped racial formation, this approach still overemphasizes the power of elite discourses and, more importantly, distorts our understanding of the power of race in fashioning everyday life. Just as colonial elites drew selectively on widespread ideas and adapted them to local concerns, colonial inhabitants too carefully drew on elite ideas about race as codified in law, choosing when to utilize those ideas, when to reject them, and when to ignore them all together.

It is precisely these daily decisions made within structural constraints that produced the concrete historical circumstances that made race real, and it is only by bringing the politics and practices of race into the same analytic frame that we can fully understand this process. Consequently, this book operates simultaneously on two levels. First, using laws, official proclamations, and official and private correspondence, it examines how those with political power wrote race into the social order. Second, it examines how New Orleanians, of all ancestries and qualities, responded to elite efforts by uncovering their everyday practices as revealed in court cases, sacramental registries, and notarial records.[7] The result is a picture of racial formation as a long and contested process, involving individuals on both sides of the Atlantic, from the officials who sought to create new societies in the Americas to the enslaved women who sought freedom and security for themselves and their children.[8] All made choices that were constrained by the decisions made by others, and all contributed to the developing racial order.

To understand how race was lived, as opposed to thought about, we need histories that are grounded in space and time. But what can we learn from the history of New Orleans, an exotic city in a region scholars have long dismissed as peculiar, exceptional, and peripheral to the main story of North American colonization (until 1803, that is, when it suddenly became central to Jeffersonian democracy and manifest destiny)?[9] Until the mid-1970s, colonial American history was, almost exclusively, the history of New England. A region blessed with rich archival sources, New England's supremacy was, in part, a legacy of the early nineteenth century, when the descendants of Plymouth trumped those of Jamestown in claiming center stage in the new nation's history. In doing so, they successfully defined slavery and racism as exceptions to the American story.[10] But these issues would not go away, and by the 1980s the Chesapeake was taking its turn in the spotlight, while the Carolinas were poking in from offstage. This scholarship demonstrated that New England, despite its significant contributions to the "American mind," stood apart from the more common experience of Anglo-American colonial development typified by instability, heterogeneity, and, most importantly, slavery and race.[11]

At the same time, colonial historians stepped up their challenges to the notion of their field as the prehistory of the United States and began looking beyond the English seaboard colonies. At first, they looked toward the Caribbean and the larger Atlantic World, uncovering the political, economic, and cultural connections that existed not just between the colonies and their metropole but also among the colonies themselves.[12] The Atlantic World has proven itself a useful unit of analysis for many questions, especially those involving the movement of peoples, goods, and ideas among the ocean's four continents. Studies of slavery and race in particular have fit well within this transoceanic approach, in part because it was built on earlier studies in the trans-Atlantic slave trade and comparative slavery.[13] But the Atlantic World approach has also discouraged other lines of inquiry. It has been difficult to construct a truly Atlantic world that crosses boundaries drawn by older imperial history, and Atlanticists have generally struggled to incorporate Indians as active participants in the making of that world even as decisions made in Indian country greatly shaped the development of colonies on the continent's margins.[14]

But peoples, goods, and ideas were not constrained within monolingual spheres. Nor were these movements simply oceanic. More recently, some historians have begun to focus inward toward North America writ large without returning to the earlier isolationist treatment of individual colonies. Many continentalists, for lack of a better term, have been particularly concerned with including the histories of non-English regions of habitation, both indigenous and immigrant, in order to reclaim the full diversity of early North America.[15] These regions, such as northern New Spain (otherwise known as the Spanish Southwest) and New France, have had their own historiographies, but these have often run on parallel tracks to the scholarship on the English North American colonies. Historians of eighteenth-century Louisiana, for instance, have to some extent marginalized themselves by focusing exclusively on the French or Spanish eras, emphasizing their own exceptionalist narratives and failing to engage with the questions driving mainstream colonial scholarship.[16]

Two books published in 1992 sought to rectify Louisiana's exclusion by taking on the breadth of its colonial history and addressing issues central to the colonization of North America in general. Daniel H. Usner Jr.'s *Indians, Settlers, and Slaves* examined the economic and cultural exchanges that bound natives and newcomers together in the establishment of American colonies, while Gwendolyn Midlo Hall's *Africans in Colonial Louisiana* traced the development of plantation slavery and African American culture.[17] Both contributed to our understanding of the range of colonial experiences and possibilities, forcing us to resituate English experiences within a larger context. Usner and Hall focus on quite different aspects of the encounters among inhabitants of the lower Mississippi River Valley, but they agree that these encounters were characterized by relative fluidity until the last quarter of the eighteenth century. At that point, local economic and political developments as well as revolutionary events taking place throughout the Atlantic led Louisiana officials and elites to impose a far more strict racial hierarchy. Although the new racial order was more rigid than the old one, it did include a distinct category of free people of color, unlike the biracial systems that dominated the Anglo-American regions by this time.[18]

Analyzing the development of colonial racial orders through the lens of intimacy, on one level, slightly modifies the chronology for New Orleans proposed by Usner and Hall but, on another, results in a more dramatic challenge to stories of racial formation in both New Orleans and colonial Anglo-America. Regulating sex was the principal way in which officials tried to define and maintain discrete racial groups, and therefore the true codification of the tripartite system with which New Orleans would be so closely identified did not happen until 1808 when the Anglo-Louisiana legislature required whites, free people of color, and slaves to find endogamous marriage partners. Thus, in the political narrative, race came to trump all other criteria of differentiation by the early nineteenth century. This is a narrative marked by quick transitions from one era to another, but it is one that is also tempered by another chronology in which intimate practices exhibited far more continuity from one political era to another and in which other criteria of identity—class, status, religion, language—continued to play significant roles well into the nineteenth century.[19] Evidence of sexual practices reveal that official desires for racial endogamy were slow to be accepted by all New Orleanians, who continued to form families across color lines well into the antebellum era. Accumulating evidence of ongoing relationships in the eastern seaboard states implies Anglo-American authorities' efforts to impose their concepts of racial order were met with similar limited success.[20] Together, these findings suggest that it is time to put aside the question of when ethnocentrism became racism and instead to investigate the ways in which race did and did not determine historical experiences.

All colonial authorities, whether English, French, or Spanish, tried to police sexual practices in their efforts to codify race, but the resulting social orders were shaped by geopolitical, demographic, economic, and cultural circumstances specific to each colony, and therefore they could be quite distinct from each other. In New Orleans, manumission was far more common than in the Anglo societies to its north and east, free people of color were more numerous, and racially exogamous relationships were more publicly acknowledged.[21] It was indeed the gens de couleur libre who were at the heart of New Orleans' racial order. They embodied the continued importance of status alongside ancestry in determining racial identity, and it was their presence that forced Anglo-Louisianan authorities to formalize a tripartite system. Numbering over thirteen hundred, about one-fifth of the city's population, at the time of the Louisiana Purchase, the gens de couleur libre were certainly the most significant free population of African descent at the time, but they were not the only one.[22] Charleston, the Anglo-American city to which New Orleans is most often compared, also had a significant population of free people of color, almost a thousand in 1800, although that was just 5 percent of the city's population. Free people of color in both cities were predominately creoles, in contrast to the increasing numbers of African-born among each region's slaves, and many claimed at least one European ancestor.[23] New Orleans' gens de couleur libre, unlike their counterparts in Charleston and elsewhere in the United States, enjoyed far more security in their legal and economic rights, although they were denied important political rights.

Despite its differences from other North American colonial cities, New Orleans is ideal for analyzing colonial racial formation. First of all, it sat at the intersection of a wide-ranging trading economy and one based on plantation slavery. European colonizers' desire to exploit resources and peoples, whether through trade or slavery, shaped their conceptions about who should be a part of the colonial order and how. But trade and slavery engendered quite distinctive intercultural relationships, so the history of New Orleans reveals the impact of different political economies on racial formation as well as the differential incorporation of Native Americans and Africans/African Americans. In addition, its succession of political regimes facilitates a comparative approach that allows one to examine how different cultural, legal, and religious practices shaped race within a single locale where other factors, such as population and geography, remained constant.[24] This experience of adapting to successive political and legal regimes, far from being unique to New Orleanians, was a fact of life for many inhabitants of North America, from indigenous peoples throughout the continent to colonial subjects from Quebec to St. Augustine, New Amsterdam to San Francisco.[25] Finally, New Orleans' historical documents, particularly its notarial and sacramental records, are rich sources for exploring the day-to-day interactions of all New Orleanians, providing a rare opportunity to examine race beyond its articulation in tracts and legal codes authored by elite Euro-American men.

These sources enable us to move beyond the image archive and focus instead on the intersection and disjuncture between the public politics and daily lived realities of race. The presence of the gens de couleur libre highlights the two areas that were particularly important at both levels: manumission and racially exogamous sex. Because racial formation in early America took place in conjunction with the development of chattel slavery, manumission played a significant role in the construction of specific racial orders.[26] If manumission was restricted, colonial authorities were able to equate specific ancestries with enslavement; more liberal access to manumission made this equation difficult to sustain and demonstrated that enslavement was not necessarily an immutable status. In addition, manumission raised questions about how the formerly enslaved would be incorporated into the social order: whether they would be treated as full members of free society, relegated to the margins, or left to form their own distinct social strata. While manumission legislation contributed to the development of racial orders, actual manumission acts shaped the everyday experiences of race.

Access to manumission fluctuated during New Orleans' first century in ways that significantly molded the evolution of the city's racial order. Although manumission was legally possible in French Louisiana, slave labor was a scarce commodity, and each individual emancipation required government approval. As a consequence, less than 150 slaves received their freedom between 1724 and 1769, and the

number of free people of color remained negligible. When Spanish officials assumed formal control over the colony in 1769, they introduced a far more liberalized manumission policy that slaves, their free relatives, and owners quickly exploited. More than two thousand slaves were manumitted during the four decades
of Spanish rule, and so gens de couleur libre became a significant proportion of
New Orleans' population by the end of the century. Manumission was dramatically curtailed following the Louisiana Purchase, a move that simultaneously restricted the growth of the gens de couleur libre population and served to further
distinguish them from slaves since, by the early antebellum period, most gens de
couleur libre were more than a generation removed from enslavement.

Even more than manumission, sex is a revealing focal point because it was
through sex that race was defined, maintained, and undermined in ideology and
on the ground.[27] On the one hand, sexual practices and mores contributed to European explanations of human difference. On the other, it was through the regulation of sexual relationships that officials and elites envisioned creating order out of
disorder and defined who would be included and excluded from colonial society
and how. Officials and some elite Euro-Louisianans attempted to regulate intimacy along racial lines by denying racially exogamous relationships the legality of
marriage, thus rendering them illicit and their offspring illegitimate. At the same
time, such relationships produced offspring who transgressed the very racial boundaries that officials were attempting to define and regulate.

Marriage regulations show most clearly how political authorities imagined the
social order. The French Code Noir envisioned a society composed predominately
of free whites and enslaved blacks. There would be just a few ex-slaves rewarded
with freedom for their loyalty, but no one of mixed ancestry. Spanish officials'
idealized society was arranged along a racialized continuum, from black to white,
in which freedom, wealth, family status, and loyalty to the regime could help one
move up the hierarchy. Marriage, in this ideal, would take place between social
equals. Authorities in Anglo-Louisiana attempted to fix individuals in one of three
groups by requiring each to marry endogamously and by solidifying the boundaries between enslavement and freedom and between whites and free people of color,
thus bringing New Orleans' tripartite racial order into being.

Sexual relationships themselves also had contradictory effects in everyday practice. As elsewhere in the Americas, most were exploitative. Using coercive sex to
subordinate women of color, Euro-American men violently reinforced the sexual,
gendered, and racial orders of colonial societies.[28] Given these circumstances,
could women of color in these societies ever truly consent to sexual relationships
with Euro-American men? Some have argued that the sharply contrasting power

positions of such men and women makes even asking this question suspect.[29] Others counter, however, that dismissing all relationships between white men and women of color as exploitative revictimizes these women and denies them any role in shaping their own lives, albeit within the highly constrained circumstances of colonization, slavery, patriarchy, and white supremacy.[30] This disagreement makes clear that we must attend to both the social conditions within which sexual relationships took place and the particular circumstances of individual relationships.

If coerced sex brutally reminded enslaved or colonized women of their subordination, relationships that became stable, long-term unions show that some rejected official efforts to dictate their intimate choices.[31] By forming families with women of color, Euro-Louisianan men undermined efforts that sought to define those women as unsuitable marriage partners for them. When they recognized, manumitted if necessary, and transmitted patrimony to their children, they similarly destabilized efforts to concentrate property in the hands of a Euro-Louisianan elite. For women of color, these relationships offered opportunities for freedom and economic security.[32] At the same time, to take a white man as a sexual partner was fraught with peril, given the possibility of violence and the lack of the benefits and protections of legal marriage. Still, significant numbers of enslaved women did achieve freedom for themselves and their children in this manner, although some waited years if not decades for freedom, and others saw their children freed as their consorts left them in slavery.

The struggle for these women was not over once they had secured freedom for themselves and formed households with their Euro-Louisianan consorts, as these families often found themselves the subject of virulent diatribes issued by officials and elites. But the latter's condemnation of interracial families was belied by their failure to take action against them and contrasts sharply with their reactions to interracial interactions among men in public spaces. Because officials linked a wide range of social interactions among men—at taverns, in gambling halls, and on plantations—with violence, petty criminality, and even anticolonial rebellions, they expended far more energy trying to police these heterogeneous male gatherings than racially exogamous families.[33] The former posed a considerable threat to the public tranquility of the city, but the latter were generally contained within intimate domestic spaces and, despite explicit official hostility, were allowed to flourish behind doors.[34]

HOME TO SEVERAL SMALL Indian nations in the sixteenth century, the area that would become New Orleans was first claimed by Spain in 1539 when Hernando de Soto asserted Spanish sovereignty over the entire southeastern region of North

America. Although Spain would not effectively establish its sovereignty outside of St. Augustine and a few other scattered settlements in Florida, Soto's entrada had significant consequences for southeastern native peoples as it introduced them to European firepower, ferocity, duplicity, manufactured goods, animals, and, most importantly, diseases that drastically reduced their numbers in the century and a half that passed before René-Robert Cavelier, sieur de La Salle, claimed the same region for France in 1682, naming it Louisiana in honor of Louis XIV.[35] Realizing that effective occupation was the surest way to assert sovereignty vis-à-vis competing European nations, France sent an expedition led by Canadian-born Pierre Le Moyne, sieur d'Iberville, that successfully established France's first permanent encampment at Fort Maurepas on Biloxi Bay in 1699.

Louisiana's early population was, like that of most other American colonies, primarily male: it encompassed sailors and soldiers from France as well as Canadian coureurs de bois who had already been expanding their trade routes out from the Great Lakes, through the Illinois country, and into the lower Mississippi River Valley. During the first two decades of the eighteenth century, colonial officials struggled to create an agricultural colony that could sustain itself and the military force needed to protect it. But many colonists refused to work the land, preferring to make a living through Indian trade and hunting. What they needed to settle, authorities decided, were wives. Initially, religious and secular officials debated the feasibility of encouraging marriages between French or Canadian men and Indian women. Some contended that French-Indian marriages would help populate and stabilize the colony with little financial investment from the Crown, but others viewed the relationships themselves as a hindrance to the establishment of a French-dominated agricultural colony. Participants in this debate drew on different elements of Atlantic ideologies about cultural differences to support their positions. Those who supported these marriages argued that differences between the French and Louisiana's native peoples were fluid and malleable, while those who opposed them saw them as innate and fixed. Chapter 1 analyzes this debate within the context of French and Indian gender roles, marital and inheritance practices, and sexual mores.

The question of French-Indian marriage was most pressing during the earliest years of the colony's growth when its political economy was based on trade and subsistence agriculture. By the late 1710s, however, slavery emerged as a competing form of economic and social organization.[36] In response to the local demand for slaves, thousands of Africans were forcibly sent to Louisiana and quickly became a majority of the colonial population. Chapter 2 focuses on metropolitan and local responses to this development, centering on an analysis of the metropolitan-authored

1724 Code Noir and its implementation, or lack thereof, by local authorities in Louisiana. Chapter 3 then shifts the focus to everyday practices of manumission and racial exogamy in French New Orleans.

By 1762, France was eager to get rid of Louisiana, as it was both difficult to maintain and a constant drain on Crown finances. In gratitude for Spanish support during the Seven Years' War, Louis XV handed the colony over to his cousin Carlos III. When Spanish officials assumed formal control over the colony in 1769, they brought with them laws regarding slavery that had been developed elsewhere in the Spanish Americas, which they then tried to impose on a sometimes hostile French elite. Particularly important was a new legal apparatus that liberalized manumission, resulting in the rapid growth of the number of free people of African ancestry during the last third of the eighteenth century. Local elites did not let these challenges to their public and domestic authority go uncontested, however. Chapter 4 examines the fault lines between Spanish bureaucrats and local elites as they struggled over the meanings of slavery and freedom and illustrates how enslaved and free people of African ancestry were able to take advantage of these conflicts in their frequent and persistent efforts to gain legal freedom.

In addition to new laws governing slavery, Spanish rule also introduced economic and cultural practices that had contradictory effects on the development of New Orleans' racial order. Spanish inheritance practices, especially the acceptance of natural children and their right to inherit from their unmarried parents, influenced the social tolerance of racially exogamous families. At the same time however, limpieza de sangre held that African and Indian ancestry stained a family's lineage, making them ineligible for certain honors and privileges, and thus was antagonistic to such families. Chapter 5 examines these simultaneous developments, analyzing the limpieza de sangre suits alongside the growing numbers of publicly recognized racially exogamous families.

At the same time that Limpieza de sangre suits offered Euro-Louisianans the opportunity to articulate a concept of their "whiteness," Spanish law also allowed people of color to conceptualize their own racialized identities as they sought to renegotiate their positions within the city's racial order. Chapter 6 focuses on two case studies of racial renegotiation. The first involves several slaves who sued for freedom, claiming that as the descendants of Indian women, their enslavement was illegal under Spanish law. Such suits engendered a conflict between slaves and their owners about the meaning of Indianness and its relationship to African ancestry. In the second case, in contrast to the first in which slaves sought to identify themselves as mestizos to gain freedom, a woman identified herself as a mestiza in order to have her daughter racially classified as white. Together these examples illustrate the different ways in which Indian and African ancestry had been racialized by the end of the eighteenth century. Whereas those of African descent were essential to colonial society, Indians were seen as existing outside of it. Those of Indian descent living within colonial society were perceived as something else but not necessarily as a person of color.

The cases examined in chapter 6 highlight the relative fluidity of Spanish New Orleans' racial order; the final chapter analyzes how this system was rigidified and codified in the aftermath of the Louisiana Purchase. When Anglo-Americans arrived to govern New Orleans, they brought with them a conception of race that sought to equate any degree of blackness with enslavement and to reserve freedom for whites. Racial denigration and harassment increased as thousands of Anglo-American and European immigrants flooded the city and as politicians in Anglo-Louisiana successfully made the boundary between slavery and freedom far less porous than it had been in the colonial era. But their efforts to force the city's racial order into a more familiar black-white mode were defeated by the legacies of eighteenth-century New Orleans, especially by those who were becoming known as the gens de couleur libre, who struggled to protect the rights they had gained under Spanish rule.

The circumstances that forced Anglo-American authorities to codify a tripartite racial system were the result of New Orleans' political, demographic, economic, and cultural history. New Orleans was the marginal capital of a peripheral colony that mattered to both France and Spain mostly for its strategic value in stemming British and later Anglo-American expansion across the continent. Thus both nations made only erratic efforts to develop the territory as a settler colony, and its population remained small. In 1785, there were just over fifteen thousand colonial inhabitants in the greater New Orleans area. Stretching from English Turn, about fifteen miles downriver from the city proper, to Cannes Brûlées, about ten miles upriver, this region was the colony's principal plantation district and the principal focus of this study.[37]

While the size of the population and its concentration along the Mississippi River facilitated daily encounters among the region's diverse inhabitants, its immigration history and demographic profile encouraged intimate interactions. The greatest concentration of voluntary and involuntary immigrants arrived in the late 1710s and early 1720s. Mortality rates were high for Europeans and Africans alike, but both populations began slowly to grow from natural increase by midcentury so that the creolization process took place without the constant inflow of new immigrants until the 1780s.[38] Race and sex ratios also facilitated, although they did not determine, interracial sex. The region's native population outnumbered

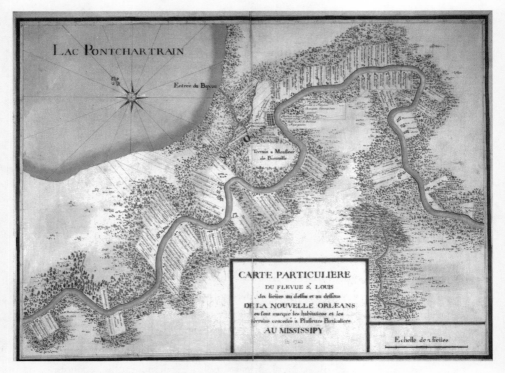

New Orleans' plantation belt stretched from Cannes Brûlées to English Turn. The long-lot land concessions that were typical of French North America meant that most plantation residents had easy water access to the city proper. Carte particuliere du fleuve St. Louis . . . , ca. 1723. Courtesy of Edward Ayers Manuscripts, Newberry Library, Chicago, Ill.

its immigrant inhabitants until the mid-eighteenth century, and Africans outnumbered Europeans as early as the mid-1720s and continued to do so for most of the century. Among Afro-Louisianans and Indians who lived within colonial society, there was a surplus of women; conversely, among Euro-Louisianans, men outnumbered women.[39]

Although the New Orleans region had a slave majority within a decade of its founding and slave labor was an integral part of its economy, colonists failed to develop any highly profitable exports until the very end of the eighteenth century. Before then, the colony's political economy was based on the production of staple and subsistence crops in combination with what Usner called a frontier exchange economy. Slaves were not solely identified with agricultural labor but rather could be found in almost every sector of the economy, including trade, which allowed some to move throughout the vast territory of Louisiana.[40] Until the last decades of the eighteenth century, New Orleans exhibited the distinguishing characteristics of a slaveowning rather than a slave society, including relatively accessible manumission, a more ambiguous status for ex-slaves, and somewhat more relaxed relations among its diverse inhabitants (although slavery itself was not necessarily any less brutal there than it was in a slave society).[41]

The colony's political and economic marginality meant that all its inhabitants were drawn into mutually dependent economic relations, while its small, concentrated population meant that relationships were mostly face-to-face.[42] Catholicism also brought New Orleans' residents together within a single church. Although French and Spanish priests in Louisiana expended less effort in converting Indians and Africans than they did elsewhere in the Americas, significant numbers of both groups were baptized.[43] As a result, compadrazgo came to link New Orleanians of European, African, and Indian ancestry, slave and free, through the creation of fictive kinship ties that significantly integrated non-Europeans into a spiritual community with Europeans. Still, Catholicism did not ameliorate the condition of slaves, as Frank Tannenbaum argued in his classic overview of the differences among Spanish, British, and French slave systems throughout the Americas.[44] Catholic or Protestant, slaveowners' treatment of slaves was shaped far more by economics and demographics than by particular theologies, just as local conditions had a greater influence on daily encounters among heterogeneous inhabitants than elite racial discourses.

French and Spanish legal regimes—Tannenbaum's other principal explanation of the differences among slave regimes—had contradictory influences on slavery and race relations in colonial New Orleans. Both colonial powers introduced slave codes, written in distant metropoles, that contained some provisions to ameliorate slavery, but local officials mostly ignored these, and therefore they did little to lessen the brutality of the slave experience. Yet French and Spanish legal regimes both contained mechanisms for manumission and delineated clear legal statuses for ex-slaves and other free people of non-European ancestry, unlike in most parts of British North America where the status of these people was ambiguous. The transition to Spanish rule solidified slaves' access to freedom through coartación, which allowed slaves to buy their freedom even from unwilling owners, a right that slaves were quick to exploit and one that was responsible for half of all manumissions in Spanish New Orleans. Spain also enhanced the economic and legal status of free people of color, overturning an earlier ban on their ability to inherit property from Euro-Louisianans and formalizing militia units that granted certain men of color the same legal privileges as their white counterparts.[45]

Political marginality, a black majority, slow economic development, and French and Spanish religious and legal regimes all combined to create the conditions conducive to the formation of a racial order that tolerated racially exogamous families and created a crucial niche for free people of color. Within the framework created by these structural factors, the actions that individual New Orleanians took—slaveowners who manumitted their slaves, judges who upheld slaves' freedom suits, Euro-Louisianan men who formed families with women of color, and, most importantly, slaves and free people of color themselves who fought for freedom and security in a society biased against them—gave practical meaning to abstract legal categories and helped to mold New Orleans' racial order. Only by attending to their actions can we evaluate the power of race in early America.

The presence and at times toleration of racially exogamous families does not mean that there was no racial discrimination or that race had not become a crucial element of the social order by the end of the eighteenth century.[46] Rather, their existence demonstrates that, for some New Orleanians at least, race was not always the most important factor affecting their decisions about with whom to form families, decisions that were also influenced by legal status, quality (a word both the French and Spanish used to encapsulate socioeconomic status and character, in addition to ancestry), religion, and culture.

It is not that race did not matter by the end of the colonial era. To a great extent it did determine identity, legal status, rights, privileges, and obligations as well as influence everyday interactions. But it might not have mattered as much as we think it did. In their laudable efforts to write race into the center of American history, historians have sometimes overemphasized its explanatory power.[47] Rather than rigidly determining status, economic opportunities, residence, and even the most intimate decisions, race was treated by early Americans as one obstacle among other everyday realities around which they negotiated their lives.

Notes about Language

In this study of racial formation, I have taken care not to impose languages of race from later eras onto the eighteenth century.[48] I do not use "miscegenation," a word that was coined in 1863 to define "the mixture of two or more races" that would inevitably lead to "the dark races . . . absorb[ing] the white."[49] Eighteenth-century New Orleanians had no single word or phrase to describe sexual relationships and families that crossed perceived racial boundaries, suggesting that they did not yet think of them as a category apart.[50] In addition, not all such relationships and families engendered the same response, so I generally specify both the participants (for instance, Indian women and French men) and the type of relationships (marital or nonmarital) at issue. I do occasionally use "interracial," as an adjective modifying sex and families, but I prefer "racially exogamous" because it stresses that social rules defined appropriate marriage and sexual partners and at the same time provides a shorthand way to refer to sexual relationships that took place between people who were perceived to belong to different racially defined social groups.

Before the very end of the eighteenth century, New Orleanians also used no single phrase to refer to those who would become known as the gens de couleur libre. French and Spanish authors employed a variety of phrases to capture this group, including "affranchis," "nègres/negros libres" and "mulâtres/mulatos libres," and "sang-mêlé." I have tried to remain close to the language of the time, reserving "gens de couleur libre" for the very late colonial and Anglo-American eras, but occasionally I have relied on terms such as "Afro-Louisianan," "people of African ancestry," and, more generally, "people of color," to stress nonwhite ancestry, when grouping together Indians, nègres/negros, mulâtres/mulatos, quarterons/cuarteróns, métis/mestizos, and the like.[51]

If I assign a racial label to an individual, I have taken this information directly from the documentary sources. During the last third of the eighteenth century, Spanish racial terms were used in the censuses, notary and court records, and sacramental registries whether or not the authors of the documents and the subjects they described were Spanish or French speakers. Since, as I demonstrate in chapter 6, individuals were frequently marked with different racial labels in documents recorded at different points in their lives, it is impossible to ascertain with confidence what these individuals were called outside of the notary's office, court, or church, whether they were described with Spanish or French terms or racial labels at all.[52] Thus, I have left all labels in the language of the documents. The same is true for proper names. That is, I have not assumed that someone named Pedro was actually called Pierre unless it is clear (usually indicated by his or her signature) that this was the case; so Francophone New Orleanians often appear in the text by the Spanish variant of their name. For the sake of consistency, however, I have silently corrected variations in proper names when they appear in both French and Spanish language sources, using the variant that either appears to be the individual's own preference or the one that appears most frequently.

Indians living within colonial settlements, mostly enslaved but occasionally free, were rarely identified as belonging to a particular nation. I have followed suit, using "sauvage" and "indio," as contemporaries did, or "Indian." Euro-Louisianans, those perceived as having no African or Indian ancestry, almost always went unmarked in the documentary record, although "blanc" or "blanco" was used as a group label, and some individual men were racially marked as white, especially at the baptisms of their nonwhite children. I realize that leaving these individuals unraced perpetuates the notion that white was the norm from which others deviated, yet that is precisely how census takers, priests, notaries, and other officials used these labels. In addition, we cannot assume that those who went unmarked in fact had only European ancestry. At times, this makes for a convoluted reading but one, I hope, that demonstrates just how race was used in everyday practice in early New Orleans.

CHAPTER ONE

Indian Women, French Women, and the Regulation of Sex

IN MARCH 1745, a dying Charles Egron dit Lamothe appeared before the New Orleans curé, Father Dagobert, to make a will. Born in Quebec in 1677, Egron had arrived in Louisiana with founder Pierre Le Moyne, sieur d'Iberville, in 1700 and had lived in various French settlements along the Gulf Coast, eventually settling in Mobile. Like many of his fellow male colonists—whether from Canada or France—Egron established a household with an Indian woman, Françoise, who may have at one point been his slave; unlike most others, however, Egron married Françoise and it was to her and their two children that he sought to leave his property. Consisting of a habitation in Mobile, some cattle, and a few slaves, Egron's property was to be divided, with one half going to Françoise, "his wife and Legitimate spouse," and the other to Marie Magdeleine and Charles, the children "from his legitimate marriage." In confirming the will, the Superior Council followed metropolitan practice by assigning the minor Charles a tutor to look after his interests. But it also followed local practice by appointing a curator for Françoise, who as an Indian woman was deemed incompetent to manage her own interests.[1]

The seemingly intimate decisions that men like Egron made—with whom to establish a household, to marry, and to have children and to whom to leave one's property—were in fact matters of great interest to colonial and metropolitan authorities. Authorities struggled, as the French began to colonize Louisiana in the early eighteenth century, to create a settler colony that would anchor French sovereignty over a vast area. They needed to establish small but stable settlements that were clearly under French control, a difficult endeavor when immigration was limited, often entailing unwilling colonists who sought to return to France as soon as possible and others who preferred to roam the colony seeking profits from furs rather than settling and engaging in sustainable agriculture. As the authorities saw it, the solution to their problems was marriage. It was only through the reproduction of

French social institutions, particularly marriage and family, that the colony could be established on a secure enough footing to become economically self-sufficient and no longer fiscally burdensome to the metropole. As Commissaire Ordonnateur Jean-Baptiste Martin d'Artaguiette wrote in 1710 to Louis Phélypeaux, comte de Pontchartrain, the minister of the marine, "There are here . . . young men and soldiers who are in a position to undertake farms; it is necessary for them to have wives. I know only this one way to settle them."[2]

Although secular and religious authorities alike agreed that marriage—as a relationship legitimated by church and state—was central to family, household, and social formation, and thus to colonial development, they disagreed about who would make suitable brides for French male colonists. The nature and contours of this disagreement can be seen most clearly in a decade-long debate between Henri Roulleaux de La Vente, the curé at Mobile, and Jean-Baptiste Le Moyne, sieur de Bienville, governor of Louisiana for much of the colony's French period.[3] Given the lack of French women in the colony and his aversion to nonmarital relationships between French men and Indian women, La Vente engaged in a campaign to legitimate these relationships. In doing so, he was advocating an older official policy of Frenchification in New France that had been sanctioned at the highest administrative levels, a policy that sought to Christianize and "civilize" native women, who would then marry French men, thus colonizing the vast regions of French North America with a limited number of metropolitan French bodies. Bienville and other secular colonial administrators, however, saw Indian-French relationships turning into marriages as itself detrimental to colonial development. Although they were not unconcerned with "concubinage among the coureurs de bois and soldiers" with Indian women, these secular authorities believed that only marriage to French women would facilitate their goals.[4]

As they argued, La Vente, Bienville, and others characterized Indian women, French men, and the influence of marriage in ways that bolstered their own points of view. While La Vente perceived differences between Indians and French as fluid and mutable, Bienville saw Indians as fixed in their ways, even as he feared that French men might become like Indians. Despite disagreements, secular and religious officials ultimately agreed that the most suitable brides were indeed French women, who were then represented as the colony's saviors. The entire episode, lasting through the 1720s, reveals how fundamental the regulation of sex and marriage was to establishing a successful colony and how constructions of race were embedded in this process, as both proponents and opponents of Indian-French marriages selectively drew on existing discourses of difference.

A Colony of a Colony?

Louisiana developed as an extension of New France, and especially during its first two decades, its economic and social development must be seen in light of its connections to New France. French explorations of the Mississippi River Valley began in New France, many of lower Louisiana's earliest colonizers were Canadian-born, and its economy, like that of New France, combined trade and subsistence agriculture. When Jesuit priest Jacques Marquette and explorer Louis Jolliet worked their way down the Mississippi River in 1672, they were seeking lands in which they might find new Indians to convert and more fur-bearing animals to trap. Although Marquette and Jolliet only made it as far as the Arkansas River before turning back, another Canadian-based explorer did make it to the mouth of the Mississippi River ten years later. When he reached the Gulf Coast in 1682, René-Robert Cavelier, sieur de La Salle, claimed all the lands drained by the Mississippi River for France.[5]

Two years later, La Salle set forth to colonize the region, accompanied by more than 250 sailors, soldiers, and laborers and just a handful of women. Unfortunately, the expedition was beset by dissension and misfortune—one ship carrying important provisions and many crewmembers were lost to Spanish privateers near Santo Domingo—and La Salle overshot the mouth of the Mississippi River, landing at Matagorda Bay near present-day Galveston, Texas, in February 1685. Within two years, La Salle's colony had disintegrated and he himself had been killed by some of his more disgruntled colonists.[6] France's efforts to effectively occupy the region, thus forestalling other European nations from claiming it, would have to wait until 1699. It was then that Canadian-born Iberville and his brother Bienville successfully established the first permanent French encampment at Fort Maurepas near present-day Biloxi, Mississippi.

From the French perspective, Louisiana could not have been colonized at a worse time. The War of Spanish Succession absorbed most of France's material and military resources, leaving the fledging colony on its own when it most needed financial support from the metropole. What little international energy the metropole had was directed toward its Caribbean colonies, which were already established and beginning to demonstrate their economic profitability. Louisiana also had the misfortune to be launched after the decline of the religious impulse that had greatly fueled the colonization of New France.[7] Thus, as a result of circumstances largely beyond the control of colonizers, Louisiana's development sputtered along. Its population grew only slowly, sometimes even declining, and was continuously dependent on both metropolitan France and neighboring Indian nations for its survival.

Although they sailed from France, Iberville and Bienville were accompanied mostly by fellow Canadians, who quickly began engaging in trade with Indians throughout the Mississippi River Valley. As in New France, the attempt to assert sovereignty over a vast area with just a few colonists made political and military alliances with the region's Indian nations a necessity. Louisiana officials worked hard to maintain the good will and support of the powerful Choctaw and Chickasaw nations, who could help them defend themselves against their enemies, Indian and European alike, and against whom they could not protect themselves. Individual colonizers often owed their very survival to the Chitimachas, Houmas, Chaouachas, and other petites nations along the Gulf Coast and the lower Mississippi River who provided them with corn and meat.[8] As such conditions persisted through the 1710s, it appeared as though Louisiana would mirror New France's sparse, heavily male, and militaristic settlement patterns as well as its economic reliance on Indian trade. Thus many of the solutions proposed for Louisiana were influenced by experiences in New France.

The earliest French presence in the lower Mississippi River Valley was exclusively male, and, among colonists, men outnumbered women throughout the French era. Reflecting the imperialist and militarist intentions of the Crown, Fort Maurepas' eighty-two residents in December 1699 included ten officers and twenty soldiers.[9] Six months later, the population had increased to 125, still all men, mostly through the immigration of Canadians, who comprised just less than one-half of the fort's residents.[10] Throughout the first decade, military personnel composed the majority of French colonizers, followed by Canadian immigrants, many of whom refused to remain within the confines of the French forts and were scattered among various Indian villages along the Mississippi River.[11]

Although La Salle's 1684 expedition had included "some young women," Iberville's contingent of colonizers did not. The year before Iberville set out, one potential investor had written to Pontchartrain discussing "whether it would be prudent that women should be taken over during the first voyage." There were, according to Antoine Alexandre de Rémonville, chevalier seigneur de Rochebonne,

> strong reasons for and against it. If they are taken, it may be the source of libertinage, debauchery, jealousy, and quarrels, as it would be impossible, in the first instance, to have all married men. On the other hand, women are very necessary for cooking and washing for the mechanics and [l]aborers. If it should be concluded to take them, the chiefs and officers should be very exact in restraining

every disorder or disturbance. Such women should also be selected who understand how to sew, knit, and do, also, all other kind of housework.[12]

In 1699, Rémonville's concern about disorder won out, and it was not until 1704,
the same year that the main site of colonization moved eastward to Fort Louis on
Mobile Bay, that the first French women arrived in Louisiana.[13] By then, however,
Louisiana's French and Canadian men had discovered that there were women
available locally who could fulfill, sometimes willingly, often not, the sexual and
domestic roles that Rémonville had highlighted, and it was these intimate choices
that colonial and metropolitan officials debated during the 1710s and 1720s as they
sought to establish order in early Louisiana.

To Remedy Disorder with Marriage

Many of the Canadian men who traveled down the Mississippi River and resided,
albeit often temporarily, in the lower Louisiana French outposts were coureurs de
bois who made their living by engaging in trade with the region's native peoples,
adapting to Indian customs and norms in order to facilitate trade. Since most
southeastern Indian peoples did not separate commercial and political relationships from personal ones, a trader's success depended on his ability to integrate
himself into both trade and kinship networks, often through marriage. If French
men's motivations were not primarily (if at all) sexual, neither were Indian wom-
en's. Some may have initiated relationships with French traders to gain access to
European goods. As conduits of these goods, they would able to gain status within
their own communities.[14] They also may have been aiding their fathers' attempts
to create military and economic ties, for as Jesuit Father Le Petit noted, the Illinois
Indians were "inviolably attached to the French, by alliances which many of that
Nation had contracted with them, in espousing their daughters."[15] Colonist Antoine Simon Le Page du Pratz suggested a third possibility when he claimed that
one Natchez woman begged him to marry her daughter in order to "fortify" her
grandchildren with "French Blood" and encourage the establishment of French
customs among the Natchez. Although it is possible that this exchange took place,
Le Page du Pratz probably misinterpreted the mother's reasons; she likely wished
to create alliances or learn more about the French by placing an intermediary
among them. Le Page du Pratz turned this around, placing himself in the role of
the civilizing and desirable European.[16]

It was not just coureurs de bois, however, who developed intimate connections
with Indian villagers. Never able to consistently feed themselves and dependent

on provisions from France, which often did not arrive or were delayed and spoiled, colonists relied upon local Indians for their daily sustenance.[17] In 1706, "seeing that the food supplies were fast diminishing and that no vessel was on the way to bring some," Governor Bienville "gave permission to several persons of the garrison to go hunting or to go live as best they could among the savage nations friendly to the French." André Pénicaut was among those who spent that winter with the Acolapissas and Natchitoches, a stay he recalled fondly in his narrative, completed in 1723. When they arrived, they were "embraced . . . [by] the men as well as the women and girls, all being delighted," as Pénicaut perceived it, "to see us come to stay with them." Lodging with the Natchitoches chief, Pénicaut wrote that he "was not sorry . . . for in his house I received every possible favor. He had two daughters that were the most beautiful of all the savage girls in the district. The older one was twenty; she was called Oulchogonime, which in their language means the good daughter. The second was only eighteen, but was much taller than her older sister. She was named Ouilchil, which means the pretty spinner."[18]

The twenty-six-year-old Pénicaut had his eyes on the younger Ouilchil, while a fellow colonist, Picard, exchanged at least one kiss with her older sister. When Bienville sent out word the following February for the colonists to return to Mobile, they were "quite melancholy." Their sorrow at leaving their native hosts, however, was balanced by their pleasure "to behold the provisions that had come for us and to find wine in the lot, which we had not had among the Acolapissas" and that "consoled us for the loss of the favors of their girls." Another group of "soldiers, workmen, and even officers" were "received with pleasure" by Biloxi and Pascagoulas Indians in 1719. Following local custom, they supplied their guests "with good hominy and sagamity, boiled with good store of meat or bear oil." Earlier, the Biloxis had traded "game of all kinds, such as buffalo, bear, deer, geese, [and] seal" with those who had remained on their concessions. Just as the colonists were despairing their survival, three provision-laden ships arrived and the Biloxis and Pascagoulas were paid for their hospitality in imported merchandise.[19]

At least one observer believed that French men were spending more time during these sojourns with Indian women than they were with Indian men. According to Le Page du Pratz, "by more often frequenting the company of [Natchez] women than men," French men were learning the feminine pronunciation of the Natchez language. As a result, Natchez women and men alike mocked them.[20] Le Page du Pratz's comment suggests the presence of a gendered frontier as well as a cultural one.[21]

Colonial officials, for their part, would rather not have sent soldiers and colonists to reside in Indian villages. In 1713, after "extreme want" had forced Bienville to "send the entire garrison into the woods . . . to seek a living among the Indians by means of hunting," the newly arrived governor, Antoine de La Mothe, sieur de Cadillac, reported that, although "the Indians [had] kept them alive as well as they could," even the officers had been reduced to a "deplorable condition."[22] Like Cadillac, d'Artaguiette was concerned with appearances. The inability of France to keep French soldiers fed and clothed meant that many were "clad in skins and this gives the Indians a miserable idea of us."[23] Louisiana officials hoped these descriptions would encourage more dependable supplies from France, but metropolitan officials responded that colonists should "apply [themselves] carefully to the cultivation of the land in order that the colony may be able to subsist by itself in difficult times when the assistance from Europe may fail you."[24] It was these material circumstances—and the pragmatic practices mobilized to combat them—as much as sex imbalances among the colonizers that encouraged sexual relationships between French men and Indian women.

When French men resided in Indian villages, whether as a temporary recourse against famine or a more permanent effort to facilitate trade, local customs and the presence of the women's kin shaped their relationships with Indian women. Such relationships were more likely to be consensual than those that took place within French outposts, where most women had been brought involuntarily and where they were isolated from their own communities. From the early 1700s, French colonizers purchased Indian slaves in a trade whose existence they often blamed on the English, though they also engaged in slave raiding expeditions themselves. Nearby Alibamon and Chitimacha Indians in particular found themselves on the receiving end of French slave raids. Colonizers usually killed the men and then enslaved the women and children.[25] Le Page du Pratz bought himself one of these Chitimacha women just a few days after his arrival in the colony in order to have someone to prepare his food and tend to his other domestic needs. This unnamed woman remained with him for many years, even, according to Le Page du Pratz, refusing her father's attempt to buy her back.[26] In 1721, there were ninety-seven Indian slaves in the Mobile area and another fifty-one in New Orleans.[27] Although French-era censuses tended not to distinguish Indian slaves by gender, anecdotal evidence suggests that most enslaved Indians were indeed women.[28]

Le Page du Pratz was not the only one to claim that he needed an Indian slave woman for domestic help. Governor Cadillac noted in 1713 that unmarried Canadians and soldiers "insist that they cannot dispense with having [enslaved Indian women] to do their washing and to do their cooking or to make their sagamity and to keep their cabins."[29] But Cadillac and La Vente were not convinced. La Vente believed that Euro-Louisianan men were purchasing Indian slave women "ostensibly to keep them as servants but the truth is that they are abusing them." Cadillac concurred, noting that these women were "almost always pregnant or nursing." La Vente was not only appalled at this "scandalous Concubinage," which he saw as "the principal reason for the public and regular irreligion" in which colonists lived; he also claimed that such abuse drove the enslaved women "to very often smother their children without even baptizing them." Further, Cadillac asserted that male owners and fathers sold their children away from their mothers. If such practices were taking place, then the relationships occurring within French villages were far more exploitative than those relationships in Indian villages, where such practices were not reported.[30]

In order to combat what they saw as scandal and debauchery, Cadillac and La Vente offered two solutions. The first sought to remove enslaved women from the households of single French men by selling them to the French islands and replacing them with either male slaves (of whom there were "enough . . . to service them") or hired French women. In a postscript, however, Cadillac noted that he had "not been able to find any [French woman] who has been willing to take charge of the washing."[31] La Vente requested "an ordinance to forbid the French of Mobile from taking Indian women as slaves and especially from living with them under the same roof in concubinage," a request that was supported by his superiors at the Foreign Missions.[32] It is clear that Euro-Louisianan men sought women who could fulfill wifely duties by providing both domestic labor and sex, but Cadillac and La Vente worked hard to separate these female roles, acknowledging that unmarried men needed someone to cook and clean for them but seeking to deny them access to extramarital sex. Reluctantly, Bienville at least partially conceded the point to La Vente and ordered slave owners "to send [their slave women] to sleep in the houses where there are French women," an action he described as "a very great inconvenience" to the owners for whom the labor of enslaved women was "indispensable."[33]

Cadillac and La Vente also sought to transform these relationships of "concubinage," as well as those taking place within Indian villages, from illicit to licit ones. In an offhanded way, Cadillac proposed that Frenchmen marry their slaves as an alternative to selling them to the Caribbean islands.[34] For La Vente, permitting French-sanctioned marriages between Christianized Indian women and French men served two purposes: it would discourage the latter from "maintaining scandalous concubinages" and would help in the missionaries' efforts to convert Louisiana's native peoples. The existence—indeed in La Vente's perception, the pervasiveness—of illicit relationships put Christianity in a bad light. Extramarital sex set an example that, "instead of attracting [Indians] to Catholicism," diverted "them out of the Christian way by giving them a piteous idea of our holy religion." Father Gabriel Marest, writing from Kaskaskias in the Illinois country, bemoaned the "pernicious example" set by some colonists, who "make more impression on the minds of the Indians" than anything he could preach to them.[35] But it was not just missionaries who were concerned with the bad example of Christian behavior that colonizers set. Commissaire Ordonnateur Nicolas de La Salle (nephew of explorer Robert) accused Canadians of "destroy[ing] by their wicked libertine lives with Indian women all that the missionaries of the foreign missions and others teach them about the divine mysteries of the Christian religion."[36]

La Vente suggested to Pontchartrain several ways officials might "suppress vice," "stop the scandals," and "restore piety." He could "purge the Colony" of "all the impious people" whose behavior "devastated" the colony or he could send "from France, newly married habitants, who will populate the country with legitimate marriages." La Vente acknowledged, however, that these were neither "quick nor easy" solutions. Still he urged Pontchartrain to recruit "some good Christian families" who could be placed throughout the colony not only to "work advantageously for themselves" but also to serve as a living example "for the edification of the sauvages." Although La Vente clearly preferred this solution, he also offered two alternatives. He requested permission to "allow Frenchmen to marry these sauvagesses" (he and other priests had, in fact, already been performing such marriages). Though he admitted disagreements "between the spiritual and temporal government[s] regarding the unions of Frenchmen with Indian women [indiennes]," La Vente contended such marriages created "closer relationship[s] with those nations" and also "incline[d] them easily to become good Christians and good subjects of the King." If Pontchartrain refused to allow these marriages, La Vente wrote, it would "be necessary to send, at least for the soldiers and the common people, a great number of girls." In addition, he should "forbid [the officers and principle habitants] from keeping their sauvagesses or from taking new ones."[37]

La Vente and other religious officials had two concerns. The first was "to bring the French who were already Christians back to their faith and good manners," combating the overall irreligiosity and licentiousness that they saw as rampant among both Louisiana's natives and its colonizers and that they blamed on secular officials. Though Father Raphaël acknowledged that "there have been bad priests who instead of repressing disorders have authorized them by their scandals," he was more critical of secular officials who, on the "pretext . . . that at the beginning of a colony it is necessary to be easygoing with people and to tolerate many things that would not be tolerated in a country already established," were "extremely indifferent" to "concubinage, extortion, [and] public impiety." The missionaries' second concern was to create new Christians among the region's Indians. They believed that marriages sanctified by the Catholic Church could serve as a "civilizing" vehicle, leading to the cultural colonization of Indian women and their children. Allowing illicit relationships to continue, however, encouraged un-Christian moralities and could even result in French men falling into "liv[ing] without any faith or law."[38] As Pénicaut noted, at least one missionary "remained in Louisiana as much to instruct the French as to convert the savages."[39]

In proposing to sanctify Indian-French relationships, La Vente was building on past policies of both missionaries and secular administrators in New France. Since 1648, missionaries had struggled to control illicit relationships between French fur traders and Indian women, while metropolitan secular authorities had sought to gain more control over the male colonists themselves. Both believed that their goals would be fulfilled by permitting and even encouraging French men to marry Indian women. In the late 1660s, Jean-Baptiste Colbert, minister of the marine, repeatedly urged local officials to follow a policy of Frenchification, whereby Christianized Indians would be settled among French colonizers so that the former's children would be raised "in our manners and customs." Colbert's idea was that by "having but one law and one master," native peoples and their coloniz-ers would thus "form only one people and one blood." The easiest way to effect this transformation, he wrote, was through intermarriage.[40] One secular administrator who tried to follow this policy in the early eighteenth century was Cadillac who, before becoming governor of Louisiana, was the commander at Detroit. Although by 1700 most policy makers and administrators in New France had moved away from Colbert's "one blood" policy, Cadillac argued throughout the first decade of the eighteenth century that "marriages of this kind" were "absolutely necessary," for they served both secular and religious ends, enhancing "the glory of His Maj-esty" by "strengthen[ing] the friendship of these tribes" and firmly establishing the Christian religion among them.[41]

Retarding the Growth of the Colony

Although Governor Cadillac continued to advocate Indian-French marriages, most of Louisiana's secular officials opposed them.[42] For Bienville, the crux of the matter was that by sanctioning these marriages, La Vente was in fact authorizing coureurs de bois to live "as libertines and under no authority, dispersed among the savage villages, under the pretext that they have married among the savages." Although he occasionally sent soldiers and colonists to live in native villages, Bienville be-lieved that for colonization to be successful, French colonizers needed to reside in French villages under French authority, not with Indians on a permanent, or even semipermanent, basis. Yet it was not only marriages within Indian villages that secular authorities sought to prohibit: La Vente infuriated Bienville by marrying "a good inhabitant" of Mobile to a "sauvagesse whose dissoluteness was public." Bienville claimed the priest was stubborn and haughty and accused him of continually subverting secular authority. He was critical of the missionaries in general, arguing their "luxuriousness stands so far apart from Christian beliefs," and denied that marriage aided in conversion.[43]

In challenging La Vente's proposal, secular officials represented both French men and Indian women in ways that they thought demonstrated that their relationships were detrimental to the colony's development. Unlike missionaries, who stressed the power of European social institutions, such as marriage, to convert and "civilize" Indians, secular officials believed that cultural differences would obviate the purported civilizing influences of marriage on the grounds that they would "be of no utility for the increase of families" in the colony. Further, Commissaire Ordonnateur Jean-Baptiste du Bois Duclos asserted, few native women would in fact want to marry French men: "Accustomed to a certain sort of licentious life," they would find the French marital regime too restrictive.[44] Misreading culturally sanctioned premarital sexual experimentation as promiscuity and infidelity, French officials like Bernard Diron d'Artaguiette portrayed Illinois women as "naturally inclined toward love," although he acknowledged that "married women indulged very little in gallantry" out of fear of their husbands' jealous wrath. Natchez women were "precocious in matters of love" and, as "mistresses of their own bodies (to use their expression)," they had "several lovers, all of whom they make happy." In particular, Diron d'Artaguiette continued, they "generally like all the Frenchmen, to whom they refuse none of their favors, in return for a few glass beads or other trifles." Some officials, including Diron d'Artaguiette, did acknowledge exceptions among Indian women. Diron d'Artaguiette noted that Arkansas women would have nothing to do with French men.[45] Henri Joutel, a survivor of the La Salle expedition, argued that Hasinai women did "not publicly prostitute themselves" and were not "naturally given to lewdness." Even in his defense, however, Joutel insisted they had "little difficulty giving in if they were urged in the least bit." In particular, he wrote, "their virtue is not proof against some of our toys," and they were easily tempted to "wantonness" with French men in exchange for "needles, knives, and more particularly strings of beads."[46]

This perception of licentiousness was furthered by representations of native women as almost naked. According to Pénicaut, although Natchez women wore dresses made out of mulberry bark linen, prepubescent girls wore only small aprons that "cover[ed] only the forepart of their nakedness, from the waist to the knees." He described Pascagoulas women as wearing only "a single hank of moss which passed between their legs and covered their nakedness, the rest of their bodies being quite nude."[47] Young Bayogoulas girls, according to Iberville, similarly "conceal[ed] their nakedness with a small bundle of moss," while adult women wore "only a sash of bark."[48]

European commentators could not separate their representations of women's near nudity and sexual behavior from native marriage practices that they also saw as immoral and unstable. For the French, a stable society required lawful marriages that legitimated and regulated families, households, children, and the transmission of property. As seigneurs or lords over their wives and other dependents, husbands were supposed to defend, protect, love, and be faithful to their wives and administer their shared property as head of the household community. Wives, for their part, were required to love, submit, obey, and try to please their husbands. Husbands were enjoined from abusing the power they held over the wives, while wives were to restrain themselves from interfering in their husbands' management of the household. Divorce was not allowed, although there were limited grounds for separation, including a husband's extreme cruelty, his lack of economic support, or a wife's infidelity.[49]

Indian premarital sexual experimentation, female sexual independence, polygyny, matrilineality, and divorce therefore made many Europeans see Indian marital practices as disorderly and Indian women as unsuitable brides for French men. Although Diron d'Artaguiette exaggerated when he claimed that polygamy was practiced "among all the Indian nations which I have seen," he was correct in noticing its presence among some southeastern Indian groups.[50] For Choctaws, some Caddo bands, and particularly Natchez, polygyny was a legitimate marital practice; chiefs and other elite men contracted marriages with several women to build economic and political alliances and to acquire status and power.[51] French elites would have understood marriages contracted to create or maintain alliances, but they could not sanction polygyny because of the Catholic character of French marriage.

Just as polygyny challenged French notions of the proper marital order, so too did southeastern practices of matrilineality. For Natchez, hereditary positions, such as chiefships, as well as property descended through the female line: a chief's sister's child, not his own children, inherited his position. Similarly, among matrilineal Choctaw, a father did not exercise authority over his own children; rather their maternal uncle was the more important male authority figure.[52] Unable to see the matrilineal logic to these systems, French commentators once again blamed women's sexual behavior, explaining that they "infer their origins from the women's side, because, they say, it is certain that the child comes from the woman," while their husbands could not be secure in their paternity.[53]

It was, however, the ease of divorce that most troubled European observers, especially when they considered Indian women as prospective brides for French men. According to Le Petit, Natchez Indians had an "indifference to the conjugal union" that resulted "from the liberty they have of changing when it seems good to them" as long as the marriage was childless.[54] Diron d'Artaguiette believed that native women left their husbands "without the least complaint being made by those whom they leave." Even if they married French men, such women would, according to Diron d'Artaguiette, "also leave them at the least trouble," and, in Duclos' words, they would "never be able to accustom themselves" to marriages with French men, let alone "remain with them for the rest of their lives."[55] François Le Marie denied that Indian marriages "deserve this name, given the ease with which they are broken."[56] Secular administrators read this sanctioning of female autonomy that permitted Indian women to choose and leave spouses as undermining French notions of patriarchal marriage that dictated wifely submission and obedience and leading to social instability, thus undercutting their attempts to secure the colony through marriage, families, and household formation.

Yet it was not just native women's sexual behavior that was blamed for the prevalence and detrimental effects of their relationships with French men. Although Diron d'Artaguiette had claimed that Natchez women were the authors of the phrase "mistresses of their own bodies," the sentiment appears in many accounts of Indian women and French men alike and even Diron d'Artaguiette's brother pointed some of the blame at French men.[57] For d'Artaguiette, the causes were threefold: "The sauvagesses are easy, the climate stimulating, and the young men, for the most part Canadians, . . . are said to be very vigorous."[58] Colonist Tivas de Gourville similarly disparaged Canadian men in his 1712 memoir. They were, he wrote, coureurs de bois and others "who are of a strong and vigorous age and temperament." Desiring "sex, and not finding any who can hold them," they roam "among the Indian nations and satisfy their passions with the daughters of these Indians." Such behavior, he continued, "retards the growth of this colony."[59] Cadillac (perhaps because of his many years in New France) called Louisiana colonists "the dregs of Canada, jailbirds" who had no respect "for religion or for government" and who were "addicted to vice principally with the Indian women whom they prefer to French women." He described one particular Canadian coureur de bois as "a real debauchee, unprincipled and insubordinate . . . [and] very much devoted to the Indian women," despite his having a wife in Canada.[60] So, at least part of the blame for disorder that secular and religious officials alike decried was placed on Euro-Louisianan men and their unrestrained desire for sex.[61]

As these statements reveal, officials saw colonists' relationships with native women as part of their general insubordination to colonial authority. As La Vente put it, these men were "always ready to go back to the forest and leave the colony behind."[62] "Voyageurs," according to one anonymous memoir, "contract sauvage manners easily. They run in the Woods . . . without shorts and with simple trousers. They please themselves."[63] Governor Étienne Périer explicitly linked relationships with native women to, as he saw it, the degeneration of French men and their increasing insubordination when he wrote that "the majority of habitants of [the Illinois country] have married sauvagesses; they have themselves become sauvages, that is to say, very difficult to discipline."[64] Officials struggled to control these men by trying to regulate their intimate lives, not just by policing relationships with native peoples, which could adversely impact the colony, but also by making coureurs de bois and colonists subordinate their own desires and goals to those of the larger colonizing project.[65] In order to make Louisiana a self-sufficient, agricultural economy, secular officials believed they needed to encourage the formation of stable families that resided under French authority.[66]

As Périer's observations suggest, some officials believed that marriages to Indian women would not either recivilize French men or civilize Indian women. When Duclos described several examples of Indian-French marriages that had lasted, it was not, he argued, "because [the wives] have become Frenchified," as missionaries like La Vente asserted they would. It was rather "because those who have married them have themselves become almost Sauvages, residing among them and living in their manner, so that these Indian women have changed nothing or at the least very little in their manner of living." He went on to argue that few Indian women would want to marry French men, unwilling to submit themselves to patriarchal authority, and that the only French men who would want to take Indian brides were those "who live in the manner of the Indians," and most of them would not willingly choose marriage either. Agreeing with Duclos that marriage would not have La Vente's proposed civilizing effects, d'Artaguiette wrote that they did not "cause . . . any great change at all in the Indians" but rather just resulted in "these Frenchmen . . . lead[ing] with these wives a life as nomadic as before."[67]

References to native women becoming "Frenchified" or French men becoming "almost Sauvage" relied on the idea that one could adapt to the cultural differences in dress, marriage practices, and sexual behaviors of another culture. Individuals of one culture could easily adopt these aspects of another. Yet in Duclos' and d'Artaguiette's constructions, Indian women were highly resistant to change, while French men were, unfortunately in their eyes, highly susceptible to abandon their natal culture for native ways.

One last series of objections to La Vente's proposal centered on children and inheritance, not just of property but also of culture and behavior. For the French, concern for the transmission of property between the generations was central to marital regulations.[68] Inheritance and marriage in French Louisiana were governed by the metropolitan Coutume de Paris, a codification of fifteenth- and sixteenth-century laws that limited the rights and prerogatives of married women yet granted widows a great deal of discretion over their husband's property, especially when compared to their counterparts in the British North American colonies. Under the Coutume, marriage created a community in which husbands and wives shared ownership of property equally, although it was solely administered by the husband. Upon a spouse's death, the surviving spouse received one-half of the community property, and the remainder was divided among the couple's children.[69]

In 1728, however, in response to a petition from Father Jean-Baptiste Le Boullenger, the curé of Kaskaskias in Illinois country, the Superior Council devised different inheritance practices for successions involving native widows of French men and métis children.[70] According to Le Boullenger, "many habitants of Illinois have married women sauvagesses of the Illinois nation, almost all Catholics." One, Guillaume Potier, had recently died, leaving a small estate, an Indian widow (Marie Achipicourata), and at least two young children. Marie offered to share Potier's estate with his relatives but they opposed her claim to the succession at all, arguing that she had "been declared an adulterer" and accusing her of "bearing the child of another, even during her husband's life."

Le Boullenger claimed that the issue was larger than just this one succession. He was particularly concerned about the disposition of property in the case of childless couples. Although widows legally owned half of the community property a marriage created, Le Boullenger clearly believed that, in the cases of French-Indian marriages, the property properly belonged to the husbands and their heirs. When such a widow died without children, her property devolved to her relatives who, Le Boullenger stated, "are sauvages who . . . take back to their villages her movables and her nègres and livestock and dispose of the lands, houses, and other grounds." Le Boullenger claimed that he knew of one case in which the Indian widow herself, "preserving love for her homeland and its sauvage manners," took her half of the community property back to her natal village.

The question, for Le Boullenger and for François Fleuriau, the procureur général, was whether the widow's relatives were "reputed as régnicoles and subject to French laws; and if they have to enjoy the same advantages as the King's subjects." Fleuriau argued that they should not. He admitted that wives, "whose state and condition" followed their husbands' and who "lived under the same laws as them," should enjoy the advantages of the king's natural-born subjects. But, he continued, "their fathers, mothers, brothers, sisters, and other relatives, who [have] always remained in their villages, exempt from French laws" should not be able to inherit what he saw as French property. He pointed out that the company's 1717 Patent Letters deemed all French subjects who emigrated to Louisiana as well as children "who are born of French habitants of said country" and raised in the Catholic religion and "foreign Europeans who profess the Roman Catholic religion" as régnicoles. They were therefore "capable of all successions, gifts, bequests, and other dispositions." He correctly noted that the Patent Letters did not grant this status to "sauvages," who thus could not "claim to enjoy the advantages belonging to the French."[71]

On December 18, 1728, the Superior Council addressed Le Boullenger's petition and Fleuriau's representation. First, it ruled in favor of Marie, declaring that her youngest child was legitimate, since it had been born during the marriage. But it then agreed with Le Boullenger and Fleuriau and issued a decree that counter-manded widows' rights under the Coutume. The Company of the Indies would confiscate such estates except for their real estate holdings, which would be managed, if the marriage had been childless, by the attorney of vacant estates (thus incapacitating the widow's legal ownership) or, if there were children, a tutor (thus deeming the widow an incompetent mother).[72] The widow was to receive a pension of one-third of the property's revenues, although she would even lose her claim to that if she returned to her natal village.[73] In his commentary on the decision two months later, Jacques de La Chaise acknowledged that it was "contrary to the Coutume de Paris" but, he continued, it was "judicious," as it was "not agreeable that the sauvages take the goods of the French among their nations."[74]

When Charles Egron died in 1745, Fleuriau had a chance to implement the decision he had helped to write almost two decades earlier and requested that a curator be chosen for Egron's widow, Françoise, "because of her status as an Indian woman." The following year, when the original curator asked to be released from this responsibility, Fleuriau now described Françoise "as an imbecile." Having legally proscribed the widow from managing her own estate, Fleuriau considered her rationally incapable of doing so. Hopefully, Françoise could take solace in the fact that her son-in-law, René Sabourin, was named the new curator.[75]

Although the 1728 decree modifying the Coutume de Paris for Indian widows was articulated in terms of property and citizenship, questions of race permeated this discussion as well as the larger debate over Indian-French relationships. Le Boullenger had dismissed Potier's widow's rights with the statement, "She is after all a Native Woman," as if that claim alone explained her inability to manage property and raise her children, a sentiment echoed in Fleuriau's treatment of Egron's widow, Françoise.[76] As for Potier's and Egron's children and others like them, it was unclear whether they were French subjects, natives, or something else, not quite French but not quite Indian. For Cadillac, they were "métisses and appear to be sang mêlé."[77] For Duclos, such children were "extremely tawny" ("basané," which translates as "bronzed," "tawny" or "swarthy"); their "Whiteness and purity of blood" was clearly "adulterated." Permitting racially exogamous relationships was not "conducive to the welfare of the colony," as it would become "a colony of mulâtres, who are naturally idlers, promiscuous [and] rogues," like those of Spanish America.[78] Cadillac, with his Canadian experience (particularly his postings at Michilimackinac and Detroit), used "métis" (and he indeed may have been the one to introduce this term into lower Louisiana), but Duclos referred to the same children as "mulâtre," perhaps having picked up the word in Spanish America where he spent some time before arriving in Louisiana.[79] As Cadillac's and Duclos' accounts demonstrate, exogamous sexual relationships and their offspring were part of a trans-Atlantic discourse that officials drew on selectively as they dealt with peopling and creating social order in Louisiana.

Mixing Good Blood with Bad

The notion that Indian-French relationships mixed "good blood with bad," and therefore degraded the former, had, by the mid-1710s, become a trope that opponents of legitimizing these relationships called on to support their position. In 1709, the governor of New France, Philippe de Rigault, marquis de Vaudreuil (whose son would later become governor of Louisiana), based his opposition on his belief that such marriages would only appeal to French men who were already "licentious, lazy, and intolerably independent" and on his view that their children were "characterized by the great slothfulness of the savages themselves."[80] Even supporters of Indian-French marriage expressed a "fear that these marriages mix good blood with bad and will produce a colony only of children of a hard and idle character."[81] It was not just the French who used the language of blood to criticize Indian-French relations. In his sympathetic rendering of the Natchez uprising of 1729, Le Page du Pratz recited a speech of the Grand Sun in which the Natchez leader complained that the nearness of French colonists served no other "purpose than to debauch the young women and corrupt the blood of the Nation."[82] La Vente and other religious officials countered these assertions that Indian-French marriages corrupted the blood of their offspring. La Vente claimed, "We do not see that the blood of the sauvages will have any prejudicial effect on the blood of the French. As we see, the whiteness of the children of French men married with the sauvagesses is equal to that of the French themselves."[83] For the bishop of

Quebec, it was illegitimate relationships, rather than racially exogamous ones, that produced children who "can only become bad subjects."[84] The separate but often overlapping issues of illegitimacy and racial exogamy—and the degenerative effects of each—would continue to influence discussions of métis and mulâtre children, especially in regard to their suitability and potential as colonial subjects. As this debate demonstrates, race as a concept that emphasized unchangeable, physical differences was already present in French Louisiana, but it competed with the idea that differences between Indians and the French were essentially cultural and could be altered or even eradicated. To a great extent, the position taken on the question of Indian-French relationships by a given official determined whether he described the differences between native peoples and French colonizers as racial or cultural.

Those who sought to describe Louisiana's native and colonial populations as racially distinct often relied on skin color, which had by the early eighteenth century become an easy referent for physical differences. As we have seen, Iberville had rejected an offer of sexual companionship by Bayogoulas Indians in 1700 by explaining that "their skin—red and tanned—should not come close to that of the French, which was white."[85] But proponents of Indian-French marriages also discussed color, illustrating that even these physical distinctions were not yet seen as immutable. La Vente used color to indicate similarities and differences between various Indian groups, on the one hand, and French colonizers, on the other. He suggested that women of the more northern regions of the colony—Tunicas, Chickasaws, Kaskaskias, and Illinois among others—would make better wives than Indian women from the southern regions, as the former were "whiter, more laborious, more skillful, better at household work, and more docile than those of the south." La Vente conflated skills he deemed appropriate for the brides of French men with similarity in skin color.[86]

Pénicaut conflated beauty rather than gender-appropriate skills with whiteness. Describing Natchitoches and Acolapissa Indians, his hosts during the winter of 1706, he compared their physical appearances, perhaps to explain his attraction to the young Ouilchil. The Natchitoches were, he wrote, "handsomer and have better figures," while the Acolapissas, men and women alike, tattooed themselves, "which disfigures them hideously. . . . That is why," he continued, Natchitoches were "so much better looking." He concluded his remarks with the almost offhanded observation that, "besides, they are naturally whiter." Étienne de Véniard, sieur de Bourgmont, also distinguished among native groups on the basis of the proximity of their physical characteristics to those of Europeans. The Omahas, he wrote were "white and blonde, like Europeans. It is the most handsome tribe of all the continents."[87] At a time when most authors described native complexion as

These images emphasized Louisiana's native peoples' similarities in stature and appearance, including their pale coloring, to Europeans. *Naturels en été* and *femme et fille,* 1758, in Le Page du Pratz, *Histoire de Louisiane.* Courtesy of the John Carter Brown Library, Brown University, Providence, R.I.

olive, reddish, tawny, or tanned, references to whiteness in these comments stands in for a variety of cultural attributes that brought "whiter" natives closer to French colonizers, while "red and tanned" skin marked their distance.[88]

French observers not only recognized a range of colors among Louisiana's native peoples; they also saw those colors as malleable. The idea that Indians' skin color came from environmental conditions, cultural practices, or both was common in French travel narratives and contemporary histories of the Americas. Officer Jean Bernard Bossu first claimed that Indians were naturally "reddish" but then credited both maternal imagination, as "the mothers, finding beauty in this color, transmit it to their offspring," and "artifice," as the Indians "paint themselves every day with rocou, which . . . makes them appear red as blood."[89] Le Page du Pratz incorporated the environment and cultural practices into his explanation. He noted, "The children of the Natives are white at birth" but their skin eventually "darkened, because they rub them with Bear's oil while young, in order to expose them to the Sun."[90] The discourse of skin color, while present in Louisiana from the very beginning, was thus one that could either reflect a belief that cultural differences were mutable, as in Bossu's and Le Page du Pratz's discussions, or that they were fixed and racialized, as in Duclos' conflation of the dissolute character of mulâtres with their tawny complexion.[91]

Racialized fears of "mixing blood" as well as perceptions of unrestrained sexual behavior on the parts of both native women and colonizing men led most secular officials in Louisiana to oppose any proposals that would legitimate racially exogamous marriages they saw as threatening to the social order. For their part, however, those in the metropole vacillated as far as Louisiana was concerned and neither authorized La Vente's proposal to recognize such marriages nor stated unequivocally that they should be prohibited, a lack of resolution shaped by their concerns with both conversion and colonial order.[92] In 1699, Louis XIV had granted Iberville's request "to allow the French who will settle in this country to marry with the daughters of the sauvages." The king saw "no inconvenience [to these marriages], provided that [the brides] be Christian." Iberville's "principal occupation" was, the king continued, to "establish the Christian religion" in his new colony "apply[ing] himself to prevent debaucheries and all sorts of disorders" to further that aim.[93] He also supported Cadillac's 1709 request to allow Indian-French marriages in Detroit over Governor Vaudreuil's opposition, which he ordered to governor to reexamine.[94]

Around the same time, however, he instructed his Louisiana governors—Sieur Nicolas Daneaux de Muy in 1707 and Cadillac in 1710—to "prevent these disorders," meaning nonmarital relationships, "from continuing" while also beginning to back away from outright support for Indian-French marriage. It is clear from his instructions, as well as from those of Pontchartrain, that, like the missionaries, metropolitan officials were concerned with the "shameless dissoluteness" in which French and Canadian men were living and with its "prejudicial" impact on both religion and "the increase of the Colony."[95]

But, like Bienville, Louis XIV and Pontchartrain also feared losing control over those men and demanded that all coureurs de bois be made to settle within French outposts.[96] Périer made the connection explicit when he noted it was necessary to post troops in Illinois country as much "to restrain the French who live there as to keep the Sauvages respectful." Illinois' French colonists were, he continued, "all coureurs de bois from Canada or Louisiana who have made establishments there in order to be independent of the governors and commandants of the posts. It would be dangerous to leave them longer in this spirit of independence, which spoils the few soldiers that we have in this post."[97] In an earlier attempt to prohibit unlicensed fur trading in New France in 1696, the Crown blamed the independent character of coureurs de bois, who abandoned themselves "to libertinage, to debauchery, and to all sorts of disorders and crimes," for undermining colonists' commitment to cultivation as well as undercutting merchants' profits.[98]

Following Louis XIV's death in 1715, his five-year-old great-grandson Louis XV assumed the throne, though Philippe, duc d'Orléans, ruled as regent until 1723. Although there was some continuity in colonial administration (for instance, Pontchartrain remained the minister of the marine), it was after Louis XV's succession that the metropole first began issuing instructions that "it is necessary to prevent these sorts of marriages as much as possible," quoting Duclos' rationales: few native women would willingly commit themselves to French marriage, requiring them to be Catholicized would be a time consuming deterrent, and children born of these marriages would be "swarthy . . . mulâtres, naturally lazy, promiscuous, and . . . mischievous." The only one of Duclos' grounds the Crown failed to reiterate in its instructions was the one that claimed few French men would willingly marry Indian women, thus minimizing the blame that Duclos and others in Louisiana had placed on French men as a cause of the colony's disordered state.[99]

Despite the 1716 instructions to "prevent" Indian-French marriages "as much as possible," there continued to be confusion in the colony about whether or not these relationships were prohibited, and missionaries continued to sanctify them. When Father Le Boullenger petitioned the Superior Council in 1728, he specifically noted that "the Code Noir prohibits completely marriages of blancs with noirs, but it does not prohibit at all those with sauvages," and, therefore, "blancs have married sauvagesses, by observing the ordinary ceremonies of the Church."[100] Le Boullenger was in fact correct, although he also seems to have been studiously ignorant of the Crown's policy of discouragement, demonstrating that priests in the outposts where these relationships were more common, who therefore could have had the greatest impact on stemming these practices, were seemingly unaware of the Crown's shift in policy.

In response to Le Boullenger's request, the Superior Council not only changed inheritance practices when native widows and métis children were involved but also prohibited "all Frenchmen and other blanc subjects of the King . . . from contracting marriages with Sauvagesses until the King makes his will known." The penalty for entering such a marriage was to be "deprived of all dispositions."[101] When, a couple of months later, Commissaire Ordonnateur Jacques de La Chaise wrote to the Company of the Indies about the 1728 decree restricting the inheritance rights of Indian widows and métis children, he noted, "I thought that there was a regulation forbidding these sorts of alliances. All we found were some letters, where it speaks of preventing them as much as possible." But, he continued, "this is not enough, for the Church never takes any notice."[102]

La Chaise was right. Four years later, secular officials were once again complaining to Minister of the Marine Maurepas that "these sorts of marriages" were being frequently performed by missionaries in the Illinois country, who defended them by asserting "there is no difference between a Christian slave and a blanc."[103] Administrators criticized missionaries for "too easily approving," and even encouraging, marriages that were "a dishonor to the nation" and that "could have dangerous consequences for the tranquility of the Colony," adding "that the children of these marriages are more promiscuous than even the Sauvages." After the usual trans-Atlantic delay, Maurepas notified the procurator for the Jesuit missions and the Illinois commandant that the king prohibited the missionaries from celebrating "any marriage[s] of this kind without the agreement of the governor and the commissaire ordonnateur of the Colony or the commander of the post."[104] Once again, then, in enunciating a ban, the Crown stopped short of making it total.

Other evidence confirms that the 1716, 1728, and 1735 policies were never completely effective and that Euro-Louisianan men continued to have relationships, sanctioned or not, with Indian women.[105] In 1718, a Christianized Chitimacha, Jeanne de La Grande Terre, married François Derbanne in Mobile, shortly before they moved to Natchitoches, which Derbanne helped to found, quickly becoming among its wealthiest residents.[106] Recognized, if not always sacramental, Indian-French relationships remained relatively common in Natchitoches throughout the eighteenth century.[107]

A similar situation prevailed in Illinois. Of the twenty-one children baptized between 1701 and 1731, seventeen had Indian mothers and French fathers.[108] In 1723, Marguerite Ouaquamo Ouoana, the widow of one French officer, married another, Nicolas Peliter de Franchomme.[109] Françoise (sometimes surnamed Missoury, but most often referred to as Madame Dubois), a Missouri woman, also had two French husbands. After her first, Sieur Louis Dubois, a sergeant and interpreter, was killed by Indians during the French-Fox wars, she married Sieur Louis Marin de La Marque sometime before 1734.[110]

It was Françoise Dubois' mistold life story that served as the basis of Dumont de Montigny's moralistic tale of the woes of racially exogamous marriages. As related in his 1753 *Mémoires historiques sur la Louisiane*, the young Missouri woman, the daughter of a great chief, was one of five Indians taken to France in 1725. While in France she was baptized at Notre Dame and married Sergeant Dubois, who had accompanied the group on their trip. On returning to Louisiana, they settled at an unnamed fort, where her husband had been appointed commandant. At this point in his tale, Dumont exclaims, "What advantages could not now be expected from the conversion of the great chief's daughter, and her marriage with a Frenchman!" But alas, tragedy ensued for the French husband and his compatriots. Madame Dubois (Dumont never does grant her a first name) was unhappy living in the fort, "either because she no longer loved her husband" or because "her own Nation's way of living suited her better." Sergeant and Madame Dubois had scarcely returned from France when "Sauvages massacred Sieur Dubois and butchered the whole garrison, not a single man escaping," except "Dame Dubois," who then "renounced Christianity, and returned to her former mode of life."[111] Far from ensuring the successful colonization of Louisiana, Dumont's moral was that Indian-French marriages would be its undoing.

Given the true histories of women like Françoise Dubois (who did not help kill her husband and remained living in French settlements until her death), Dumont could not have been more wrong about the long-term consequences of marriages like hers. French outposts throughout upper Louisiana were established by French and Canadian traders, who frequently had Indian wives. At Kaskaskias, founded in 1703, habitants and their Indian neighbors worked and worshipped alongside each other. After a generation or two, habitants tended to marry the daughters of these earlier marriages rather than native women themselves, and by 1752, at least eleven of Kaskaskias's sixty-seven male householders were or had been married to Indian or métis women.[112] They included Louis Alexandre Tibierge, merchant and husband of Françoise Dubois' daughter, also named Françoise. In the neighboring outpost of Fort de Chartres, at least four of forty-four households had identifiable connections to Indian kin, including Louis Marin de La Marque, the widower of Françoise Dubois herself.[113] Perhaps in recognition of the colonizing work done by French habitants and their Indian wives, Bienville settled an Illinois property dispute in 1734 by ruling that habitants with Indian wives should have first claim to lands recently vacated by Illinois Indians, some of them relatives of these habitants.[114] This ruling came six years after the Superior Council attempted to ban Indian-French marriages and despite Bienville's own earlier antagonism to them. In this instance, pragmatic concerns overrode any ideological opposition to racially exogamous marriages.

Almost all of these sanctified relationships took place outside of New Orleans and the older post of Mobile, far from the vigilance of secular officials. Charles Egron and his wife, Françoise, were among the very few formally married

Indian-French couples living in either colonial capital. In 1727, métis Angelique Girardy, daughter of Joseph Girardy and Françoise, "indienne," married the first of her two husbands (the first was French, the second Canadian).[115] Four years later, Mathurin L'Horo married Marie, a sauvagesse libre, in the earliest, clearly identifiable Indian-French marriage in extant New Orleans sacramental records.[116] Later that same year, Hippolite, "daughter of a sauvagesse named Catherine, formerly the servant of Nicolas Chauvin de La Fresnière," married Canadian Joseph Turpin; La Fresnière was present to witness the marriage, possibly an indication that the bride was his daughter.[117]

Most Indian-French relationships in Mobile and New Orleans, however, took place within the context of slavery and did not result in sanctified relationships or paternal recognition of métis children. When Mobile curé Alexandre Huvé baptized newborn Pierre Ignace in 1720, the midwife who had attended the birth testified that the mother, an unnamed Indian slave of Joseph-Christophe de Lusser, asserted the father was Pierre de Manadé, the surgeon-major of the fort. Priests did not lightly accept attestations of paternity from the mothers of children born outside of marriage, so Huvé's willingness to attribute paternity to Manadé in the sacramental registry is significant.[118] It was common knowledge that another prominent colonist, François Philippe de Mandeville, officer and commandant at Mobile in the early 1720s, had at least two natural children with his own Indian slaves.[119] By 1726, Father Raphaël could applaud that "the number of those [French men] who maintain young sauvagesses or négresses to satisfy their intemperance has considerably diminished," though he continued to grumble that there were "still enough to scandalize the church and to call for an effective remedy."[120]

Missionaries not only continued to sanctify Indian-French relationships while complaining about nonmarital ones, but they also continued to argue for them, although increasingly as an expediency rather than a positive good. In 1717, François Le Marie dismissed La Vente's suggestion that "whiter" Indian women would make suitable brides for French men, stating that "every sauvagesse is always a sauvagesse, that is to say fickle and very difficult to bring back once they get into evil ways." But, he argued, missionaries had to have the discretion "to sometimes allow these sorts of marriages" when they determined "there [was] no other way to prevent the scandals that desolate their missions."[121] In a 1738 memoir written to "explain . . . the effect of the [1735] law prohibiting marriages with the sauvages," Jesuit René Tartarin argued that "despite the court's will," missionaries were forced to "continue performing these sorts of marriages . . . because of the awful disorder that some Frenchmen lived in and some presently do so."[122] Where secular officials had emphasized the dangers of Indian-French marriages to the colony and downplayed the moral issue of concubinage, Tartarin, like other religious officials, emphasized the moral dangers of allowing unsanctified relationships to continue.

Praising the king for being "zealous for the establishment of the Religion" and criticizing secular authorities for tolerating "those true disorders" and being unconcerned with "the establishment of religion," Tartarin bemoaned the "unbearable . . . scandal" that directly challenged all the king's support for the missionaries and the church. Echoing earlier missionaries, he wrote, "The sauvages can only have a bad judgment of the Religion just by seeing the French living in such disorders." Therefore, the missionaries had to "remedy these disorders with marriage." For Tartarin, racially exogamous marriages were clearly the lesser of two evils; he agreed with the court that they were "disagreeable," but without any other viable option, he felt missionaries had no choice. He further argued that it was "better for the state to perform these marriages" because métis children would be born regardless of official policy and missionaries' actions, and "bastards [are] more dangerous than the legitimate métis."

> The legitimate métis are established among the French by education, and by the inheritance of their father's goods, and the greatest number behave truly as Frenchmen. In twenty years, only one retired among the sauvages. . . . Métis bastards, on the contrary, have always remained among the sauvages in greater numbers, without education, without hope, without any inheritance[;] the savage blood dominates them, they make more men for the different nations from which they came.

It was precisely by denying métis children the "hope of establishing themselves among Frenchmen and Frenchwomen" that "this multitude of bastards" contributed to the "perpetual" disorder of the colony. Only marriage, integration into French families, and education could overcome "the involuntary misfortune of their first birth." Abandoning them and their mothers to perpetual concubinage would force "the bastard métis" to live "without faith, without law," not to mention "the public scandal and shame on the Religion" that perpetual concubinage would elicit. Tartarin did acknowledge the strength of "sauvage blood" that French husbands struggled to eradicate, but he concluded by arguing that "legitimate métis children" abandoned their native kin and "desired to be true French Creoles." Partly distinguishing and partly conflating the consequences of illegitimacy and the mixing of blood, Tartarin believed that the cultural context of legitimacy could overcome any degenerative consequences of mixing blood.

For missionaries like La Vente and Tartarin, nonmarital relationships were the greater disorder, one that could only be remedied through marriage. For most secular officials, on the other hand, illicit but transitory relationships that took place within French villages were preferable to sanctioned ones that would bind French men to Indian kin and facilitate their escape from French control. As La Vente astutely saw it, the colony's secular administrators had determined that it was "less embarrassing and more convenient" to allow colonizers "to have [Indian] concubines" rather than Indian wives.[123]

Although the debate split largely along ecclesiastical and secular lines, between those concerned with moral order and those with social order, it was also caught up in officials' conflicts over authority and even in their personality disputes.[124] The Crown's ultimate resistance to outright prohibition (revealed in the fact that it failed to establish punishments such as exiling French men married to Indian women from the colony or imposing sanctions on those who performed such marriages) in part reflected the tension between its religious and political goals. Both Louis XIV and Louis XV stated time and again that the establishment of Catholicism among Louisiana's native peoples was one of their principal goals, but they also sought to establish their authority over Louisiana's colonial subjects as well as its native inhabitants.

A change in economic goals also played a role in the shift from promoting Indian-French marriages to discouraging them. In the very early years of colonization, Louisiana looked as if it would replicate New France's extractive economy, whether of furs or oft-sought after but elusive minerals. The growth of such an economy would be facilitated by regularized and harmonious relationships between colonizers and native peoples. Once it became clear, however, that Louisiana's furs were not of the same quality as those of New France and that without the development of sustainable agriculture the colony would remain an excessive burden on metropolitan finances, the same marriages that facilitated a trading economy threatened to undermine an agricultural one by draining off French men needed as farmers and settlers.[125] Despite their disagreements over which was the lesser of two evils—marital or nonmarital relationships—there was one thing that all authorities, from La Vente to Bienville to Pontchartrain, could agree on: French men needed wives to become colonial settlers, and European, not Indian, women were the most suitable conduits to facilitate that transformation.

We Ought to Send Women

Metropolitan and local authorities alike believed that the problems of racially exogamous relationships and fixing French men to French outposts could be solved by increasing the number of European women in the colony. When Pontchartrain noted in 1716 that Indian-French marriages should be "prevent[ed] as much as possible," he followed it with a pledge to send "girls from here as soon as we are able to."[126] For d'Artaguiette, "the surest remedy" for deterring "the course of concubinage" was "to send women there." Without wives, he had written earlier, coureurs de bois "will run away in the woods."[127] D'Artaguiette's predecessor, Nicolas de La Salle, also explicitly linked the emigration of French women with "preventing disorders and debaucheries that [Frenchmen] commit with the sauvagesses."[128]

Over and over again, Louisiana administrators wrote to France begging for more French women, stressing that only marriage to French women would encourage the colony's young Frenchmen, many of them coureurs de bois or discharged soldiers, to establish farms. As such, they saw the presence of French women as central to the goal of establishing a more stable and permanent economy based on family farming rather than a transient economy of Indian trade. French and particularly Canadian men had been at least partially blamed with their "vigorous" appetites for "debauchery," but through marriage to French women, they could, it was thought, ultimately be redeemed.[129]

Euro-Louisianan men themselves also submitted requests for French brides. In 1709, one group of Canadians declared to Bienville and d'Artaguiette that without wives, "they would not settle down" and cultivate the land as requested.[130] Bienville and La Vente might disagree over the appropriateness of Indian-French marriages and over the extent of their respective authorities, but they could agree that the immigration of French women was the most dependable way to complete the colonization of Louisiana.[131]

Most French women of the early eighteenth century, however, like most French men at the time, showed little inclination to migrate across the Atlantic for an uncertain life in an unfamiliar colony.[132] Despite the hardships brought on by the War of Spanish Succession (1701–14), which persisted even after the Treaty of Utrecht, few were inclined to emigrate. Skilled workers continued to find employment in France, and unskilled workers who did seek emigration traveled to the French West Indies where opportunities were better. Discharged soldiers and farmers also preferred to remain in France. Knowledge of Louisiana was vague, but most people knew enough about its dire living conditions to want to avoid emigrating there at all costs. Death rates were high for arriving immigrants, and colonizers continued to rely on France for some of their most basic daily needs. In addition, as an anonymous memoir written from Louisiana in 1714 declared, "No one wants to emigrate to an abandoned land where there is no security."[133] Only the poor, unskilled, and ignorant found themselves on ships heading for Louisiana.

In 1714, Antoine Crozat, whose monopolistic control of Louisiana began in 1712, proposed establishing a lottery that would fund the transportation of those willing to emigrate but unable to pay their way. Although supported by Pontchartrain, Crozat's lottery was rejected by the comptroller general of finances, who argued that it would be a drain on the French population, which was still recovering from losses during the recent war. For similar reasons, officials in New France rejected proposals to allow the free migration of families from their colony. In 1716 and 1717, the Council of the Marine did its part to encourage emigration by granting free passage and sustenance for those going to Louisiana while mostly rejecting requests for those seeking transportation to the French West Indies. Poverty and unemployment in France, along with a somewhat more positive popular view of the colony, also helped to slightly increase immigration. But, by March 1717, there were still probably no more than six hundred Euro-Louisianans of both sexes in lower Louisiana, concentrated at Mobile and Biloxi.

Following the establishment of the regency in 1715 and of the Company of the West, which took over Crozat's monopoly in August 1717, immigration to Louisiana underwent a dramatic shift. Philippe, duc d'Orléans, who thought of the colonies as little more than places to send the unwanted and undesirable, ended the ban that Louis XIV had placed on forced migration, and the first ship carrying unwilling immigrants—prisoners convicted of salt smuggling and women taken from the poor houses—set sail in 1717. The following year, Philippe ordered all the vagabonds in the Paris area to be arrested and deported. For two years, unwilling migrants formed a substantial minority of those arriving in Louisiana, until complaints from colonists as well as from the company forced Philippe to prohibit the deportation of "Vagabonds, people without known occupations, Cheats and Criminals" to Louisiana, although they could still be sent to other French-American colonies. Although the company realized the importance of underwriting substantial immigration to the colony, by 1720 it was complaining that involuntary migrants became unwilling colonial subjects and even more reluctant workers.[134]

The forced migrations of the late 1710s badly damaged Louisiana's reputation once again, and John Law, director of the Company of the West, initiated a propaganda campaign that extolled the colony's fertile and productive lands, its gold and silver mines, and the harmonious relations between colonizers and native peoples, as illustrated in François Gérard Jollain Jr.'s *Le commerce que les indiens du Mexique font avec les françois au Port de Mississippi*, a painting from about 1720 that the company distributed. Law's campaign was fairly successful in recruiting concessionares, laborers, and artisans as well as German, Swiss, and Alsatian families, although less so in convincing skilled workers to emigrate. When the Company of the West became the Company of the Indies in 1718, it attempted to increase voluntary migration by offering free transportation to the families of engagés and by promising support for women willing to go find husbands. In all, somewhere between four and six thousand Europeans arrived in Louisiana between 1719 and 1721, of whom more than twelve hundred had embarked unwillingly.[135] Eight years later, however, only twenty-two hundred Europeans remained in the colony (though that did represent a sixfold increase from 1718). As many as two thousand had returned to France, spreading "the most frightful accounts" that discouraged further emigration, while many others had died.[136] After 1721, migration slowed to a trickle, and when Bienville returned in 1733 he "found the colony in a much worse condition" than when he had left nine years earlier, blaming its demise on "the want of provisions, of merchandise and of money" and "because of the considerable decease in the number of the colonists."[137]

The limited number of immigrants, alongside the construction of native women as unsuitable brides, reemphasized the importance of recruiting European women—from France, elsewhere in Europe, and Canada—and the centrality of their role in the development of the colony. European women were valued for both the cultural and reproductive work they could perform. Women "who understand how to sew, knit, and do, also, all other kinds of housework" were deemed "useful to the colony" in that they could illustrate proper gender roles for "the daughters of the Indians." But, most importantly, they would bind young male colonizers to the colony. Recognizing the vital role European women would play in populating the colony, Commissaire Ordonnateur Hubert recommended furnishing single women who arrived in the colony "with supplies to feed them until they get married."[138]

Initially, Louisiana officials listed few criteria in their requests for more French women. De Gourville suggested recruiting women from the Paris asylums who would not be missed. To persuade these women to emigrate, he recommended granting them free passage and supporting them for almost two years after their arrival.[139] Other Louisiana administrators were more specific and asked for "hardworking people and girls who know how to do something useful" who could perform the labor necessary in a young colony: cultivating the land, raising families, and teaching Indian men and women. D'Artaguiette wrote that the best immigrants would be "families of farmers, selecting those in which there are many girls who would be married to the Canadians." Not only would this "make that many more settlers," but, d'Artaguiette claimed, it "is the only way to put at one stroke the establishments of this colony in a position to do without the assistance from France for material existence." For its part, the metropole acknowledged

LE COMMERCE QUE LES INDIENS DU MEXIQUE FONT AVEC LES FRANÇOIS AU PORT DE MISSISIPI.

In an effort to encourage immigration from France, the Company of the West distributed this fanciful engraving illustrating the riches of the colony, including peaceful trade with Indians. François Gérard Jollain Jr., *Le commerce que les indiens du Mexique font avec les françois au Port de Mississippi*, ca. 1717. The Historic New Orleans Collection, accession no. 1952.3.

that sending marriageable young women would "increase the number of households and families as much as is possible."[140]

In January 1704, Pontchartrain sent word to Bienville that the first group of épouseuses—women specifically sent "to be married to the Canadians and others"—would be arriving aboard *Le Pélican* later that year. They had "been brought up in virtue and piety and [knew] how to work." He promised that he would send only "those of recognized and irreproachable virtue" and requested Bienville "to marry them off to men capable of supporting them with some sort of comfort."[141] The women arrived at Mobile in July under the watchful eye of their chaperon, Father Alexandre Huvé, and were greeted by colonists like Pénicaut, who described them as "quite well behaved," noting that therefore "they had no trouble in finding husbands." Indeed, Bienville reported in September that "all the girls [had already] married the Canadians and others who are in a position to support them." At least one, however, had not. Françoise Marie Anne Boisrenaud was still single as late as October 1706, when Bienville wrote to Pontchartrain asking if it had been his intention that these women "should be obliged to be married when they find a good match." He requested permission to make Boisrenaud marry "since there are several good suitors who are sighing for her." The king responded that if she failed to marry, the governor could force her to return to France unless it was found that she could be otherwise "useful to the colony."[142]

It would be eight years before another ship brought single young women to the colony, and they would be received quite differently from their predecessors. On June 5, 1713, twelve young women arrived aboard *La Baron de Fauche*, the same ship that delivered Cadillac to his appointment as governor. He had been instructed by the king "to give extreme care to the girls . . . in order to marry them as quickly as possible." Cadillac was to prevent them from engaging in "libertinage" or "debauchery" and ensure that they lived "in the discretion and modesty suited to their sex."[143]

During the voyage, however, Cadillac and his wife, who was charged with supervising the women, were unable to prevent the seduction of Madame Cadillac's own chambermaid and perhaps others by fellow passenger Sieur Louis Poncereau de Richebourg, whom Cadillac accused of "indulg[ing] in all sorts of debaucheries." Upon the arrival of *La Baron de Fauche,* some Canadians who had also been aboard "spoke ill of [the women] as soon as they landed."[144] In addition to stories about their onboard activities, these women were reported by Duclos as being "so ugly and malformed that the habitants and especially the Canadians have no desire for them." In future, he continued, "more attention should be directed toward the girls' figures than towards their virtues. The Canadians, especially the coureurs de bois, . . . are not very scrupulous about the girls' past conduct, before they desire them, and if they had found some more attractive to their taste, they would have been able to marry them and get themselves established here, which would increase the colony."[145]

Cadillac concurred, stating that besides being "very poor," the "girls" had "neither linen nor clothes nor beauty." Yet despite rumors of immodesty and alleged unattractiveness, one woman had already married by mid-July, and Duclos believed the others would not remain unmarried for long. Three months later, however, Cadillac reported that only three had married and one had died, leaving eight who were "living in misery." He recommended abandoning this project in favor of "send[ing] boys or rather sailors because we could make good use of them."[146]

Rumors of immodesty, and therefore unmarriageability, only increased when women were included among the unwilling recruits sent from France after October 1717. Passenger lists of this era included women who were "sent by the king" or "exiled" to the colony.[147] Not all the more than twelve hundred women who arrived between 1712 and 1721 had been rounded up in the duc d'Orléans' sweeps of city streets, prisons, and hôpitaux, however. Eighty-eight épouseuses arrived in January 1721 aboard *La Baliene*, under the supervision of three nuns, whom the company directors had ordered to "maintain the said girls in the purity of their honor."[148] According to Dumont, "As soon as these girls disembarked, they were all lodged in the same house with a sentry at the door. During the day, leave was given to go see them and choose from amongst them, those that suited one better; but as soon as night fell, entry to their house was forbidden to all persons. These girls were not long in being provided for and married."

Demand for "these girls" was such, Dumont continued, that "a very serious dispute" arose over one named Hélène. Although she was "anything but beautiful and had the air of a Soldier of the Guards rather than a girl," two young men almost came to blows over her. The quarrel was settled when the commandant had the men draw straws. Dumont concluded that if "as many girls arrived as there were Soldiers and Workers on [Dauphine] Island, there would not be a single one who remained without a husband."[149] The final, sponsored shipment of épouseuses arrived in 1728. Referred to as the "filles de la cassette," or "casket girls," for the "little trunk of linens and clothes, caps, chemises, stockings, etc.," they were given for their new lives in Louisiana, Dumont reported that they were "more distinguished than their predecessors"; they "did not have time to be bored in the houses they were given on their arrival, and it did not take long to find husbands."[150]

Although seen as the colony's saviors—the ones who would put wayward French men on the path to successful colonization—French women's presence could lead to its own disorders. As Rémonville had noted to Pontchartrain in 1697 before Iberville set off for Louisiana, French women could also "be the source of libertinage, debauchery, jealousy, and quarrels."[151] Father du Poisson wrote ironically that the incoming women were "taken from the hospitals of Paris, or from the salpêtrière, or other places of equally good repute, who find that the laws of marriage are too severe, and the management of a house too irksome."[152] In 1722, Nicolas-Michel Chassin, the company's garde magasin (storekeeper) in Illinois country, complained that these women were unsuitable for officers to marry: "Several are becoming impatient but we let them grumble. The Company has already sent four or five hundred girls, but officers and those who hold any rank cannot make up their minds to marry such girls who in addition to the bad reputations that they bring from France give reason to fear that some also bring remnants of infirmities of which they have been imperfectly healed." He therefore suggested that girls be recruited from Canada but feared that was not a perfect solution either since "a libertine who came here from that country makes us fear that among those who might come from there might be some of the same sort."[153] Later that year, Chassin himself married a prominent local métis woman, Agnès Philippe, the daughter of militia captain Michel Philippe and his wife, Marie Rouensa, one of the region's staunchest Christian converts and daughter of a Kaskaskia chief.[154]

Unfortunately for the Louisiana administrators who espoused the civilizing effects of French women, the colony seems to have had the opposite effect on the women. Although some of them may have been prostitutes in France, it is more likely that they turned to this occupation in Louisiana because they had few other options.[155] Cadillac complained of one married "woman who is so scandalous that she prostitutes herself to all comers, sauvages as well as blancs." La Chaise complained that "there are many other women . . . who have no husbands and who are ruining the colony," recommending that all the immigrants—men and women—who had been forced to Louisiana (presumably only those who were not being productive) be returned to France. A few months later, the Superior Council argued for "the necessity of purging the colony of these vagabonds and especially of a number of women of bad life who are entirely lost."[156] The following year, complaining about the "many women and girls of bad life here," Périer and La Chaise recommended the building of "a house of correction" in which "the women and girls of bad lives who cause a public scandal" could be put. Another possibility was to have the Ursuline nuns "take care of the girls and women of evil life."[157]

By 1732, Périer and Commissaire Ordonnaleur Edme-Gatien Salmon were claiming that most of the "dissolute women" had been purged from the colony and that there was "no need at all" for "a house of correction." They did, however, argue that the company should continue to support orphan girls and widowed women, who would otherwise be "abandoned to their evil fate" and become "so many libertines."

With charitable support, such women could become "good mothers of families."[158] Thus, while administrators had earlier believed that French women would secure the establishment of families and farms in Louisiana, by the late 1720s they found themselves faced with many women "who are useless and who do nothing but cause disorder," betraying their simplistic belief that French women were better suited than Indian women at subduing Euro-Louisianan men.[159]

François de Mandeville, sieur de Marigny, doubted the transformative effects of marriage even as he added his voice to the demands for more French women. While arguing that, once married, Canadian men "would work to support their families in mutual rivalry," he also noted that even "the married and settled people live in . . . slothfulness," as they had little faith in the colony's permanency. For him, the presence of more French brides was but only one issue that had to be addressed; the king also had to demonstrate his commitment to the colonization of Louisiana by sending more troops and colonists, especially peasants who could teach the Canadians, who had "been in the woods for a long time," how to cultivate the land.[160]

EVEN WITH INCREASING NUMBERS of French women arriving in Louisiana, administrators and clerics were unable to eradicate relationships between Indian women and Euro-Louisianan men, and both nonmarital and marital relationships continued to occur. That the post-1716 policies discouraging Indian-French marriages had to be reiterated time and time again indicates how ineffective they were. As late as 1751, Governor Pierre de Rigault de Vaudreuil had to instruct the new Illinois country commandant that "an essential point of public order which directly concerns solely M. de Macarty is to prevent the marriages which the French have hitherto contracted with the native women. This union is shameful and of dangerous consequences because of the familiarity it encourages between the natives and the French, and because of the bad race it produces."[161]

In addition, although local and metropolitan authorities reacted in an increasingly hostile way to relationships between native women and colonizing men, such marriages did not, in fact, challenge French attempts to build alliances or exploit Indian lands; indeed they continued to be accepted informally because they could aid in this process, especially in upper Louisiana where Indian trade remained a mainstay of the regional economy.

Although these relationships continued throughout the eighteenth century, and officials made sporadic efforts to combat them, the intensive debate of earlier decades receded from public view.[162] This ebbing of concern over Indian-French relationships coincided with lower Louisiana's transformation from an extractive colony to a protoplantation society. With the arrival of African slaves in large numbers beginning in the late 1710s, the lower valley (although not the Illinois region) began to move out from under the shadow of New France—with its legacies of intermarriage and demand for female immigrants—and local and metropolitan officials turned their gaze southward, toward the French Antilles, for a new vision of social order. Despite, or perhaps because of, the colony's utter dependence on African labor, there was never any serious consideration that Africans, who arrived almost exclusively as slaves, would participate in building colonial society in the way that at least some officials thought Native Americans could. The metropole almost immediately prohibited African-French marriages, and there was no one who argued otherwise—there would be no decades-long debate over or missionary support for African-French relationships, as there had been with respect to Indian-French marriages. This stark contrast illustrates how particular political economies helped to determine colonial sexual and racial politics as least as much as either demographics or racial ideologies.

The contrast between the Code Noir's absolute ban on African-French relationships with officials' earlier failure to impose significant penalties on French-Indian relationships highlights their ultimate ambivalence about the latter, given that they were useful in building alliances with native nations and facilitating trade relations. That successive so-called bans allowed marriages to take place with the consent of a secular official demonstrates that underlying the disdain for Indian-French marriages by secular officials was a greater desire to control French male colonists, Indian women (and, perhaps through them, their male relatives), and even religious officials, who could appeal to the king's religious sentiments in opposition to local secular authority.[163] As secular officials sought control and religious ones sought morality and religiosity, both called on ideologies of cultural and racial differences to bolster their cases. Yet metropolitan policies and imported racial ideologies did not always reflect emerging colonial attitudes, which were dependent on the particularities and contingencies of certain places and certain times.

CHAPTER TWO

Legislating Slavery in French New Orleans

IN 1736, Marie, a young slave woman, ran away, claiming she was being "cruelly treated without cause." Marie's legal owner was Françoise Larche, who had recently inherited her father's estate. However, Françoise was a minor and Marie was under the control of Françoise's uncle and guardian, Joseph Chaperon and his wife, Louise Le Coq, who used her to nurse their young child. Marie first fled to the Jesuit priests who had hired many of the other slaves from the Larche estate and then, when the priests said they could not hire her without informing Chaperon, to Jacques Larche, the deceased's brother. "Fearing . . . Chaperon's fury," Marie hoped that Jacques would hire her out to someone else as "she could not return to Chaperon as she would die." Having previously seen how hired slaves were mistreated by people "who were not their real masters," Jacques filed a declaration with the Superior Council. In response, Le Coq declared that Marie had run away and that Jacques himself had "influenced her to desert her post," and the council ordered Marie to return to Chaperon.[1] The following year, Chaperon came to the attention of the Superior Council again when it was notified that a fifteen-month-old child of an unnamed slave woman (perhaps Marie again, as the woman was identified as belonging to the Larche estate) was "unable to stand, slightly swollen, and affected with diarrhea," a condition the investigating doctor diagnosed as brought on by "bad food and neglect."[2]

Chaperon's violence was well known and was directed toward Euro-Louisianans in addition to slaves, both those under his command and those belonging to others.[3] He even makes a cameo appearance in Jean Bernard Bossu's account of mid-century Louisiana, where Bossu wrote that Chaperon "forced one of his Nègres into a hot oven, where this wretch expired, and as his jawbones had been drawn back, the barbarous Chaperon said: I believe that he is still laughing, and he took up a pitchfork to stir up the fire. Since then, this habitant has become the bugbear [épouvantail] of the Slaves, and when they are disobedient to their masters, they threaten them by saying: *I will sell you to Chaperon.*"[4] Notwithstanding this wide-spread knowledge of Chaperon's violence toward Afro- and Euro-Louisianans alike, there is no clear evidence that Chaperon was ever punished for his mistreat-ment of the enslaved, despite provisions in the Code Noir of 1724 that criminalized "barbarous and inhumane" treatment of slaves. The case of Chaperon clearly il-lustrates that the metropolitan-authored code was not simply accepted by either the colony's ruling elite, who adapted metropolitan policies to suit themselves, or its ordinary residents, who often ignored both metropolitan and local policies gov-erning slavery.[5]

The Code Noir was the metropole's response to the emergence of slavery in lower Louisiana. By the early 1720s, it became clear that the region's economy was moving away from that of New France, with its dependence on Indian trade and family farms, toward the Caribbean model of plantation agriculture and enslaved labor. As such, the Crown looked to the islands to determine how to govern Loui-siana, and in 1724, it rewrote the Code Noir that had been implemented there in 1685 to regulate the relationships between slaves and their masters, the enslaved and the free, and those of African and of European descent. These 1724 regulations would shape how racial identities—with their particular rights and obligations—emerged in lower Louisiana, but they were, to a great extent, defined by a distant metropole that was responding to situations within Louisiana, elsewhere in its co-lonial empire, and in France itself, as it sought to regulate racially exogamous relationships, manumission, and the status of free people of African ancestry. Codifying status and ancestry as important determinants of rights, privileges, and obligations, the 1724 Code Noir reflected the transition from a status-based hierarchy to one rooted in race, thus creating a niche for free people of African ancestry, albeit one that few were able to take advantage of during the French era.

While metropolitan officials attempted to clarify and codify social relationships from a distance, local officials and elites had to live in and attempt to rule over a fragile colony in which hunger, sickness, poverty, and death affected Africans, In-dians, and Europeans alike. The common hardships through which all Louisian-ans struggled created conditions similar to those Peter Wood has described for early South Carolina: ones of "forced intimacy and tenuous equality."[6] As such, social relations were more fluid and social hierarchies less established than they would become with the entrenchment of plantation agriculture in the late eigh-teenth century. Local officials were selective about which aspects of the Code Noir they chose to enforce and which to ignore, as they adapted metropolitan-authored laws to conditions in the colony.

Everybody, Gentlemen, Is Asking for Negroes

The development of slavery in Louisiana was driven primarily by concessionaries and habitants, who demanded slaves as early as 1706.[7] As we saw in chapter 1, the colony suffered from an extreme shortage of labor because of a high mortality rate and an unfavorable reputation exacerbated by engagés' complaints about their "slavish treatment" and unpaid wages, which the Superior Council admitted was "too common for connivance."[8] Despite this continuing labor shortage, the Crown was unable, and Antoine Crozat's proprietary company unwilling, to make the investment that would be required to supply Louisiana with African slaves. Additionally, some worried about the consequences of an enslaved labor force. Father Pierre François Xavier worried that nègres were "always Foreigners" who would never think of Louisiana as their native land and were "attached to us only by fear." He urged authorities to rely on engagés rather than nègres since the former eventually "become Habitants, and increase the number of natural Subjects of the King."[9]

Louisiana did have a market in Indian slaves but habitants complained that Indian slaves "desert when they are hard pressed" and that they could "not get nearly as much service from them as from the negroes."[10] Local authorities were particularly concerned with maintaining good relations with nearby Indian nations, on whom they were dependent for food, trade, and alliances, and correctly perceived that slave raids would imperil these relations. In seeking to ensure that Indians sold as slaves to habitants were "taken only from the nations that have killed Frenchmen," Bienville forbade colonists in 1711 from purchasing slaves from European middlemen and required Indian slave traders "to bring the slaves that they take in the future themselves in order that I may know from whom they have taken them."[11] In 1728, Governor Périer argued that the use of Indian slaves was "contrary to the welfare of this colony," in part because it encouraged warfare among Indian nations that often threatened to involve the French colony as well. He realized that it was only by seeking to keep "all the nations in peace among themselves" and refusing to trade in Indian slaves, thus convincing them that the French were "better friends of theirs than the other European nations," that the French could hope to keep the English from turning neighboring nations against the fledging colony. But Périer also argued that, regardless of the circumstances of their capture, Indian slaves were "of very little service to us." They were "not suited for anything else than for fishing and hunting" and often fled "to their nations" or to other nations that were closer. In addition, "these Indian slaves being mixed with our negroes may induce them to desert with them, as has already happened, as they may maintain relations with them which might be disastrous to the colony when there are more blacks."[12] For these reasons, the number of Indian slaves living among the colonists was kept low and colonial administrator Jean Bochart, chevalier de Champigny, could report in 1744: "There are very few savage Slaves, because we are at peace with all the Nations." He justified the possession of those few, claiming they "were kept in former Wars, and we keep them."[13]

Bienville nevertheless supported habitants' request for permission to sell Indian slaves to Caribbean planters in exchange for African ones, claiming that it "accomplishes a great good for the colonists."[14] Although Pontchartrain initially agreed that "this proposal . . . seems advantageous for the establishment of the colony," ultimately he and Louis XIV determined it was "not practicable" since, as one habitant warned, Caribbean planters "do not get rid of their negroes unless they know that they are bad and vicious."[15] A Caribbean official later confirmed these fears when he requested permission from the minister to send to Louisiana those "blacks who are bad characters," including "poisoners [and] flagrant maroons," since he was running out of prison space and, he claimed, "the blacks are better controlled by their masters" in the mainland colony than on the islands.[16]

Even though the colonists did not receive permission to import slaves from the West Indies, African slaves did start to trickle into Louisiana by 1709. It was not until 1719, however, that the Company of the West decided to encourage tobacco cultivation and began to import African slaves in substantial numbers "from the Islands, or from *Guinea*."[17] In less than fifteen years, more than six thousand Africans were imported into the colony. By 1731, two years after the Natchez destruction of the French village at Fort Rosalie that both bankrupted the Company of the Indies and undermined metropolitan investors' confidence in the Louisiana tobacco production centered at the fort, the slave trade to Louisiana had virtually come to a halt. At the same time, Saint-Domingue's sugar revolution was under way and its planters, seen as a better risk, absorbed all available credit. Without the company or metropolitan investors willing to supply them with credit, habitants were unable to purchase new slaves in any great numbers until the 1770s, when the new Spanish governors reopened the slave trade to Louisiana. Notwithstanding this limited trade and despite a mortality rate for arriving Africans of nearly one-third, a majority of lower Louisiana's colonial population was black and enslaved by 1726, and it would remain so until the 1780s.[18]

Nearly three-quarters of these slaves ended up on plantations within a twenty-five-mile plantation belt surrounding New Orleans, beginning downriver just below English Turn and continuing up through Cannes Brûlées. Slightly fewer than one-third of all households in this region owned slaves. Of those, more than one-half owned fewer than five; a quarter owned just one. But while most owners possessed just a few slaves, two-thirds of slaves were part of holdings of twenty or more. Indeed, six slaveowners owned almost 50 percent of the region's slaves. The colony's largest was Governor Bienville, who owned 145 slaves on a concession just downstream from the city on the opposite bank. The other five largest slaveowners all owned concessions at Chapitoulas, about three leagues upriver from New Orleans. The three Chauvin brothers, who together owned 263 slaves, had, according to Andre Pénicaut, "the finest and best cultivated of all the concessions in the country." Next door to the Chauvin brothers were Sieur Claude-Joseph Villars Dubreuil and his fifty slaves; by the time of Dubreuil's death three decades later, his holdings had increased by about two hundred.[19]

Despite having a black majority, with enslaved Africans outnumbering Euro-Louisianans by as many as eight to one at Chapitoulas, greater New Orleans did not develop into a slave society until the late eighteenth century, though it was something more than a slaveowning society before then.[20] Although a substantial portion of the population was enslaved and slavery was the dominant form of labor, slaves were not confined to agricultural labor but rather could be found in almost every unskilled sector of the economy and many of its skilled ones too. In this, greater New Orleans most resembled its nearest British North American neighbor before the expansion of rice cultivation. Like late seventeenth-century South Carolina, eighteenth-century New Orleans relied on a mixed economy, suffered from a shortage of labor, and was an unprotected outpost exposed to external dangers.[21]

Slave-based plantation agriculture contributed to the colony's economy, but it competed with what Daniel Usner Jr. has called a "frontier exchange economy," only fully supplanting the latter with the cotton and sugar revolutions at the end of the century.[22] Until then, greater New Orleans was characterized by relatively fluid race relations because of the dependence of Euro-Louisianans on Afro-Louisianans for labor and defense, and the steady growth of a population of free people of African ancestry. Most slave regions in the Americas experienced similar "frontier phases," although New Orleans' transition to a full-blown slave society was particularly drawn out, taking almost a century. Its status as a "frontier slave society" for most of the eighteenth century, as well as its early and lasting black majority, profoundly influenced the ways in which definitions of race developed in colonial New Orleans.[23]

Plantation agriculture was slow to develop for a variety of reasons. For the Crown, Louisiana was a military outpost, intended to defend the interior of the North American continent and the very profitable French Caribbean colonies, but it had little economic value itself. Realizing a profit was clearly a concern for Crozat, John

Law, and the Company of the Indies, but each failed in some fundamental manner. Crozat, interested more in easily extractable resources, did little to people the region with slaves or colonists. The collapse of John Law's Company of the West in a speculative panic known as the Mississippi Bubble resulted in his flight from France and the reorganization of his monopoly as the Company of the Indies. The company did invest heavily in Louisiana, but it soon realized just how much would be necessary before a profit could be achieved. Crozat, the Company of the Indies, and even eventually the Crown, in its cession of the territory to Spain in 1762, all gave up on the colony in great part because its costs far outweighed its profits or other benefits. The Crown only held on to the colony for so long because it was important for geopolitical reasons.[24]

The colony was not without economic potential, however. In 1712, Tivas de Gourville reported: "There is corn in abundance and as many buffalos and deer as one wishes to kill."[25] That same year, Commissaire Ordonnateur d'Artaguiette described the country as "productive and fertile," suggesting that wheat, rice, timber, skins, mining, and trade would provide a solid foundation for the colonial economy.[26] Two decades later, after substantial numbers of African slaves had been imported, Périer and Ordonnateur La Chaise reported they did "not doubt the success of [tobacco] at all, provided the colony has workers and attention is given to supplying it every year with at least one thousand negroes."[27]

Not everyone, however, was as optimistic. Governor Cadillac attacked such reports as "pure fables. They have spoken about what they have not seen at all, and they have too readily believed what was told them." For his part, Cadillac believed Louisiana was "an unhealthy country" where wheat would not grow and tobacco was attacked by vermin. He did acknowledge that indigo and silk might become profitable, but he felt development of these crops would take at least ten years, and he was not sure Crozat would be that patient. "The colony," he summarized, "cannot be poorer than it is at present."[28]

Many concessionaries and habitants believed that the road to success lay in slaves, and they did not wait until they had found a reliable and profitable export crop before clamoring for them. As early as 1706, Bienville notified Pontchartrain that colonizers "eagerly ask for negroes to clear the land."[29] Calls for more slaves never ceased during the French era. Again and again in the 1740s and 1750s, colonists requested a "great many nègres," complaining that they "cannot succeed without that."[30] Yet the desire for slaves far outstripped colonizers' ability to pay for them. In 1722, at the height of the slave trade to French Louisiana, the Company of the Indies charged an average of 1,000 livres for a pièce d'Inde, as a prime hand was called, the same price it charged the much wealthier planters in the French

Caribbean. A few female slaves sold for as much as 1,600 livres, 400 livres more than even a skilled male slave and three times as much as an Indian slave, suggesting that at least some buyers recognized the reproductive potential of enslaved women in such a tight market.

Because so few Louisiana habitants could afford these prices, the company worked out a variety of solutions to enable them to acquire slaves, from requiring slaveowners to relinquish their slaves for one month each year to work on public projects to liberally extending credit. Despite Périer and La Chaise's claim that they "always observed the practice of preferring the good payers and those who work to the others in distribution of negroes, giving . . . preference to those who pay cash for them," by the end of its reign over the colony, the Company of the Indies was owed several million livres by habitants, mostly for slave purchases.[31] Without this willingness to extend credit, Louisiana would have remained a society with a handful of slaves rather than becoming a frontier slave society.

When slaves arrived, they were put to work without delay. Habitant Andre Pénicaut reported seeing slaves disembarking and then immediately being used to unload munitions and merchandise from the very same ship.[32] More often, they were confined to warehouses by the river or put to work on the company's own concession opposite New Orleans until distributed among the habitants. Some slaves were retained by the company or royal officials and put to work at the wharf, in the warehouses, or on public projects. Of the eighty-eight slaves who arrived aboard the *Expédition* in 1723, fifty were kept to work on the levee, three were determined to be good sailors, and only thirty-five were distributed to various concessions.[33] But most new slaves, like the 175 Senegalese who arrived aboard *Le Maréchal d'Estrées* in 1721, were distributed among the concessionaires and habitants, who used them to start clearing their lands before producing such export and subsistence crops as tobacco, silk, indigo, cotton, and rice.[34]

Although Louisiana would later come to be known for its sugar and cotton plantations, neither crop was dominant in the eighteenth century. There were, by the 1750s, several "perfectly successful" cotton plantations but, as Commissaire Ordonnateur Honoré Michel de la Rouvillière noted, "the seeds . . . are rather difficult to detach."[35] A visitor to the colony at the end of the French era noted that the colonists "have attempted sugar" but that "they do not make it turn out to great account."[36] Sugarcane takes fourteen to eighteen months to mature; before then, its juice is too watery and makes inferior sugar. The cane cannot be allowed to freeze so the possibility of cold spells during Louisiana winters shortened the predictable growing season to just nine months. Although the Jesuits began experimenting with sugar cultivation and processing in the 1750s, it was not until the 1790s that Étienne Boré was successful in crystallizing sugar from immature cane.[37]

Before then Louisiana's main export crops were indigo and tobacco.[38] Indigo, grown mostly on plantations within twenty-five miles of New Orleans, had much higher start-up costs and required more slaves than tobacco, restricting it to concessionaires who were already wealthy or had access to credit or to important colonial officials. Tobacco, on the other hand, could be grown by almost anyone, and indeed many habitants had small tobacco plots in addition to their principal crops. After the destruction of Fort Rosalie in 1729 by Natchez Indians, a second, smaller plantation belt, focused mainly on tobacco, grew up around Pointe Coupée, about one hundred miles upriver from New Orleans. At midcentury, Michel reported that the year's tobacco yield was small but "of good quality" and that the indigo harvest "was in general bountiful." Two other important crops were corn and rice, which fed the "poor habitants and the negroes of the colony" and was also exported to the West Indies.[39]

Tobacco was the most profitable export crop, but neither it nor indigo could support the colony, nor did their production require the labor of all of Louisiana's slaves. Rather, as an Anglo-American visitor to the colony in 1766 noted, Louisiana's "principal Staple is their Trade for Furs and Skins from the Illinois [since] their want of Negroes keep back the Indigo making."[40] As Usner has shown, "Inhabitants of the Lower Mississippi Valley pieced subsistence and commercial endeavors together into a patchwork of farming, herding, hunting, gathering, trade, and transportation activities."[41]

Afro-Louisianan slaves were also "very useful to the service [of his Majesty] and they [were] never unemployed." Slave men worked on boats up and down the Mississippi and on the docks as caulkers, carpenters, and other skilled craftsmen, while slave women unloaded vessels at the docks and cleaned the king's warehouses. They also cultivated "a little rice or garden produce for their own use."[42] Many of these activities brought slaves into daily contact with Indians, both slave and free, and a wide range of Euro-Louisianans. It was these everyday interactions that officials in France and Louisiana attempted to regulate through the introduction of the Code Noir in 1724.

Les Codes Noirs

In large part, Louisiana's Code Noir copied the one implemented in the French Caribbean islands in 1685: both sought to regulate the treatment of slaves as well as the relationships among slaves, affranchis, and Europeans.[43] The 1724 code's first three articles focus on religion, indicating that Catholic doctrine informed the entire code.[44] In the seventeenth-century Anglo colonies, religion had operated as one of the first markers of human difference, as the earliest laws distinguished between Christians, who could not be enslaved, and non-Christians, who could, rather than between Englishmen and Africans. Difficulties began to arise when Africans and Indians converted to Christianity, leading the Virginia assembly to decree in 1667 that baptism did not confer freedom on slaves (who nevertheless would continue to claim freedom on the basis of conversion and baptism through the 1690s).[45] Despite metropolitan customary law that emancipated baptized slaves, French metropolitan authorities did not have the same qualms as Virginia legislators about whether baptism would free slaves in their colonies. Rather, they insisted that slaves were to be converted and baptized—and remain enslaved. Even as France moved away from the evangelical fervor of previous centuries, the Crown's commitment to Catholicism as a universalist religion made it unsuitable as a marker of difference, unlike in Anglo-America where early discriminatory laws focused on the Christian/non-Christian divide.[46]

The code's remaining fifty-one articles can be divided into four categories. Nine articles defined slaves as moveable property, regulating the ways in which they could be sold, inherited, and leased.[47] Another six placed restrictions on slaves' behavior, including prohibiting them from carrying offensive weapons, "gathering, by day or night" with slaves belonging to different masters, and selling or trading "any sort of commodity" without "express permission from their masters."[48] The majority of the code's articles, however, governed the everyday treatment of slaves or delineated the legal status of slaves, affranchis, and freeborn (né libre) blacks.

Masters were ordered to instruct their slaves in Catholicism, to have them baptized, and to bury baptized slaves in consecrated ground. Slave families were recognized and protected in law. Masters could not force slaves to marry against their will (although slaves who wanted to marry were required to obtain their masters' consent), and they were prohibited from selling husbands away from wives and parents from their minor children. They were prohibited from working their slaves on Sundays and from abandoning old or sick slaves. They were obligated to provide their slaves with provisions and clothing and were forbidden from substituting alcohol for these provisions as well as from making slaves provide their own food even if granted time to do so (although this practice did become the custom of the country).[49]

As noted earlier, masters could also be prosecuted "for barbarous and inhumane crimes and treatments," while slaves could file grievances if they were not properly fed and clothed.[50] Two articles limited the corporal punishment masters

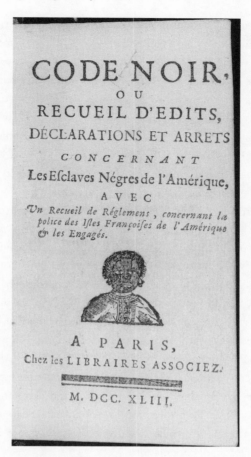

The title page of a 1743 edition of the Code Noir included a stereotype of an African head. *Code Noir ou recueil d'édits, déclarations et arrest concernant les esclaves nègres de l'Amérique* (Paris: Libraires Associez, 1743). Courtesy of the Enoch Pratt Free Library, Central Library/State Library Resource Center, Baltimore, Md.

could inflict on slaves, threatening masters with criminal prosecution if they, or someone acting under their command, killed or mutilated a slave.[51] While limiting masters' own ability to punish their slaves, the Code Noir decreed harsh court-sanctioned punishments. Slaves who were convicted of running away could have their hamstrings cut, a fleur de lis branded on their shoulders, or be executed. A slave "who struck his master, his mistress or the husband of his mistress, or their children with bruising or shedding of blood" could likewise be executed.[52]

The Code Noir also governed intimate relationships between masters and their slaves, and it was in the discussion of these relationships that the Louisiana code differed most from its Caribbean antecedent. According to article 9 of the 1685 code, "hommes libres who have had one or several children from their concubinages with . . . slaves" were to be fined 2,000 livres in sugar, with a similar fine levied against the masters of such slaves for permitting these relationships. If the accused man was also the slave's owner, he was to be "deprived of the slave and children," who were to be sold for the benefit of the hospital "without ever being able to be manumitted." The code did not prescribe any punishment for nonreproductive relationships, perhaps on the assumption that all, or at least most, sexual relationships would result in children or, alternatively, because its authors were not concerned with relationships that did not produce children.

Yet, though article 9 only punished relationships that resulted in children and therefore seemed intended to prevent the growth of an Afro-European population, there are two aspects to this article that undermine this interpretation of it. First, the article was, at least rhetorically, race neutral but status specific in that the prohibited relationships were between *free* men and *enslaved* women. Second, and more telling, was the proviso that if the "free man was not married to another person during his concubinage with his slave" and if he married her "in the forms observed by the Church," she "will be granted freedom in this way" as will her children, who will be simultaneously "rendered . . . legitimate."[53] All of this gave enslaved women a considerable incentive to engage in relationships with free men, regardless of ancestry, in the hope that marriage and therefore freedom would result. The concern at the heart of article 9 was nonmarital relationships, regardless of status or ancestry, and its primary motivation was to impose metropolitan religious mores on the colonial population.

By 1724, however, metropolitan authorities decided that several important changes regarding racially exogamous relationships were necessary. Article 6 of the Louisiana code (which replaced article 9 of the earlier code) stated: "We forbid our white subjects, of either sex [nos sujets blancs, de l'un et de l'autre sexe], from contracting marriage with Blacks [les Noirs] under penalty of punishment and fine; and all cures, priests, or secular or regular missionaries, and even ship chaplains, from marrying them. We also forbid our said white subjects, and likewise the enfranchised or free-born Blacks [Noirs affranchis ou nés libres], from living in concubinage with slaves." The 1685 code permitted marriages between free men, whether noir or blanc, and slave women; the 1724 code, on the other hand, prohibited marriages between all blancs and noirs, whether slave or free. The 1724 code also explicitly referred to white women, who were conspicuously absent in the earlier code.

Yet, although the prohibitions were gender neutral, the specified punishments were aimed only at free men and enslaved women. As in 1685, fines were levied against fathers and masters (300 livres each) and slaves were confiscated, never to receive freedom, if they had children by their own masters. A slave woman and her children could still receive freedom through such a relationship but only if she were "living in concubinage with" an unmarried "black man, manumitted or free [l'homme noir, affranchi ou libre]" who married her.[54] This change from the earlier code meant that enslaved women no longer had an incentive to engage in relationships with European men but only with free men of African ancestry.

In its somewhat complicated manner, article 6 prohibited nonmarital relationships between blancs or free noirs, on the one hand, and slaves on the other, although it was silent on the question of nonmarital relationships between people of the same status and ancestry. And while encouraging the legitimation of relationships between free black men and their enslaved partners through marriage, the article forbade marriages between blancs, male or female, and noirs, whether enslaved or free. Finally, nonmarital relationships between free blacks and whites eluded the code's scrutiny. The article defined people of African ancestry as unsuitable marriage partners for people of European ancestry and also sought to discourage what were defined as illicit relationships involving slaves.

The gender-neutral nature of the Code Noir was not uncommon, as most bans on racial exogamy from the colonial era through 1967 were, in Peggy Pascoe's words, "technically gender-blind."[55] A few, like Maryland's 1664 law that prohibited relationships between "freeborn English women" and "negro slaves," were gendered as were enforcement practices. Relationships between white women and nonwhite men were perceived differently from those between black women and white men because the former, as Martha Hodes has noted, "threatened racial slavery in a way that sex between white men and black women did not." All children born of racially exogamous relationships challenged the attempts of those who would make "black" and "white" into distinct and discrete social categories, but in the British North American colonies the paternal European ancestry of those born to enslaved black women was erased or at least suppressed in a way that the paternal African ancestry of those born to European women could not be. The latter's children also, in Hodes's words, "endangered the equation between blackness and slavery" as, born of free European women, they themselves would be free but of African ancestry.[56] Relationships between European men and African women were either formally (by omission from legal prohibitions) or informally (through social practice) elided. Since reproductive relationships between white men and enslaved women increased the slave population, the sexual exploitation of enslaved women did not threaten, and indeed underwrote, the logic of racial dominance.

The French codes noirs challenged the usual gendered and racial logic of such regulations, particularly the 1685 code, which allowed the children of enslaved women to become free through the legitimation of their mothers' relationships with free men, whether African or European. Rather than bolstering racial dominance through sexual exploitation, the 1685 code provided some protection for an enslaved woman as well as an incentive to have sex with her white master. Such protection was fraught, however, since the woman's punishment—perpetual enslavement with no chance for manumission—might have discouraged her from denouncing a sexually abusive master, even though by so doing she would be removed from his possession.

Both French codes were distinctive in their lack of value-laden language. Anglo-American provisions of the seventeenth century decried racially exogamous relationships as "shameful matches" that defiled, dishonored, and disgraced English bodies, God, and nation and brought forth an "abominable mixture and spurious issue." Even Massachusetts, with its small slave population, criminalized sex between a "negro or mulatto" and any of "her majesty's English or Scottish subjects, nor of any other Christian nation," in order "for the better preventing of a spurious and mixt issue."[57] Such sentiments do begin to appear in French colonial edicts but slightly later. In 1731, the metropole urged Saint-Domingue authorities to prevent marriages between hommes blancs and négresses or mulâtresses because, as the edict declared, "it was a stain upon the whites."[58] In France at least, if not also in the colonies, the fear that this kind of language expressed did not emerge until the late eighteenth century, indicating that article 6 of the 1724 code was not primarily motivated by a concern for maintaining racial purity.[59]

Viewing the 1724 Code Noir's proscription of racially exogamous relationships both within the context of the entire code and side by side with its 1685 precursor demonstrates that the later code was enacted during the period in which ancestry was replacing status as the determining factor in the prohibition of such relationships. By 1724, metropolitan authorities had not yet fully articulated an impulse to segregate, or at least to distinguish, the free from the enslaved and those of European ancestry from those of African ancestry. At the same time, however, they acknowledged the existence of free people of African ancestry. These tensions are most clearly revealed in the articles concerning manumission and the legal status of affranchis.

Although both codes noirs prohibited the manumission of slave women who lived in concubinage with white men, they did allow some legal avenues to freedom, and here again the 1724 code differed in important ways from the 1685 code. According to the earlier code, owners over the age of twenty could "manumit their slaves, by all acts between the living or because of death, without being held to give reasons for their manumission nor needing the advice of their parents."[60] By the 1724 code, however, owners had to be over twenty-five and could only manumit their slaves with the prior approval of the Superior Council, a provision that was intended to prevent owners from setting a price on their slaves' freedom, thereby "inciting the said slaves to theft or robbery." Slaves manumitted without the council's permission were to be reenslaved but confiscated from their previous owner.[61] While the 1685 code granted automatic freedom to slaves who were "made universal heirs by their masters, or named executors of their wills, or tutors of their children," the 1724 code—which made slaves incapable of "claim[ing] anything by succession, disposition between the living, or because of death"—retained the provision only for those appointed as tutors.[62]

In making the Louisiana code's manumission articles more restrictive, the Crown was responding to demographic changes in its Caribbean colonies, hoping to prevent similar demographic changes from occurring in Louisiana. Initially encouraging manumission, in part to prevent "a dangerous state of despair" from developing within the slave population and to create a middling class of artisans and other skilled workers, by 1721, the Crown was concerned with the size of Saint-Domingue's rapidly growing gens de couleur libre population: from five hundred in 1700 to fifteen hundred in 1715. Upon emancipation, most affranchis migrated to urban areas, leaving behind the plantations—and plantation labor—a circumstance the Crown decried as "ruining the plantations for which they are fitted, and causing considerable harm to the colony that depends principally on the labor of negroes."[63] In 1736, it forbade priests from baptizing children born of enslaved women as free, a "dangerous abuse" slaveowners had been practicing as a form of manumission, unless the mothers could prove their own free status.[64] When it tried to limit owners' prerogatives to manumit slaves, however, the Crown found itself faced with members of a hostile planter class, who customarily freed their own enslaved children when they became teenagers. In a position of economic and political power to resist this imperial attempt to regulate their intimate lives, Saint-Domingue planters continued to manumit their children, and the metropole backed down (at least temporarily).[65] In revising the 1685 code for application to Louisiana, the Crown sought to leave "the hope for liberty" which could "sustain or animate the fidelity of the slaves," while limiting Louisiana slaveowners' ability to release their slaves from bound labor, thus maintaining a very scarce and valuable labor source.[66] The 1724 code's other statements on manumission aimed at preventing the growth of an affranchi population unable to support itself by insisting that owners continue to support those affranchis who were disabled or ill.[67]

Upon emancipation, both codes noirs declared that affranchis were to be granted "the same rights, privileges, and immunities enjoyed by persons born free"; indeed manumission in a French colony was deemed to confer the same advantages granted to a native-born subject of the Crown.[68] However, neither code completely erased all distinctions between the freed (affranchis) and the freeborn (nés libres), nor did it grant complete equality between those with African ancestry and those without; thus both status and ancestry were used to define rights and privileges. The 1724 code acknowledged that there were "exceptions" to the rights and privileges to be enjoyed by the free. Both affranchis and freeborn people of African ancestry were incapable of receiving donations or inheriting from blancs, a prohibition that had not been included in the 1685 code. Indeed, as we have seen, under the earlier code slaves could be named universal heirs, an action that resulted in their freedom as well as inheritance of property.[69] Both codes ordered affranchis "to convey a singular respect to their former master, their widows, and children," even though they were "freed and released from all other duties [and] services" their former masters might try to claim from them. If an affranchi were to insult his former master, he would "be punished more seriously" than if he had insulted another person.[70]

The 1685 Code Noir made status the most important determinant of rights and banned extramarital sex between the free and the enslaved (but granted freedom to slave women who married free men); the 1724 code, on the other hand, utilized both status and race in distinguishing the rights and obligations of free persons of African descent from those of both Euro-Louisianans and slaves.[71] The codification of status, alongside ancestry, as an important determinant of individual rights, privileges, and obligations prevented the simple equation of blackness with enslavement, which characterized most British North American slave codes of the eighteenth century.

In addition to outright freedom, affranchis and nègres libres enjoyed certain other rights and privileges the enslaved did not. Although the former may not have been able to inherit from whites, they could, unlike slaves, own property and distribute it as they saw fit.[72] Free people of African ancestry, but not slaves, could sue and defend themselves in civil cases as well as act as witnesses in civil and criminal trials, in contrast to slaves who could only testify if they were "necessary witnesses, and only when Blancs are lacking."[73] Free and enslaved people of African ancestry were tried "with the same formalities as free persons," although for slaves there were certain exceptions. They were to be "severely punished, even with death" if convicted of an act of violence against a free person. Punishments for theft ranged from death to being "beaten with rods by the executioner of the high court and branded with a fleur de lis."[74]

The Code Noir not only distinguished between the free and the enslaved in defining certain punishments for particular crimes but also between free persons of African and of European ancestries. Affranchis were grouped with slaves in the crime of aggravated theft (which included theft of livestock). Regarding one other crime—harboring runaway slaves—affranchis and nègres libres received different punishments from "other free persons." The latter were fined 10 livres for each day they harbored a runaway slave; the former were fined 30 livres. In addition, if unable to pay their fines, affranchis and nègres libres were to "be reduced to the condition of slaves and sold." The 1685 code also imposed different punishments, but it distinguished between affranchis and "other free persons," thereby grouping freeborn persons of African ancestry with blancs rather than with persons freed during their lifetimes, and it had not threatened them with reenslavement.[75] That the singling out of affranchis was not accidental was confirmed by a Martinique administrator in 1704, when he reported that the affranchis and freeborn nègres were not treated equally; the former, he observed, had fewer rights than the latter and owed certain obligations to their former masters.[76] The changes between the two codes indicate that metropolitan concepts of social order and individual privileges were beginning to be principally based on racial categorizations, so that one's European or African ancestry was becoming more important than one's status as free or enslaved in creating one's legal identity. The 1685 code demonstrated a fear that the recently manumitted would have loyalties to the enslaved that needed to be discouraged through higher fines; the 1724 code extended those perceived loyalties to those of African descent, even if born free. As such it posited a community of racial identification rather than one of status and, in threatening to enslave freeborn nègres as a form of punishment, suggested that freeborn persons of African descent did not have an unassailable or irreversible right to freedom.[77]

Because it was concerned with both status and race, the 1724 code used a variety of labels to define who was subject to its various provisions. These categories differ from the labels that the 1685 code used in important ways. Both codes use "esclaves" most commonly to refer to slaves, although the 1724 code specifies "esclaves nègres" in one place, and both occasionally use "nègre" alone when clearly referring to slaves.[78] "Maître" ("master") and "personne libre" (used, for instance, when declaring that slaves should be governed by the same marriage regulations as free persons) oppose the category of "esclave." When not set against slaves, free inhabitants of the colonies are variously referred to as "habitants" and "sujets" (sometimes followed by the phrase "of whatever quality and condition they may be").

Although both codes distinguish affranchis from slaves and from other free persons, the 1724 code also distinguishes between affranchis and nègres libres (sometimes specified as "nés libres"), making one's birth status also noteworthy.[79] The 1724 code also refers to Europeans as "blancs," unlike the earlier one.[80] Curiously, outside of the title, the word "noir" does not appear in the 1685 code and is used only twice in 1724. These linguistic differences further demonstrate that the 1724 code was moving toward relying on racial categories—especially in its usage of "blanc" and "noir"—to determine rights and privileges even as status—whether one was enslaved, freed during one's lifetime, or born free—continued to be important in that determination. That the regulation of sex was implicated in this process of increasing racialization is clear: two of the four uses of "blanc" and both uses of "noir" in the 1724 code are in article 6, prohibiting racial exogamy. Euro-Louisianans are only referred to as blancs when they are banned from having sex with Afro-Louisianans.

To Observe His Majesty's Ordinances

That metropole officials had developed more rigid racial ideologies is apparent in their rhetoric and colonial legislation after the mid-eighteenth century, but Euro-Louisianan attitudes during this period are less clear. Only a handful of locally authored slave codes were enacted during the French period, and most of them were concerned with regulating social order, such as prohibiting colonists from trading with slaves or giving them alcoholic beverages.[81] In 1714, when there were probably no more than a couple hundred slaves throughout the colony, almost all of them Indian, the Superior Council passed its own very brief series of slave regulations.[82] Clearly indebted to Caribbean-authored legislation and the 1685 Code Noir, the council ordained death for esclaves and sauvagesses who struck their owners or other Frenchmen.[83] Threatening to strike an owner brought a whipping, although it was left to a judge's discretion what the punishment should be for a slave who threatened to hit a Frenchman other than his owner. The regulations detailed excessive corporal punishments for slaves who deserted their masters, assembled in the woods, or stole from their owners, including being placed in irons or receiving twenty or thirty lashes, sometimes to be repeated for three consecutive days. The council did proscribe fewer strokes for those under eighteen, yet even those under ten were to receive six lashes for running away. It banned all slaves from carrying weapons except for those sauvages whose owners let them hunt. Recognizing that African slaves were a far scarcer commodity than Indian ones, the council decreed that the owners of nègres slaves condemned to death would be compensated 300 livres, double what they would receive for sauvages.[84]

Almost forty years later, after thousands of African slaves had been brought into the colony and their numbers surpassed those of Euro-Louisianans, Governor Vaudreuil and Ordonnateur Michel enacted their own regulation. Most of its thirty-one articles reflected officials' continuing obsessions with drinking, assembling, and thieving, but a few articles were significantly harsher than the Code Noir. Vaudreuil and Michel complained that some owners were too paternalistic and did not punish their slaves sufficiently. They encouraged owners to chastise their slaves "at all opportunities" and threatened to confiscate insufficiently disciplined slaves "in order to make some severe examples." They expanded the Code Noir's required submission on the part of "nègres" (a term that, by 1751, was clearly synonymous with slave) and "other slaves" toward blancs. Those who failed to "have enough respect and submission[,] . . . who, in short, forgot that they are slaves," would be whipped with fifty lashes and branded with a fleur de lis on the buttock.

But Vaudreuil and Michel distinguished between the respect that nègres owed all blancs and the right of any blanc, soldiers in particular, to assert authority over nègres. Nonowners could confront slaves who refused to cede the road to them and demand justice, but they were not given free license to "mistreat a nègre who is not misbehaving." The regulations allowed for the reenslavement of "all nègres and négresses who have obtained their liberty" (implicitly excluding the freeborn) who harbored runaways, encouraged "slaves to steal from their masters," or led "a scandalous life in contempt" of law and religion. The penalty for French colonizers who were "infamous enough" to similarly incite slaves was a public whipping followed by a life sentence in the galleys. The 1751 regulations concluded by stating that, on all other matters, the Code Noir remained the law of the land.[85]

Neither the Superior Council's nor Vaudreuil and Michel's regulations had anything to say about slaves' legal personalities—whether they were moveable property or could testify in court—nor about owners' religious obligations and daily management of their slaves.[86] They were also silent on manumission and, except for Vaudreuil and Salmon's threat of reenslavement, on the status of affranchis. Since the Code Noir's enforcement was left in the hands of Louisiana officials and the Superior Council, whose members were mostly local slaveowners, it is possible to discern local ideologies at work in the council's actions. By and large, the council upheld those provisions of the code that restricted slaves or punished their misbehavior and ignored those that restricted the behavior of owners. For the slaveowners who dominated local government, slaves were ultimately property that should be managed at the discretion of their owners. Eventually, however, they would have to confront owners who recognized more humanity in their slaves than council members thought wise. These differences of opinion regarding the humanity of slaves became most noticeable when owners sought to manumit their slaves and even more so when they tried to leave property to their former slaves. When the council considered François Viard's testamentary bequest to manumit his female Osage slave in 1729, it approved her freedom. After all, she was Viard's property and he should be able to alienate his property if he so wished. But, citing article 52, it denied his cash legacy to her, thus restricting his property rights but fulfilling the code's larger goal of restricting slaves' and affranchis' access to property. Although it convinced itself that it was enforcing the code, the council in fact fulfilled Viard's dying wishes for his former slave to be educated in the Catholic faith by transferring the cash legacy directly to the Ursuline nuns to pay for her room, board, and education.[87]

Other provisions of the code that the council occasionally upheld included article 24, restricting the use of slaves as witnesses to only those instances in which they were "necessary" and "Blancs are lacking." In June 1751, Councilor d'Auberville determined that he did not need to hear the testimony of enslaved négresses Isabelle and Marianne in the case of *d'Erneville v. Battard* as there were sufficient white witnesses to the events in question.[88] There were, however, numerous cases, both criminal and civil, in which slaves were allowed to testify. In a dispute over the estate of her deceased owner, the court believed Calais' testimony regarding the location of some lost goods.[89] Slaves Boucary and Diaucour were summoned to testify in a case of assault among Euro-Louisianans, while Manon had to testify to her own condition in a redhibition case.[90] Perhaps the most dramatic case involved soldier André Baron, who was accused of bestiality in 1753. Of the several people who testified against him, only two, including negro slave François Xavier, were eyewitnesses to Baron's crime. Xavier was called before the court four times: twice to be interrogated and twice to be confronted by the accused. During the second confrontation, a mare that Xavier identified as the beast in question was also brought to the court. Baron tried to defend himself by labeling Xavier "a miserable fellow," "a rascal," "a beggar and a wretch," although he did not denigrate the Frenchmen who had testified against him. The court, however, clearly gave weight to Xavier's testimony, as it questioned Baron about his failure to complain about the slave's accusation if it was indeed false.[91]

As for the code's stipulations that slaves receive a Christian education, there is little evidence that the Superior Council was concerned with enforcing them. In the mid-1720s, Father Raphaël complained that "the instruction of the negro and Indian slaves is entirely neglected." Owners were far more concerned, he continued, with "deriving profit from the work of these poor wretches without being touched by concern for their salvation." His objection is belied, however, by the sacramental registries that show that two-thirds of those baptized in the early 1730s and again two decades later were slaves. Raphaël also criticized slaveowners who allowed Christian slaves to marry "slaves who are still infidels." Abbé Raguet, Father Raphaël's superior, decrying the owners who were "rendered horribly criminal by joining thus the light with the darkness," informed him that such marriages were null and that he should not "tolerate such concubinages." When they arrived almost five decades later, Spanish priests believed that little had changed. In his first letter to the bishop of Havana, Father Cirilio de Barcelona wrote that what gave him "the greatest concern" was "that the negros marry without parish priests and thus live and die in concubinage" and, even worse, that they did so with their owners' knowledge. He urged the bishop "to oblige the masters to follow the law" on this matter. In this instance, the sacramental records confirm these perceptions; only one-third of the couples who married in the early 1760s were slaves. Most slaves do appear to have been buried, alongside Euro-Louisianans, in the church graveyard, and one slaveowner, the city's treasurer, was fined by the Superior Council for burying a young baptized négresse slave outside of the cemetery. Citing the king's will "that masters be obliged to inter the bodies of their baptized slaves in the cemetery, with the ceremonies of the Church," the council also ordered her body to be disinterred and reburied in consecrated ground.[92]

Nor did the council concern itself with upholding the code's provisions to prevent slaves from working on Sundays and feast days, protect enslaved families, and provide them with adequate food and clothing. Raphaël hoped, "for the sake of religion, that the rules of the Code Noir against masters who abuse their slaves and who make them work on Sundays and holidays would be enforced."[93] No owner was prosecuted for selling a husband away from his wife or parents from their minor children, although some owners were influenced by the sentiments behind this restriction and worked to keep enslaved partners together. In 1737, Noel Soileau exchanged a nègre slave of his for one of Joseph Larche's because the slave was married to "one of Larche's negresses and spen[t] all his time with her and his children." Soileau was willing to participate in this exchange despite his belief that the marriage was illegitimate.[94] The following year, La Coste, who was about to move to Pointe Coupée, requested permission to sell a nègre named Beller "so as not to separate him from his wife."[95] Similarly, individual owners may have paid more attention to the code's articles on providing for slaves, as indicated by Sieur Georg

August de Vanderkeck's contract with Christian Grever to oversee his plantation at the German Village. "In order to observe the ordinances of His majesty," Grever was required to provide each nègre and négresse with an outfit of clothing each year.[96]

The Superior Council's selectivity in enforcing the Code Noir is clearest in cases involving cruelty toward slaves. When such cases did emerge in the court records, it was because council members were concerned with property rights rather than inspired by humanitarian or benevolent concerns. One case of abuse that received substantial attention involved Councilor Raymond Amiot d'Ausseville and Jacques Charpentier dit Le Roy, who had leased d'Ausseville's property just downriver from the city. In January 1730, d'Ausseville sued Le Roy, accusing him of mismanaging his concession and mistreating his slaves, killing at least one of them. According to d'Ausseville, Le Roy worked the slaves to the point of exhaustion, fed them only rotten beans, and caused the death of Brunet, a nègre slave who died of a gangrenous-infected bruise, a result of Le Roy's punishment. Further, d'Ausseville charged that Le Roy inflicted corporeal punishment on pregnant women, causing many of them to have spontaneous miscarriages, and that he was particularly cruel to women who had rejected his sexual advances. Portraying Le Roy's sexual exploitation as an abuse of his power and authority, d'Ausseville sought to have his lease revoked and asked for the exorbitant sum of 20,000 francs in damages. The council did permit slaves to testify against Le Roy, who had "managed to conceal most of his crimes from white witnesses," but it expressed little concern in leaving them under his management while it debated the situation. The council allowed the case to drag on throughout 1730 when eventually the matter became moot, as Le Roy's lease came to an end on December 31.[97]

In a similar case, François-Louis de Merveilleux, commander at Fort Rosalie, sued overseer Pierre Gaullas for the inhumane treatment of one of his slaves. As punishment for running away, Gaullas inflicted more than six hundred lashes on Choucoura, binding his wrists tightly during the whipping. As a result, Choucoura lost three fingers on one hand and two on the other. Gaullas, however, blamed Choucoura, claiming that the slave had "lost his fingers by thrusting them into boiling water after wounding his hands by struggling while bound." Merveilleux was not opposed to harshly punishing slaves: in an earlier letter to the overseer, he had urged Gaullas "to punish lazy *Alexis* by lashing till blood flows." In Gaullas' defense, Father Philibert de Vianden testified that the overseer was a diligent employee who worked from dawn to dusk in Merveilleux's absence, "neglecting no part of his service," while the surgeon Lasonde certified Gaullas had, of his own initiative, requested the surgeon's help in treating Choucoura. Other witnesses declared that at least one of the slaves "provoke[d] Mr. Gaullas with abusive language" and that Merveilleux tried to bribe witnesses against Gaullas. Despite these testimonials, Gaullas was ordered to compensate Merveilleux 200 piastres for the damages to Choucoura and to pay the surgeon's fees.[98]

Many other cases of abused, mistreated, and overworked slaves emerge from the Superior Council records, very few of which resulted in prosecution of the offenders.[99] Charles de Morand charged the butcher Pairoc with brutalizing his slave Scipion, while veuve La Croix filed suit against Dupre Terrebonne Junior for killing one of her slaves and wounding another. Dame Jeanne Catherine Loquet de La Pommeraye won a judgment of 2,000 livres against Sieur Gabriel Joseph Dubois for causing the death of her slave Coffy through overwork and malnutrition.[100] In none of these cases did the owner seek criminal prosecution of the assailant; rather monetary reparations were their goal. When Lasonde accused Coupart of beating a sauvagesse slave so viciously that she might die, he was trying to get his money back for this recently purchased slave.[101] For owners, a violent attack on slave property was, in some ways, no different from an accidental wounding, as when Jean Prat sought compensation for the injury to his slave, a very valuable indigo maker, who was "dangerously wounded" while hired to veuve Dautir.[102] Nor were the suits that arose from such attacks different from ones that involved damage to other property, from livestock to cornfields.[103] Although no slaveowners were prosecuted for injuring their own slaves, it was not uncommon for those who hired or leased slaves to be ordered to pay damages and medical costs to slaveowners.

A few Euro-Louisianans, particularly those without wealth or political connections, did face criminal punishment. Gambest, a young, unemployed Euro-Louisianan, had to pay 500 livres in damages and was imprisoned for having wounded two slaves.[104] A soldier, Pierre Antoine Dochenet, was sentenced to death for stabbing two négresses: Babet, who was owned by the Ursulines, and Louison, who belonged to the King. His conviction rested on the testimony of three soldiers and three slaves in addition to that of Louison and Babet, the latter of whom was near death and fairly incoherent.[105] As the victims of the assault, Louison and Babet were probably deemed "necessary witnesses," but the council also allowed the other slaves to testify despite having available Euro-Louisianan witnesses to the crime. Even with the support of Euro-Louisianans, slaves could not bring their abusers to account when the latter were also their owners. Charles Leconte and Laurent Lerable both filed petitions on behalf of slaves who complained of abuse but in neither case did the council deem it necessary to issue a response.[106] It similarly dismissed the two cases of abuse brought against Joseph Chaperon in the mid-1730s described at the beginning of this chapter.

Additional accusations of cruelty emerge in the testimonies of runaway slaves, who often tried to justify their flight with claims of mistreatment and abuse on the part of their owners but to no avail. In the summer of 1748, Bayou and Mamourou fled their owner, De Gruy, an officer in the Illinois country. Traveling on foot, they remained at large for two weeks and got as far downriver as Bayogoulas. When arrested, they accused their owner of physical abuse, forcing them to work everyday and failing to adequately feed and clothe them, thus violating articles 5, 18, and 38 of the Code Noir. They claimed they were trying to reach New Orleans, not to escape enslavement, but to ask Madame Aufrère, De Gruy's mother-in-law, to assist them in getting a new owner. Dismissing their claims of abuse, the Superior Council ordered the slaves back to De Gruy, who was to "administer . . . such correction as [he] shall judge proper."[107] Guela, a nègre slave belonging to Governor Périer's concession, found to his detriment that claims of floggings, constant beatings, and too little food could bring yet more abuse from the Superior Council itself. Ignoring Guela's assertions of cruelty, the Superior Council convicted him of running away and sentenced him to be branded with a fleur de lis on his shoulder and to have both his ears cut.[108] This was, in fact, the precise punishment prescribed by article 32 of the Code Noir, thus once again demonstrating the Superior Council's selective enforcement of the code's prescriptions.

The Superior Council had no hesitation in upholding the Code Noir when slaves transgressed its provisions, but it tended to prosecute violations by Euro-Louisianans only when other Euro-Louisianans complained about damages to valuable slave property, and even then, it did not do so consistently.[109] When Captain Ignace Broutin sued Pierre Claveau for causing the death of one of his slaves, not only did the council not prosecute Claveau; it also upheld his countersuit for wages that Broutin was withholding.[110] Furthermore, the council prosecuted violations of the code's religious provisions only when priests forcefully pursued the matter. Although article 6, banning marital and nonmarital relationships between blancs and noirs, was a matter of concern to the priests, for example, few bothered to discuss African-French relations, in marked contrast to their concerns with Indian-French ones. A rare public condemnation came from Father Raphaël, who complained that colonists "live in a scandalous disorder with their slaves." Two years later, he acknowledged that "the number of those who maintain young Indian women or négresses to satisfy their intemperance is considerably diminished," though he emphasized "there are still enough to scandalize the church."[111] But, as was the case with complaints about owners' religious failures, Raphaël's concern was with the failure to inculcate morality rather than the interracial nature of these relationships. And, other than d'Ausseville's charge that Le Roy sexually exploited enslaved women, no one was ever prosecuted for violating the Code Noir's ban on racially exogamous sex, even as evidence of such relationships emerges from this and other court records, as will be seen in chapter 3.

Of All the Nègres I Have Known

The Superior Council's selective efforts to enforce the Code Noir reveal its disagreements with the metropole over how to govern a slave society, but few local officials recorded their thoughts on matters of race. One prominent planter who did so was Antoine Simon Le Page du Pratz, who arrived in Louisiana in 1718 at the age of twenty-three. First settling at Bayou St. John, he moved upriver after two years to establish a concession near a Natchez village that he worked with two African and three Indian slaves, including a Chitimacha woman with whom he may have fathered children. In 1728, he was hired by the Company of the Indies to manage its concession on the west bank of the Mississippi opposite New Orleans, making him manager of the largest single slave holding at the time. To oversee 230 Indian and African slaves, Le Page du Pratz was assisted by four other Euro-Louisianan men, two of them engagés.[112]

After sixteen years in Louisiana, Le Page du Pratz returned to France in 1734 and began writing his *Histoire de Louisiane,* published in 1751. Part ethnography and part memoir, the book concludes with a section suggesting a "manner of governing Nègres," written to advise future slaveowners. In his experience, he wrote, "Nègres are a kind of men that it is necessary to govern differently from Europeans, not because they are noirs, nor because they are Slaves, but because they think differently from Blancs." If "prudence requires that your Nègres are lodged at a sufficient distance, so as not to trouble you," he recommended a balance between having one's slaves "near enough for you to observe what is happening among them" yet far enough away as to not to be disturbed by "the stench that is natural to some Nations of Nègres." Warning parents to keep their children away from nègres because they could "never learn anything good from them, not in morals, education, or Language," he reserved particular disdain for parents who allowed their children to have intimate contact with slaves, especially in the form of wet-nursing. Describing milk as "the purest blood of the woman," Le Page du Pratz believed that children could be contaminated through cross-racial breastfeeding, making such parents—particularly mothers, who had "all the conveniences" and "nothing else to do but breastfeed her child"—"truly the enemies of their posterity."[113] This theme was elaborated by Jean Bernard Bossu, who argued that "black, tanned, or red slave women [esclave noire, bazanée, ou rouge]" had "corrupted blood" that "affects the inclinations of the young children." He had "often seen," he wrote, children who had become "innocent victims of the disordered life of their nurses," a situation he found "disastrous to the propagation of the human species."[114]

Antagonism toward cross-racial wet-nursing, which existed in many American colonies, was related to a more general anti-wet-nursing sentiment that had developed in Europe, beginning in the late sixteenth-century England. Defending her decision to breastfeed her own children, Queen Anne reputedly asked, "Will I let my child, the child of a king, suck the milk of a subject and mingle the royal blood with the blood of a servant?"[115] That children could imbibe unwanted qualities from their wet nurses was linked to the belief that breast milk was women's highest form of blood, able to pass on social and moral qualities (albeit a less powerful transmitter of qualities than men's highest form—semen).[116] Although neither Le Page du Pratz nor Bossu explicitly mentioned racial exogamy, their anxieties concerning the mixing of blood through wet-nursing provided a further ideological justification for the metropole's impulses to separate enslaved people of African ancestry from free people of European ancestry.

Yet Le Page du Pratz did not universally denigrate Africans, and he reserved great praise for the Senegalese. Although they were "the blackest," they had "the purest blood" and he claimed he had "never seen one who has the odor" (indeed, Le Page du Pratz asserted that the Africans who "smell the worst are those who are the least black"). Linking "physical" factors such as skin color, smell, and quality of blood with social qualities, Le Page du Pratz goes on to describe the Senegalese as having

> more fidelity and a better understanding than the others and are consequently better suited for learning a trade or how to serve. . . . They are very grateful, and when one knows how to attach them to oneself, they have been seen to sacrifice their own friends to serve their masters. They are [such] good Commandeurs of other Nègres because of their fidelity and gratitude that they seem to be born to command. As they are proud, they can be easily encouraged to learn a trade or to serve in the house, by the distinction that they will acquire over the other Nègres and the cleanliness of dress that this condition will entitle them to.

The Senegalese were the only group Le Page du Pratz recommended for domestic service, in part because of their demonstrated fidelity and in part because "they are not so robust as the others for working the fields nor resisting the great heat."[117] Praise for the Senegalese was not unique to Le Page du Pratz. Diderot's *Encyclopédie* portrayed them as "the finest [slaves] in all of Africa," describing them as "full, well built, and hav[ing] a smooth skin without any man-made marks."[118] French admiration for the Senegalese may have been shaped by the latter's role as traders and go-betweens in St. Louis and Gorée, two West African outposts of the French slave trade.[119]

Promoting a climactic justification for slavery, the *Encyclopédie* defined Africans generally as "by nature vigorous" and therefore better suited for work in "the excessive heat of the torrid zone" than Europeans. Bienville agreed that Africans, not Frenchmen, were suited for work in the tropics. In a 1743 letter to Pontchartrain, he complained "there are very few [soldiers] who make good settlers because in a country as hot as this one it is impossible for a Frenchman to endure the work of an establishment without the assistance of some negroes."[120] Bienville stopped short of declaring that Frenchmen were incapable of working in Louisiana's subtropical climate but he implied that Africans were better suited to it. Diron d'Artaguiette was less equivocal. Writing in 1721, he noted that the colony would never prosper if nègre slaves were "not sent in sufficient numbers" because they were "better suited than the blancs for working the land." He particularly credited their ability to "do wonderfully well in the climate."[121]

Yet not all were convinced that Euro-Louisianans were naturally incapable, or less able, to labor in Louisiana's climate. Bienville's successor, Vaudreuil, and his commissaire ordonnateur, Michel, found another explanation for soldiers' inability to become good colonizers, one that blamed culture rather than nature. Euro-Louisianans lacked, they wrote in 1751, the "ambition and strength to undertake to clear a tract of land" not because they were by nature unable to function in Louisiana's climate but because "they have lived all their lives in great debauchery and without restraint, and that has ruined their constitutions." Vaudreuil and Michel went on to request "good peasants" and "good laborers," who, alongside "a supply of negroes," would allow the colony to flourish.[122]

Whether or not Euro-Louisianans believed enslaved Africans were naturally suited to such work, such workers were clearly valued by Euro-Louisianans desperate for reliable workers. Complaining "he could not use white men or white women as much for their laziness as their libertinage," Delorme hired a company négresse named Margot as his cook. After he was forced to return Margot on his dismissal as a company director, she was quickly bought by Superior Council member Jacques Fazende for 1,000 livres.[123] Slaveowners' reliance on, and trust in, their slaves was demonstrated by their use of slaves as commandeurs, or overseers. In the 1763 census for Chapitoulas, with forty-two plantations and just over one thousand slaves, only two Euro-Louisianans listed commandeur as their occupation; the other plantations were presumably overseen by slaves.[124]

THERE WAS NO CONSENSUS in the colony as to whether Euro-Louisianans or Afro-Louisianans were better workers and whether the cause was cultural or natural. And although Le Page du Pratz distinguished among Africans—not ascribing the same essentialized qualities to all those he deemed nègres—he was beginning to encode cultural differences as racial ones, especially by linking them to physical or biological factors, such as smell, skin color, and blood. As illustrated in chapter 1, a similar process was under way in the racialization of Indian women. Though Africans were, for Le Page du Pratz, clearly different from Europeans, he also acknowledged that despite being "slaves, it is also true that they are men and capable of becoming Christians."[125] This refusal to deny the humanity and suitability for Christianity of slaves of African ancestry was also present in the Code Noir. But the tendency to grant enslaved Africans the capacity for spiritual equality existed at the same time that metropolitan and local officials were beginning to erect legal and social boundaries between the enslaved and the free and between those of African and of European ancestries, albeit boundaries that cut at least three ways. The Superior Council mostly enforced the code's provisions that emphasized slaves' status as property, but a few Euro-Louisianans, like Le Page du Pratz and especially those who manumitted their slaves or formed families with women of color, seem to have respected those that emphasized Afro-Louisianans' humanity. As the following chapter shows, however, these Euro-Louisianans were few, and thus free Afro-Louisianans and those of both European and African ancestry, while recognized in the Code Noir as occupying a distinct rung in the city's socioracial hierarchy, remained a nascent segment of the social order during the French era.

CHAPTER THREE

Affranchis and Sang-Mêlé

IN AUGUST 1725, two New Orleanians stood before Father Raphaël at New Orleans Parish church to partake in the sacrament of marriage. The groom was Jean Baptiste Raphael, a native of Martinique, and the bride was Marie Gaspart, daughter of Jean Gaspart, a drummer in the company of Louis-Claude Le Blanc, and Agnes Simon, a native of Bruges. Though Simon attended her daughter's wedding as a witness, and presumably supported her daughter's choice of husband, Raphael's parents, Jean Raphael and Marguerite de St. Christophe, did not; they probably still resided in Martinique. Other witnesses included a drummer, a soldier, and a sailor in the employ of the Company of the Indies. What made this wedding singular among the thirty-one others that took place in New Orleans in 1725 was that Raphael was a free black man and Gaspart a white woman. This marriage would have been unusual anywhere in colonial North America, especially by the eighteenth century (in particular because it united a European woman with a man of color), but it also directly contravened a prohibition in Louisiana on marriages between blancs and noirs enacted in the 1724 Code Noir. The presiding priest, Father Raphaël, must have been aware of this, as he married the couple only after Commandant General Pierre du Gué de Boisbriant granted his permission, allowing Raphaël to declare he could not "ascertain . . . any impediment to affect this marriage."[1]

Sometime after the ceremony—whether days, years, or even a century is unclear—a marginal notation was added identifying both parties as nègres libres.[2] Such notational changes were not uncommon in the sacramental records from the eighteenth and early nineteenth centuries. However, evidence within the sacramental registers suggests that the bride's marginal classification as a négresse was mistaken. Raphael is explicitly labeled as a nègre libre in the text of the entry, but Gaspart and her parents are unraced, thus, according to the convention of the time, suggesting that they were white. When Raphael and Gaspart's daughter Marie was baptized six years later, Gaspart continued to be unmarked by race, although her daughter was labeled a négresse, born, the priest noted, "in legitimate wedlock."[3] Finally, no other surrounding marriage entry refers to governmental permission before proceeding with the marriage, demonstrating that Father Raphaël was aware this marriage was different from those that united either European partners or free persons of African descent.[4]

Several aspects of this marriage and of Marie's baptism are noteworthy. Raphael and Gaspart's marriage itself, although unusual, is evidence that legitimate marital relationships between New Orleanians of European and African ancestry were possible and highlights the willingness of individual colonists (including, in this case, the bride's mother and the witnesses) as well as both secular (Boisbriant) and religious (Raphaël) authorities in the colony to ignore or override prescriptions emanating from the metropole. In addition, Raphael, who migrated to the colony as a free man, and his daughter, who was born to free parents, were unusual among free people of African ancestry during the French era, as most experienced some period of enslavement before gaining their freedom through manumission. Restricted by the Code Noir and by economic incentives, however, few slaveowners freed their slaves before 1769 and thus the city's population of free people of color remained small. Finally, the recategorization of Gaspart in the marginal notation of her wedding, the failure to label her at Marie's baptism, and Marie's own labeling as a négresse rather than a mulâtresse all reveal the inchoate conception of race that was emerging in French Louisiana.

Said to Be His Daughter

Although Raphael and Gaspart's 1725 marriage is the only clearly racially exogamous marriage to appear in the French marriage books, a few others are evident from other sources. The Superior Council records note that Le Roy, a white locksmith, and his unnamed négresse wife were accused of theft in May 1723 by Joseph Chaperon (the abusive slave owner described in the previous chapter).[5] And the ship's log for *Le Galathée,* which arrived in Louisiana in 1727 from Senegal, included among its passengers a Senegalese mulâtresse who was joining her husband, Jean Pinet, a French gunsmith, who had earlier been deported from Senegal for an unspecified crime.[6]

Later Spanish-era sacramental registers, however, indicate relationships that took place during the French period. When Jean Lafrance married Marie Charles in 1767, neither spouse was marked with a racial label. The first four of their children went similarly unmarked at their baptisms. Yet when their fifth child, Antonio, was baptized in 1779, the ceremony was recorded in the book for nonwhites, where he was noted as a "child of color," albeit a legitimate one. Antonio's racial designation was later crossed out with a heavy scribble, making the original comment barely legible. Their two subsequent children were baptized as blancos. It is possible that the priest at Antonio's baptism had indeed erred and that Lafrance and Charles were both Franco-Louisianans. In 1788, however, Lafrance asserted that their daughter Catherine was a cuarteróna, suggesting that his wife was a mulata. An alternative reading, that both Lafrance and Charles were persons of color is less plausible given that six of their seven children were either unmarked or designated as blanco at their baptisms. Rather it appears to be a fairly clear case of a marriage between a Franco-New Orleanian and a mulata whose children were generally treated as white.[7]

Three other French-era marriages are mentioned in the Spanish sacramental records. When mulatos libres Juan Bautista Charrayse and Maríana Barco married in 1777, both claimed to be natives of New Orleans and the legitimate children of an unraced father and a negra libre mother.[8] It is possible that Charrayse and Barco lied to the priest, Father Cirilio de Barcelona, a Spaniard who had arrived in New Orleans in 1772. Two years after Charrayse and Barco's marriage, in 1779, Cirilio once again took the word of a mulato libre who asserted that he was the "legitimate son of [unraced] Pedro Longlis [Langliche] and Juana María, negra libre, his parents."[9] That Cirilio was willing to accept that mulatos could have been born from legitimate marriages between Euro-Louisianan men and Afro-Louisianan women is significant in itself, although it says more about Spanish understandings of such relationships than actual French practices in the years before 1769.

Subsequent evidence from Pierre Langliche, the second groom, illustrates how dominant cultural expectations determined how those responsible for recording information about racially exogamous relationships reacted to such relationships, in turn shaping the content of the information they recorded. When an elderly Langliche dictated his will in 1816, the notary, Christoval de Armas, wrote that Langliche was the natural, rather than legitimate, son of Sieur Langliche and négresse libre Jeanne Marie; Langliche was illiterate—signing his will with an x—and thus could not have known if de Armas properly recorded his own description of his parents' relationship. De Armas was a native of the Canary Islands who had migrated to New Orleans with his family no later than 1783, when he married into a prominent Franco-Louisianan family, and by 1816 he had lived under Anglo-American rule for thirteen years.[10] Whether Langliche himself was no longer willing to claim legitimacy in the face of Anglo-American hostility to racially exogamous marriages or whether de Armas negated Langliche's claim by declaring him to be a natural son is impossible to determine. This example illustrates the diffi-culty of uncovering the true extent of such relationships, both marital and non-marital, as our evidence depends on the priests' and notaries' understanding of or hostility toward them.

It is also possible, however, that Charrayse's, Barco's, and Langliche's parents were indeed married in the church but that the records of their marriages have vanished. Langliche was born in the early 1730s, Charrayse probably in the late 1750s, and Barco in the early 1760s.[11] If their respective parents had married be-tween 1734 and 1758, any record of such a ceremony is now lost to history. Time, humidity, and the fires of 1788 and 1794 damaged or destroyed many sacramental registers from the first half of the eighteenth century. For the French period (1718–66), complete baptism records exist for the years 1731–33 and 1744–66, supple-mented by some scattered records for 1729–30. But there are no records at all for the years 1720–28 and 1734–43. The marriage records are even more scanty: there are two runs of complete records covering the years 1721–33 and 1759–66 with a few additional entries from 1720, but there are no extant records for a twenty-five year period beginning in 1734.[12]

Thus baptism records are missing for just under half of the French years and marriage records for just over half. These gaps in the archival record make it espe-cially difficult to determine the prevalence of long-term, perhaps even marital, relationships in which Euro-Louisianan fathers recognized their children with women of color. Particularly disheartening is the lack of both baptism and mar-riage records between 1734 and 1743 and the continuing absence of marriage rec-ords through 1758, formative years in the development of New Orleans' society. Thus, although racially exogamous marriages were clearly rare, there may have been others, like those of Charrayse's and Barco's parents, that were recorded in books that are no longer extant. Scattered evidence from the baptismal registries and other sources, as well as a growing number of people identified as mulâtres, however, make it clear that both long-term, nonmarital relationships and more casual ones took place with greater frequency than the extant evidence uncovers.

One case in particular reveals the usually indifferent responses of officials to them as well as the fraught dynamics of nonmarital relationships. In 1751, a mulâtresse teenager named Charlotte fled her owner, Pierre-Henri d'Erneville, an infantry captain. She found refuge at the house of Sr. Battard, a captain temporarily staying in New Orleans. She claimed that her master "torment[ed] her" and sought Bat-tard's assistance in removing her from d'Erneville's possession. Battard approached Madame de Vaudreuil, the governor's wife, who seemed sympathetic to Charlotte's plight and apparently agreed to obtain a pardon for her if Battard would return her to her owner. Battard also offered d'Erneville 1,500 livres to purchase Charlotte, but d'Erneville refused. With the assistance of his father-in-law, Procureur Général François Fleuriau, d'Erneville harassed Battard, posted a guard outside his house, subjected him to "disagreeable inspections," and lobbied the Superior Council to cite him "for having debauched and sequestered the said mulâtresse." Charlotte was found at Battard's house—in his bed, "naked, with only a skirt," although Battard himself was absent. According to the soldiers sent to arrest her, she "threw herself on her knees," offering them 100 piastres if they would let her go or take her to Vaudreuil's, where she could receive her pardon. But the soldiers refused her bribes and took her to prison.

D'Erneville sought compensation for Charlotte's absence and requested that Battard be fined for his actions. For his part, Battard sought reparations and damages for being unjustly pursued. The Superior Council declined to credit either man's claims, although it did order Battard to have nothing more to do with Charlotte. According to Commissaire Ordonnateur Michel's account, a flustered Fleuriau was not satisfied; he accused Battard of being a "rouge" and "a miscreant . . . who deserved the rope" and continued to pursue the case. After hearing witnesses for both parties, presiding councilor Vincent-Guillaume Le Sénéchal d'Auberville apparently ended the proceedings with no resolution. Perhaps he agreed with Michel that the matter was a civil one, not a criminal one, as Battard had not truly harbored a runaway as defined by the Code Noir. Or, perhaps, the news that, in Michel's words, Charlotte was "said to be [d'Erneville's] daughter" led him to silently drop the matter.[13]

Michel's suggestion of d'Erneville's paternity has to be considered in the context of his letter to the minister that included his description of this affair. Michel was hostile to both d'Erneville, whom he described as a "troublesome man," and Fleuriau, who was, he wrote, haughty and "an extremely limited and insipid man"; he accused both men of abusing their powers in their vendetta against Battard. Michel was far more sympathetic to Battard, who was, he wrote, "reputed to be well born" and had "served with distinction" during the recent war. As for Charlotte herself, Michel denigrated her as "the mulâtresse" and as "naturally libertine," suggesting that she earned her wages through prostitution because her mistress "obliged her to go to work every day in the city in order to earn wages, [insisting] that she bring back every evening fifty sols." This was, he continued, "absolutely prohibited by the Police regulations; but as the daughter of the procureur général . . . , [Charlotte's mistress] doubtlessly thought she was authorized." Thus, it could be suggested that Michel's accusation of paternity was simply one more charge in his campaign to discredit his rivals in the eyes of the minister. But d'Erneville's paternity was affirmed fifty years later by Charlotte herself when, in her will, she claimed to be the daughter of d'Erneville and a négresse named Jeanneton.[14] Michel's apparent nonchalance about d'Erneville's paternity suggests that this situation was not unusual, while the Superior Council's failure to pursue either d'Erneville or Battard indicates its willingness to turn a blind eye to racially exogamous relationships, relationships that ranged from Jacques Charpentier dit Le Roy's abuse of enslaved women under his authority to Charlotte's possible participation in prostitution to the marriage of Raphael and Gaspart described at the beginning this chapter.

Charlotte's experiences, and those of her mother, were undoubtedly more typical for women of African ancestry who had sex with Euro-Louisianan men than negra libre Juana María's marriage to Pedro Langliche. Charlotte was probably born from a coercive relationship between Jeanneton and the young d'Erneville, whose purchase of his daughter from her mother's owner demonstrated at least some limited paternal feelings. Unlike other reputed fathers, however, he failed to free her at that time. In the late 1740s or early 1750s, he married Pelagia Fleuriau, the procureur général's daughter, while continuing to keep Charlotte enslaved. About 1754, Charlotte gave birth to a son who most likely grew up alongside his grandfather's legitimate children. By 1766, Charlotte, although still a slave, was listed in the census as heading her own household, which included five other slaves. In 1771, when Charlotte was in her late thirties, d'Erneville finally promised to free her but not until his death. Two and a half years later, Charlotte gave up waiting for him to die and purchased her own freedom for 400 pesos. D'Erneville continued to hold his grandson Charles in slavery, although he may have been allowing him to live freely as a Charles Derneville appears on a "list of mulâtres libres" compiled about 1770. In 1775, with little or no money of her own, Charlotte negotiated to free Charles by convincing Santiago Landro to pay d'Erneville 600 pesos for his freedom and then obligating herself to work for Landro without pay.[15] D'Erneville's insistence that Charlotte purchase freedom for herself and her son demonstrates that Euro-Louisianan paternity was not a guarantee of freedom. D'Erneville did leave Charlotte a small bequest at his death, "for the good services that I have received from her in my sickness," but even this was partially negated by his claim that she owed him 160 pesos. Unlike many others, therefore, Charlotte received few advantages from her father and yet she was able to acquire a significant amount of property during her life. In the aftermath of the 1788 fire that burned much of the city, Charlotte listed the value of her destroyed property at 2,497 pesos. Despite these losses, at the time of her death, she owned a house, some land, and one slave, to whom she willed manumission.[16]

Enjoying Full and Complete Liberty

Unlike Charlotte and her son Charles, who had to wait for the more liberal manumission policies of the Spanish era, other Afro-Louisianans were freed during the French era, as some slaveowners did take advantage of the 1724 Code Noir's manumission provisions, restrictive though they were. And yet the code's overall discouragement of manumission was clearly heeded, as the numbers of manumissions and of free persons of African descent remained small. The code granted authority to the Superior Council to determine whether a particular manumission was "legitimate," but manumissions of slave consorts and children were not permitted, since article 6 punished them with perpetual enslavement. Yet at least one Euro-Louisianan defied the code, declaring that mulâtresse Marie Louise "should enjoy full and complete liberty being the daughter of a Frenchman."[17] It is not surprising that slaveowners were reluctant to confess transgressing the Code Noir, especially as it should have nullified any attempted manumission. When seeking council authorization to manumit their slaves, most owners declared they wished to reward their loyalty and good services. Councilor François Trudeau used just such language himself when he petitioned for authorization to free his négresse Jeanneton, stating "she has always served him with zeal and fidelity."[18]

Yet paying careful attention to the circumstances of individual manumissions suggests intimate and familial relationships between manumitters and the slaves they sought to manumit. Just over sixty slave owners declared their intentions to free around 140 slaves during the French era. Unfortunately, the state of the extant records makes it impossible to determine the exact number of slaves who were actually manumitted. Of the 146 slaves in connection with whom manumission is mentioned, 55 definitely received their freedom, another 18 probably did, and 8 probably did not, while the status of the remaining 65 is unclear.[19]

More than half of the slaves whom owners tried to free were women, who they sought either to manumit alone or with their children, or were children. Some were clearly not the consorts of their manumitter. When Manuel Sanchez de St. Denis freed his Indian slave Félicité in 1758, she joined her already free husband, Julien.[20] Another young woman, négresse Adrienne, was manumitted on her own in 1767 by her godmother, Adrienne Houmard, widow of Jean Baptiste Lottiere.[21] Jeanne Kerrourette, another of the very few women who sought to manumit their slaves, wanted her faithful domestic, La Mirre, to be freed on her death.[22]

Négresse Jeanneton was the consort of her would-be manumitter, although she failed to gain her freedom, illustrating the precariousness of sexual relationships between slave women and their owners even when manumission was a possibility.

She had been promised her freedom sometime before August 1736 when, for un-stated reasons, her owner, Pierre Garçon dit L'Eveillé, nullified his earlier promise. Almost a year later, Garçon had Jeanneton imprisoned for running away, but Jean-neton defended her actions, declaring she was six weeks pregnant by her owner, and asked to be taken away from him.[23] Perhaps Garçon originally offered manumis-sion to persuade Jeanneton to have sex with him but, for whatever reason, he later revoked his offer, although the relationship must have continued since Jeanneton became pregnant eight or nine months later.

Négresse Marianne was more successful than Jeanneton, demonstrating that some women could achieve freedom for themselves and their children through sexual relationships with Euro-Louisianan men. Born a slave, by 1745 Marianne was living as a free woman with Claude Vignon dit La Combe, who manufactured pitch and tar on the shores of Lake Pontchartrain. Her two mulâtre sons, Joseph and Pierre, however, were still owned by Pierre Boyer. At his impending death, Boyer freed both boys and left them his property. Two years later, Vignon dit La Combe wrote his will, confirming that all three were free and bequeathing them 300 piastres, in addition to several head of cattle he had previously given them. It is possible that either Boyer or Vignon dit La Combe were the father of Marianne's sons. Boyer's paternity is suggested both by the given name he shared with one of the sons and by his bequest. But Vignon dit La Combe also left the bulk of his estate to Marianne and her children; in addition Joseph appears to have taken La Combe as his surname.[24]

When very young slaves were manumitted, they were clearly being rewarded for something other than their years of good service to their owners. Lucas Villanausa obligated himself to free a six-month-old métis girl when he purchased her from Jean Hubert in July 1765; the girl's mother, Louisan, was noted as consenting to the sale, perhaps in recognition of the Code Noir's ban on selling children apart from their parents.[25] That same month, Gardelle Gaspard paid Jacques Lemelle an ex-cessive 800 livres for a six-month-old quarteron under the condition that the infant remain with his enslaved mother, Jacqueline Lemelle, for another year; beyond that, however, Gaspard would have to pay Jacques Lemelle 20 sols per day for main-tenance. It is probable that Gaspard was acting for Joseph Dusuau de La Croix, who would later claim Jacqueline's son, Louis, born about this time, as his own.[26] Other Euro-Louisianan men suggested their paternity when they freed young slaves and promised to have them educated, as did Henry DeCuir and Jean Baptiste Ducarpe when they freed four-year-old mulâtresse Rosette and six-year-old mulâtresse Françoise, respectively. Despite indications of probable paternity in these promises, which contravened the Code Noir's restrictions, Governor Louis Billouart de Kerlérec approved these manumissions, suggesting that local selectivity once again overrode the metropolitan code.[27]

Mulâtresse Marie Charlotte was promised freedom by her probable father, Pierre de St. Jullien, but because he did so on his deathbed, he was not around to ensure that she received her freedom, and it would take her almost a decade to see her father's promise fulfilled. In 1735, shortly before he died, St. Jullien sent Marie Charlotte to live at the Ursuline convent to receive an education. She must have expected freedom on her father's death, but Raymond Amiot d'Ausseville, the attorney for vacant estates, invalidated her manumission, claiming that St. Jullien's debts far outweighed his assets and that no official consent had been received. Marie Charlotte remained with the Ursulines for two years, until the nuns requested 449 livres 10 sols to cover the cost of her board. On Commissaire Ordonnateur Salmon's orders, d'Ausseville paid the nuns and then bought Marie Charlotte for himself for 1,500 livres. But Marie Charlotte did not give up. In November 1743, after several verbal protestations and a written petition, she convinced Procureur Général Fleuriau that d'Ausseville had illegally "secreted [her] manumission" and denied her freedom, "which she had never enjoyed to this day." Prominent Euro-Louisianans—Superior Council member Jean-Baptiste Raguet and Company of the Indies agent Jean-Baptiste Prévôt—were willing to testify on her behalf that St. Jullien's estate was not as indebted as d'Ausseville had claimed. Fleuriau also noted that d'Ausseville should have turned the manumission request over to the council rather than making the decision himself. On Fleuriau's petition, Vaudreuil and Salmon granted Marie Charlotte her freedom on payment of 1,500 livres to the heirs of the now deceased d'Ausseville. Although finally able to enjoy her freedom, Marie Charlotte was not content to leave it there. A year and a half later, she sued the executor of d'Ausseville's succession for wages to be paid against the 1,500 livres she owed. Claiming that "it is not just that a free woman should have been kept in slavery through a trick" and citing article 20 of the Code Noir, which allowed for slaves to request judicial intervention for their mistreatment, she requested 20 livres a month from the day that he purchased her until his death.[28]

Although women and children were more likely to be promised and to receive freedom, adult men were manumitted as well, often for services to the state rather than to individual masters. In 1730, La Chaise proposed freeing some of those slaves who had fought with the colonizers following the Natchez uprising, and eventually fourteen were rewarded for their "proofs of valor and attachment to the French nation."[29] One other nègre earned his freedom by agreeing to become the colony's executioner. In November 1725, Louis Congo, a company slave, bargained not only for his own freedom but also quasi freedom for his wife, two arpents of land, rations, and payments for each hanging, whipping, and branding he performed. Procureur Général Fleuriau protested Congo's demands but, describing him as "very strong" and knowledgeable, he realized it would be difficult to find someone else and recommended that the council accept his conditions.[30]

Other than Louis Congo and those who were freed for military service, adult men were rarely manumitted on their own. Among those few were Jean Baptiste Poulierdon, who later redeemed his wife from slavery, and Jacques, whose owner, Dominique Brunel, had taught him the craft of jewelry making. Jacques was the only one of Brunel's slaves that he freed, demonstrating the selectivity of manumission. In addition, Brunel left his former slave all of his jewelry-making tools.[31] A few more men received their freedom alongside their wives and children. Louis Connard, his wife, Catherine, and their four children were freed by will after the death of their owner, Captain Jacques de Coustilhas, who also left them a small plot of land.[32] Others were freed in pairs, presumably husbands and wives, most often in their old age. Laplante was about sixty, and he and Françoise had served their Pointe Coupée mistress and her deceased husband for more than forty years. Jorge, freed with his wife, Marie, by Bienville, died shortly afterward, while ten years later Marie was dubbed "veille Marie." Caton and his wife, Manon, were both described as very old and indeed dying.[33] Although the Code Noir did not prohibit manumitting elderly slaves, it did require owners to pay a daily fee to the hospital for their maintenance in order to prevent owners from merely abandoning their slaves.[34] When Lalande Dalcourt requested permission to manumit sixty-year-old Marie Anne, he acknowledged that she was feeble but claimed her children were willing to take care of her. Governor d'Abbadie approved the request and released Dalcourt from the obligation of paying the daily maintenance fee.[35]

Pledges of freedom, even when formally recorded in wills or in the Superior Council registry, were not always realized, as Garçon's Jeanneton learned when her owner revoked his earlier declaration of intent. For others, freedom was eventually achieved but not until after the death of their owners or their departure from the colony, until which time each was to continue to "serve as a slave."[36] Still others, like Marie Charlotte, were imperiled by the indebtedness of their owners. Despite being promised his freedom by Madame St. Hermine, François, a twelve-year-old mulâtre, was purchased by St. Hermine's testamentary executor, and his manumission was judicially annulled, as the estate's debts exceeded its assets.[37] Jean Louis Azemar acknowledged that his debts might overwhelm his estate when he stated that he wanted to free forty-year-old nègre Spadille. If there was not enough to pay his creditors, he requested that Spadille at least be able to choose his new master. Whether Spadille had a say in the matter or not, he was bought by Baure a week after his master's death for 1,000 livres.[38] Sieur Jean-Baptiste de Chavannes, former secretary of the Superior Council, made sure that his manumission of négresse Marie Angelique dite Isabelle would be granted by attaching proof that he had fully paid her purchase price to the Company of the Indies.[39]

Slaves, especially those who were manumitted by testament, could have their liberty threatened not just by creditors but also by heirs, who protested the loss of valuable property. Veuve Jaffre's attempt to prevent the manumission of Jean-neton and her six-year-old daughter Marie Jeanne may have been motivated by spite, as Jeanneton may have been her deceased husband's consort in earlier years. Under Bernard Jaffre dit La Liberté's 1740 will, Jeanneton and her daughter were to receive their freedom following La Liberté's death and after Jeanneton had worked at the hospital for two years. Claiming half ownership of the two slaves, veuve Jaffre opposed their manumission, although she eventually agreed to it on payment of half their value. Jeanneton served her two years at the hospital, and in June 1742 Bienville and Salmon decreed that she and her daughter should hence-forth "enjoy all the privileges and rights of free people."[40]

The Code Noir decreed that, for manumission acts to be valid, formal permis-sion had to come from the Superior Council. In 1735, however, the Superior Coun-cil denied itself this authority, putting it in the hands of the governor and the or-donnateur alone.[41] Although many slaveowners did seek formal permission, some manumitters ignored the formalities and found their own ways to free their slaves. Some used the baptismal registry to mark particular individuals as free, as Louis Rançon had done in 1751 for his son, a practice that became more frequent after 1760.[42] Although not a legitimate mechanism for manumission under the Code Noir, as it bypassed the Superior Council's judgment, priests apparently accepted a master's declaration "that he wishes the said [child] to be baptized as free," as Jacques Lemelle stated when he had the children of Jacqueline, his mulâtresse slave, baptized. He later ensured their freedom by registering their manumissions under more liberal Spanish policies.[43] Occasionally, a baptized child was clearly labeled as free even when she was born of an enslaved mother. In these cases, either the priest made no mention of liberty being granted to the child or else mention of the mother's enslaved status was crossed out, implying that she and therefore her child were free.[44]

Other former slaves for whom there is no extant manumission record neverthe-less appear in various records as free. It is possible that these records have been lost, although it is also possible that some owners acted on their own to free their slaves or merely allowed them to live as free as Pierre-Henri d'Erneville apparently did with his grandson Charles. Antoine Meullion, a widowed surgeon living at Pointe

Coupée, promised freedom to his Senegalese slave Charlotte and her two-year-old son in 1746, decreeing they would be free when he died or left the colony. Twenty-one years later, Meullion was still residing in the colony and, though no formal act of manumission is extant, he declared Charlotte, her son, and a daughter born after 1746 already free in his will. In addition, he requested that his heirs take care of them.[45] Similarly, Jean Charles de Pradel, a former officer and wealthy planter, informally freed his slave, St. Louis. Pradel's cook, and a slave about whom his brother often asked, St. Louis was punished in the early 1750s when Pradel sent him to the quarters to work alongside the other field slaves for suspected theft and nighttime carousing. In a 1755 letter to his brother, Pradel referred to St. Louis derisively as "Monsieur St. Louis" and noted that "he does not like" field work "very much." By 1763, however, St. Louis must have earned Pradel's respect once again as he was free and working for his former owner, who entrusted him with large sums of money. Pradel now reported to his brother that St. Louis, despite having "his liberty," was "too grateful for all the kindness I have shown him during his slave days to forsake me at a time when I need his help." St. Louis continued to serve the Pradel family; in 1765, he was sent to France by the widow Pradel to accompany her daughters home to Louisiana.[46]

Not all free Afro-Louisianans achieved their liberty through the benevolence of Louisiana slaveowners. Martinique-born Jean Baptiste Raphael and Jamaican Thomas Hos, both nègres libres, arrived in Louisiana as free men sometime before their respective 1725 and 1730 marriages. In addition to Jean Pinet's mulâtresse wife, who arrived in 1727, nègres libres Simon Vanon and his future wife, Marie Anne, emigrated from Senegal sometime before their 1731 marriage.[47] Several Afro-Louisianans migrated from France, including Marie, Jean Baptiste Cesar, Perrin (noted as a cook), and Isaac Matapan, all of whom appear on passenger lists for ships that left France between 1718 and 1721 and who were bound to work on various concessions in the colony.[48] John Mingo arrived in Louisiana in 1726, having fled slavery in South Carolina, and was declared free by Jonathan Darby, director of the Bernard Cantillon concession.[49]

Other Afro-Louisianans, including Mingo's wife, had their freedom purchased by their husbands. In November 1727, John Mingo married Thérèse, a négresse belonging to the Bernard Cantillon concession. In granting his consent to the marriage, Darby also agreed to allow Mingo to purchase Thérèse, "pay[ing] as much as he clearly can each year to redeem 1,500 francs." Once the price was paid in full, "Thérèse shall have her liberty" as would any children she had borne. In the meantime, Darby would continue feeding and clothing Thérèse. Two years later, Mingo contracted to work for de Chavannes as commandeur for 300 francs a year, 8 percent of the plantation's produce, and a jug of brandy each month. De Chavannes also hired the still-enslaved Thérèse as a domestic for 200 francs a year, with payment going to Darby until Thérèse's purchase price was paid off. In November 1730, however, Mingo complained to the Superior Council that Darby "makes difficulties" and was not crediting him fully for payments made in kind. In response, Darby claimed to have been "correct and conscientious" in his dealings with Mingo, whom he had treated generously, and suggested that perhaps it was the translations between Mingo's English and Darby's French that had caused confusion, a somewhat disingenuous claim since Darby later identified himself as an Englishman. The Superior Council ruled that Thérèse should "be restored" to her husband, but that Darby was still entitled to payment.[50]

Like Mingo, François Tiocou (a Senegalese nègre freed for participating in the war against the Natchez), Jean Baptiste Marly, and Jean Baptiste Poulierdon also worked to redeem their wives from slavery. "Wishing to procure the liberty of Marie Aram, his wife, Négresse Esclave," in July 1737, Tiocou agreed to work for the charity hospital, his wife's owner, for six and a half years without wages.[51] Tiocou had already paid 450 francs toward her purchase price, an amount he had received from the settlement of a wage dispute. In March 1744, the hospital's director and curé petitioned Vaudreuil and Salmon to honor their agreement with Tiocou, declaring that he and "his wife have worked and served the Hospital well and faithfully." Confirming her manumission, Vaudreuil and Salmon granted her "the privileges of persons born free."[52] Similarly, Marly contracted with Jean Joseph de Pontalba, an officer at Pointe Coupée, to cook for him in exchange for food, medical attention, and the freedom, after three years, of his wife, Venus. In a dilemma that would face many free Afro-Louisianans seeking to redeem their relatives, Marly had to chose between Venus and their griffe daughter, who would only receive her freedom if Venus died before Marly's term of service was completed.[53]

Clearly not all, or even most, manumitted slaves received their freedom because they were the sexual partners or children of their manumitters, nor did all Euro-Louisianan men free their consorts or children. Even with the problems of undercounting free people of African descent in the French period (discussed below), it appears that far more individuals identified as mulâtres remained enslaved than were freed. The 1771 census of New Orleans, taken just after the end of the French regime, enumerated 41 mulâtresses and 27 mulâtres as free, while more than 250 lived in slavery. The same census demonstrates that certain people of African descent were more likely to enjoy their freedom than others. Being female and/or identified as mulâtre significantly enhanced an individual's chances of enjoying freedom: women were more likely to be free than men, mulâtres more likely than nègres, and mulâtresses most of all. Studies of manumission elsewhere in the Americas generally confirm that, at least in urban areas, women were more likely to acquire freedom than men.[54]

Women were slightly more than one-half of the New Orleans population of African descent but over two-thirds of the free population. Similar calculations regarding racial identifications cannot be made with as much confidence, given the imprecise use of such labels by census takers, and thus have to be taken as rough indications. According to the census numbers, about one in five slaves were identified as mulâtres. By contrast, more than two-thirds of the free people of African ancestry were identified as mulâtres. Mulâtresses were overrepresented among the free to an even greater extent. Only one in eight Afro-New Orleanians were mulâtresses compared to two of every five free Afro-New Orleanians.[55] On the one hand, it is possible that more mulâtresses—women with perceived African and European ancestry—received their freedom than did mulâtres, nègres, or négresses, supporting the argument that New Orleans' gens de couleur libre population owed much, but not all, of its origins to racially exogamous relationships.[56] Mulâtresses, just 11 percent of the slave population, were 41 percent of the free. In contrast, nègres were 35 percent of the slave population but only 5 percent of the free. Négresses and mulâtres were both just over one-quarter of the free population, although the former were 45 percent of the enslaved and the latter just 10 percent. On the other hand, it is probable that female affranchis were more likely to be designated as mulâtresses. Possessing freedom placed freed women of color higher on the status hierarchy than enslaved women, an increased status that often slipped over into their racial categorization as well.[57]

Regardless of whether they were identified as mulâtresses or nègres, free status brought significant benefits, not least of which was freedom itself. Among the rights that affranchis clearly did acquire were those to make contracts, hold property, and engage in lawsuits. Nègres libres could hire themselves out to habitants and concessionaires, whether for wages or to redeem their families from slavery, as Mingo, Tiocou, and Marly did. They could also sue and, in general, received their due process in court. Nègre libre Raphael, like many other engagés, contracted to work for a Louisiana concessionaire and left France bound for the colony in about 1719. His employer, Jean-Baptiste Faucon Dumanoir, was to pay him 200 francs a year and provide him with an outfit of clothing. Raphael first appeared in court in 1724 when, like many Euro-Louisianans, whether wealthy or not, he sued to have a debt repaid. On March 16, he had lent Sieur Paulin Cadot 200 francs to be paid within one month. When Cadot had still not paid by early May, Raphael sued and the council ordered Cadot to pay the debt plus interest and court costs.[58] Having had success before the council, Raphael filed another suit two months later, this time against his employer. Despite having served Dumanoir "with fidelity and affection," Raphael complained that his employer had shortchanged him on his wages and clothing and had also seized his trunk with his possessions. Although this case dragged on somewhat longer than his suit against Cadot—which had been settled in just two days—in September, the council finally ordered Dumanoir to settle his accounts with Raphael and return his trunk. Raphael was also allowed to leave Dumanoir's service for a new employer, and Dumanoir was to advance him 100 francs to tide him over.[59]

Ex-slaves were, however, subject to the possibility of reenslavement and the Superior Council did reenslave at least three affranchis. In 1743, twenty-year-old Jean Baptiste Coustilhas, who had been freed in 1739, was accused by his employer of stealing some shirts and handkerchiefs. Jean Baptiste was found guilty and condemned to be sold into slavery to the highest bidder.[60] Jean Baptiste's sister, Jeanette Coustilhas, managed to hold onto her freedom for another four years but she too was eventually reenslaved after being convicted of theft and unable to pay her creditors. Condemned on April 8, 1747, she was sold three days later for 1,900 livres.[61] Another Jean Baptiste was reenslaved in 1757 for licentiousness. Originally condemned to be sold outside of Louisiana, Jean Baptiste remained imprisoned in New Orleans until 1763, when officer Jean Trudeau beseeched the council to allow him to remain in Louisiana and offered to purchase him for 1,000 livres.[62]

But accusations of criminal activity did not always lead to reenslavement. Jean Baptiste Coustilhas had defended himself by accusing Joseph Pantalon, a thirty-five-year-old nègre libre from Senegal, but Pantalon was exonerated by the council after he voluntarily turned himself in and denied Jean Baptiste's accusations. In addition, most nègres libres convicted of crimes were not sold back into slavery. When Laroze was convicted of stealing from the Company of the Indies stores in 1722, he was flogged and imprisoned for six years.[63] Négresse libre Jeannette, who was reprimanded by the council for hosting nighttime gatherings of slaves and servants, was admonished never to do so again, but she was neither fined nor reenslaved for this crime.[64] The threat of reenslavement, even if rarely realized, symbolized the precarious legal status of free people of African ancestry during the French era even as they were able to exercise the "rights, privileges, and immunities enjoyed by persons born free."[65]

Defining Mulâtres, Métis, and Quarterons

Just how many free blacks, like Raphael, or individuals of mixed ancestry, like his daughter Marie, there were in French Louisiana is difficult to ascertain as census takers, along with priests and other official record takers, were uncertain in their use of racial labels, demonstrating that an ambiguous relationship between race and status existed during this period. Officials used censuses, in part, to make a population legible. By selecting only certain criteria worthy of enumeration, they simplified individual complexity, turning it into manageable data.[66] As such, analyzing which categories they included and how these changed over time reveals their understanding of the social order. Slaves were first enumerated in the 1708 census for the entire colony, which included 80 slaves, all "sauvages and sauvagesses from different nations." Another 120 people made up the garrison, which was divided into ten quite narrow categories, from staff officers and soldiers to priests and cabin boys. Outside of the garrison and slaves, the residents were enumerated as habitants (here indicating male heads of households), women, and children.[67]

By 1721, officials had decided on a simpler classification system that divided the colonial population into unraced men, women, and children, French servants ("domestiques français," sometimes called "domestiques blancs"), nègre slaves, and sauvage slaves. In addition, the census includes a segregated list of men and women "de force," involuntary immigrants including prisoners, exiles, and others who were forced to migrate to Louisiana, a category that disappeared from censuses after 1731.[68] In subsequent French censuses, adult Euro-Louisianans were simply counted as "maîtres" or "men carrying arms" and "femmes," but at the same time that any hint of unfree status was removed from Euro-Louisianans, slaves, both nègres and sauvages, began to be enumerated more carefully by sex and age.[69]

Free people of African ancestry first appeared in a 1727 census for New Orleans and its nearby settlements. Louis Congo, the former company slave turned executioner, lived along the road to Bayou St. Jean just north of the town with his wife. Both were called "nègres affranchis" but were enumerated as engagés since there was no category yet for affranchis or other free people of African ancestry.[70] Similarly, in 1731, nègres libres Simon and Scipion, owners of habitations along the Mississippi River opposite the growing plantation district of Chapitoulas, were enumerated among the unraced "men carrying arms," and their wives were counted as unraced women.[71] There was still no place to count free people of color in the following year's census of New Orleans, although a mulâtre category appeared for the first time, the same year that the term was first used in the sacramental records. Five of the six mulâtres counted in 1732 were nameless residents within households headed by identifiable Euro-Louisianan men and therefore were most likely slaves. The sixth, however, was householder Xavier, labeled a mulâtre libre. The only other identifiable free person of African ancestry on the census was Marie, a négresse libre, who owned a house a few doors down from Xavier on Rue Bourbon. Unlike Xavier, however, Marie was not enumerated in any column; the census taker clearly felt that she did not fit in any of the three available categories of unraced women, mulâtres, and enslaved négresses.[72] According to the 1732 census's conceptualization of the social order in this decade-old city, mulâtres had emerged as a enumerable category (despite their limited numbers). Mulâtres could be either slave or free; free nègres, on the other hand, still did not quite fit into any category. There are also several free nègres who appear in other records but do not appear in these censuses at all.

Unfortunately, only the totals are extant for the next census, taken in 1737, and that survey includes neither a category for mulâtres nor one for affranchis.[73] It was more than a generation before another census was taken, in 1763, which identified fifty men and fifty-eight women living in New Orleans as mulâtres, while another twenty-seven mulâtres and twelve mulâtresses lived in the city's environs. All are categorized as slaves. The 1763 census is the first to enumerate separately free people of African ancestry; it counted a mere nineteen—six nègres, eight négresses, three négrillons, and two negrittes—living within the city. Twenty-six more lived upriver at Chapitoulas, and downriver, at English Turn, thirty-five individuals formed what was identified as a "canton of nègres libres," where ninety-two-year-old Bernard Raphael, his wife, five grown children, and five grandchildren lived. Though the census taker at English Turn included mulâtres and nègres among the affranchis and libres, other districts lumped all free people of African descent together as nègres.[74]

A census three years later illustrates that French census takers were still uncertain over how to count free people of African ancestry. The census begins with a summary of all the Europeans (5,556) and slaves (5,940) in Louisiana, as well as an estimate of the number of "Indians capable of carrying weapons" (this group—presumably comprising only adult men—vastly outnumbered the colony's immigrant population at 15,955). Slaves were once again lumped together with no distinctions by race, sex, or age enumerated, while free people of African ancestry disappeared as a category.

Yet affranchis and libres do appear in the census itself, and the individual district census takers enumerated them in different ways. At English Turn and Chapitoulas, where the largest concentrations of libres had lived three years earlier, the census takers grouped them together at the end of their districts' lists. At English

Turn, the census taker carefully enumerated each nègre libre household, using the same columns as the rest of the census to count men with arms, wives, and children, and young and old of each sex. However, the seven nègre libre households are carefully blocked off from the surrounding households and their fifty-one residents are excluded from the totals that immediately follow and that are labeled "Families of Blancos." At Chapitoulas, the census taker identified each household under the general heading "mulatos" and described its residents (for instance, "Carlota, her mother, 2 brothers and 2 sisters") without using the census's columns. Like his counterpart at English Turn, he failed to include these fourteen residents in his district's totals. New Orleans census takers similarly described households headed by nègres and mulâtres libres without enumerating them. Although they scattered them throughout the census, the recapitulated totals at the end fail to account for any of those residents identified as free people of African descent.[75]

French census takers not only were not quite sure how to account for affranchis and libres; they also clearly undercounted them. Given the absence of separate columns in the censuses, the only identifiable free people of African descent are those household heads whom the census taker explicitly noted as such. Individuals who resided in households headed by Euro-Louisianans were most likely counted among the unraced. This enumeration of free people of African ancestry among the unraced is suggested by four lists generated for Spanish governor Alejandro O'Reilly in 1769 or 1770, purporting to record free men of African ancestry in New Orleans and its environs. A list of "mulâtre libre de la Nouvelle Orleans" contained forty-four names, a list of "nègres libres" in New Orleans and its environs had twenty-nine, and another of the city's "mulâtres and nègres libres" had twenty-nine identified as mulâtres and twenty-seven as nègres. Although there is significant overlap among these three lists, there are enough names that only appear on one to suggest that there was confusion among the list takers as to just who was a free person of African ancestry.[76]

A final list of the "quantity of the naîgres [sic] libres" in New Orleans, compiled by nègre libre Nicolas Bacus, included 195 free men of African ancestry just within the city.[77] Assuming a conservative estimate of an additional 2 people of color for each man, the free population of color for New Orleans and its environs was at least 87 and could have been as high as 585, far more than the 47 enumerated in 1763 and comprising anywhere from 2 to 14 percent of the region's total population. We need to be similarly cautious in relying on the censuses' racial categories in trying to uncover absolute numbers of Afro-Europeans and, by implication, the extent of racially exogamous relationships; still, in considering the construction of racial categories, it is illustrative that someone in 1763 (either the census taker, the individual reporting on a particular household, or the enumerated individuals themselves) believed that more than one hundred of New Orleans' inhabitants were mulâtres.[78]

Priests were also participating in the sorting of New Orleanians into racial groups. The sacramental records reveal more about the local development of a racialized language of categorization than even the censuses; in addition, they occasionally expose the presence of racially exogamous sex. The first child to be labeled "mulâtre" in the extant sacramental records was eight-day-old Catherine, who was buried in July 1732, the same year that "mulâtre" emerged as a distinct census category.[79] By mid-1753, fifty-nine baptized children were similarly categorized. In thirty-five of these cases, the mother was identified with a racial label, making it possible to begin to determine how priests were using this category. Nineteen mothers were described as négresses, fourteen as mulâtresses, and two as sauvagesses, including the mother of Marie, baptized in 1733, who was categorized as "a mulâtresse born of [a] sauvagesse."[80] If French priests were carefully calculating perceived racial heritage based on ancestry, we might assume that nineteen of the fathers were white, fourteen probably mulâtres, and speculate that in the last two cases the priest was using "mulâtre" as a more generic term for mixed ancestry ("sang-mêlé" does indeed turn up as a racial category in Spanish-era censuses).

In those four cases in which it is possible to identify the fathers, it becomes clear that the priests were using a broader and less consistent definition of "mulâtre." At her baptism in 1748, seven-month-old Charlotte was described as both a mulâtresse (in the text) and as a négritte (in the margin); her parents were "a nègre and a sauvagesse, slaves of Mr. Le Bretton in legitimate marriage."[81] Four years later, Etienne, mulâtre, son "of an unknown nègre father" and Marion, mulâtre libre, was baptized. The phrase "of an unknown father" would become increasingly common in the second half of the eighteenth century but, in these cases, the father was rarely classified as nègre.[82] The final two cases involved the only named fathers in all fifty-eight baptisms. In January 1750, Spaniard Don Jose Rohedeng appeared at the baptism of Nicholas, the mulâtre son of Marianne, a mulâtresse libre, and declared his paternity.[83] The following year, unraced Louis Rançon, a merchant, not only declared his paternity of négresse Marie Jeanne's son Louis François; he also obtained his son's freedom, and so three-day-old Louis was baptized as a mulâtre libre.[84]

French dictionaries of the period also defined "mulâtre" and other racial labels in imprecise ways. For instance, the entry for "mulâtre" in Furetière's 1701 dictionary includes the offspring of nègres and Indians. It also notes, however, that "the Spanish called *Mulates,* children born from a father and mother of a different

Religion, as from a Moor and a Spanish woman." The same entry includes definitions for "métis" ("born from an Indian man and a Spanish woman") and "jambos"
("born from an Indian man, and a *Métice* woman"). The entry for "metif" begins
with those "who are engendered by a father and mother of different quality, country, color, or Religion," such as those with "a slave father and a free mother [or] a
male Moor and a Spanish woman." It adds that those born of "an Indian man and
a Spanish woman, or vice versa" are also called "métif," a message it reiterates in a
separate definition for "métis." Such children shared in their parents' traits, "as a
mule shares its two natures." The entry concludes that "this word is a great insult
in Spain," as it was derived from "*mule,* an animal engendered by two different
species."[85]

Additional sacramental entries illustrate the priests' fluid use of racial categorizations. During the same years, eleven children were baptized as métis. Of the six
identified mothers, four were sauvagesses and the other two négresses. Only one
father is identified: the unraced Simon Coussot was the father of seven-and-a-half-
year-old métisse Françoise whose mother was sauvagesse Terese. Françoise's baptism took place six months after the birth of Coussot's first child with his wife;
perhaps legitimate fatherhood made him feel some responsibility toward his premarital child.[86] Pierre, baptized as nègre, was the son of a mulâtresse and unidentified father.[87] Some baptized children received multiple racial designations:
François and Philbertin were both labeled "négrillon mulâtre" ("little negro mulatto"), while Marthe was described as a "negritte métisse."[88] Occasionally, racial
identifiers were changed, as with Monsieur Dubreuil's slave Cecile. She was first
defined as a "negritte," but then that was crossed out and replaced with "mulâtresse."[89]
"Quarteron," a very rare label in the French period, first appeared in 1751 when
Marie, the daughter of Marianne, mulâtresse libre, and "an unknown white father," was described as a "quarteronné by birth."[90]

In the same sample, at least ten children were baptized without a racial label
where the entry contains indications that they should have been, including three
children whose parents were both nègre slaves, a fourth whose mother was an enslaved négresse, and two who were themselves slaves but for whom no parental
information was given.[91] Marie and Anne were the children of mulâtresses and
unidentified fathers, and Françoise was the daughter of a négresse slave and an
unknown white father.[92] At the baptism of the unraced Jean Paul Leflot in 1747,
Jean Leflot, who was also unraced, "declare[d] he is the father and . . . he wants to
marry the mother," mulâtresse Christine, thus making him the first unraced father
to declare paternity of a child of African descent in the extant baptism records.[93]
Unlike Spanish priests later in the century, who carefully (although not always

accurately) calculated perceived racial heritage based on ancestry before attributing a particular racial label, French priests seem to have been fairly casual in their use of racial labels, indicating a still inchoate use of race.

If French New Orleans had mirrored the social order envisioned by the Code Noir, there would have been no mulâtres, since there would have been no racial exogamy, and only a few nègres affranchis who occupied the precarious space between free Euro-Louisianans and enslaved Afro-Louisianans. Missing registries and official record-keeping practices, especially a haphazard use of racial labels, make it difficult to determine with any accuracy the numbers of slaves manumitted or sang-mêlé children born, but it appears as though the restrictions and prohibitions of the Code Noir successfully kept both manumissions and racially exogamous marriages relatively rare, although they were probably more frequent than the extant records indicate. That these were metropolitan impositions, however, rather than local commitments is demonstrated by the explosion in manumissions in the years immediately following the transfer of Louisiana to Spain and its introduction of more liberalized manumission policies and the rise in publicly acknowledged racially exogamous relationships that occurred a decade or two later, as the following chapters suggest.

CHAPTER FOUR

Slavery and Freedom in Spanish New Orleans

IN JUNE 1773, Catherina, a thirty-six-year-old mulata slave belonging to the estate of Juan Bautista Destrehan, filed a coartación petition for herself and her five-year-old daughter Félicité, requesting the court appoint appraisers to determine the price of their freedom. She argued that she had "merited the right to buy her freedom for cash as she ha[d] been a slave of this estate all her life and was a servant to all her master's children," and she claimed that "some persons, in recompense for her services, have promised her the money" she would need. Responding a few months later, one of the estate's executors, Étienne Boré, asked that her petition be dismissed because "in no manner will he consent to giving her her freedom considering her bad conduct, her iniquity, her dissimulation, and what she had done to herself to become infirm so as to be valued more cheaply." As it would do in many other cases, the Spanish court overruled an owner's opposition to a slave's desire for freedom, appointed appraisers, and allowed Catherina to purchase her freedom for the determined price. On November 6, having received the adjudicated price of 320 pesos from Catherina, Boré was forced to grant her and Félicité their freedom.[1]

Catherina's case illustrates one of the most important policy changes that occurred under Spanish rule: the introduction of coartación. It also demonstrates the extent to which slaves understood those new policies and the role that the Spanish government took on itself in mediating the relationship between slaves and their masters, at times even upholding slaves' rights against those of their owners. When Spanish officials assumed formal control over the colony in the late 1760s and introduced these new laws and policies regarding slavery, they found themselves confronting a sometimes hostile Francophone elite.

In seeking to establish their own authority and bring tranquility to the multiracial and multicultural colony they had inherited from the French, Spanish officials endeavored to organize New Orleans' society into three corporate bodies:

Euro-Louisianans, libres, and slaves. They imposed a new legal apparatus that encouraged manumission and strengthened the rights of both slaves and freed persons of African descent, thus profoundly reinforcing the development of New Orleans' tripartite racial system that the Code Noir had initiated by codifying the distinctive position of free Afro-Louisianans within it.

But it was not just Spanish policy and bureaucrats who facilitated the growth of the gens de couleur libre population. Slaves quickly became cognizant of their new legal rights and engaged in frequent and persistent efforts to gain their freedom. Some local whites aided slaves in their pursuit (whether because of intimacy, kinship, or religious, social, or economic ties), but others saw liberalized manumission as a threat to their domestic and public authority and tried to reverse these developments through a slave code that harked back to the 1724 Code Noir.

These contestations over slavery and freedom—between Spanish officials and local elites as well as between owners and slaves—were shaped by the economic, demographic, and political developments of the last third of the eighteenth century. When Spain inherited the colony in the 1760s, its economy was struggling, producing sufficient subsistence crops but few reliable export ones and still depending on a trade economy that linked Indians, Euro-Louisianans, and Afro-Louisianans. By the time France regained the colony in 1800, it had been transformed: New Orleans was now the flourishing commercial center of a thriving plantation economy. That transformation had been made possible through an increase in the number of laborers, a process Spain initiated when it reopened the slave trade in 1777.[2]

The successful shift to a plantation economy and the arrival of thousands of enslaved Africans over the following two decades had contradictory consequences for the development of slavery in lower Louisiana. On the one hand, the region's growing dependency on slave labor exacerbated the exploitation that lay at the heart of any system of plantation slavery. In addition, as slave prices declined in the early 1790s, slave owners could afford to treat their slaves more callously than when slaves had been scarcer or more expensive. On the other hand, the commercialization of New Orleans created new opportunities for slaves to hire themselves out, while the increased availability of slaves at lower prices encouraged manumission, as owners could more easily replace those they freed, and slaves themselves had a better chance of acquiring their own freedom price.[3] But, perhaps most important for slaves seeking freedom was the introduction of Spanish rule and the precariousness of Spanish authority over the inhabitants of the formerly French colony. The Spanish regime provided slaves with greater options than had been the case under the French, and they quickly learned how to take advantage of them. Spanish laws did little to mediate the actual experience of enslavement, especially in conjunction with a rising plantation economy, but the codes and the response they engendered from local elites reveal how competing interests shaped the developing constructions of race and offered slaves a chance to remake themselves as free.

Metropolitan and Local Slave Codes

Conflicts between Spanish officials and colonists emerged not long after Louisiana officially became part of the Spanish-American empire in February 1763. The colony's inhabitants were unaware of the change of government until the fall of 1764, when the Superior Council published news of the event, throwing the habitants, according to an Anglo-American observer, into "the greatest Confusion."[4] Spain delayed further in asserting authority over its new colony. Antonio de Ulloa was appointed as the first Spanish governor in April 1765, but he did not arrive in Louisiana until March 1766. Although Ulloa was instructed to make "for the present, no change in the system of its government" and to regard Louisiana "as a separate colony" from the Spanish-American empire, a group of New Orleans' planters and merchants feared that the new Spanish government would undermine local governance and impose new trade regulations and other fiscal policies to their detriment. At first they petitioned Louis XV to reclaim his former colony, and when that failed, they unceremoniously ran Ulloa out of the colony in November 1768. It was not until the arrival of General Alejandro O'Reilly the following August that Spain effectively established control over its new colony. Shortly after arriving, O'Reilly had the revolt's ringleaders arrested and tried, and several of them were then executed.[5] With such an inauspicious start, it is unsurprising that tensions existed between the Francophone elite and the Spanish governors and bureaucracy for much of the Spanish period. Slaves and free people of African ancestry moved swiftly to take advantage of these tensions, especially once they learned that officials, seeking loyalty from other elements of the colony's population, would listen to, if not always act on, their complaints and petitions.[6]

Following the 1768 revolt, the Crown reversed its previous intentions to leave the colony's government, laws, and practices intact. Instead, it ordered O'Reilly to unite "the province to the rest of [its] dominions," a unification to be achieved in part by establishing Spanish law over the colony.[7] O'Reilly's Ordinances and Instructions, published in November 1769, abolished the Superior Council (citing the role it had played in the 1768 revolt), established a local governing council—a cabildo—in conformity with Spanish colonial practices, and implemented Spanish law as embodied in the Siete Partidas and the Recopilación de las Indias.[8]

O'Reilly initially issued a proclamation that reenacted the 1724 Code Noir as the law of slavery for the colony, but he and his successors in fact quickly implemented Spanish slave policies.[9] Some were written by metropolitan officials far from the day-to-day circumstances of American slavery as part of a larger project to reorganize the Spanish empire. Local Spanish officials promulgated others as they sought to both integrate Louisiana into the Spanish empire and adapt imperial laws to the local environment. Local Francophone elites resisted these new policies and attempted to assert their own ideas about race into the colony's social order.

Contemporaries on both sides believed that Spanish policies were more moderate. Spanish officials defended their laws as "just and fair," while local elites protested they were too lenient and inadequate for their circumstances.[10] From the very beginning of the Spanish era, local elites complained that Spanish officials undermined owners' authority over their slaves. Attempting to justify its expulsion of Ulloa in 1768, the Superior Council claimed that the Spanish governor had extended legal protections to enslaved nègres while treating French colonists like slaves.[11] Just three years later, Governor Luis de Unzaga y Amezaga acknowledged that "our laws [are not] as harsh as those of the French here."[12] Free people of color too expressed a preference for Spanish governance. In the 1790s, negro libre Pierre La Violeta feared the return of French rule, declaring that free people of color "have always been for the Spanish, and if they were to fall under the domination of the French they would be ill-treated." Mulato libre Esteban Lalande was careful not to criticize the French but credited Spanish officials with bringing freedom. In 1812, Paul Macarty was accused of expressing "a hope that the Spanish flag would soon be raised in the state."[13] The slave system in Spanish Louisiana was as thoroughly imbued with violence as elsewhere, and protective laws were often ignored by governing officials, whether Spanish or French. But Spanish bureaucrats, local planters, and people of color saw significant differences between Spanish and French slave policies, and both proponents and opponents alike perceived Spanish policies as more beneficial to slaves than French policies had been.

It is important to keep in mind that however contemporaries perceived Spanish policies, they were indeed intended to perpetuate rather than eradicate slavery. The philosophy behind Spanish slave policies is best represented in the 1789 Código Negro, the Crown's attempt to impose a comprehensive slave code over all its American colonies, including Louisiana. Local elites articulated theirs in both their protestations against the Código Negro and their attempt to write their own slave law, the Code Noir ou Loi Municipale of 1778. Neither code was in fact implemented: the Código Negro was revoked in 1794 after colonists throughout the

Spanish Americas protested against it, and the Code Noir ou Loi Municipale never received official sanction. However, both provide important insights into divergent views of slavery, race, and social order held by the Spanish metropole, members of the colonial bureaucracy, and the local planter elite.

Like the 1724 Code Noir, both these codes began by requiring that the slave experience be mediated by the framework of Catholicism: owners were "required to instruct their slaves in the principles of the Catholic religion," have them baptized, and oversee daily prayers. Both codes ordered owners to provide slaves with sufficient food, clothing, and housing and to tend to the needs of elderly and infirm slaves. In exchange for owners' "sustaining, educating, and employing them in useful labors," slaves were required to obey, respect, and submit. Both addressed how slaves should be treated and what recourse they had for mistreatment. Both defined crimes and proscribed punishments.[14]

Both codes considered slaves to be simultaneously persons and property, but the Crown paid slightly more attention to slaves as persons while the planters emphasized their status as property. The Código Negro, for instance, required owners to facilitate marriages among their slaves, even if that meant purchasing a spouse or potential spouse from another owner. Justified as an effort to "avoid illicit dealings of the two sexes," the metropole's promarital policy was also informed by a belief that marriages would dampen slave discontent. The Code Noir ou Loi Municipale, on the other hand, prohibited owners from allowing their slaves to marry slaves belonging to others, a practice it saw as merely a "pretext to leave their master's habitation by day or night." It described marriages as "prejudicial to the Master" and assumed that most slave unions were "illicit conjunctions" that could not be avoided.[15]

This tension between slaves as persons and as property is also reflected in the codes' different provisions on slave punishment and abuse. The Código Negro allowed owners to inflict punishment on their slaves for disobedience and other minor infractions but restricted them in their choice of weapons and the number of lashes they could inflict. More serious infractions were to be tried in local courts and under the same laws as free criminals; penalties of death or mutilation of limb had to be approved by the audiencia. The Código Negro enumerated fines for owners who failed to properly provide for their slaves and proscribed criminal prosecution for those who "cause[d] slaves serious contusion, effusion of blood, or mutilation of limb." Any slave victimized in this way was to be sold to a new owner. It required priests and local officials to root out slave abuse and heed slaves' complaints, holding them liable if they failed to assist slaves in such circumstances, and ordered the city council to conduct visits of neighboring plantations three times a year. Whereas the Código Negro positioned itself and its local representatives "as protector[s] of the slaves" and limited owners' power over slaves, the Code Noir ou Loi Municipale offered slaves only minimal protection from cruelty and maltreatment, failing to authorize any mechanism for removing mistreated slaves from their abusers.[16]

Spanish judicial records contain evidence that the courts were willing to prosecute incidents of slave abuse, and in this they went beyond their French predecessors, whose only concern had been for owners who sought compensation for maimed or dead slaves. Spanish officials, on the other hand, not only investigated and prosecuted those who abused slaves belonging to others but also owners who mistreated their own slaves. Occasionally, they removed slaves from abusive owners, for example, María Santilly, whose owner, "moved by passion, or cruelty has inflicted [on] this poor unfortunate woman . . . some frightful punishment or torture."[17] At other times, they fined the abusers. Don Juan Antonio Lugar was charged the costs of prosecution after pardo libre Francisco Pechon accused him of mistreating his negro slave Juan Bautista, while mulato libre Josef Forstall was fined 10 pesos in addition to 48 pesos for damages and court costs for wounding Don Francisco Broutin's slave who had refused to run an errand for Forstall. Broutin, the former notary, was also on the receiving end of an unusual case whose resolution is unknown. Don Basilio Ximenes requested that Broutin be ordered to shoot his dog, which had bitten Ximenes's slave Gimi. Don Guy Dreux had to pay a more substantial 338 pesos for killing his own slave Agata, in a case initiated by Agata's son.[18] At least two Euro-Louisianans were also sentenced to prison: Don Vicente Lesassier was sentenced to just under a year for mistreating a young slave girl, and Don Claude Tremé was sentenced to five years for killing another man's slave despite claiming in his defense that he had discovered the slave attempting to rob his house. Less than ten years later, Tremé was once again charged with cruelty toward a slave.[19] This handful of cases clearly does not reveal the full extent of slave abuse during the Spanish era and, as under French governance, most cases that received the court's attention involved violence against a slave belonging to another owner.

The protective aspects of the 1789 Código Negro should not be overemphasized. As interpreted by local bureaucrats, the Crown's concern with slave treatment had far more to do with preserving tranquility and perpetuating the institution of slavery than with protecting individual slaves. The Código Negro's own preamble began by declaring that its purpose was "to consolidate scattered laws . . . compatible with slavery and public tranquility." In 1776, when José de Gálvez, minister of the Indies, appointed his nephew Bernardo de Gálvez as governor, he instructed him to tend to "the good treatment" of slaves in part to abide by "the rules of humanity and justice" but, more importantly, to prevent "the uprisings of these people." Directing him to "forcefully pursue" fugitive slaves and "rigorously punish" any who assisted them, he also wanted Bernardo to "admonish" slaveowners "not [to] use excessive harshness with [slaves] nor treat them with the tyranny that some have been accustomed to, . . . which is the cause of their defiance and despair." Nearly two decades later, following the discovery of a slave conspiracy at Pointe Coupée, Governor Francisco Luis Héctor, baron de Carondelet, continued to stress the importance of "maintain[ing slaves] in such a state of contentment, and Subordination, as may banish from their minds the notion of acquiring a liberty." Five years later, acting civil governor Nicolás María Vidal criticized planters who, citing the Haitian Revolution as an excuse, sought to write harsh new slave laws that would authorize owners "to inflict rigorous and oppressive punishments" to be "impose[d] at will." Vidal countered that it was the planters themselves who were to blame for "insolent" slaves because of their indiscriminate punishments and neglect in providing proper provisions. The Crown, he continued, would never approve such a code; the behavior of these owners "greatly oppose[s] . . . the pious and kind intentions of our Sovereign."[20]

Whether the Código Negro proscribed mistreatment of slaves for benign or pragmatic reasons and whether or not its policies were enforced, planters perceived it as a challenge to their authority over their own slaves.[21] Even before the metropole codified its slave policies in 1789, Louisiana planters acted to write their own slave code. That they did so within a decade of the Spanish takeover indicates their dissatisfaction with Spanish policies governing slavery. In 1778, in anticipation of a growing slave population following the 1777 reopening of the slave trade, the cabildo commissioned two of its members to draft its own comprehensive slave code. Several months later, Francisco María de Reggio and Joseph Ducros submitted their draft, which was then circulated around the colony "in order that the inhabitants [could] express their views." The cabildo itself held two meetings devoted to discussing the draft code and then invited "the most prominent citizens of this Jurisdiction" to a quasi-public discussion in March 1779 that concluded with unanimous approval of the code and a request to send it to the king for his approval.[22] The code was apparently never sent to Spain, however, and never received official sanction. Five years later the cabildo acknowledged that the Spanish laws of the Indies, rather than its own code, governed the treatment and punishment of slaves in Louisiana.[23]

Having failed to enact their own code, planters continued to resist the implementation of what they perceived of as leniency on the part of Spanish officials.

When the Código Negro arrived in the colony in 1790, the cabildo declared that, if enacted, "great damage will result to this Province." It appealed to Governor Esteban Miró to suspend the code until it had a chance to communicate to the king how "detrimental" such a code would be "to the inhabitants of this Province."[24] Such complaints echoed throughout Spanish America: local governments in Havana and Venezuela independently suspended the Código Negro; in Puerto Rico, provisions were selectively applied; and in Santo Domingo and New Granada, it was never published. In response, the Crown repealed the Código Negro in 1794.[25]

In criticizing the Código Negro, planters in Louisiana and elsewhere articulated several concerns. They pleaded poverty, claiming it would be impossible for owners to support a priest on every habitation or purchase spouses for their slaves. They suggested that metropolitan officials were ignorant of colonial labor regimes and rejected restrictions on what hours and days slaves could be made to work. Although they credited the king's "spirit of prudence and . . . feelings of humanity," they predicted that granting slaves the right to complain about mistreatment would lead to continual, malicious lawsuits, forcing many planters to abandon "the pursuits of agriculture in order to avoid seeing themselves so frequently and so causelessly exposed to vexations and contumelies." Sometimes, the planters made contradictory claims. They contended, on the one hand, that the Código Negro merely codified existing laws, and therefore was not needed, but asserted, on the other, that the code would result in "the ruin of agriculture, the destruction of trade . . . , and the subversion of public tranquility."

Finally, the planters blamed slaves themselves. Claiming a knowledge of slaves' characters superior to that of officials in the metropole, acquired from their "long experience among the negros," the planters described them as "indocile and inquiet"; they had a "dissatisfied and rebellious humour" and were capable of creating fanciful accusations against their owners. Slaves were also responsible for rejecting Catholicism and the sacrament of marriage because, according to the planters, slaves believed marriage to be "a source of disgusts and miseries," a form of "double servitude." All efforts on the part of owners "to establish and encourage that institution among them have always proved fruitless," because negros, they wrote, "have an almost insuperable aversion to marriage."[26]

The planters' racialized depictions of the "character of the negros" indicate that, as racial projects, the two codes also differed significantly. For the metropole, slaves were workers whose "first and principal occupation" was "agriculture and other labors of the field." Its Código Negro was truly a slave code that sought to regulate a particular system of labor and set of labor relations. It treated slaves as a corporate group and focused on defining the legal rights and obligations of owners and slaves. The Code Noir ou Loi Municipale, on the other hand, sought to regulate race relations more generally. Unlike the Código Negro, the Code Noir ou Loi Municipale included provisions on gens de couleur libre, interracial sex, and manumission.[27]

For planters, the problem of free people of African descent was their possession of freedom within a slave society. As the code noted, there was no "perceptible sign that distinguishes the nègre slave from the one who is free," making it easy for slaves to "falsely declare themselves free." Therefore, it decreed that nègres libres who wished to carry arms or ride horses had to carry written declarations of their freedom. Fearing that free people of African descent would be more likely than blancs to assist runaway slaves, the code imposed extra penalties on the former. Affranchis could even be reenslaved. The Code Noir ou Loi Municipale additionally restricted gens de couleur libre by reintroducing the 1724 Code Noir's bans on gens de couleur libre receiving inheritances or other donations from blancs and on marriage and concubinage between blancs and noirs or mulâtres. It also added a prohibition on marriages between nègres libres and slaves, citing "the multitude of abuses that result" from them.[28]

Far more than the 1724 code it often replicated, the planters' 1778 code conveyed a pervasive principle of racial discrimination, a result of its local rather than metropolitan origins and also perhaps of a growing concern with the increasing numbers of sang-mêlé in the colony. As with the earlier code, the planters' code required "affranchis to convey a very great respect toward their former Masters, their Widows, and their Children" and "punished [them] more seriously" for assaults against former owners. But the planter-authored code went beyond its metropolitan predecessor in decreeing deference from all affranchis toward all blancs, not just their former owners. They were ordered "never to expose to insult, abuse, nor beat Blancs, nor to claim to be equal to them" but rather to "yield to them" and to address them only with respect.[29] Yet the 1778 Code Noir was not universally negative to gens de couleur libre. Again echoing its 1724 predecessor, gens de couleur libre were to "enjoy the same rights, privileges and immunities enjoyed by persons born free," except where specified elsewhere in the code.[30]

Although the Code Noir ou Loi Municipale used both the categories "affranchis" and "libres" (which qualified the labels "nègres" and "mulâtres"), it is clear from the textual context that the code's authors did not mean to distinguish between those freed during their lifetimes and those born free (nèe libre) as both the earlier French codes noirs had done.[31] In collapsing this distinction, the 1778 code implied that all free people of color had literal or at least figurative connections to slavery. The legal entities subjected to the provisions of the 1778 code were most often referred to as "esclaves" and "maîtres" ("masters"), although "blanc," "nègre" (most often modifying "esclaves" but occasionally qualified by "libre"), and mulâtre (mostly qualified by "libre") were also used. "Noir" appeared only once: in the article prohibiting racial exogamy, perhaps because it was copied from the 1724 code. One article—the one declaring that affranchis generally enjoy the same rights as persons born free (personnes nées libres)—also denied "manumitted blacks or free mulattoes [affranchis nègres ou mulâtres libres]" the right to inherit from whites. Although the authors may not have intended to make this distinction, their wording implies a correlation between nègres and enslavement, on the one hand, and mulâtres and freedom, on the other, although it did acknowledge that nègres could achieve freedom through manumission.[32]

Redeeming Themselves from Slavery

As might be expected from a code that took a more discriminatory view toward free persons of color, the Code Noir ou Loi Municipale sought to reverse the liberalization of manumission practices that had begun with Spanish rule. This liberalization had happened in a piecemeal fashion rather than through any single decree. Indeed, the 1789 Código Negro failed to mention manumission except to state that "nonuseful slaves" could not be manumitted unless their former owners continued to provide for them.[33] Yet, as early as 1771, New Orleans' notaries were recording manumissions without reference to government permission, as had been required by French law. That is, owners were freely manumitting their slaves for whatever reasons motivated them to do so; they were not choosing from a limited range of legitimate reasons nor were they defending their act before a government or judicial official. They were also freeing their slaves through a variety of means, from baptizing them as free to bequeathing freedom in their wills.

Even more important than voluntary manumission, however, was the concept of coartación. Developed in Cuba, coartación drew on provisions of the Siete Partidas, especially the notion that "all laws should protect [liberty] whenever an opportunity presents itself."[34] Coartación allowed slaves to be freed at their own initiative, even if they did not have their owners' consent, although the latter received some form of compensation for their loss of property. During the late seventeenth century, Cuban owners and slaves slowly worked out a system according to which they negotiated a fixed price for freedom that slaves could pay in installments over time, sometimes decades. Such arrangements were honored by new owners if the slave was sold or inherited. Coartación received royal recognition and legal sanction in the late 1760s—just as the Spanish arrived in Louisiana—when the Crown decreed that "when the slaves deliver to their owners the amount of their value, acquired permissibly by honest means, whether from their own industry or from relations or friends . . . , in order to be redeemed from captivity or servitude, the said owners are obligated to grant them, simply and legally, a freedom letter."[35]

By the time coartación arrived in Louisiana it was a well-developed practice that acknowledged a slave's rights to personal property (in order to acquire the funds with which to purchase their freedom) and to act as legal agents capable of making contracts, at least when their own freedom was at issue, while at the same time recognizing an owner's right to compensation.[36] In addition, there was an established mechanism for determining an individual slave's price if owner and slave could not mutually agree on a figure. In such cases, the slave and her or his owner named their own arbitrator, each of whom would determine a just price for the slave. If the two assessments varied, the court could appoint a third appraiser of its own, whose valuation was usually final. Upon receipt of the full payment (which could be in the form of a lump sum or installment payments and could come from a third party), owners were forced to issue an act of manumission whether or not they had initially consented to the process.

Slaves (and owners) did not lose time in taking advantage of the increasing opportunities for freedom under Spanish law.[37] In the month following O'Reilly's imposition of Spanish law, seven slaves were manumitted. Louis Claude Lechert used his will to promise freedom to his négresse slave Nanette and her four mulâtre children; Jean Bordenave allowed Louis Mallet to purchase the freedom of his négresse Jeanne; and Father Dagobert declared at the baptismal font that Pierre Joseph, son of Madame Prévôt's mulâtresse slave Madeline, was freed "by an act of liberty."[38] It took only four years under the Spanish for the number of manumitted slaves to surpass all those freed during five decades of French rule. Almost two thousand slaves received their freedom during the four decades of Spanish rule.[39] In the 1770s, an average of forty-four slaves were manumitted each year; by 1803, this number had doubled.[40] At the same time, however, the slave population of the New Orleans region almost tripled, from just under three thousand to more than eight thousand.[41] In the early 1770s, 1 slave in 126 became free; by the end of the Spanish era, only 1 in almost 300 did. Although this was a significant decline, slaves in New Orleans were still almost three times as likely to obtain their freedom than those in post-Revolutionary Virginia where only 1 in 875 slaves was manumitted annually.[42]

A slave's chances of gaining freedom were shaped by the ups and downs of the slave trade. The first significant increase in the trade came in 1777 when the Crown permitted Louisianans to purchase slaves from the French Caribbean. In 1782, they were permitted to import slaves, duty free, from friendly or neutral countries. Four years later, however, Governor Miró banned imports from the French and British Caribbean, and all slave imports were banned between 1795 and 1800 and then again in 1804.[43] But the relationship between slave imports and manumissions was not a simple one. Certainly the increased availability of slaves encouraged some owners to reward an individual slave or two with freedom, knowing they could easily replace them. But owners began manumitting their slaves in dramatically higher numbers before the trade reopened in 1777, and the number of manumissions increased in the years following the 1795 ban.[44] At least some owners, then, were responding not to market forces but rather to the legal changes introduced by Spanish rule, suggesting that more slaves would have been freed during the French era if manumission policies had not been so restricted.

Yet even if some Franco-Louisianans had chafed under the earlier restrictive rules, it is not surprising that the elites on the cabildo responded to the relaxation of manumission policies and the dramatic increase in the numbers of manumissions by reinstating the requirement of judicial consent. Under the unimplemented Code Noir ou Loi Municipale, owners would have had to petition the court, participate in an "inquiry into the life and morals of the said slave," and produce four witnesses who would affirm their "legitimate and true motives" for emancipation. The code justified these onerous steps because, as it noted, emancipation made "a Citizen of a Slave" and, therefore, "one has to take all possible precautions to insure the regularity of his morals, the docility of his character, and of his disposition to work." The code also sought to exile emancipated slaves from the city for work in the country unless the slave was already trained in a trade and his current master "certified to [the slave's] good conduct" and would continue to employ him.[45]

Not only did the planters propose a new, highly restrictive mechanism for manumission; they also undermined existing manumission practices with additional provisions. The code prohibited slaves from hiring themselves out, thus restricting slaves in their ability to earn their own purchase price. It denied slaves the right "to have anything of their own"; therefore, even if they could earn money to purchase their freedom, they could not retain possession of it.[46] Even though the planters' restrictions were never implemented, and thus slaves continued to negotiate for freedom throughout the Spanish period, the draft code clearly revealed planters' opposition to Spanish reforms.

The almost two thousand manumissions granted during the Spanish era took a variety of forms. Four of every ten slaves who gained their freedom received it freely and voluntarily, without the owner receiving any form of compensation and without the interference of the courts. The remaining 60 percent of manumissions were compensated in some way or another. Of those only a very few—just seventy-two in the entire period, or under 4 percent—required the manumitted slave to perform additional services for his or her owner before being granted liberty. The great majority of compensated manumissions, and just over half of all manumissions, involved coartación. The ratio between unconditional and compensated manumissions changed over time. During the 1770s, slaves were slightly more likely to be freed voluntarily but by the end of the Spanish era, two-thirds of slaves were compensating their owners in some way.[47]

Certain slaves had a greater chance at freedom than others. Gender, age, and appearance also influenced the type of manumission that any given slave was granted. As during the French era, female slaves were more likely to receive their freedom than male ones despite an almost equal sex ratio within the enslaved population. In New Orleans during the last third of the eighteenth century, women comprised between 51 and 54 percent of the city's enslaved population, but they received just over 60 percent of the manumissions. Male and female children were manumitted in roughly equal numbers, but nearly two and a half times as many adult women were manumitted as men. As elsewhere in Spanish America, particularly in urban areas, enslaved women cost less to free, they often had greater opportunities to earn cash through petty trade, and they were more likely to enjoy intimate relationships (sexual or otherwise) with their masters that might lead to unconditional manumissions.

Although negros and mulatos were unconditionally manumitted in roughly equal numbers, negros were more than four times as likely to purchase their own freedom. In contrast, mulatos were one and a half times more likely to have their freedom purchased for them by a third party. In addition, negros were almost twice as likely to resort to the courts in order to obtain their freedom. Among negros, women were three times as likely to receive unconditional freedom as men and almost twice as likely to have their freedom purchased, either by themselves or by a third party. In her analysis of Spanish-era manumissions, historian Kimberley Hanger concluded that the lighter one's skin, the more likely one was to be freed young and through the actions of others, while those of a darker complexion were more likely to be freed at a more advanced age and through their own initiative.[48]

The relationship between ascribed complexion and freedom is a complex one. According to the 1771 and 1791 censuses, the fastest growing segment of the population was the one defined as "sang-mêlé," which included mulatos, pardos, cuateróns, and mestizos. In 1771, 316 New Orleanians were marked as sang-mêlé (68 libres and 248 slaves), a category that distinguished them from blancos and negros. Two decades later, there were almost three times as many sang-mêlé (594 libres and 285 slaves), with the free accounting for most of the increase. There are two plausible explanations for this pattern. As Hanger argues, those with mixed European and African ancestry were more likely to be freed than those with only African ancestry. But it is also likely that free persons of African ancestry (or those in the process of becoming free) were far more likely to be perceived (and therefore labeled) as belonging to a lighter skin color: that is, freedom whitened or at least lightened.

Under Spanish law, when an owner wanted to unconditionally free a slave, he merely had to appear before a priest or a notary and two witnesses. A small number of slaves were freed at the baptismal font, beginning, as we have seen, just one month after O'Reilly's Ordinances and Instructions were announced, when Father Dagobert baptized Madame Prévôt's slave Pierre Joseph as free. Three decades later, Ursula, négresse slave of Thomas Saulet, appeared before the priest to have her daughter baptized, bringing a note from her owner requesting that María Manuela be baptized as free. Mulata Rosa brought a copy of her cuarteróna daughter's notarized manumission act when she had her baptized, and so the priest duly noted her as free.[49] Other baptized infants were described as free while their mothers were described as slaves but with no explicit mention of liberty being granted to the infant. It is possible that in these cases the priests erred either in identifying the infant as free or the mother as enslaved. In the 1773 baptism record of Gaspar, for instance, his mother was initially described as the slave of Mr. Bas, but that notation was then crossed out and "libre" was added to Gaspar.[50] It is also possible, however, that enslaved mothers were surreptitiously trying to gain freedom for their children.

At least one owner petitioned to have such a baptism corrected. In 1800, Pierre Genti wrote to Bishop Luis Peñalver y Cárdenas, complaining that his mulato slave Thomas had been baptized two years earlier as free without his permission. The bishop questioned Thomas's godparents as well as Father Antonio Sedella, who had performed the baptism. Thomas's godmother denied that she had declared Thomas free, knowing that he was the son of a slave, while his godfather did not recall any mention of freedom at the baptism. He added, however, that he had later heard that Thomas had been baptized as free. In his response, Sedella noted, "Concerning the free or slave state of infants baptized," officiating priests could "rely only on the word of those assisting at the baptism," and he acknowledged that "it is easy to be deceived." Since Thomas had been baptized two years earlier, Sedella claimed "it is almost impossible to remember why he recorded the child as free." The bishop ruled that the notation of Thomas as free did "not affect his slavery or freedom," and he ordered Sedella to make a note to this effect in the baptismal registry.[51]

Most owners who manumitted their slaves voluntarily did so at the notary's office, renouncing there any claims to ownership of the slave. Although not required to do so, owners often listed their reasons for granting their slaves freedom. Very few manumitters claimed to have spiritual motives for unconditionally freeing their slaves, suggesting that religion played an insignificant role in their decision.[52] Equally rare were manumitters who described themselves as being moved by "pity and commiseration" as were those who referred to "the will of our Sovereign to redeem from captivity all who are so held, and as the law provides."[53] The most frequent motives cited by manumitters were "gratitude" felt for the "good services" received from their slaves, or sometimes from someone else's slave, and the love they had for the slave. Sixty-year-old Francisco was freed by Antonio Barnabe for "the love he bears him, and because he has served him faithfully and well for many years."[54] Doña Luisa Dutive freed the three-year-old mulatica María Estenne "for the love that I have for her, and the good services that I have received from her mother, Victoria." Doña Luisa's love, however, was not all that great, although the services may indeed have been good, and she decided to keep Victoria enslaved.[55]

Care has to be taken, however, when interpreting the language owners used to describe their motivations. Phrases like "for the good services" and even "for the love I have" appear frequently, and the latter seems especially hackneyed when paired with an acknowledgement that money had changed hands.[56] In one case, François Dusuau de La Croix Demazilière freed his mulata slave Fanchon because "of the love I have for her and her good services," but the following year, he tricked her into going to Saint-Domingue where she was sold back into slavery.[57] The language of these acts was also influenced by the notary who recorded them. For instance, manumitters who appeared before Jean Baptiste Garic, a French notary who continued practicing until 1779, regularly cited religious reasons as their motivation, whereas those using other notaries rarely mentioned spiritual motives.[58] This suggests that it was the notary, rather than the owner, who provided somewhat formulaic language with which to describe individual motivations, although it is evident that the owner could choose from a variety of phrases that best suited his or her situation.[59]

Yet despite the hackneyed declarations of love and notaries' boilerplates, it is clear that at least a substantial minority of owners who freely and unconditionally manumitted their slaves as well as those third parties who purchased a slave's freedom did so because they had an intimate relationship of one variety or another with those they manumitted. Some slaves were freed by their godparents; others by the grown-up children they had helped to raise, although few were as explicit as Don Bartolomé Francisco de Bretton, who noted that he was freeing fifty-five-year-old negra Juana because she had been his wet nurse.[60]

Relations of intimacy, especially sexual partnerships and paternity, were what motivated many graciosa manumissions and perhaps most third-party coartacións.[61] Although it was rare for blancos to admit paternity of a slave they were in the process of manumitting, a few did. Antonio Guichard initiated a coartación for an unnamed mulato newborn in 1782, declaring that the slave was "his son, therefore he would like to buy his freedom," while Carlos Begin credited "the love and fondness that I profess for my son" when he freed ten-month-old mulatto Carlos in 1793.[62] Pedro La Croix and Don Pierre Bonne waited until their mulata daughters were far older before freeing them but, in doing so, both explicitly claimed them as their natural daughters. In La Croix's case, he had just purchased the thirty-two-year-old Juaneton from Don Esteban Carnaby for 600 pesos; perhaps he had not been able to afford, or Carnaby unwilling to sell, her earlier.[63]

Others were not so explicit, but paternal motivations are often suggested by circumstantial evidence, including purchase followed quickly by manumission or third-party coartación, the manumission of a very young child, who could not have earned his or her freedom through good services, a given name shared by manumitter and slave, and mulato or cuarterón children born of negra or mulata mothers. Jean Audebert's manumission of a six-month-old mulatico typifies all four of these, purchasing and manumitting Juan, whose mother was negra Isabel, on the same day.[64] Juan Doriol purchased three-year-old mulatico Juan Luis and his mother, negra María, "in order to give them freedom for the much love and fondness that I have for them" and freed them the following day.[65] Luis Jousson waited twenty months before freeing his mulato namesake, but it is hard to imagine he received much labor from the boy, who was five months old when he purchased him.[66] Similarly, it is hard to take Don Luis Lalande Daprémont at his word when he claimed to be manumitting a three-year-old mulatico "in remuneration of his loyalty and various services."[67]

Owners who manumitted their slaves graciosa did so for a variety of complex and sometimes unrecoverable reasons; compensated manumissions, on the other hand, are much easier to understand, if only from a straightforward economic point of view. For many owners, coartación was an easy choice; the compensation they received enabled them to purchase a new slave, perhaps younger, healthier, or otherwise more suitable, if they desired. Others may have hoped, as did Spanish officials, that by holding out the promise of freedom for a price, slaves would utilize their spare time in productive enterprises, although there was always a concern that slaves would steal or work for wages rather than for their masters in order to earn the money to purchase themselves.

For slaves, coartación was the surest avenue to freedom, one they could initiate themselves and one, they quickly learned, the courts were willing to enforce against reluctant owners, although few in fact were forced to appeal to the courts. Given that coartación had evolved in Cuba, it is likely that Louisiana slaves learned about the practice from the free pardo and moreno militia men from Havana who accompanied O'Reilly in 1769, many of whom may have acquired their own freedom through coartación.[68] In March 1771, the elderly negro Bautista was the first slave to request a carta de libertad for a price from his owner, Joseph Meunier, who granted him his freedom for a meager 30 pesos.[69] The first litigated case of coartación began on November 15, 1771, when mulata Juana Catalina petitioned the governor for her "rescate" ("ransom" or "redemption"), a "favor," she noted, "that the laws concede to her." She pointed out that she had "made special services to [her deceased master] Destrehan and his wife during their lives" and requested an appraisal in order to set her freedom price. Valued as a group with her husband and son at 900 pesos in the inventory of the Destrehan estate on November 26, she was appraised alone at 300 pesos. Within three weeks, Juana Catalina paid the sum and received her carta.[70]

Within just two years of O'Reilly's imposition of Spanish policies (including, implicitly, coartación), then, slaves in New Orleans were cognizant of their right to request their compensated freedom. Knowledge of these rights, as well as of the process of coartación and the ideology underpinning it, quickly became widespread, as several petitions from the early 1780s illustrate. Echoing Juana Catalina's petition, María Theresa requested permission to "redeem herself from slavery through legal means" and stressed "her right to ask [for her freedom] according to law and the Royal Ordinances of the Sovereign." Michel asserted his right to "the franchise the law concedes to him to claim his freedom," and Maríana (also called María) drew up her petition "using the faculties conceded to her by law." Libres also filed petitions "in conformity to law" when they sought appraisals for their enslaved relatives.[71]

In most cases of coartación, slaves and their owners agreed on a freedom price, and thus slaves did not have to resort to the courts. When negra Maríana paid her owner, Don Martin Navarro, 500 pesos for her freedom, he went to the notary to have her carta drawn up.[72] Owners also appeared before notaries to record contracts with their slaves in which they obligated themselves to grant freedom in the future once the agreed-on price had been produced. In 1784, Francisco Muñoz, the warden of the city's prison, set a price of 250 pesos for his negra slave María and stated his "wish that whenever she can exhibit [this] sum . . . her freedom will be given to her immediately . . . with the full understanding that she need not be appraised." He ordered his executor to accept whatever payments she could afford to make, however small, until her full price was paid.[73]

If a slave and his owner could not agree on a price or if the owner refused to negotiate at all, the slave could ask the courts to intervene. Although less than 15 percent of coartación cases required judicial intervention, it is clear that slaves' ability to call upon the court—and the court's willingness to rule in their favor—caused more owners to negotiate voluntarily.[74] In a typical petition, negro Michel claimed that he had asked Francisca Girardy many times "to grant him his liberty for a just price," but since she had "never been willing to draw up an Act of Emancipation," he appealed to the court to authorize an appraisal.[75] The appraisal process, initiated by the slave's petition, involved the appointment of two appraisers: one named by the slave and the other by the owner. When the court notified an owner that a coartación case had been instigated, it warned the owner that the court would appoint an appraiser if the owner failed to do so, making noncompliance an ineffective way to thwart a slave's freedom. When Francisco Maney failed to respond to a coartación petition, Governor Unzaga ordered the post commander to "notify the defendant to either come to the city himself or appoint some one to answer this demand."[76]

Appraisers, chosen for their knowledge of the local slave market and for being "versed in such matters and [knowing] about the talents and the capabilities of the said negro," met with slaves and their owners in the presence of a court official. Examining slaves "most carefully and minutely," inspecting them for signs of age and infirmities, and assessing their "talents, age, and robustness," the appraisers determined their value.[77] At times, the two appraisers reached the same estimate.[78] However, if the appraisers differed in their valuations, slaves could request that the court appoint a "third in discord," whose determination was usually deemed final. Typically, owners' appraisers came in with the higher valuation of the two, and they were often, but not always, supported in their judgment by the court-appointed appraiser.[79]

Owners sometimes attempted subterfuge to prevent or at least delay their slaves' freedom. When Bernarda Arciny, negra slave of Francisco Daniel Dupain, successfully sued "to redeem herself from slavery" at an adjudicated price of 800 pesos, her owner left town, preventing her "from the enjoyment of her freedom for a greater length of time than necessary." In a common display of slave initiative, Arciny petitioned the court to force Daniel Dupain, her owner's father, to draw up the carta, knowing that he held power of attorney over his son's affairs during the latter's frequent absences from the city.[80] Seven years earlier, Juan Suriray de la Rue went further and imprisoned his negra slave, María Juana, in an effort to prevent her from being able to present a coartación petition to the court.[81] Perhaps aware of Suriray's imprisonment of María Juana, Arciny had included in her initial petition a request that Dupain be prevented "from taking action against her, to have her punished or imprisoned, as he has threatened to do so."[82] Marie-Françoise Girardy tried to thwart María Theresa's coartación first by failing to respond to the slave's petition—forcing the court to name an appraiser for her—and then by insisting on a second appraisal since the court had proceeded "without her participation." All of Girardy's efforts failed, however, and when she finally appeared before the notary, she reported that the alcalde had ordered her to issue María Theresa's carta.[83]

Slaves not only knew how to navigate the local court system; they were also aware that unfavorable decisions could be appealed to a higher court in Havana. When María Isabel and Rosa did so in 1776, they successfully forced a New Orleans alcalde to overturn his earlier decision against them. In May 1775, their owner, Renato Chouteau, had freed María Isabel, Rosa, and Rosa's daughter "on condition that [they] serve him as long as he lived," and he confirmed their manumissions in his will. Although Chouteau had explicitly ordered that "after his death, neither his heirs nor assigns may contradict [their freedom] nor reclaim them in any manner," his heirs did just that when the estate was being settled the following year. The estate's executors, arguing that the manumissions would disadvantageously impact Chouteau's wife, two sons, and his creditors, sought to have their conditional manumissions revoked. Ruling that Chouteau had violated his marriage contract by disposing of property to the detriment of his wife, Alcalde Pierre-Henri d'Erneville revoked the manumissions.

"Demanding their rights under their acts of emancipation and their late master's will," María Isabel and Rosa petitioned Governor Unzaga. They protested that d'Erneville had made his ruling without advice from the letrado and requested that Unzaga send their case to Havana for legal advice, which he did.[84] With a report from Havana in hand, d'Erneville overturned his previous decision, and with the consent of all parties, he decreed that the emancipations were valid. He did, however, hold the slaves responsible for reimbursing the estate for part of the debts it incurred as a result of their manumissions "before they may enjoy the full use of their freedom." Despite this partial remaining obligation, the slaves' recourse to a higher judicial authority resulted in their eventual freedom.

María Isabel and Rosa's case also set a significant precedent. When Chouteau first promised them their freedom, he included Rosa's daughter María Juana. By the time of his will, Rosa had a second child, whom Chouteau was careful to note as also freed. The Havana letrado determined that Rosa's son should be considered freeborn, as he had been born after his mother had received her conditional manumission, and he was therefore not included when the slaves' debt to the estate were calculated.[85] The ruling demonstrates that women who had already received a legal promise of freedom—whether a conditional emancipation or a coartación agreement—could then pass freedom onto their children despite the fact that the mothers themselves were still legally slaves.

In addition to knowing their legal rights, slaves also knew their own value, which they could have arrived at by discovering their original purchase price, what their owners had tried to sell them for, how much they had been valued in an estate inventory, or their value in comparison to other slaves of a similar age or skills. Maríana named her inventoried price in her coartación petition.[86] Catherina complained in 1773 that the appraised price of 450 pesos for her and her daughter was excessive, since two years earlier, Catherina had been inventoried together with her all three of daughters at just 500 pesos.[87] In the inventory of his deceased owner's estate, Silvestre, a fifty-year-old negro carpenter, had been valued at 300 pesos. A few days later, his brother, negro libre Valentin, initiated a coartación, offering to pay the inventoried price for Silvestre's freedom. The estate's executor, Francisco Marie de Reggio, refused, however, claiming that such a valuation was "nothing more than a legal formality taken so as not to cause confusion at the auction sale," where slaves often brought in two to three times their inventoried price "on consideration of the different talents he might possess, which naturally will not have been noted by the appraisers." De Reggio did not reject the coartación out of hand; instead, he sought to have a new appraisal to determine Silvestre's price.[88]

In Silvestre's case, as in many others, slaves, their free relatives, and owners all attempted to negotiate for the best price. Having failed to free his brother for 300 pesos, Valentin offered no objections to de Reggio's request for a new appraisal, but he added a request of his own: that Silvestre be examined by a surgeon to determine "whether he suffers from any infirmity and the exact state of his health." Two surgeons discovered that Silvestre had a dislocated right knee that made it difficult for him to practice his trade, although they considered him only "slightly injured" and not "totally crippled." Valentin's attempt to have his brother's price lowered did not work, however, as even with this knowledge, the appraisers eventually determined Silvestre's value to be 800 pesos.[89] Catherina too highlighted her infirmity when she requested a third appraiser, one who knew "the state of her health and . . . of her habitual infirmities," as a result of which her value was reduced from 450 pesos to 320 pesos.[90]

Negra libre Elena also tried to manipulate the appraisal process when, in August 1780, she petitioned to purchase freedom for her son, Maylois, from Henrique Desprez. After Maylois was appraised at 600 pesos and 800 pesos, the court followed its usual practice and named a third appraiser, who concurred with the lower estimate. At first, Alcalde Pedro Piernas approved Maylois' manumission at 600 pesos, but then he ruled that a fourth appraiser should be appointed, since the first three did not agree. This fourth appraisal came in at 800 pesos. At this point, Elena requested the case records in order to respond to this unusual occurrence. Her subsequent petition made a twofold argument. First, she asserted that the use of a fourth appraiser is "contrary to law, which speaks only of a third in discord," and therefore, the initial assessment at 600 pesos should stand. Second, she denied that her son had the talents and abilities that Desprez claimed, and asserted that, on the contrary, "he is a thief and a drunkard and that he has been arrested." To further challenge the high price placed on her son's freedom, she cited several other cases of coartación: Carlos, a mulato joiner; Andres, an expert blacksmith; and Luis, a master carpenter, who were all freed for between 750 and 800 pesos. How, therefore, could her "poor miserable son," "a negro without a trade, a drunkard and a thief," be worth as much as these skilled tradesmen? Alcalde Piernas denied Elena's petition and appointed a fifth appraiser, who confirmed Maylois' value at 800 pesos.[91]

Although slaves and their relatives sought the lowest price for freedom, they were also willing to appeal to their owners' economic interests, even if that meant paying a higher price. Nicolas' owners had been trying to sell him for 400 pesos. For four years, however, they were unable to find a willing purchaser at this price "for a man without any trade, or occupation, and suffering much from stomach troubles." After a coartación appraisal, Nicolas purchased his freedom for 800 pesos, twice as much as his owners had been seeking (although 400 pesos less than their appraiser had valued Nicolas).[92] Clearly, in this case, Nicolas was willing to pay more for his freedom than other potential owners were for his labor. Other slaves highlighted their own age or infirmities and pointed out that their owners would be better served by investing in younger or more able slaves. Catherina argued that it would "be of greater interest to the estate to sell her to herself for cash, invest the money in a young negro boy, capable of working and earning for it, than to continue to hold her in bondage when her health will no longer permit her to work." Although she failed to convince one of the estate's executors, who actively opposed her manumission, the others consented "that her freedom be given to her and to her child at the price of their valuation so as to employ the produce in other negroes who will be more useful to the estate."[93]

It was not just slaves who sought to manipulate appraisals; owners too tried to get the best deal for themselves and often played on a slave's desire for freedom to get a higher price. After two appraisers agreed that María Theresa, fifty-year-old slave of Marie-Françoise Girardy, was worth 500 pesos ("because she is a good seamstress, washer, and ironer"), Girardy complained "the appraisement is gravely prejudicial to her" and requested a second assessment that would "take into consideration that her slave is one of the most perfect servants in this Province, a good washer and ironer, also a seamstress and embroiderer, as well as an excellent cook, in a word she has all the talents for a house domestic." When two additional assessments came in at 500 and 900 pesos, María Theresa herself complained that Girardy's appraiser had not taken into account "the 25 years she has been in the service of her owner, nor her advanced age." The court-appointed "third in discord" then valued María Theresa at 600 pesos, a price she accepted.[94] Another owner failed miserably when he tried to extort an unreasonable price from Antonio Guichard for the freedom of Guichard's mulato son. In 1782, Guichard offered to pay Francisco Daniel Dupain 100 pesos for the infant, just eight days old. Dupain, according to Guichard, demanded more "out of all reason," forcing Guichard to resort to the courts. The appraisals came in at 10, 50, and 60 pesos. Governor Miró ordered Dupain to free the infant for 60 pesos, far less than the father had initially offered.[95]

In some instances, owners consented to inventoried prices amicably and did not try to extort higher prices. When mulato libre Joseph Casenave petitioned to free negra Magdalena and her mulato son from the succession of Marie Eva LaBranche, he respectfully requested that they "not be put up for sale at public auction but that they might be given letters of emancipation so that they may enjoy their freedom in the future." In accepting this request, the heirs and executors of LaBranche's estate, like the great majority of owners involved in coartación cases, voluntarily agreed to free their slaves for a price and negotiated that price without judicial intervention.[96]

Owners' willing participation in the coartación process can also be inferred by the gap between the prices they demanded for a coartación and those they had to pay to purchase a new slave. Prices for slaves and for coartacións fluctuated in correlation with each other during the last third of the eighteenth century. Both increased steadily during the 1770s, decreased slightly during the 1780s (as more slaves were available for purchase), and then rose again during the 1790s (in response to increased demand with the success of sugar cultivation and a new ban on slave imports in 1795). Despite rising prices and demand, the cost of a coartación became increasingly cheaper in relation to the cost of a creole slave (who was more likely to be freed than a new African-born slave). During the 1770s and 1780s, the average price of a coartación was nearly two-thirds of the mean price for a creole slave but it dropped to around one-half during the 1790s and to about two-fifths by 1803.[97]

Like Magdalena and her son, as well as Guichard's son who, at eight days old, could certainly not have purchased himself, about one-half of coartacións were funded by someone other than the slave being manumitted. Although Guichard was one of the very rare blancos who openly acknowledged his familial connections to a slave he was helping to free, just over one-quarter of these benefactors were white. More frequently, however, the money came from libre relatives seeking to "remove [their relatives] . . . from the state of slavery."[98] Mulata libre María Theresa purchased her mother's freedom; negro libre Valentin freed his brother Silvestre; and mulata libre Marguerite made arrangements to free her mother, Genevieve, and brother Louis after her death.[99] Less frequently, slaves purchased the freedom of other slaves, mostly paying for their children's freedom alongside their own but sometimes freeing their children while themselves remaining in slavery.[100] For slaves without access to sufficient funds, freeing a child was a far less costly endeavor than trying to free themselves.

Although the strict understanding of coartación was that only well-behaved slaves would be allowed to purchase their freedom, there were, in fact, instances of coartación in New Orleans in which unruly (in the eyes of their owners) and even runaway slaves were allowed to free themselves. Catherina, whose manumission opened this chapter, was able to purchase her freedom despite Boré's declaration of "her bad conduct, her iniquity, [and] her dissimulation."[101] Elena, trying to reduce her son's value, had raised the issue of his troublesome conduct, including the fact that he had been arrested.[102] When negra libre Margarita sought to purchase her daughter, Naneta, from Maríana Lerable, viuda Lecomte, Lerable responded with a somewhat contradictory declaration. She both described Naneta as "one of the most perfect creole servants in this Colony, with all the required qualities to make a good house maid, cook, laundress, and has many other talents well known in this city" and asserted that "Naneta has been a fugitive from her house for the last eighteen months." As a runaway—one of the most disobedient acts a slave could perform short of murdering her mistress—Naneta should not have been eligible for coartación. Yet, once Margarita produced the assessed value of 1,000 pesos, Naneta was freed, although she was ordered to reimburse her former owner 136 pesos (8 pesos for each of the seventeen months she had absented herself from her owner's service).[103]

As the cases of Elena, Margarita, and Catherina demonstrate, libres and slaves alike often found support in the Spanish courts in their pursuit of freedom. In 1794, negro slave Luis Dor successfully sued the estate of deceased mulato libre Esteban Lalande for payment of a debt of 230 pesos, slightly more than the amount he needed to purchase his freedom from Don Joseph Dusuau de La Croix. Dor's success came despite opposition from Lalande's widow, parda libre María Gentilly, who argued that her signature on Dor's note had been forged and that her dowry should be protected from seizure, even when the money was to go to such a worthy cause as freedom. She even criticized owners such as Dusuau who demanded payment for their slaves' freedom; if Dusuau truly wanted to partake in "an act so humane as to manumit his slave," he should do so without compensation. But Gentilly's protests were in vain; Dor was awarded his money and purchased his freedom.[104]

When slaves who had been promised freedom by their deceased mistress, Pelagia Lorreins, complained to Alcalde Guy Dufossat that Lorreins' testamentary executor had failed to fulfill Lorreins' bequest, Dufossat ordered their emancipations to be issued within one day.[105] One alcalde went beyond ordering an owner to issue a carta, eventually enacting it himself. In March 1798, negro Josef Ginefry appeared before Don Pedro Marin Argote declaring that he had paid his owner, Don Nicolas Verbois, 400 pesos for his freedom. Argote ordered Verbois to issue Ginefry's carta. Two months later, however, he learned, probably from Ginefry, that Verbois had ignored his order. Once again he ordered Verbois to appear before a notary and grant his slave freedom. When Verbois still had not done so five days later, Argote himself went to the notary and issued Ginefry's carta.[106]

Recourse to the Spanish courts did not guarantee success to all slaves who sued their owners. Some unfortunate slaves learned that proper legal documentation to a coartación agreement and witnesses who could testify to payments made were crucial; without them, it could be difficult to prove that one's owner was reneging on promised freedom. María Luisa Saly claimed that her owner and former consort, Mateo Parin dit Canon, had agreed to free her when she repaid him for her purchase price, but he had reneged and had begun "to treat her with extreme cruelty." Since Saly could not produce proof of their agreement and Canon's witnesses denied any agreement existed, Alcalde Jacinto Panis sentenced her "to perpetual silence," forbidding her from making any future demands for freedom and ordering her to "respect him as a slave should her master." Why Panis ruled against Saly is unclear. Canon was not a man of status, and, as an alcalde, Panis upheld several freedom suits, including the highly contested Guillory case I discuss below. He also played a pivotal role as a witness in another case that was hindered by the lack of written documentation. In 1780, Maturina sued her owner, mulata libre Naneta

Chabert, claiming that Chabert had, at the time of her purchase, agreed to free her upon repayment of the 250 pesos she had cost. Several witnesses testified to having served as intermediaries, passing money along to Chabert from Maturina, including Panis, who testified to having received 100 pesos from Maturina and to knowledge of Chabert's promise of freedom. Alcaldes Guy Dufossat and Pierre de Verges chose to believe only Panis—the other witnesses were all free women of color—and Maturina was defrauded of 92 pesos. Panis was clearly not opposed to manumission in general, as his actions in these other contested cases demonstrate, as does his own graciosa manumission of an elderly slave who had served him for just a year and a half.[107]

Other slaves also lost their battles for freedom. Josef, a slave belonging to the recently deceased Pierre Degout Fleury, tried unsuccessfully for several years to free himself. In a case that began before Governor Miró in August 1783, Josef claimed that Fleury had often talked about emancipating him "as a reward for his good and faithful services," and, indeed, several blanco witnesses testified to this fact, claiming even that Fleury had written out a note to this effect but had failed to sign it. One asserted that just forty-eight hours before his death, Fleury had declared "It would not be just that he should remain a slave." The attorney for the estate's heirs, however, dismissed Josef's demand as "unfounded" and declared "he has neither the right nor any legal grounds for claiming his freedom, because he has not presented any document authorizing it, and the testimony . . . his witnesses have given does not amount to anything, since Fleury was nearly always drunk." Josef's case was lost when one of the court's own escribanos, Fernando Rodriguez, testified that the day before Fleury's death, the owner had rejected Josef's request for freedom in the escribano's presence. Although it failed to provide his freedom, Josef's case demonstrates Euro-Louisianan support for Afro-Louisianan claims to freedom. Not only did several blancos testify in support of Josef's claim, but Juan del Póstigo, the court's letrado, twice recommended that the court rehear Josef's case on two subsequent petitions in 1790.[108] Póstigo's willingness to repeatedly open the door to Josef's claims illustrates the role the Spanish government took in facilitating slaves' desire for freedom, even though those desires were not always satisfied.

Not all Spanish officials were as receptive to slaves' requests as Póstigo, however. Governor Bernardo de Gálvez attempted unsuccessfully to end the practice of coartación, arguing that it was a function of Cuban law inapplicable to Louisiana. His opportunity came during a long and drawn-out case that began in February 1776, when negra María Juana petitioned Gálvez's predecessor, Unzaga, requesting her coartación. She accused her owner, Juan Suriray de la Rue, and his wife of cruel treatment, which she blamed on the fact that she had been Suriray's consort before his marriage. María Juana appealed to Unzaga "to entreat the fair administration of justice that His Lordship distributes." Despite initially appearing sympathetic to María Juana's case, Unzaga revoked his first order for the coartación to proceed after Suriray filed suit against Englishman Edward Jenkins and mulata libre Maríana Deslattes for harboring María Juana as a fugitive and abetting her in her pursuit of freedom, thus beginning a legal battle that lasted fourteen months and involved judicial officials in New Orleans and Havana.[109]

According to María Juana and her witnesses, she had pleaded with Jenkins to buy her from Suriray, detailing the cruel abuse she suffered for two years. Jenkins and Deslattes attempted to negotiate with Suriray but could not agree on a price, and shortly thereafter all parties found themselves in court. The case quickly spiraled out of control as Jenkins and Suriray accused each other of all sorts of illicit behavior. Seeking counsel, Unzaga sent a copy of the case records—comprising more than three hundred pages—to letrado Don Guillermo Veranes in Havana. Veranes's advice arrived back in New Orleans in May 1777, and Gálvez, having replaced Unzaga, called the parties back into court to hand down his decision. Following Veranes's recommendation, Gálvez dismissed the case against Jenkins, ruling that Suriray had failed to prove that Jenkins was guilty of abetting María Juana's escape.

As for María Juana's request that began this dispute, however, Gálvez pointedly disagreed with Veranes's recommendation that her carta be drawn up for the estimated price "as is customary in this island, in like cases." In her original plea to the court, María Juana had claimed that "her master cannot and must not deny her her liberty nor is there a law to the contrary"; indeed, she argued, "Divine Law [was] in her favor [as] no Christian is obliged to remain in captivity as she, herself, is continually exposed to punishment where through suffocation or desperation she might die." Suriray had responded that she had "no right to extract her liberty. . . . In the laws of Spain there is no obligation for the master to free or alienate a slave or to destroy his property." On the contrary, he continued, "the master is the absolute owner of his slaves as well as his other property with the faculty to free and to dispose of them at his own free will." Gálvez concurred with Suriray and dismissed María Juana's claims to a right of liberty or to be freed from abusive captivity. He denied that the 1768 royal cédula confirming coartación in Cuba had any authority in Louisiana, a colony that was "governed by the general laws of the Kingdom as it has been previously arranged."[110]

María Juana had the misfortune to have her case pending when Gálvez succeeded Unzaga as governor. Unzaga had shown himself to favor coartación, earlier noting that it was "done in the interests of His Most Christian Majesty," and it is likely that he would have followed Veranes's advice to allow María Juana to purchase her freedom.[111] Gálvez, on the other hand, was hostile to the idea that slaves could force their owners to free them, even though the latter were compensated for the loss of their slaves' labor. More than any other Spanish governor, at least through 1795, Gálvez appears to have sympathized with the local elite on matters of race and slavery; the year after María Juana's case, he would side with the cabildo in their failed effort to enact a more stringent slave code.[112] Yet despite Gálvez's denial that Louisiana slaves had a right to freedom, coartación in fact continued to be practiced. More than one hundred uncontested cases and at least ten litigated ones would present themselves during the remainder of his five years in office.[113]

Although slaves could not always rely on the government to enable their freedom, as the cases of Maturina, Fleury's slave Josef, and María Juana demonstrate, the Spanish courts and bureaucrats generally upheld slaves' right to coartación and facilitated their ability to achieve freedom. They also protected that freedom if owners attempted to revoke it. In November 1780, Gálvez, who had three years earlier had denied that coartación applied in Louisiana, ruled for libre María dite Mariquine in her suit against her former owner, Pedro Methode, who was trying to sell her as a slave. María produced a document dated April 1779 and signed by Methode, which stated "that he permits her to go with her son, Charles, where she please, to live, because he has given her her freedom, since July, last, which he ratifies by the present." In addition to documentation of her freedom, she asserted that she had in fact "enjoyed her liberty peacefully as is known to everyone in [New Orleans]" since July 1778. Methode claimed, however, that far from being a carta, his letter was merely "a license, or a permit, that he wrote for her so that she might travel honorably as he is accustomed to do with all his slaves." He argued that he had never promised her freedom and, even if he had, he could not have afforded to do so because of his debts. Gálvez rebuffed Methode's assertions and ordered him to issue María a formal carta, threatening him with another suit if he failed to do so.[114]

Like María, negra Margarita successfully defended herself against her former owners' attempts to reclaim her and her children as slaves despite their reasonable claim that the manumission had been illegal. In 1770, Gregoire Guillory freed Margarita and her children on the condition that she "remain in his services" until his death. As a resident of the rural post of Opelousas and without access to a notary, Guillory drew up a "simple note" containing the promise of freedom and the conditions stipulated; later that year, he had the document notarized during a trip to New Orleans. The problem, as Guillory's sons later pointed out, was that Margarita in fact belonged to their mother, and thus Guillory had no right to manumit her. They accused their father of pressuring them into signing their marks on the manumission note and forcing them at knifepoint to relinquish Margarita.

Sometime before April 1778, Margarita moved to New Orleans, leaving her children in the possession of the Guillory sons. Later that year and again the following one, Jean-Baptiste Guillory, the eldest son, petitioned unsuccessfully to have Margarita returned to him and his brothers as her "proper owners" and to have her manumission annulled, as it had not been passed by her legitimate owner. In 1781, another of the sons, Claude, traveled to New Orleans, found Margarita, and had her arrested, asserting that she was a runaway. In a hearing before Alcalde Jacinto Panis, Margarita produced her carta de libertad and had her freedom declared valid. The following year, Margarita petitioned the court to force the Guillory brothers to "declare her children free," prevent them from "remov[ing] them, secretly, beyond the limits of the Colony," and "leave them in peaceful possession of [their freedom]." For the next twelve months, petitions went back and forth between Opelousas and New Orleans until eventually Margarita and the Guillorys reached a compromise: the Guillory brothers agreed not to contest Margarita's freedom, while Margarita promised to pay 600 pesos for the freedom of her children.[115]

In another case, Fanchon's previous owner did not merely try to revoke her freedom but physically sold her back into slavery. François Dusuau de La Croix Demazilière had freed sixteen-year-old mulata Fanchon in December 1773 after she had nursed him back to health when he had been "seriously ill and in danger of death." Sometime the following year, however, he sent her to be sold in Saint-Domingue, where she was eventually bought by Pierre Fauché for 4,000 pesos. Several years later, in February 1783, New Orleans resident Pierre Gauvin sued Fauché for the return of Fanchon, declaring that she was truly free, although she had lost her carta and so was unable to prove it to the Saint-Domingue authorities. Gauvin had a copy of her carta sent to the island's governor, who confirmed her manumission and ruled the sale to Fauché null and void. Fauché then successfully sued Demazilière for the return of her purchase price.[116]

As the cases of Margarita and Fanchon demonstrate, even having a carta was not always a guarantee of freedom. Nor were promises of freedom always realized, whether because owners failed to properly notarize such promises or because executors contested testamentary manumissions. Crucially, most slaves did not have owners who were willing to free them graciosa, and they themselves did not have the resources for a coartación. Despite all the obstacles in their way, however, a substantial number of slaves did achieve freedom during the Spanish era, creating a population whose legal status lay between enslaved people of African descent and free Euro-New Orleanians. Within the first decade of Spanish rule, the number of free people of color in New Orleans more than tripled (although some of that increase is probably a result of undercounting during the French era), and their numbers continued to increase significantly through the end of the century, reaching 1,500 in 1805.[117]

SPANISH RULE HAD MIXED consequences for people of African ancestry. On the one hand, far more people of African ancestry found themselves enslaved in Louisiana as the reopened slave trade fueled the growth of a plantation economy, which, in turn, created rapidly deteriorating conditions for the enslaved. On the other hand, the Spanish government opened new avenues to freedom and often defended the rights of slaves against their owners. Spanish law institutionalized manumission as a feature of the slave system and secured the social and legal position of free people of African ancestry, granting them full rights to sue, form contracts, and own, sell, inherit, and transfer property.[118]

Greater legal opportunities to pursue freedom and greater judicial protection of free status once achieved were significant developments of the Spanish era. Liberalization of manumission law allowed owners to free their slaves without the judicial oversight that French law had demanded, and many did so for various reasons. Some certainly sought to rid themselves of elderly or invalid slaves, but affectionate relations moved others to free their children, consorts, godchildren, or the women who had raised them. But, although Spanish bureaucrats and some masters facilitated the process of manumission, far more important was the agency of the slaves themselves who desired freedom and, as quick students of Spanish law, readily exploited disagreements among officials and elites to act on those desires. Willing to call on Spanish judicial officials who demonstrated their readiness to defend aspirations for freedom, slaves pressured owners into freeing them unconditionally or through uncontested coartacións. Through the intersection of Spanish law and slave agency, people of African ancestry redeemed themselves from slavery. Not only did the population of free people of African ancestry increase dramatically during the last third of the eighteenth century, but so too did the number of those individuals who had African, European, and occasionally Indian ancestry, a consequence of the growing numbers of families formed by women of color and Euro-Louisianan men. It was this combination of freedom and mixed ancestry that became the essence of the gens de couleur libre by the end of the Spanish era.

CHAPTER FIVE

Limpieza de Sangre and Family Formation

IN DECEMBER 1779, Doña Céleste Eléonore Elizabeth Macarty married future governor Don Esteban Miró. Before she could do so, Spanish law required her to demonstrate her limpieza de sangre.[1] Like coartación, limpieza de sangre was another Spanish legal principle introduced into New Orleans after 1769, and at least twenty New Orleanians filed petitions during the last quarter of the eighteenth century to prove their purity of blood. Originating in mid-fifteenth-century Spain, limpieza de sangre was an exclusionary principle designed to prohibit undesirables from holding "honorable positions" and prevent marital "alliances that may dim [familial] honor." Initially defined by religious criteria, which named Jews, Muslims, heretics, and their descendants as those whose blood was unclean, in the Spanish-American colonies, the list of those who did not possess pure blood had expanded to include all those with Indian or African ancestry. In their petitions, New Orleanians declared that their families "were persons entirely and known to be white, of clean blood, and distinguished origin; . . . and known as Christians of the old faith."[2] Conflating honor and status with lineage, limpieza de sangre constructed a socioracial order that was based on a concept of whiteness that held that only those of pure European ancestry possessed honor, legitimacy, respectability, and rank.[3]

Céleste Macarty succeeded in demonstrating her nobility. Her paternal grandfather was a member of the Irish aristocracy who had left his native land for France in the early eighteenth century. He joined the French army and was eventually granted membership in the Royal and Military Order of St. Louis, granting him the right to call himself a chevalier. Two of his sons, members of the same order, emigrated to Louisiana in 1730, where they held important military offices. Marriage and godparentage linked the family not only to colonial governors but also to attorney generals, alcaldes, and wealthy landholders. The Macartys were, according to one testimonial, "originally as well as presently, persons of the most prominent and principal class among the families of this colony."[4]

The Macartys may have been among New Orleans' "principal class" but they were also well known for their relationships with women of color. In his will, Céleste's older brother, Jean Baptiste François, recognized and bequeathed property to his natural cuarterón son, despite having three legitimate children from his marriage to a blanca. Céleste's younger brother, Eugene, appeared in the St. Louis Cathedral to declare his paternity of the children of a mulâtresse libre. One of her cousins, future mayor of New Orleans Augustin François, had a series of relationships with women of color until, in 1799, he settled into a relationship with Céleste Perrault, yet another woman of color, that would last almost five decades.[5] Like Jean Baptiste François, many Euro-New Orleanian men had publicly known relationships with women of color either before or after their marriages to Euro-New Orleanian women. Like Eugene and Augustin François, many others forewent marriage altogether and established households and families with women of color. And, also like the Macarty men, many Euro-New Orleanian men, including prominent officials, wealthy merchants, and planters as well as men of lesser means, legally acknowledged their consorts and children of color and transmitted their property to them. For a woman of color, a stable, long-term relationship with a blanco could bring freedom and prosperity. And indeed, free women of African descent, had, by the mid-1790s, acquired about one-quarter of the city's propertied wealth, much of it (although not all) from blanco consorts and fathers.[6]

At the same time that Céleste participated in a discourse that denigrated racially mixed lineages as impure by filing a limpieza de sangre petition, her brothers and cousin contributed to the blurring of racial boundaries that was becoming more prevalent in New Orleans as the eighteenth century came to a close. Many changes had taken place in New Orleans during the half century that had passed between the 1725 marriage of nègre libre Jean Baptiste Raphael and Marie Gaspart (a description of which opened chapter 2) and Céleste Macarty's to Esteban Miró in 1779. The city itself had grown from a minor colonial outpost of less than one thousand inhabitants to an economically important entrepôt whose numbers would reach five thousand in 1785. Although blancos were a majority in the city proper (which, in eighteenth-century censuses was within the confines of the present-day French Quarter), they were outnumbered by slaves almost two to one within the plantation district of more than fifteen thousand inhabitants that stretched from English Turn downriver to Chapitoulas upriver and behind the city to Lake Pontchartrain. The liberalization of manumission policies ushered in by Spanish rule meant that increasing numbers of people of African ancestry had achieved their freedom, becoming almost 20 percent of the city's population by 1791.[7] Perhaps most important in regard to the limpieza de sangre cases, those described as sang-mêlé were also increasing. By 1791, 18 percent of the city's population was enumerated as sang-mêlé; two-thirds of them were free. The city's demography began changing in one other significant way during the last quarter of the eighteenth century, as more and more Anglo-Americans and non-French Europeans moved into the area, soon outnumbering those who traced their roots back to the French era.[8]

Seen within this context, it is possible to interpret limpieza de sangre as providing petitioners with a language of whiteness through which they could express their anxiety at this increasing racial and cultural diversity. Yet it is important not to read too much into these petitions that were, after all, a legal requirement for women who wanted to marry Spanish officers and men who sought appointments as priests or officers.[9] The formulaic nature of the petitions further suggests that bureaucratic necessity, rather than racial anxiety, motivated petitioners, especially when considered alongside the behavior of the men in families like the Macartys. Limpieza de sangre was a cultural discourse about race, one that used a language of blood to define categories of social difference and elite status, but it was one that many New Orleanians rejected in their everyday lives.

Held and Respected as White Persons

Initiated during the last quarter of the eighteenth century, each of the limpieza de sangre petitions filed by Euro-New Orleanians followed the same general pattern.[10] Submitting themselves to the "formalities" required of those who wished to "contract marriage" or hold prominent offices, they requested permission to establish their legitimacy and purity of blood with certified copies of their and their parents' baptisms and testimonials from several witnesses.[11] Doña Juana Catalina Dubois' petition, filed because of her impending marriage to Spanish lieutenant Manuel Perez, included the interrogatory, or written list of questions, that she and every other petitioner asked their witnesses. The first three questions asked her witnesses to confirm that she, her father, and her mother had all been born of legitimate marriages, properly "solemnized by the Church," and that they had been "nursed, educated, and fed" by their respective parents, who had publicly and routinely acknowledged them as their child. The witnesses were then asked to testify that she, "her parents, and grandparents and the rest of her ancestors in the paternal and maternal lines are Christians, pure of all bad races of Moors, Jews, Mulatos, and Indians," who had not recently converted nor been prosecuted by the Inquisition but rather had "always had a good reputation for habits and purity of blood."

The final question asked the witnesses to describe the petitioner's "general rumor and reputation."[12]

Lineage, and the legitimacy of that lineage, was thus the first issue to be established. Petitioners stressed that limpieza de sangre could only be guaranteed through legitimate, church- or state-sanctioned, racially endogamous marriages. In and of itself, legitimacy conferred "great honor and advantage." Only legitimate children could receive holy orders from the church and secular honors from the state, and they were the privileged inheritors of their parents' estates. Witnesses stated that they knew the petitioner to be "the legitimate child of the lawful marriage" of the petitioner's parents. But being born of a lawful marriage was not enough. They also swore that the petitioner had been "educated, fed, and recognized" as a legitimate child by his or her parents. Or as one petitioner asserted, his parents "called me their son and I called them my parents."[13] These assertions of being "fed" by one's parents could be implicit denials that one was breast-fed by a slave wet nurse, a practice that at least some Euro-Louisianans believed could taint an infant's blood and corrupt its upbringing, as seen in chapter 2. It is also possible that legitimacy had to be demonstrated through upbringing, both physical and mental (as in education and religious training), as well as through the public recognition of the parent-child relationship.

Once the petitioners' legitimacy was established, the witnesses moved on to their religious faith, racial purity, and honorable reputation, as Dubois' interrogatory indicates. Although religious criteria had lost some of their earlier centrality in defining limpieza de sangre, they remained important. Every witness in every case testified that the petitioner's ancestors were "old Christians . . . not recently converted," nor had they ever "been punished by the Holy Tribunal or the inquisition." Moors and Jews were still considered impure or unclean, as the petitioners' families were asserted to be "clean of all stain of . . . Jews and Moors."[14] The continuing references to Jews and Moors, very few of whom resided in Louisiana, illustrates how the concept of limpieza de sangre retained much of its metropolitan meaning even though that meaning could find no purchase in the colonial context.

An absence of heretical ancestors or those belonging to other faiths was not sufficient, however. Only those "entirely free of all bad races" and "clean of blood, without stain or mixture" could possess limpieza de sangre. In the language of the petitions, the blood of blacks, Indians, mulattos, or "any other bad mixture" could "infect" or "stain" one's lineage, causing it to be unclean or impure. But it was not good enough to be white; one had to be publicly acknowledged as possessing whiteness. One family, according to its witnesses, had been "known, respected, held, and considered . . . as white persons," while another was "entirely and known to be white, of clean blood and distinguished origin."[15]

Limpieza de sangre was more than just the absence of certain kinds of ancestors. It also embodied social qualities such as honor, occupation, faith, and respectability.[16] Using the language of blood, these characteristics were naturalized, deemed inheritable, and thus racialized. Petitioners had, in the words of the witnesses, held "distinguished employment[s]," including offices and appointments "only conceded to the Nobles" and to "those subjects of [the] most eminence." A witness testified that "the occupations of [the petitioner's] family have always been respectable; that he has not heard or known of any inferior position they have held." One petitioner asked her witnesses to confirm that "I have always conducted myself with the decorum my state demands, frequenting the sacraments, and engaging in Christian and devout acts." Conduct was also seen as indicative of the quality of one's blood. Another petitioner asked his witnesses to testify that his parents were "of honorable conduct" and that he did not frequent taverns or other "indecorous public places."[17]

Perhaps as important in the minds of petitioners as their actual legitimacy, faith, social position, occupation, and honor was their reputation as individuals who possessed these qualities and public acknowledgment that they possessed them. One petitioner's kin were praised for the "good reputation [they enjoyed] for their habits," while "the fathers and grandfathers of [another] petitioner, both paternal and maternal, are of noble birth and have always been held and are respected as such." Another "enjoyed a good name and has always been accepted publicly for their good qualities . . . and held in constant and well-known esteem." As proof of this public acceptance, this witness noted that the petitioner's home "has been visited by the most prominent people." For this petitioner himself, it was not enough that his wife's parents were "known, held and respected as persons of fine and distinguished origin"; he stressed that they were also "looked up to and treated with respect."[18] Through these public declarations, limpieza de sangre petitioners were able to have their reputations legally acknowledged.

After the petitioners collected their witnesses' testimonies, they submitted the entire document to the governor or other high-ranking official, who was required to approve the petition before forwarding the case to the king. In their endorsements, these officials declared themselves convinced of the petitioners' "legitimate birth, pure blood, . . . recommendable circumstances, and . . . good habits," declaring "it is evident that there exists in this [petitioner] the well-known qualities of birth and fortune." They requested their superiors' "favorable support" in presenting the case to the king.[19] Each petition was apparently well received and served its purpose. The male petitioners took up their positions as priests and military officers; the female ones went on to marry their intended spouses.

Preventing Unequal Marriages

One goal of limpieza de sangre was to prevent "unequal marriages." Although the Crown did not categorically prohibit racially exogamous marriages in Spanish New Orleans, it did pass regulations to discourage interclass and interracial marriages so as to further the consolidation of property among the elite and protect their position at the top of the socioracial hierarchy. According to the pragmática sanción issued in 1776, marriages that took place without parental consent could result in "the most serious offenses against God our Lord, family discord, scandals, and other of the gravest transgressions against morality and society." Acknowledging that marriage was a sacrament and yet asserting royal authority over its civil effects, the pragmática sanción required priests to obtain parental consent for those under the age of majority. Everyone, "from the highest classes of the State, without any exception, to the most common townsfolk," was required to get parental permission because they all owed an "indispensable and natural obligation of respect to their parents and elders, who hold their position by natural and divine right." Marriages involving those under the age of consent that took place without parental consent were deemed to have no civil effects, making children born from them illegitimate and ineligible to inherit and allowing the couple's parents to disinherit their children. Children could, however, appeal their parents' "irrational dissent."[20]

Two years later the Crown acknowledged that circumstances were quite different in its American colonies. Fearful that improper marriages would have even greater "prejudicial effects" there, it explained how the pragmática sanción was to be applied to the colonies. Two conditions in particular concerned the Crown: the "diversity of classes and castas" that was present in the colonies and the difficulty residents might have in obtaining parental consent. Addressing the issue of the castas first, the cédula of 1778 exempted "mulatos, negros, coyotes, and individuals of the castas and similar races" from the requirement of parental consent. The cédula assumed that castas were most likely illegitimate themselves, would not know who their fathers were (mothers, in this instance, were ignored), and would rarely seek sacramental marriage themselves. The only castas excepted from this exemption were those who "served [the king] as officers in the Militias or are otherwise distinguished by their reputation, good behavior, and services," who were understood as having "the natural obligation of honoring and venerating their parents and elders." "All other inhabitants of the Indies" were required to follow the pragmática sanción's provisions. Addressing the second concern, the Crown permitted colonial inhabitants whose parents lived in "very distant provinces," thus making it difficult to obtain their consent, to substitute the approval of a local district judge.[21]

The 1776 pragmática sanción, and the modified form of it that was enacted in the colony in 1778, must be placed within the context of power struggles between the church and state, and particularly the Bourbon monarchy's attempts to counter Pope Benedict XIV's encyclical of 1741, which permitted priests to perform marriages of conscience secretly without publishing any banns.[22] In that light, the bolstering of colonial hierarchies that resulted from granting parents the authority to prevent interracial marriages would have been an unintended side effect of the pragmática sanción, as its initial concern was for marriages that united individuals of different calidades, or qualities, a concept that included but was not reducible to race. However, when clarifying its stipulations for the colonial context, the Crown wrote most castas out of this status system altogether, denying them the obligation that even "the most common townsfolk" of Spain had toward their parents. Yet in requiring militia officers and other "reputable" castas to obtain parental consent, it granted that honor was something that individual castas could earn.[23] Nor did the regulation actually prohibit unequal marriages; rather, it allowed parents of minor children to object to such marriages if they so desired.[24] But, even then, prospective spouses whose parents objected to their union could appeal and had, therefore, at least a chance of marrying over their parents' opposition. The Spanish metropole was not unconcerned with cross-racial marriages, but it treated them as a subset of a larger group of problematic marriages that united spouses of different calidades, and thus they were not addressed in its 1789 slave code.

The locally authored 1778 code, on the other hand, as we have seen, prohibited a variety of relationships, marital and nonmarital, that crossed race or status lines. It banned concubinage between blancs and négresses or mulâtresses, enslaved or free, threatening enslaved women with confiscation and owners with a fine. Because of "the multitude of abuses that result," it banned marriages between enslaved and free nègres as well as those between slaves belonging to different owners. And, replicating the 1724 Code Noir almost word for word, it "absolutely prohibited all Blanc Subjects of one or the other sex, from contracting Marriage with Noirs or Mulâtres," leaving these latter categories unmarked by status.

The earlier French code had proscribed "an arbitrary fine" for racially exogamous marriages, but the planters' code decreed that such partners were "to be shamefully hunted from the colony," thus echoing the more emotionally laden sentiments of Anglo-American laws that were absent from the earlier French code.[25] It is clear that for the authors of the 1778 code, preventing cross-racial relationships and, more importantly, denying them the legality of marriage was paramount. In contrast, the Spanish metropole was more interested in imposing sexual morality, as can be seen in various provisions of its 1789 code, including its requirement that owners facilitate their slaves' marriages, that single slaves be housed in rooms segregated by sex, and perhaps also in its recommendation that slaves be assigned to sex-segregated tasks.[26]

When Bishop Luis Peñalver y Cárdenas informed the priests of Louisiana and West Florida about marriage regulations in 1795, he failed to mention racial exogamy, as the church, in contrast to the state, did not prohibit interracial marriage. Bishop Luis's instructions incorporated principles from both the Council of Trent and the pragmática sanción. He asserted canonical authority over the sacrament of marriage by insisting that all marriages take place in church following the publication of banns. But he also ordered priests to obtain parental consent (or, in their absence, that of a local judge) before they issued a marriage license. He granted couples the right to petition secular authorities to overrule parental opposition and conceded, albeit reluctantly, that parental objections would sometimes have to be overruled in order to prevent what he perceived as a greater problem than unequal marriages: concubinage.[27]

In May 1800, Bishop Luis was forced to consider a parental objection to a racially exogamous marriage. Late in 1798, mestizo Josef Faffar dit Makons and blanca Elisabet Olivos had, according to Josef, run off together because her parents objected to their desire to marry, while Elisabet's sister claimed Josef had abducted Elisabet. Whether they eloped or Elisabet was kidnapped, in March 1799, they appeared together before Ouachita post commander Juan Filhiol and convinced him to ratify their marriage contract, promising to marry in the church as soon as possible. When Elisabet's parents learned of the marriage, they complained to Bishop Luis that it had taken place against their will. Their daughter's groom, they claimed, was insufficiently churched, and Elisabet's sister Susana testified that she had never "seen him make the sign of the cross." This was not the first time the Olivoses had opposed the marriage of one of their children to someone they deemed ignorant of religion. Yet religion was not their only concern. According to Elisabet's parents and her sister, Josef's parentage and upbringing were also relevant to their opposition, as they noted his father was Huron, his mother Natchez, and "he went in and out of the woods like a savage."

Bishop Luis was not only concerned about Josef and Elisabet's marriage taking place against her parents' objection but also about Filhiol's assumption of the priestly authority to oversee the sacrament of marriage. Filhiol did have the authority to notarize marriage contracts (and in the 1790s, he oversaw about twenty), but he was not a priest, though other Ouachita residents defended Filhiol's actions because, they testified, there was no priest at their post. Filhiol, who had married both Elisabet and her brother over their parents' objections, defended his actions by claiming he had initially tried to convince Elisabet to leave Josef and return to her parents, even offering her sanctuary in his home while reconciliation took place. When she refused, however, he felt compelled to recognize their marriage in order to prevent the worse scandal that would result from their continued extralegal relationship. In April 1800, Josef and Elisabet finally followed up on their promise to Filhiol and appeared in church to receive the sacrament of marriage, a move that required receiving a dispensation for having previously married clandestinely. Sent by Bishop Luis to investigate, Father Juan Brady wished to separate the couple but, he wrote Bishop Luis, they were poor and already had a young son whose welfare would be endangered if they were forced apart. Josef and Elisabet begged Brady to intercede with the bishop on their behalf, and Josef himself traveled to New Orleans to testify. The final report, prepared by the ecclesiastical court's attorney general, stressed that, for subjects of a Catholic king, marriages had to be contracted before a priest and recommended informing Filhiol about his obligations under the Council of Trent and the 1776 pragmática sanción to obtain parental consent. That said, the report recommended, and Bishop Luis granted, the dispensation that Josef and Elisabet sought.[28] Once again, the church's commitment to eradicating concubinage and upholding individual will worked against the state's interest in supporting an endogamous marital regime, allowing some cross-class and cross-racial marriages to take place.

Blancos Married to Mulatas

As with French priests, who in the first decades of the eighteenth century had promoted marriages between Indian women and French men, Bishop Luis and his subordinates saw it as their duty to eradicate concubinage.[29] A considerable number of New Orleanians, regardless of their socioracial status, failed to marry before the church, living in extralegal relationships that ranged from permanent to temporary, from the socially sanctioned to the barely tolerated.[30] According to a report compiled by Bishop Luis in 1795, many New Orleanians "live[d] in public sin" and neglected to avail themselves of sacramental marriage. He relayed the comments of one priest, who asserted "there are parents who, when their sons reach the age of puberty, give them a negra or mulata," thus "inducing their sons to shame." Despite instructing his subordinates to "discreetly and prudently" discourage their parishioners from "living a scandalous life in concubinage," he was still complaining four years later that "the military officers and a good many inhabitants live almost publicly with colored concubines."[31]

Various circumstances combined to discourage New Orleanians from participating in the sacrament of marriage. Many were thwarted by the high cost. In 1795, Bishop Luis set marriage fees at 48 reales for blancos and libres and 40 reales for slaves; intended spouses also had to pay 2 reales for each of the three banns that had to be published.[32] But even those who could afford these fees often delayed their weddings while actually entering into what to all appearances looked like a marital relationship, establishing households and beginning to have children, sometimes long before appearing in church to receive formal recognition of their relationship.[33]

Spanish bureaucrats and military officers faced additional hurdles. They were discouraged from marrying into the local population and were required to obtain the Crown's consent if they wished to do so. By preventing bureaucrats from marrying local women, as well as moving them from colony to colony, the Crown could instill loyalty to the metropole among its officer core, control bureaucrats' relations with creoles, and maintain absolutist monarchical control.[34] A few Spanish officers decided to forgo seeking official permission to marry and established extramarital households, most often with women of color. This practice was also encouraged by the metropole's decision to move its bureaucrats frequently from colony to colony. Nicolas María Vidal left behind two natural daughters, both free women of African descent, when he was sent from Cartagena to New Orleans as auditor de guerra and lieutenant governor in 1791. He then established a household with mulata libre Eufronsina Hisnard, herself the acknowledged daughter of a blanco, with whom he had two daughters. Although he was not present at their baptisms, he did acknowledge Hisnard's children as well as his older daughters in his 1798 will. Never legally married and with no legitimate descendants, he left his entire estate to be divided among his four natural daughters.[35]

Officials who decided to seek permission to marry found themselves subject to delays of a year and longer. When Lieutenant Pedro Piernas failed to include certain vital documents in his petition to marry Felicitas Portneuf, the metropolitan authorities could have required him to resubmit his request, adding several more months to the process, but, taking pity on the groom-to-be, his request was granted "in order to avoid delay due to the distance."[36] At least in this instance, metropolitan officials acknowledged that requiring royal permission for military officers and other government officials could unduly delay legal marriage.

One prominent official who did not let bureaucratic regulations prevent him from beginning a family was the future governor Manuel Gayoso de Lemos. He and Margaret Cyrilla Watts declared their intention to marry in January 1796 but did not receive permission to do so until March 1797. Despite the birth of their first child in July of that year, the couple waited until December to marry, baptizing their five-month-old son at the same time.[37] Clearly, they had not waited for royal permission to begin their family. Similarly, Captain Pierre-Joseph Favrot and Marie-Françoise Gérard contracted marriage in December 1783, but they had to wait a year before receiving royal consent. Three days before their nuptials, their five-month-old daughter was baptized.[38] While New Orleans' religious might have decried such situations as "public sin," these extralegal relationships had no long-lasting social or economic consequences for the couples involved nor for their children, who were legitimated retroactively by their parents' marriages.

It was indeed the practice of retroactive legitimation, more so than bureaucratic regulations, that made legal marriage less urgent for much of the population.[39] Under Spanish inheritance law, children who were born of unmarried parents were automatically legitimated upon their parents' subsequent marriage. Spanish law clearly distinguished among four different statuses: legitimate, natural, legitimated, and illegitimate. If a child's parents were in a validly contracted marriage at the time of her birth, she was born legitimate. A natural child was one whose parents could marry but had not. As with Gayoso's son and Favrot's daughter, the status of natural children was changed to legitimate as soon as their parents married, even though they had been born outside of marriage; they could also be legitimated by a royal decree.[40] Illegitimate children were those born of relationships prohibited by canon law and were the only ones who could not be retroactively legitimated. The three principal impediments to marriage were the preexisting marital state of one of the partners (making the relationship adultery), consanguinity within the fourth degree between the sexual partners (making it incest), and religious vows of celibacy taken by at least one of the partners. Children of such unions were deemed "spurious" and were excluded from any possibility of inheritance. Unlike English common law, then, which decreed children born outside of marriage forever illegitimate and denied them any right to inheritance, Spanish law allowed for both the transformation of children's status from extramarital to legitimate and, even without that transformation, granted them a right to inherit from their parents.

O'Reilly's 1769 Ordinances and Instructions incorporated these principles into Louisiana law. Legitimate children were given preferential treatment; they were deemed "forced heirs" to whom their parents were required to leave the bulk of their property (thus giving power to the pragmática sanción's punishment of disinheritance). But even parents with legitimate children were free to bequeath up to one-fifth of their estates to whomever they pleased, including their natural children, whom O'Reilly defined as "those born of a free girl, to whose marriage with the father of the said children no legal impediment existed." But natural children were not excluded from inheriting their parents' entire estates if the latter had no legitimate descendants. Assuming that maternity was surer than paternity, O'Reilly's ordinance decreed that a natural child could inherit his or her mother's entire estate even if she died without making a will. Fathers without legitimate descendants could bequeath their entire estates to their natural children, to the exclusion of any surviving ascendants or collateral relatives, but only if they wrote a will. Only "the children of ecclesiastics, or monks" were prohibited from "in any manner inherit[ing] from their parents or kindred."[41] Unlike the Code Noir, then, which declared freed and freeborn nègres "incapable of receiving from Blancs any donations," the concern of Spanish inheritance policies was the legitimacy, not the race, of heirs. And as with Spanish judicial support for slaves' right to self-purchase, Spanish legal practices and Spanish officials' willingness to uphold these policies worked in tandem with the actions of New Orleanians of African and of European ancestry to bolster the legal, economic, and social position of New Orleans' libres.

The pragmatic reasons for getting married—to legitimate children and facilitate the transmission of property—as well as the high cost of doing so combined to encourage wealthy elites to marry while discouraging other New Orleanians from doing the same.[42] Couples who did enter a sacramental marriage tended to be of similar calidades, yet there is evidence of a handful of exogamous marriages. The earliest in the Spanish era was probably the one that Governor Ulloa allowed to take place within his home in 1768 between a blanc and négresse slave. Indeed, this marriage was one of the complaints that Francophone elites directed against Ulloa during their revolt, noting that Ulloa had allowed his chaplain to confer "the Sacrament of Marriage" to this couple "without the permission of the Curé, without any publication of banns, without the forms or solemnities required by the Church." This marriage took place, they continued, "to the great scandal of the Public, to the contempt of the Council of Trent, and against the precise intention of our Prescriptions, civil as well as canonical."[43]

The following year, blanco Jean Paillet and Catherine Villeray, the natural daughter of mulata libre Charlotte and Sieur Joseph Roy Villeray, declared their intent to marry by filing a marriage contract with the Superior Council, a contract on which Villeray's signature was far surer than that of her husband-to-be, suggesting that despite being a woman and one of color at that, Villeray had received more education than Paillet.[44] Their marital state was confirmed at the baptisms of their children, all of which were registered in the libro de blancos. When the census takers made their rounds in 1778 and 1791, they also failed to mark any family member as other than blanco. Paillet's marriage did not hurt his status; indeed it improved over time until, in 1787, both he and Villeray were granted the honorific titles "don" and "doña."[45] Just one other such marriage appears in the sacramental records. On May 1, 1779, negro libre Bautista Rafael Fancon, a New Orleans native and the legitimate son of negros Rafael and María Magdalena Fancon, married María Andrea Gotié, the widow of Vilime Aleman.[46]

Yet the absence of other entries in the sacramental records does not mean that these were the only racially exogamous marriages to take place in Spanish New Orleans. Evidence outside of the registries indicates that marriages between Euro-Louisianans and people of color occurred more frequently than the registries suggest, although to be sure they were not common. Parda libre María Theresa Cheval had her breach of promise suit taken seriously in 1779, even though she was accusing blanco Phelipe Lafarga of reneging on his promise to marry her.[47] In 1793, Father Firso de Peleagonzalo assumed that blanco Juan Antonio Lugar and parda libre María Juana Prudhome were married, "as there were," he claimed, "in New Orleans other blancos married to mulatas."[48] But the most revealing evidence lies in the minutes of a meeting that took place among the Ursuline nuns in 1797. Debating "whether they were willing to admit to the day school for instruction and within the convent as half boarders the Mulaticas who were applying for this arrangement," the sisters decided unanimously against it, but at the same time they also decided to continue accepting "the legitimate daughters whose fathers were Blancos and mothers cuarterónas as they have been received until now."[49] The nuns would not have conferred legitimate status on children unless they knew their parents had married according to the church.

María Clara Toupart could have been one of those cuarteróna daughters. When her mother, Charlotte Lafrance, married Juan Bautista Toupart in 1785, the marriage was recorded in the white book, as was María Clara's 1793 baptism; but when Charlotte's sister Catherine married grifo libre Bartholomé in 1788, the marriage was recorded in the nonwhite register where she was noted as a cuarteróna. Their father, Jean Lafrance, in fact opposed Catherine's marriage because of the "inequality of the marriage partners," she being a cuarteróna and her spouse-to-be being a grifo.[50] No doubt there are other marriages like Charlotte's that painstaking research could uncover. Charlotte, unlike her sister, seems to have passed as white in the sacramental records, but there is also another explanation for the legitimate daughters that the Ursulines were willing to admit to their school. Charlotte's children were, in the detailed Spanish casta system, octavóns, or octoroons. Yet that label never appears in eighteenth-century New Orleans records. Sometimes the children of cuarterónas and blancos were labeled cuarteróns as well, but at other times they went unraced.[51] That is, for some priests and notaries in late eighteenth-century New Orleans, the offspring of blancos and cuarterónas were in fact white, especially, as in the case of both Charlotte's and cuarteróna Catherine Villeray's, if they were legitimate.

He Says He Is the Father

Even accounting for an additional number of marriages uniting blancos with women of color that were not marked as such in the sacramental records, it is clear that far more racially exogamous relationships did not receive religious sanction, and thus their offspring were marked by illegitimacy in addition to racial mixture. Sacramental registers and notarial records from the Spanish period reveal many more relationships between Euro-Louisianan men and women of African ancestry than do those from the French period. Although it is possible that these relationships were more frequent in the earlier period and that evidence of them has been lost in the destroyed sacramental registers, it is more likely that they did indeed increase in frequency during the Spanish period, despite the evening out of sex ratios within both the Euro- and Afro-New Orleanian populations.

By the second half of the eighteenth century, people of African and of European ancestry probably knew each other far better than their parents or grandparents had. Because both African and European immigration into the colony had virtually ceased after the early 1730s, by midcentury, Louisiana-born Africans and Europeans were coming into their own. Whereas language, culture, and religion had separated the previous generation, those becoming adults in the 1750s and 1760s grew up with each other, speaking French and sharing Catholic religious practices. Cultural endogamy had probably deterred family formation, although not more casual and exploitative sexual relationships, between Africans and Europeans earlier in the century, but by midcentury the city's second and third generation creoles of African and European ancestry shared enough language, religion, culture, and customs that their relationships had become culturally endogamous even as they remained racially exogamous.

Such a shared creole culture, and the familiarity it engendered, would not last long, however. Beginning in the 1770s, it was again under siege by the large-scale importation of slaves directly from Africa and the arrival of Anglo-Americans and other European migrants unfamiliar with the city's cultural milieu. Yet these new waves of migrants probably also enhanced the sense of shared community among New Orleans' French-speaking Catholics of both European and African ancestry. Thus, while many Euro-New Orleanians sought to form families with those who shared European ancestry, despite cultural, linguistic, and religious differences, others seem to prefer cultural familiarity to shared European ancestry.

Many of these relationships were publicly acknowledged, usually at the birth of a child or the impending death of one of the partners, and, as the century came to a close, more and more blancos were acknowledging them by appearing at the baptisms of their sang-mêlé offspring or leaving property to their consorts and children.[52] Baptism records and wills—the two sets of documents that most frequently reveal such relationships—had different standards of proof for asserting familial relationships. For a father to be acknowledged by a priest in the baptismal registry, he had to be present or otherwise explicitly claim his paternity; the priest would not accept the word of the mother or, for that matter, anyone else. Notaries, on the other hand, were willing to accept the word of testators as to their familial relationships. When a mulata mother, like Marion Dubreuil, declared that she had five natural children with blanco Raimond Gaillard, Pierre Pedesclaux accepted her assertion of Gaillard's paternity of her children.[53] Given the intimate size of New Orleans at this time, such paternities may well have been public knowledge, even if they had not been recorded at baptism. For instance, though Gaillard had not acknowledged his own children at their baptisms, by 1797 he was appearing at those of his grandchildren.[54] It is also possible that notaries were able to discourage women from naming blancos as fathers when the notaries knew the men had not publicly acknowledged the women's children.[55]

But many Euro-Louisianan men were publicly acknowledging their nonwhite children, much to the chagrin of Bishop Luis, who complained in 1795 that they did "not blush at carrying the illegitimate issue they have . . . to be recorded in the parochial registries as their natural children."[56] By the 1780s and 1790s, more and more blanco fathers were doing so. During the last two decades of the French era, increasing numbers of sang-mêlé children appeared in the baptismal registries: mulatos born of negra mothers or cuarteróns born of mulatas by, in most cases, "an unknown father."[57] The priest occasionally recorded "unknown white father," but most often whiteness went unremarked, even when children were marked as possessing a lighter phenotype than their mothers. Beginning in the mid-1780s, however, these children were acknowledged more frequently by their blanco fathers. Nicolas Rousseau's signature indicates his presence at the 1782 baptism of his mulato son Pedro. A decade later, Pedro Cázelar declared, at his daughter's baptism, that "he is her father."[58] When mulata libre Margarita Meunier's son Francisco de

Paula Tribuño was baptized in 1783, the priest originally wrote "father unknown." But Josef Tribuño must have then stepped forward and claimed his paternity, as he signed the register and allowed his son to carry his name. "Padre incógnito" was crossed out, and the priest highlighted Tribuño's connection to his son with the phrase "the natural Father."[59]

Entries in the baptismal registries often hint at stories that can be difficult to reconstruct. Crammed at the bottom of a page of one baptismal registry for negros and mulatos is an entry for Helena Hazeur, cuarteróna libre daughter of Don Louis Hazeur Delorme and mulata libre Felicite. Hazeur signed and the priest affirmed that he was her natural father. Although both Helena and her mother were noted as free, they in fact belonged to Louis' sister, Doña María Hazeur, viuda Dreux. Three months after the baptism, María gave Helena to Louis "for the much love and fondness that I profess for my brother," and Louis immediately manumitted her. Two weeks later, María allowed Louis to purchase Felicite's freedom for 600 pesos. Louis and Felicite went on to have at least three more children, all of whom he acknowledged at their baptisms.[60] It is likely that it was after their manumissions that Helena's baptism was recorded in an attempt to make it seem as though she and her mother were freeborn rather than former slaves.

Some blancos failed to recognize the first of their children born to women of color, but, as the relationship continued, they acknowledged subsequent children. When mulata libre María Juana Prudhome's cuarterón son Ramon Juan Antonio was baptized in 1791, his father was noted as unknown. Two years later, however, Juan Antonio Lugar proudly claimed Prudhome's daughter Rita Josefa as his own at a ceremony that was witnessed by "a large crowd of white and free black persons," followed by a private party at their home attended by military officers and government officials. It was at this baptism that Father Firso de Peleagonzalo mistakenly assumed that Lugar and Prudhome were married. Lugar was almost certainly Ramon Juan Antonio's father as well. He allowed Rita Josefa and a subsequent daughter to carry his surname. Despite Prudhome's marriage to mulato libre Joseph Cabaret a few months before Lugar's death, the relationship must have ended amicably because Lugar gave Prudhome 325 pesos as a marriage gift and named his two natural daughters as his heirs.[61]

Lugar was far from the only blanco to pass on his patrimony to his nonwhite family. Franco-New Orleanian Pierre Dauphin divided his estate between his consort, negra libre Marta, and their eleven mulato children, ranging in ages from twenty-five years old to fourteen months. Dauphin acknowledged the children as his own and, in an unusual step, named Marta his testamentary executor.[62] Don Barthelemy Toutant Beauregard, ancestor of the Civil War general Pierre Gustave

Toutant Beauregard, had a twenty-year relationship and four children with negra libre Margarita Toutant. In his will he named Margarita his universal heir and bequeathed her his entire estate, including two houses, slaves, furniture, and cash. The estate, which passed on to her on his death in 1792, was then to pass on to their four mulato children at her death. Although Toutant Beauregard declared himself single, one of his children, Luisa Toutant, may have been one of the sang-mêlé daughters that the Ursulines recognized as legitimate and admitted into their school.[63]

The 1778 pragmática sanción did indeed make racially exogamous marriages rare, but when wealthy blancos like Toutant Beauregard bequeathed property to their extramarital nonwhite families, they undermined its efforts to create a social order in which race, status, and class were conflated and in which racialized identities were clearly defined and circumscribed. Yet their challenges to this order only went so far. In the first place, many were slaveowners and slaves were among the most significant property they bequeathed to their families. In addition, although some blancos demonstrated concern for their own children, they could be far from compassionate toward their stepchildren.

Widower Don François Dusuau de La Croix Demazilière, the one who manumitted Fanchon in 1773 only to sell her back into slavery the following year, purchased María Bienvenu, a thirty-six-year-old negra, in 1779. A year and a half later, Bienvenu bore him a son, Pedro Baltazar, whom Demazilière manumitted, along with his mother, when he was four months old. The following year, they had a second son, Pedro Augusto. When Demazilière wrote his final will in 1787, he bequeathed to Bienvenu a life interest in a large habitation at English Turn, a house in New Orleans, livestock, and slaves. Among those slaves were her three older children. But Bienvenu could not manumit or otherwise alienate them, as they, along with the rest of this property, were to pass on to Pedro Baltazar and Pedro Augusto after her death. The two brothers kept their half siblings enslaved, freeing one in 1794 and another in 1801, only after another half sibling initiated their coartacións. The third was finally freed, graciosa, in 1803, long after Bienvenu herself had died.[64]

Other blancos were more generous to their consort's children by other men. Lugar not only named his own cuarteróna daughters as his heirs but also bequeathed 500 pesos and part of a house to his consort's eldest daughter.[65] Spaniard Don Marcos Olivares left his daughter with negra libre Maríana Voisín, his house, three slaves, and 2,000 pesos while leaving land and slaves to Voisín's other children.[66] Although often difficult to reconstruct, these racially exogamous households must have been complex ones, where half siblings and stepsiblings, both free and enslaved, lived with their mothers and their blanco consorts. Mulata libre Marion Dubreuil and blanco Raymundo Gaillard's household in 1778 included their five sang-mêlé children as well as Dubreuil's three older children by negro libre Bautista.[67] In a more unusual instance, blanco André Jung's household included his blanca wife and three sang-mêlé children, each born of a different woman before his marriage. A successful merchant, Jung acknowledged his three natural children in his will, noting they had "been fed, educated, and maintained in his home as his own family" since their births and leaving them 5,000 pesos.[68]

Blancos like Jung and Demazilière, who were widowed and had no living children from their marriages, or like Dauphin and Toutant Beauregard, who had never been legally married, had no competing legitimate heirs and were thus free to disperse their estates as they saw fit. Others, however, had serial relationships, with a nonwhite family coming before or after their marriage with a blanca. These men, such as merchant Don Beltran Gravier, were more likely to donate small amounts of property to their consorts and children. Gravier donated a small plot of land (inherited from his deceased wife) to two young cuarteróna libres, his probable daughters, who had been born before his marriage to a blanca.[69]

Even when testators had legitimate forced heirs—those who had to inherit—they could still leave some property to their natural children. Franco-New Orleanian and infantry officer Don Pierre Devergé had three legitimate daughters, all born in the early 1770s, with his wife, Doña Catalina Poupart. In 1779, he purchased mulata Maríana, freeing her four years later, before the birth of any of her children. Although Devergé did not acknowledge Maríana's cuarteróna children as his own, his will requested that his legitimate daughters give "all aid and assistance possible" to them, tending to their "food, clothing, [and] education."[70] Blanco testators often willed blanco relatives to distribute their nonwhite children's inheritances or otherwise tend to their needs. Antonio Jaillot Demouy left one-fifth of his estate to the mulato children of negra libre María Josefa, naming his brother Francisco Monplaisir Beaulieu as executor and universal heir. When the estate was settled in 1778, Beaulieu obliged himself to invest the children's property and to turn over the proceeds on their request.[71]

Although blancos who had relationships with women of color during their marriages to blancas were far less likely to acknowledge extramarital sang-mêlé children, since they were the product of adultery, a handful in fact did so. Don Luis Forneret, an interpreter of Indian languages for the Spanish government, acknowledged several sang-mêlé children who had been born when he was still legally married. His first child with his negra slave María was born in 1772, five years before he legally separated from his Franco-Louisianan wife, with whom he had no children. Forneret kept María enslaved, along with the eight children she bore, until 1786. In March of that year, he appeared at his son Joseph's baptism and claimed paternity, the first time he had done so. Four months later, he freed them all for 2,500 pesos paid, according to the notarial act, by María herself. Requiring such a substantial payment would suggest that Forneret was not the father of María's other seven children, yet, in his 1791 will, he named them along with their mother as his heirs.[72]

Don Joseph Dusuau de La Croix was unusual both because of the number of women with whom he had children who he would acknowledge and because at least two of his sang-mêlé children were born during his marriage to a blanca. Born in France, Dusuau was a lieutenant in the Louisiana infantry. In 1762 and 1763, he had two daughters with his Franco-Louisianan wife, but he then had a daughter with mulata libre Rosa in 1764 and a son with the enslaved mulata Jacqueline Lemelle in early 1767 before having two more sons with his wife. After his wife's death, Dusuau then had four children with mulata libre María Dusuau. Not only did he recognize all six sang-mêlé children in his will, but he also left them bequests ranging from 600 pesos to 1,200 pesos plus an eleven-year-old negrito slave. Further, he appointed Jacqueline's son as tutor for his half siblings, María Dusuau's four minor children, and gave him 400 pesos for their care.[73]

Dusuau's marital indiscretions and his recognition of his sang-mêlé children do not appear to have harmed him or his legitimate family's reputation. His two legitimate daughters entered the Ursuline convent, becoming choir nuns in 1780; his two legitimate sons married well; and his property at the time he wrote his will included a habitation on the other side of the river, more than fifty slaves, and several houses in New Orleans. Nor was Dusuau socially ostracized. During his relationship with María Dusuau, he served as godfather to one of his grandchildren and a stepgranddaughter from his deceased wife's first marriage.[74] Although it is impossible to determine what daily relations were like within this extended multiracial family, the fact that Dusuau named his eldest legitimate son as his testamentary executor suggests that he had faith Barthelemy would uphold his father's wishes regarding the bequests to his half siblings.

A few blanco relatives, however, were less willing to facilitate the transmission of property to nonwhite heirs, especially when they would benefit by having such inheritances denied. One such case involved negra libre Angélica, who had received her freedom and a house from Juan Perret sometime before June 1770. When Perret died in 1774, he left Angélica all his furniture, movables, clothes, and linen while dividing the rest of his estate between his eleven grandchildren. Although two of the grandchildren and the curator ad lites for several others formally consented to Angélica's inheritance, Carlos Jouet, the husband of one of Perret's granddaughters, contested it. He argued that article 52 of the Code Noir prohibited freed slaves from receiving donations or inheritances from blancos, but the court ruled in favor of Angélica, thus giving further evidence that by that point Spanish legal practices had supplanted French ones. Yet Jouet's attempt to disinherit Angélica should not necessarily be seen as a specific attack on libres inheriting from blancos, as he also protested several other aspects of Perret's succession in an ultimately successful attempt to win his wife a greater share of the estate. In order to deny Angélica her inheritance, Jouet reached for the only argument he could.[75]

When Doña Marie Corbin Baschemin, veuve de Darby, contested her son's will, she too tried to read the law to her own advantage. Her son Don Pedro Darby acknowledged his seven mulato children in his 1803 will and named them as his universal heirs. Never married, Darby had lived with negra libre Naneta for more than three decades; their oldest child, François, was thirty-three, the youngest just ten. At the time of his death, his estate included two habitations in Attakapas, livestock, and a single slave. He bequeathed the slave and half his livestock to Naneta and the remainder of his estate to their children, naming François as his siblings' guardian. In June 1804, Baschemin filed suit, claiming that as Darby's mother, she was his "only and unique forced heir" since Darby had "died without having any lawful progeny." In filing her suit just after the recent rapid transitions of sovereignty from Spain to France to the United States, Baschemin attempted to take advantage of the confusion over which nation's laws governed marriage and inheritance and just what those laws were. Baschemin mistakenly contended that Louisiana law had always and absolutely prohibited racially exogamous marriages and, as such, that "mulattos who are born of whites and blacks" could never be considered as natural children, whose parents could, but had not, married. Finally, she requested that Darby's children be required "to prove their title of freedom" before they were allowed to appear before the court. Baschemin won her case in the lower court, which voided Darby's will, but François successfully appealed the judgment as "contrary to the laws of the land."[76]

As with Jouet's opposition to Angelica's inheritance, it is possible to read Baschemin's actions as not solely motivated by antagonism toward her son's sang-mêlé children. Baschemin was a particularly litigious individual, who sued another son's blanca wife over control of his property.[77] Such challenges to a testator's efforts to transmit his patrimony to extralegal, nonwhite families were, in any event, rare during the Spanish period, a situation that changed noticeably in the aftermath of the Louisiana Purchase. Before then, most blancos who bequeathed parts or all of their estates to their natural children did so successfully and were assisted rather than hindered by their blanco relatives.

Godparenting practices also demonstrate that some blanco relatives were supportive of racially exogamous families. Don Joseph Foucher's white kin named him as a godparent, and included him as a marriage witness, even after he acknowledged a child with mulata libre Francisca Bernoudy.[78] Men particularly seem to have condoned their brothers' choices, as Louis François Xavier Hazeur (who had his own nonwhite family) and Juan Macarty did when they agreed to be their nieces' godfathers. But blancas were not averse to taking on this important spiritual responsibility either. Marie Céleste Livaudais, nee Marigny, served alongside her brother Bernard Xavier de Marigny de Mandeville as godparents to one of the sons of their mulata libre half sister. María Hazeur Dreux was godmother to at least one of her brother's children with mulata libre Marguerite Duval. Perhaps most unusual was Louise Marguerite de La Chaise, whose godson was one of the children of her deceased husband's cuarteróna daughter.[79] The baptismal registries, as well as notarial records that reveal economic interconnections among New Orleanians of all calidades, balance the portrayal of racially exogamous families that emerges from court records, which are, after all, skewed toward conflict and overemphasize those blancos who, in challenging wills and property donations, condemned their relatives' familial choices.[80]

However, since almost all racially exogamous relationships were extramarital, women of color involved in them lacked legal claims to the community property that was formed on marriage under both French and Spanish law. They could rely only on the generosity of their children's fathers to bequeath them anything. Brothers Don Pedro and Jayme Badia, for instance, had donated slaves and land to their probable children while alive, but neither left a will and so their nonwhite families stood to inherit nothing of their estates.[81] Despite these challenges, some free women of color were able to achieve the security and wealth that a legal marriage would have brought. These individuals surveyed their options as women of African descent living in a patriarchal slave society and, as much as possible, sought to make decisions that would improve their lives and those of their children.

For enslaved women far more was at stake than mere wealth: the chance of freedom for themselves and their children was the very least they hoped for from their relationships with blancos.[82] Some women were forced to wait years. Forty-year-old negra Catalina received her freedom in 1788, at least twenty-five years into her relationship with Joseph Duval Demouy. Catalina had had her first child in about 1764; at the time of their manumission her youngest was just ten months old.

Freed alongside Catalina were her nine children and her two grandchildren; thus, three generations had to wait before Demouy chose to grant them their freedom.[83] What life was like in this household in which a blanco kept his consort enslaved for most of her life before rewarding her and her children with freedom is difficult to imagine.

Other women had to wait until their consorts' deaths for their freedom. Negra María Juana was first promised freedom in 1775 by widower Joseph Meunier in his will. In an updated will written two years later, he now promised freedom to María Juana, her young mulata daughter Margarita, and three other apparently unrelated negro slaves. Meunier's paternity of Margarita is suggested because, whereas he had named his brother as his universal heir in his earlier will, the second will bequeathed his estate to Margarita and her mother.[84] Other men seem to have neglected to free their consorts and children until death was pending. Perhaps it was only then that they realized failure to do so would condemn their descendants to perpetual enslavement. Henrique Mentzinger manumitted negra Gabriella and her two mulato children the day before he wrote his will, which, although it failed to acknowledge his children, left each one a slave and named Gabriela as his heir, small comfort, as there was little else to this sergeant's estate.[85] When Juan Garro, the father of negra Rosa's son Juan José, wrote his will, he acknowledged the five-year-old mulatico as his natural son, deeded him his freedom, and named him as his universal heir. The following day, he returned to the notary to add a clause granting Rosa her freedom as well, perhaps after Rosa expressed her disappointment in having been neglected. Mother and son were formally freed two months later by Garro's executor.[86]

A few women saw their children freed but gained their own freedom with more difficulty. Negra Maríana convinced her consort, Don Marcos Olivares, to free their daughter when she was four but was forced to purchase her own freedom three years later.[87] Don Luis Lanonier used his will to acknowledge his three mulato children, confirm their freedom, and name them as his heirs. At the same time, he ordered his testamentary executor to free their mother, twenty-two-year-old negra Catarina, "graciosamente" at his death, which occurred three days later.[88] Bautista Trenier similarly freed his two acknowledged mulato sons during his life but left their mother, his negra slave Francisca, enslaved until his death. In a 1792 will, he promised freedom to Francisca and her daughter, who was probably not his, while leaving his smallish estate to his two sons. Unfortunately for them, Trenier was still alive seven years later, and they were still his slaves.[89] But Catarina and Francisca at least eventually realized their hope for freedom; countless others could congratulate themselves only on seeing their children freed. Negra Maríana must have found little comfort even in that, however, when negro libre Luis Maxent, the father of her three-and-a-half-year-old son, sold her away to Havana after freeing their son.[90] Like Maxent, who clearly acted callously in separating Maríana from their son, some fathers clearly valued their children's freedom far more than that of their consorts. But fathers who used third-party coartaciós to free their children may not have been able to afford the additional cost to free an adult woman.

Enslaved women were clearly more constrained in their options when trying to use a sexual relationship with blancos to better their lives and those of their families. Tenacity, however, did sometimes pay off. Mulata Jacqueline Lemelle gained not only freedom for herself and her children (by three different fathers) but saw her children inherit property from their fathers. Jacqueline's principal relationship was with ship captain and merchant Jacques Lemelle, which began by September 1759 and lasted until Jacques' death twenty-five years later. Jacques bought Jacqueline in 1762, when she was thirty-two years old, two years after their first daughter was born. Two more daughters were born in 1769 and 1771. Although he declared each child free at her baptism and requested permission to manumit Jacqueline in 1765, it was not until the year after the youngest's birth that Jacques formally manumitted Jacqueline and their children, crediting "their good services, loyalty, and in remuneration of other matters." Less than one month after her own manumission, Jacqueline purchased the freedom of another daughter, twenty-two-year-old María Juana, as well as that of her granddaughter from Jacques' brother François for 200 pesos.[91]

María Juana had been born several years before Jacqueline's relationship with Jacques began, but Jacqueline almost jeopardized her freedom by bearing the child of another blanco during this relationship. In late 1765, Jacques left for a trip to Europe that kept him away for just over a year; he left Jacqueline in charge "of his effects and slaves." During that time, Jacqueline became pregnant by the notorious Don Joseph Dusuau de La Croix. On Jacques' return, he tried to revoke Jacqueline's manumission, claiming "she had lacked respect and obedience." Within six months, however, Jacques had dropped his efforts to reenslave Jacqueline and agreed to manumit her infant son for an exorbitant 800 pesos. Perhaps Jacqueline had been concerned that Jacques would fail to return from Europe and so had decided that she needed to cultivate a new patron, one who indeed looked out for his son over the years.[92] Jacques too would take care of his extralegal family. On his death in 1784, he left the bulk of his estate to Jacqueline and her daughters, although he still failed to acknowledge them as his own. It was, however, common knowledge that they were, and various merchants filed claims against his estate for merchandise that had been delivered to "his daughter, Agatte." After paying his creditors, a substantial bequest to his brother François, and smaller ones to other relatives, Jacqueline and her daughters were left with several houses and a large lot on Royal Street, household furniture and effects, two negra slaves, and almost 1,500 pesos in cash.[93]

Women of color whose consorts failed to provide for them sometimes pursued other strategies. Mulata libre Janeta Ducoder sued Juan Bautista Darby for 200 pesos, claiming it was payment for her five years of services "as wife and servant in sickness and health" and support for their two children; they eventually reached a private agreement, and Ducoder dropped her suit.[94] Negra libre Fanchon and her probable consort Pierre Bonne similarly came to an out-of-court settlement after Fanchon sued Bonne for nearly 2,000 pesos in 1783. Fanchon claimed she had lived with Bonne for sixteen years as his housekeeper but that he had never paid her. If the arrangement had been strictly an economic one, it is unlikely that Fanchon would have continued working for Bonne without being paid for so many years, nor would she have occasionally used his surname as her own. After the court ordered Bonne to testify, the parties notified the court that they had reached a compromise and wished to have the order rescinded.[95]

Mulata libre Magdalena Canella sued her former companion for a gift he tried to recover once their relationship was over. Canella contended that she had lived with Louis de Beaurepos for eight years, during which Beaurepos had given her a plantation on the river opposite New Orleans and a negra slave named Adelaide in compensation, she argued "for the concubinage that he had with her and for the advantages of their two children." Two years after their relationship ended, Beaurepos reclaimed Adelaide, and Canella sued for her return. She called several witnesses, including free women of color and two blancos, who confirmed their relationship and that Beaurepos had given her the plantation and the slave. After being arrested for refusing to return Adelaide to Canella, Beaurepos countersued, asserting that he was the slave's true owner. When questioned by Canella's attorney, Beaurepos claimed to have forgotten all about their relationship and daughters, declaring that "when he has committed any sin and confessed it, he did not think about it any more." He dismissed her witnesses as "mulâtresses, libertines like herself," ignoring the testimonies of the two blancos, and accused her of currently "living in a state of concubinage" with Luis Lioteau, a colleague of the court's escribano. The alcalde ruled in favor of Beaurepos, and Canella appealed to Havana, but unfortunately the extant records do not reveal the final outcome.[96]

Undoubtedly, many relationships did not result in stable, long-term commitments, and evidence of more transitory and often violent relationships occasionally appears in the documents. Some enslaved women found themselves abused by their owners' wives, who suspected them of having sex with their husbands. Margarita petitioned for a new owner, citing the constant whippings she experienced at the hands of her mistress.[97] María Juana, whose failed coartación case was examined in chapter 4, claimed that, following the end of her relationship with her owner, she experienced "extreme cruelty" from both the owner and his new wife.[98] Similarly, María Luisa Saly complained that her ex-consort Mateo Parin dit Canon "treat[ed] her with extreme cruelty" after their relationship ended and had reneged on an earlier promise of freedom.[99] Other court records include numerous references to interracial socializing and living arrangements among New Orleanians of more moderate circumstances.[100] Violence frequently imbued these relationships. Carpenter Pedro La Cabanne dit Titon assaulted mulata Magdalena after she refused "to concede him favors as she had been accustomed to do before." Forcing his way into her house and finding her "in bed with one called Chabote," Titon wounded both Magdalena and Chabote with a knife.[101]

Although the alcalde in Magdalena's case deemed her assault "a crime worthy of punishment," other officials would have been more likely to accuse her of prostitution. Colonel and sometimes acting lieutenant governor Francisco Bouligny, in a 1776 memorial to the king, decried the "number of Mulatas Libres who [are] given over to vice, live in public concubinage, in grave detriment and scandal to Religion." He recommended exiling them if they did "not mend their ways and adopt an honorable and upright way of living."[102] Ten years later, Governor Miró tried another approach. Declaring he would not tolerate "the idleness of mulatas and cuarterónas libres" who had "licentious lives" and "carnal pleasures," he proclaimed that he would "punish with all severity of the law all those who live in concubinage."[103] At least one parda libre defended herself against the suggestion that women of color were naturally libertines when she declared that "I have not earned my freedom on my back."[104] Indeed, María Cofignie's blanco father had given her 400 pesos with which she purchased it.[105]

Some Euro-Louisianans indeed poured scorn on the sang-mêlé and the relationships that had produced them, and it was not just religious officials who were concerned about the prevalence of concubinage. Franco-creole planter Pierre-Joseph Favrot listed "the mixture of blood, which each day continues to multiply," among the "abuses that should be reformed and eliminated, as they are most prejudicial to the citizens of this capital."[106] The Marqués de Casa-Calvo, acting military governor during the waning years of Spanish New Orleans, condemned "the blancos, the habitants, [and] the nobles who forget their principles and engage in commerce with [women] of color, even with their own slaves." The recipient of Casa-Calvo's diatribe was none other than Nicolas María Vidal who, of course, himself engaged in such commerce.[107]

At the same time that Vidal was acknowledging his four natural daughters by three different women of color and making them his heirs, he was also, as lieutenant governor, endorsing limpieza de sangre petitions.[108] And, as we have seen, members of the Macarty family likewise engaged in articulating ideas of racial purity through limpieza de sangre petitions at the same time that they contributed to the blurring of racial boundaries by not just having sex with women of color but establishing stable, long-term relationships with them, acknowledging their children, and passing on their patrimonies. It is hard to know what Céleste Macarty thought of her brothers' behavior; unlike some other blanco relatives, she never served as godmother to any of her nonwhite nieces or nephews. Perhaps, despite its formulaic nature, she did internalize the language of limpieza de sangre and denigrate her brothers' children as illegitimate, dishonorable, and unrespectable and see them as a threat to her own lineage's purity. It was her husband, after all, who disparaged mulatas and cuarterónas libres in his 1786 bando.

The simultaneous and contradictory actions of Vidal and of Céleste Macarty and her brothers caution against reading the limpieza de sangre petitions as accurate reflections of Euro-New Orleanians' racial ideology. It is true that limpieza de sangre introduced a concept of whiteness that theoretically excluded anyone of traceable African or Indian ancestry regardless of whether petitioners fully accepted its principles or whether they were just fulfilling bureaucratic requirements and following prescribed guidelines. Yet, by the last quarter of the eighteenth century, many New Orleanians had tangled ancestries and, as the following chapter demonstrates, some sought to take advantage of the city's complex racial order to define their own identities.

CHAPTER SIX

Negotiating Racial Identities in the 1790s

IN SEPTEMBER 1799, Doña Clara Lopez de la Peña, a twenty-old-year-old native and vecina of New Orleans, appeared before Bishop Luis Peñalver y Cárdenas to request that he correct a clerical error concerning her daughter Luisa's baptism. Then almost five years old, Luisa was, according to her mother, subject to "notorious prejudice" because her baptism had been recorded in the sacramental registry "corresponding only to Negros." At her baptism in 1795, Luisa and Clara were both noted as mestizas libres, which Lopez de la Peña did not deny; what she did deny was that having Indian ancestry made them not white. Five witnesses testified on Lopez de la Peña's behalf, tracing her maternal lineage back to her grandmother, who, they swore, was "a mestiza," "the daughter of a hombre blanco and an India without any mixture of negro and mulato."[1] Lopez de la Peña thus requested that her daughter's record should be erased from the negro registry and entered into the book of blancos.

By the end of the eighteenth century, New Orleanians utilized a casta system that was both more restrictive than what had come before and yet allowed for more flexibility in the categorization of certain individuals. One's calidad in New Orleans was not determined solely by racial ancestry but also by social status, including whether one was free or enslaved. In addition, rather than the presence of African ancestry, it was the percentage of European blood that suggested one's racial identity. This racial order involved a more complex hierarchy than those present in contemporary Anglo-America, but there was one important similarity: in New Orleans' casta system and in Anglo-America's dualistic racial order, Indians qua Indians had come to be excluded from the colonial system and were seen as existing outside of it.

Indians had been erased from the city's racial order through a process that Ruth Wallis Herndon and Ella Wilcox Sekatau have called "documentary genocide."[2] Louisiana's native peoples had been a part of colonial society from the very beginning of the century: as slaves, consorts, and wives. Some officials had reservations about the enslavement of native peoples, not because they didn't think they weren't suited to be slaves (they did) but rather because they were concerned about the possible pragmatic political and economic ramifications of enslaving them. Indians were, in any event, quickly outnumbered by an ample supply of African slaves. At the beginning of the century, officials had also debated whether or not Indian women could be incorporated into colonial society as the wives of French colonists. As we have seen, metropolitan and local officials, on the one hand, ultimately decided to prevent "marriages of this sort . . . as much as possible"; secular officials, on the other, tolerated French-Indian extramarital relationships, demonstrating that they were at least willing to consider the incorporation of native peoples into colonial society. This was in stark contrast to the almost immediate metropolitan prohibition on marriages between noirs and blancs and on extramarital relationships between free (whether blancs or noirs) and slave laid down in the 1724 Code Noir, which engendered no local debate or opposition.[3]

The different prescriptions regarding Euro-Louisianan marriages to Indians and to Afro-Louisianans illustrate that, as colonial authorities attempted to order the colony along racial lines, they had different ideas about the roles that Indians and Afro-Louisianans should play. They encountered Indians as the indigenous inhabitants of the land they hoped to colonize; they had to negotiate with them, and they depended on them for defense, food, and trade. They realized, therefore, that intimate relationships might be necessary to create alliances between colonists and native peoples. Afro-Louisianans, on the other hand, had only their labor to offer, and the colonists took that by force. No alliances had to be built, no negotiations made. In a plantation economy, assimilating enslaved Afro-Louisianans into French creole society through intimacy served no useful purpose, even as the frontier nature of that plantation economy allowed for greater social fluidity and closeness.[4]

By the end of the century, however, Afro-Louisianans had increasingly come to be seen as an essential part of the colonial social order, while Indians had come to be seen as existing outside of it. Yet the reality was different, and Indians continued to play active roles in and around the city. One late colonial observer of New Orleans commented on the "various bands of natives" who gathered "in the city and its vicinities" each winter for diplomacy and trade with the Spanish government. Another noted that "some hundreds . . . lived with their wives and children on the outskirts of New Orleans."[5] And Benjamin Latrobe and others noted the presence of Choctaws, Creeks, and Chickasaws as well as other, unidentified, Indians, particularly in the city's marketplace.[6] Indians and people of Indian ancestry had thus not disappeared from New Orleans by the beginning of the nineteenth century, but their increasing marginality to the colony's economy and security led them to be classified in such a way that made them difficult to see.

There is still much to learn about "neighboring Indians," as James Merrell has called them: "Those smaller Indian groups situated in the midst of colonial settlements and towns." But in order to begin uncovering that history we must first recognize how colonial administrators, in their legal and political discourses, inconsistently addressed the presence of Indians in colonial societies—sometimes identifying them as separate peoples, other times lumping them with "other slaves" or generic "people of color"—and were often indecisive about the place of Indians and their descendants within the colonial social order. Such ambiguity served largely to obscure the presence of actual Indian and mestizo peoples, although this was not necessarily a bad thing. Precisely because Indian and mestizo rarely appeared as official racial categories, people of Indian ancestry were able to camouflage themselves from official gaze, making themselves, as Merrell argues, inconspicuous, which in turned enabled them to survive within their ancestral homelands.[7]

The causes for the apparent disappearance of Indians and their descendants in colonial New Orleans were many, but perhaps the most important were shifting population ratios, a transformed economic base, and changing political regimes. Prior to permanent French colonization in the lower Mississippi River Valley, there were an estimated 59,000 Indians in the region (a great majority of them Choctaws and Chickasaws), but by 1775, these numbers were had decreased to just under 18,000, and the non-Indian colonial population had surpassed it at 20,500. At the same time that the Indian population was in the process of recovering from its 1745 nadir of 16,800, the colonial population was growing at a greater rate, and Indians would never again be a majority in the lower Mississippi River Valley. Simultaneously, Euro-Louisianans' frontier exchange economy, in which Indians were vital participants, was being supplanted by a plantation economy. In this new economy, planters turned away from Indian laborers and relied almost exclusively on African slaves.[8]

This erasure of Indians from the socioracial order made it possible for some people who claimed Indian ancestry to renegotiate their status. Clara Lopez de la Peña identified herself as a mestiza in order to have her daughter classified as white, but the 1790s also saw several slaves bring freedom suits in which they asserted their right to be free because of their Indian ancestry. Taken together, these two sets of petitions offer rare insight into how people of color themselves articulated their identities and also illustrate the different ways that Indians and Africans had been racialized by the end of the eighteenth century. Since Indians were perceived as existing outside the colonial order, those of Indian descent living within it must be something else; yet as the example of Lopez de la Peña reveals, that something else was not necessarily a person of color.

Gente de color

By the time New Orleans came under Spanish rule in the late 1760s, the Spanish had developed an elaborate casta system during two and a half centuries of colonization in the Americas that had brought together Europeans, Africans, and Indians. At first, culture, language, and religion had been the most important indicators of social status, but, by the late sixteenth century, colonial populations had become increasingly diverse and were made up of significant numbers of people of mixed ancestries. At the same time, it had become more difficult to distinguish among colonial population groups by culture, language, or religion, as those of African and Indian ancestries had become, to a great extent, Hispanicized, at least in urban areas where most Spaniards and those of African ancestry resided. Thus race, alongside economic factors, "emerged as the primary criterion of social differentiation," according to historian John Chance. Already by the mid-sixteenth century, racial labels, such as "mestizo" and "mulato" and the catchall term, "casta," had become common in law, where they were used to define privileges and obligations, as well as in everyday practice, where they were evoked to describe individuals in sacramental records, notarial acts, and trial transcripts.[9]

The complexity of Spanish-American racial taxonomies received its most concrete illustration in the genre of casta paintings produced in the eighteenth century, principally in Mexico.[10] Born of Enlightenment efforts to organize and categorize, each series of paintings depicted twelve to sixteen couples of different racial types and their offspring, either on separate canvases or on one large canvas subdivided into separate frames containing each family grouping. Through dress, behavior, occupation, phenotype, and settings, the casta painters sought to illustrate social status and its links to racial categorization. No similar taxonomies, whether visual or written, appeared in New Orleans until the mid-nineteenth century. In addition, the casta paintings represent a far greater variety of racial types than were used in daily practice, at least in the written record, in much of Spanish America and certainly in Spanish New Orleans, where the most commonly used labels were "negro," "moreno," "mulato," "pardo," and "cuarterón," with less frequent appearances of "mestizo" and "grifo."[11]

In New Orleans, as throughout Spanish America, racial categories were used in

1ᵃ **Español, e Yndio, Mestizo.**

4ₙ **Español, y Negro, Mulato.**

Two of O'Crouley's fourteen panels representing Mexican castas. *Español, e yndio, mestizo,* and *español, y negro, mulato,* 1774, in Pedro Alonso O'Crouley, *Idea compendiosa del Reyno de Nueva España.* Biblioteca Nacional, Madrid, Spain.

both laws and social practice. New Orleans officials, however, rarely made systematic distinctions among the gente de color in defining legal privileges and obligations, the one exception being the putative ban on enslaving those of Indian ancestry, which gave them a greater right to freedom than other people of non-European ancestry. Spanish censuses, for instance, enumerated blancos, negros and mulatos libres, and negro and mulato slaves. In day-to-day life—whether at baptisms or marriages, appearing before a notary to engage in a financial transaction, or testifying before a judge—most individuals of African or Indian ancestry were described by their perceived racial type, while those of apparently exclusive European ancestry went unmarked, except in the baptism registries of the late eighteenth century where the phrase "de color blanco" was common.

For the Spanish, noting the whiteness of infants was redundant. Unlike French priests, who had recorded all baptisms in a single registry, Spanish priests kept two parallel sets of books beginning in 1777: one for blancos and the second for all others (variously titled *Libro de negros esclavos y mulatos, Libro de negros y mulatos libres,* or *Libro de gente de color*). This practice was well entrenched, in New Orleans at least, long before Bishop Luis instructed priests throughout the diocese of Louisiana in 1795 to keep separate books for blancos, on the one hand, and indios, pardos, and morenos, on the other.[12] The link between these record-keeping practices and the efforts of the Crown's pragmática sanción to prevent unequal marriages was made clear by a Puerto Rican vicar in 1787, when he complained that castas were having the "defect" of their birth hidden when their baptisms were recorded in the "libros de españoles." As a result, he continued, those who were "truly white" sometimes unwittingly married those "who had the mixture of mulatos." This was "a matter of so much importance" that the Crown ultimately ordered parish priests to record baptisms in the libros de españoles only when they knew the "real quality of the parents of the recently born," to take great care of the sacramental registers so that they could not be stolen or have "notes written surreptitiously in them," and to deliberate with great caution and not easily accept the word of unfamiliar witnesses who sought to "correct" previously recorded baptism entries.[13]

Alterations in New Orleans' sacramental records, especially in the nonwhite books, were not uncommon. In most cases, it is impossible to determine who initiated these changes, although a very few, like Luisa Declouet's, have marginal notations that point to judicial decrees forcing the priests to correct their sacramental records.[14] Fathers initially unidentified were later named, and natural children were rewritten as legitimate ones, with important implications for their inheritance rights. More common, however, were racial alterations. When María de la Paz's daughter was baptized in 1793, for instance, both she and her daughter were initially marked as cuarterónas; later, the entry was changed to "mestiza of India and blanco."[15] Mulatos frequently became cuarteróns or mestizos; negros even occasionally became mulatos. Some had their racial labels completely scored through, making them unreadable today.[16] A number of these changes appear to have been genuine errors on the part of the priests; others seem to have occurred when a priest realized he had "miscalculated" an infant's racial identity. Far more so than their French predecessors, Spanish priests had clear ideas about what types of parents produced what types of offspring, ideas that matched the representations in the casta paintings. Blancos and negros produced mulatos; blancos and mulatas produced quarterons, but so occasionally did two mulato parents. The children of cuarterónas and blancos were most often identified also as cuarterónas but occasionally went unraced, although their baptisms were still recorded in the book of negros and mulatos.[17] "Octoroon," the racial label that would become so identified with New Orleans in the late nineteenth century, was not used in the colonial sacramental records.

Fathers were often not identified, but their children did not necessarily receive the same racial designation as their mothers, suggesting that priests used either knowledge about the fathers that they decided not to record or visual cues to decide what to label a child. Whether slave or free, the children of negra mothers were frequently marked as mulatos; less frequently, the children of mulatas with unknown fathers were classified as quarterons.[18] Some combinations of parents, however, challenged the priests' simplistic calculations. They generally agreed upon the term "grifo" for the children of negros and mulatos, although it was also used, though rarely, to designate the children of negros and indias.[19] The children of mulatos and cuarterónas were sometimes marked as mulatos and sometimes as cuarteróns, except one child who was labeled "tierceron," the only appearance of that label found in the colonial baptismal records.[20] Priests rarely used "pardo" and "moreno," two labels that sometimes substituted for "mulato" and "negro," respectively, and suggested reliance on skin color rather than parental ancestry; one priest did note that a baptized infant was "of the color pardo."[21]

The ways in which priests, who thought in terms of limpieza de sangre and descent, used labeling practices suggested that individuals had a true racial identity that was determined by the identities of one's parents, but entries in which some individuals received different racial labels within the same record suggest otherwise. Francisco Fazende, son of the unraced Don Julio Fazende and mulata libre Genoveva Simon, was described as a "mulato or cuarterón." Anastasia Glod, born of a cuarteróna and an unknown father, was noted as a "mestiza or cuarteróna."[22]

Although the priests rarely indicated they were unsure of an individual's racial identity, other record keepers were either less sure or less concerned. The notarial records, for example, are littered with examples of racial variability. Clara Lopez de la Peña, for instance, was referred to as "mulata," "cuarteróna," "mestiza," and occasionally, even before her 1799 petition to the bishop, she was marked as unraced. Her mother, Luison Brouner, was usually labeled "mulata libre," sometimes "parda libre," and less frequently "mestiza libre." In most cases, it is likely that the priest, census taker, or notary attributed these identities to her, but in her own will, written in 1794, five years before her daughter's efforts at racial reclassification, Brouner identified herself as the daughter of María Juana, india.[23] Although the writing was the notary's, it is possible that Luison identified herself as the daughter of an india. The frequency of such instances of racial variability reminds us that we cannot assume attributed identities are accurate statements of an individual's ancestry and that we need to understand the contexts within which these identities were ascribed.[24]

Among the least used racial labels, whether in laws, sacramental and notarial records, or censuses, were those that suggested Indian ancestry. As census categories, "Indian," "métis," and "mestizo" do not appear in French censuses after 1732, and they are also missing from all but one of the Spanish censuses, which otherwise carefully divided the colonial population by gender, age, free or slave status, and race (blanco, mulato or sang-mêlé, and negro). The 1771 census is the only Spanish-era census to enumerate Indians in either the city or the colony as a whole. The first census taken by the United States after the Louisiana Purchase made explicit what all the other censuses implied: "Indians not taxed." Neither subjects nor citizens, they were not seen as permanent residents within colonial communities. And if they were residents, they had to be something other than Indian.[25]

In some baptism entries, from both the French and Spanish periods, children who had Indian ancestry were often given a racial label that suggested African rather than Indian ancestry. In 1733, Marie, daughter of a sauvagesse, was labeled a mulâtresse. Charlotte, whose parents were a nègre and a sauvagesse, both slaves, was called both a mulâtresse and a négresse at her 1748 baptism. María Francisca Foucher, baptized in 1781, was initially labeled "mulata libre"; this was later changed to "mestiza libre," and her mother's own racial label—"mulata libre"—was crossed out.[26] In one particularly confusing entry, Antonia, baptized in 1782, was classified as a mulata in the text of the entry but referred to in the margins as an india. Her mother was a mestiza; her father's identity was unknown. Later, however, Antonia's Indian ancestry was recognized and the labels "mulata" and "india" were crossed out and replaced with "mestiza."[27] This process of documentary genocide was made obvious in those records where the mother's Indian ancestry was recognized. Many people of Indian ancestry were silently reclassified, especially after 1769, when Governor O'Reilly declared that Indian slavery was illegal, providing slaveowners with a tremendous incentive to deny any Indianness in their slaves.[28]

Mestizos Who Want to Pass for Free

As slaves, Indians had been a part of colonial life since at least 1704, when there were about a dozen Indian slaves living among a few hundred Frenchmen at Fort Louis de Louisiane. Within four years, the number of Indian slaves in the colony had increased to around eighty, most of them women.[29] By the early 1720s, however, African slaves had become increasingly available to Euro-Louisianan planters, and colonial administrators' desire for stable relations with Indian trading partners and potential allies, as well as planters' fears about the ease with which Indian slaves ran away, deterred additional enslavement of Indians. Over time, both the absolute numbers of Indian slaves in Louisiana and the percent of the work force they made up declined. In 1721, 161 Indians were 17 percent of all the colony's slaves, but by 1771, only 120 Indians were identified as slaves, or less than 3 percent of all slaves.[30] But, although Indians and their descendants may have been a declining part of the enslaved labor force, they were a persistent one. According to the first U.S. governor of the territory, in 1808 there were "several hundred persons held as slaves, who are descended from Indian families."[31]

It is impossible to determine with any greater precision how many Indians and people of Indian descent were held as slaves during the Spanish era because owners stopped identifying any of their slaves as Indians following Governor O'Reilly's 1769 ordinance against Indian slavery, an ordinance that was necessitated by French practices that contravened Spanish law. Informing "all inhabitants and residents of this province . . . that the wise and just laws of His Majesty very expressly forbid any subject of any quality or condition whatsoever to make an Indian a slave or to possess any such, under any pretext whatever," O'Reilly sought to bring the now-Spanish colony in line with the rest of Spain's American colonies, in which Indian slavery had been outlawed since the New Laws of 1542. In theory, then, Louisianans of Indian ancestry had a right to freedom that was far more secure than that possessed by free persons of African ancestry, who could find themselves reenslaved if convicted of a variety of crimes.[32] In reality, however, O'Reilly's decree modified Spanish law to accommodate French practice by prohibiting only the future enslavement of Indians and permitting "present owners" to retain the slaves they already had, although they could not sell or otherwise transfer ownership of them, until the Crown made its wishes on the matter known.[33]

Interactions between Indians and Afro-Louisianans took place not only within colonial society but also in Indian villages, as this sketch illustrates. Alexandre de Batz, *Desseins de sauvages de plusiers nations,* New Orleans, 1735. Peabody Museum of Archaeology and Ethnology, Photo 41-72-10/20, Cambridge, Mass. © 2007 Harvard University.

Several slaves of Indian ancestry were freed in the two decades following 1769, but very few of these manumissions mentioned O'Reilly's decree. In 1770, Pierre Clermont conditionally manumitted his twenty-five-year-old slave Luison, a member of "the Sioux tribe" according to his owner, with the proviso that Luison serve him for another three years.[34] Pedro Francisco Santilly and Marie Touneur promised freedom to six slaves in 1773, five of whom were described as mestizas, but they gave no indication of what motivated them to do so.[35] Natchitoches resident François Moran de Bernard was one of the few to claim he was motivated by O'Reilly's decree when he freed twenty-five-year-old Marie Anne and her son, "Cennecin" Indians (Apaches) whom he had recently purchased from Caddo traders.[36] Before 1790, at least two slaves of Indian ancestry freed themselves through coartación, but they did not mention their right to freedom under O'Reilly's decree. In her suit, mestiza Juaneta included her baptism certificate, which showed her to be the daughter of "a savage" and unknown father, but went on to base her claim on her right "to free herself at her just price."[37]

It was not until 1790, twenty-one years after O'Reilly's decree was published, that any slave sought to gain freedom under the principle that Indians were not supposed to be held in slavery.[38] The reasons for this long silence are unclear, but it is possible to deduce what gave rise to the first suits. In the spring of 1786, seven Indian slaves ran away from their owners at the St. Louis post. Governor Miró took this opportunity to explain Spanish policy on Indian slavery to post commandant Francisco de Cruzat, noting O'Reilly's ban on owners purchasing, selling, or leasing Indian slaves. He also ordered Cruzat to republish O'Reilly's decree, which the post commandant dutifully, but apparently reluctantly, did.[39] Cruzat did not, however, make any efforts to emancipate his own mestizo slaves, siblings Pedro Morau and María Page. Sometime before his death in July 1789, Cruzat moved to New Orleans, taking his slaves with him. When Cruzat's heirs sought to sell the two along with the estate's other slaves, Pedro and María sued, claiming that as indios mestizos they could not be sold and were entitled to their freedom. Both received their cartas de libertad a few days later. Their half brother, indio sambo Baptiste, had successfully sued his owner, Manuel Bourgignon, a few months earlier. Baptiste must have learned about O'Reilly's ban from his siblings who, in turn, had learned it from their owner, Cruzat, as early as 1786. Because his owner was a flat boatman based in Ste. Genevieve, Baptiste had the opportunity to travel widely with his owner. He must have taken advantage of a trip to New Orleans to file suit in January 1790. The siblings' success in gaining their freedom was made possible by Governor Miró's acceptance that their mother, Catherine, was an india.[40]

Although O'Reilly's decree allowed owners to keep slaves of Indian ancestry, they were explicitly banned from transferring ownership of them. Pedro, María, and Baptiste's owners had all contravened this ban. Cruzat purchased Pedro in the early 1780s, and his heirs sought to sell both Pedro and María, leading to their suits. Bourgignon purchased Baptiste in 1788. A year after Baptiste was granted his freedom, Bourgignon sued the heirs of the man who had sold Baptiste to him, successfully arguing that the seller had misrepresented the slave as a mulato (and indeed, the original act of sale did describe him as a such) and recovering 400 pesos of the original purchase price.[41]

Despite the successes of Pedro, María, and Baptiste, the next freedom suits were not filed for another several months. On January 13, 1791, Marianne and Juan Baptiste Morel both filed petitions, and another four slaves did the same over the next few months. All six won their freedom.[42] From this it would appear that, as with coartación, slaves quickly learned that claiming Indian ancestry was another avenue to legal freedom and one that, initially at least, received the support of Spanish officials. Yet no extant suits have been found for the period between August 1791 and July 1793, and by late 1793, the tide began to turn against slave petitioners for a variety of reasons. By this time, Governor Miró had been replaced by the baron de Carondelet, who freed at least three slaves who filed suit between July and September 1793. However, at the behest of resisting planters, he then began to rethink the ease with which some slaves were gaining freedom.[43]

At the heart of the planters' resistance, as well as of the slaves' own petitions, was the meaning attributed to the slaves' ancestries and thus their racial identities. Those owners whose slaves had won their freedom before late 1793 generally did not contest their slaves' representations of themselves as indios mestizos or indios grifos. In her suit against Don Josef Verloin De Gruy, María Theresa produced an act of sale from 1781 that briefly traced her history. First owned by Andres Solisus, as a two-year-old she was sold to Guillermo Uran, who raised her in his household. When she was sixteen, Uran then sold her to De Gruy, describing her as a "salvage," for 350 pesos. Presented with such clear evidence of her identity and accepting that Indians were free by birth, De Gruy renounced his ownership of María Theresa, and then, like Baptiste's owner, sued for reimbursement of her purchase price.[44] Other slaves produced baptismal certificates to prove their ancestry. Cecilia's certificate showed that her mother was a sauvagesse slave of Jean Decuir. She elaborated on her genealogy, declaring that her parents were "an India named María of the Patoucas Nation and a Negro." In case this certificate was not sufficient evidence, she offered the testimonies of four negras libres who could bear witness to her mother's identity.[45] At best, in these early cases, owners denied knowledge of O'Reilly's ban or asserted, like Bourgignon, that they thought the slaves in question were mulatos, but they did not contest the slaves' own claims to Indian ancestry.

By late 1793, this brief trend of uncontested freedom suits started to slow down. First, the numbers of slaves claiming Indian ancestry began to increase, as did the numbers of owners potentially affected. For instance, the recently freed Cecilia filed a petition in October 1793 on behalf of her sister María Juana, several of María Juana's children, as well as some grandchildren belonging to four different owners in Pointe Coupée, Opelousas, and Attakapas.[46] Second, some owners being sued began to resist their slaves' attempts to gain uncompensated manumission. Finally, Carondelet faced accusations that he was overly sympathetic to slaves—this as the Haitian Revolution was underway—and sought to demonstrate to owners that he had their interests at heart.[47] In early 1794, Carondelet suspended all pending suits and ordered the slaves back to their owners to wait for word from the Crown.[48]

The case that first engendered planter opposition was probably the one another María Juana filed in September 1793 against her owner, Manuel Monsanto, and the owner of her two children, Julien Poydras. Describing herself as "the daughter of an india and a negro," María Juana asserted her right "to be free for coming from Indians, according to the state of the laws." Monsanto did not contest María Juana's petition, although like other owners he claimed he thought she was a mulata. Poydras, on the other hand, insisted that she was a mulata and thus that neither she nor her children were descendants of Indians or had a right to claim freedom.[49] In a February 1794 letter to Carondelet, Poydras and twenty-two other habitants asserted that these petitions were "unjust lawsuits, fomented by malignant seducers . . . under the specious pretext of supposing themselves to be descendants of free Indians." If Carondelet allowed the lawsuits to go forward, they continued, their property rights would be undermined by slaves demanding uncompensated manumission, and "irreparable wrong" would be done "to all in this colony." Although the petitioners' numbers were still small, the owners worried that a "contagion" could spread throughout the slave population.

Yet not all owners denied the Indian ancestry of their slaves. Rather, they argued that the ancestors of their slaves either had been legitimately enslaved as Natchez, who were "reduced to slavery for having revolted and committed cruel atrocities in the Time of French Domination," or as war captives, who had been rescued by French slave traders from a "cruel death that other Indians, their Enemies, had prepared for them." The latter, the owners asserted, should thank the slave traders for saving their lives rather than insubordinately requesting their freedom. Finally, they argued that as third-party owners "who acquired [the slaves] with just title and in good faith," they should not be penalized for the original owners' violations of O'Reilly's decree.[50] Even as they implicitly acknowledged the validity of O'Reilly's ban against Indian slavery, then, they defended their right to continue holding mestizos as slaves by blaming the Natchez for waging war against the French, Indians for enslaving Indians and selling them to the French, and previous owners for misleading them about the identity of the slaves they bought.

Importantly, slaves and owners also disagreed about how ancestry should be interpreted. Most petitioners emphasized their maternal ancestry, identifying the mother by name, and occasionally by nation, but leaving the father anonymous, either describing him simply as "a negro" or not mentioning him at all.[51] Ex-slave Cecilia went one step further in downplaying her paternal ancestry. In her freedom petition, she described herself as the "daughter of an india . . . and a negro," but in two subsequent petitions to free relatives, she had reinvented herself as an "india libre," thus erasing her paternal African ancestry.[52] Mestizo slaves of the late eighteenth century were almost twice as likely to have had an Indian mother than an Indian father, but that is not sufficient to explain why the petitioners all claimed Indian mothers.[53] Perhaps, following the principle that slave status was passed through the maternal line, they thought that they could inherit freedom because of Indian ancestry only through their mothers. For their part, owners emphasized the petitioners' paternal, African ancestry, contending that their slaves were "nearly all Mestizos from Negros, [who] want to pass for free Indians."[54]

Who was right? Were petitioners mestizos or not? Clearly, both petitioners and owners had a vested interest in the answer. Owners were quick to defend their property rights and emphasizing paternal African ancestry was just one way to do so. For their part, petitioners realized that, while all slaves had a right to freedom through coartación, claiming descent from an Indian woman was the only way to gain uncompensated freedom from an unwilling owner. It certainly is possible that some slaves falsely claimed Indian mothers and grandmothers. One case suggests this might have happened. When María Juana filed her petition in 1793 claiming freedom for herself and her two children, she described her son, Antonio Sarazin, as a mestizo. However, nearly twenty years earlier, when Antonio had unsuccessfully sued for his own freedom, he had described himself as a mulato and had made no claims to Indian ancestry.[55] Despite this discrepancy, however, we cannot dismiss all such renegotiations of racial identity as merely strategic ploys; census data and the sacramental records demonstrate that Indian and mestiza women were enslaved and that they were indeed having children with slaves of African ancestry.[56]

A year and half after Carondelet ordered the suspension of all suits "until his Majesty issues a resolution on the status of Mestizo and Indian slaves," he still had no word from the Crown, and so he began issuing his own guidelines for dealing with these cases.[57] First, he ruled that all mestizos who requested freedom would have to remain slaves for two years because their manumission "would ruin a number of families, who do not have any Slaves other than Indians or Mestizos or Descendants of both." He then distinguished among those whose ancestors were Natchez, those purchased from other Indians, and all others. Since Natchez Indians had been lawfully reduced to slavery "in punishment" of their "perfidy," their descendants were to remain slaves, although like other slaves, they were eligible for coartación. Mestizos whose ancestors had been "redeem[ed]" from a "violent death" could purchase their freedom for 250 pesos. All others, who he noted were "very few," who could prove their maternal Indian ancestry "are declared free at the end of one year from the date of publication [of this decree]," giving owners "sufficient time" to "replace them with Negros without detriment to their projects."[58] Unfortunately for the slave petitioners and any others who might identify themselves as mestizos, the issue was never resolved, and there was no blanket emancipation of mestizos in the following years. When the Council of the Indies received Carondelet's letter and the inhabitants' petition in late 1795, it searched its archives for O'Reilly's 1769 decree. Unable to find it (which perhaps explains why the Crown had never responded), the council neglected to return to the question of mestizo slaves during the remaining few years of Spanish control of Louisiana.[59]

The issue reemerged, however, in the early nineteenth century, as slaves once again took advantage of a transition in sovereignty and all the legal confusion that it engendered. Three cases reached the supreme courts of Louisiana and Missouri in which slaves reasserted claims that Indian ancestry granted them a right to freedom. In December 1807, "a person of color" named Seville filed a complaint on behalf of himself and his siblings against Gerard Chrétien in Ascension Parish court. According to various witnesses, Seville's grandmother Angelique was a sauvagesse who was sold by a French trader to Joseph Chrétien, Gerard's father, at the Opelousas post in about 1765. She soon died but not before having a daughter, Agnes, "who remained peaceably with Chrétien, as his slave" until the 1790s. During a trip with her owner to New Orleans, however, she initiated proceedings against Chrétien for her freedom, but Carondelet must have ordered her to return to Chrétien, as she remained with him until his death.[60] Seville won his initial case, but it was subsequently overturned on appeal. He sued again in 1816, but this time he lost in the lower court, a decision that was upheld by the Louisiana Supreme Court.[61]

In Seville's case, the parish and supreme courts focused on two questions—whether Indian slavery had been legal under the French government and whether Spanish practice undermined O'Reilly's ban—but they also addressed the sticky issue of what happened after "the cession of any part of the dominions of one sovereign power to another." They focused on the cession from France to Spain, though clearly their decision spoke to concern among Anglo-Louisianans seeking to understand which colonial laws still held sway in the region. Several witnesses testified that "it was not only the custom and practice, but also the law of the French government to make slaves of Sauvages" before 1769. However, when the city's notaries searched the archives in 1816, they found that "no document exist[ed] . . . being or purporting to be a proclamation or ordinance of the French Government, King, or Regent by which the slavery of Indians was authorized in Louisiana."[62]

Since the court could not determine whether or not Indian slavery had been legal under French rule, it looked instead on practice. It heeded the witnesses who had testified that, regardless of legality, "a great number of persons owned" Indian slaves during the French era and that, even after O'Reilly's decree, Indian slaves were "sold in public with the consent of the Spanish government." The court acknowledged that O'Reilly's declaration confirmed that Indian slavery was contrary to Spanish law but found that it also "confirmed the inhabitants in their possession of such Indian slaves." Furthermore, Carondelet's decision in the 1790s to return slave petitioners "to their masters to be treated and considered as previously" demonstrated that "the establishment of the Spanish government" had not created a right to freedom, and thus the court denied Seville's claim.[63]

In another case, Uzlere and his sister Françoise first filed suit in New Orleans Parish court in 1812, claiming that their mother, Marianne, was "an Indian woman of the Chickasaw nation" who had been "by various undue means, entrapped" and sold to Mademoiselle Manette Songe during the Spanish era. Like Agnes, Marianne "made a personal application to" Carondelet for her freedom. Unlike Agnes, Marianne was, at least according to her children, freed. She died in New Orleans about 1794, having left her children in Songe's care. Since Songe's death, they alleged, her heir Jean Baptiste Poyfarré had "continued unjustly to hold them as slaves, and to treat them as such." They sought their freedom and 5,000 dollars in damages. Finding that they were indeed "descended from an Indian woman of the Chickasaw tribe," in part because their color showed "them to be of Indian origin," the jury freed Ulzere, Françoise, and her two children.[64] The jury found that "reducing Indians to slavery [was] prohibited by the French, as well as the Spanish government," but its judgment was dismissed by the Louisiana Supreme Court, which stated that the matter concerned a question of law that should not have been submitted to the jury. Ulzere and Françoise's suit was remanded for a second trial. In 1824, their persistence was rewarded when they finally gained their freedom, although only partially on the grounds of the illegality of Indian slavery.[65]

The 1824 decision in *Ulzere* contradicted, although not explicitly, the interpretation of French and Spanish law and legal practice contained in *Seville* seven years earlier. The Missouri Supreme Court reached similarly opposing interpretations in two cases involving the same parties it heard in 1828 and 1834. In her suit for freedom, fifty-year-old Marguerite claimed to be the daughter of María Jean, also known as Marie Scipion, who in turn was the daughter of a Natchez Indian woman and Scipion, a negro. According to Marguerite's witnesses, her mother's owner, Joseph Tayon, was clearly aware of O'Reilly's decree and had declared "Marie Scipion and her children would be free at his death" because of it. Witnesses for Chouteau, Marguerite's owner, argued instead that Marie Scipion "was of negro blood," even as they acknowledged that there were "few blacks" and "many slaves of Indian blood" at Fort de Chartres at the time.[66] In its 1828 decision, which kept Marguerite enslaved, the court acknowledged that there were good reasons to consider negros prima facie as slaves and Indians prima facie as free, given that "all negroes imported into North America were brought in as slaves." But it ultimately decided that "Indians taken captive in war" before 1769 and their descendants were "lawful slaves."[67] Six years later, Marguerite reiterated her argument that Indians, in contrast to negroes, should be considered free. "Indians," she insisted, "were around and among the settlements of white men, in the full enjoyment of their personal liberty, acknowledging no inferiority to white men and treating them either as national friends or national enemies. To show a descent from this race," she concluded, "it is contended to show right to freedom." This time she convinced the court, which reversed its earlier decision to declare that "in Louisiana, under the French Government, Indians could not lawfully be reduced to slavery."[68]

Marguerite's contention that Indians were essentially free, while those of African descent were not, was echoed by other witnesses in these nineteenth-century cases. Testifying in *Seville,* Antoine Blanc averred that "no people clings so fiercely to its rights and so jealously to its freedom" as Indians, while fellow witness Louis Charles de Blanc described "the importance they placed on their rights and their liberty." Admittedly, these declarations came in an effort to displace onto Indians themselves the blame for the enslavement of other Indians; both witnesses claimed that if colonists had attempted to enslave Indians, freedom-loving "nations would have revolted against such as an act of violence."[69] For their very different purposes, Marguerite and the Blancs both drew upon the racial ideology of the early nineteenth century, which held that Indians had an innate love of liberty while those of African descent were naturally suited for the subordinate status of slavery.

Two visitors to New Orleans in the 1790s articulated these distinctions. Louis-Narcisse Baudry des Lozières, a Frenchman, wrote that the Indian did not make a good slave because "he dies a short while after losing his liberty. His constitution is very different from that of the nègre." Although Indians, Baudry des Lozières continued, were "ignorant and cruel," they were also more intelligent than nègres, who were superstitious, "stupid, and fierce." Indians could be "enlighten[ed] and humanize[d]," whereas "one promises in vain to inoculate [the nègre] with the right sense."[70] Similarly, Berquin-Duvallon, a refugee from Saint-Domingue, argued, "Nature seems to have intended one kind of man [nègres] for slavery, by the turn of their spirit, their disposition to allow themselves to be led, their moral incapacity," and their "innate passiveness." This was, he noted, "completely different from the sauvages or natives of America, who are the enemies of subjection just as nègres are naturally inclined."[71]

Slaveowners, like Poydras and his co-memorialists, clearly would have disagreed with Berquin-Duvallon when he suggested that reducing Indians to slavery was "a well-recognized impossibility." Berquin-Duvallon and others claimed that Indians and Africans possessed essentially different and innate characteristics, that they were qualitatively different from each other; slaveowners in the 1790s, on the other hand, implied that Indians and Africans were races of a different sort. When they argued the petitioners were "all Mestizos from Negros, [who] want to pass for free Indians," they did not deny that their slaves might have some Indian ancestry but, following the logic of hypodescent, they implied that whatever Indian blood their slaves may have had was overwhelmed by the African blood coursing through their veins.[72] Others, like Clara Lopez de la Peña, would argue that Indian blood could also be negated by European blood.

Where She Belongs

The perception that Indian blood was weaker than either African or European blood, as well as the failure of New Orleans' racial order to fully incorporate people of Indian ancestry, is demonstrated, once again, in the sacramental records. Although priests did use the label "mestizo," the ways they did so suggested that mestizos could be either white or people of color. Baptisms of children identified as mestizos appear in both the white and nonwhite registers. Those with nonwhite fathers were always entered into the book of gente de color, while those with white or unknown fathers appeared in both.[73] One of the mestizo children with a white father whose entry was recorded in the nonwhite registry was Clara Lopez de la Peña's daughter, Luisa Declouet. Her baptism entry reads as follows: "On twenty-five of January of one thousand seven hundred and ninety-five, I the undersigned lieutenant Curé of the Parish of Saint Louis of New Orleans, supplied Baptism ceremonies for Luisa, mestiza, born on twenty-one December last[,] . . . daughter of Clara Peña, free mestiza, and of Don Louis Declouet."[74] Luisa was the first child of Lopez de la Peña and Declouet. Because of her subsequent petition to the bishop, it is possible to trace Lopez de la Peña's lineage back three generations, although the details become fuzzy precisely at the pivotal generation, the grandmother on whom Lopez de la Peña's assertion of Indian ancestry depended.

Born in 1778, Clara's own baptism was recorded in the book of blancos, just one year after the practice of separate books began, where she is noted as the natural daughter of Don Josef Lopez de la Peña and Doña Luisa Marigny de Mandeville. Neither Clara nor her mother were identified by race in this entry.[75] Yet Clara did not base her petition on this "proof" of whiteness, most likely because common knowledge that she and her mother were women of color made a claim of no non-European ancestry untenable. They appeared in numerous notarial and sacramental acts variously labeled "parda," "mulata," "cuarteróna," and "mestiza."

Two other elements of Clara's baptism entry are noteworthy: her mother is granted the title "doña," one of the rare times Luison (as she was more commonly known) was so honored, and her surname is that of an old and prominent Franco-New Orleanian family. In Clara's 1799 petition to the bishop, she claimed that Luison's father was Monsieur Mandeville, an "official in the service of France."[76] Clara and Luison alike made strategic use of the Mandeville surname. In most notarial records, Luison has the surname Brouner (or Brunet), while in many sacramental records, she was called Mandeville. In the latter—records that were used to trace genealogies—Luison's claim to the Mandeville surname gave greater prestige to her children, grandchildren, and even her godchildren. In addition, the use of the Mandeville surname severed Luison from her own history of enslavement, at least in these important genealogical records.

By contrast, Brunet was the surname of Luison's former owner, whose widow manumitted her in 1770 when she was twenty-three.[77] Apparently childless while enslaved, Luison had a daughter, Sofi, with one N. Esteves in the early 1770s.[78] By the late 1770s, she was involved with Clara's father, although it appears that they did not live together. In June 1778, just a few months after Clara's birth, Luison was listed as the head of a household on Ste. Ursulle with her two daughters (all were labeled as mulatas libres) and two slaves, one of whom belonged to de la Peña. It is likely that de la Peña was making financial contributions to Luison's household, as she later sought to return 400 pesos he had lent her, without interest, "for [her] own necessities."[79] A Spaniard in his mid-twenties (and thus a few years younger than Luison), de la Peña was a lieutenant in the Louisiana Regiment and probably in between wives during his relationship with Luison, which must have ended before September 1785, when Luison married mulato libre Francisco Durand. A few months after Luison's wedding, de la Peña married his second wife.[80]

Far less is known about Luison's mother. The only records to mention her are Clara's petition, in which her witnesses testified that they knew Luison's mother to be a mestiza named María Juana, and Luison's 1794 will, in which she declared herself to be the "daughter of María Juana, India."[81] If a mestiza, María Juana was probably born into slavery in the 1720s or early 1730s, the daughter of an enslaved Indian woman and a white man, if Clara's witnesses can be trusted. If María Juana herself was Indian, she may have been captured and sold to a French habitant as a child or young woman.[82] Whichever was the enslaved Indian woman, María Juana or her unnamed mother, she could have established a family with a fellow slave, mostly likely from the thousands of Africans who entered the colony in the 1710s and 1720s. That many enslaved Indian women chose this path is demonstrated in the genealogies constructed as part of the freedom petitions discussed above as well as in the baptism registries. Equally plausible, however, is that she had a sexual relationship with a Euro-Louisianan man, most likely her owner.

Clara's witnesses asserted that Luison's father was Monsieur Mandeville, mostly likely Antoine Philippe, a lieutenant in the French troops and officer during the Spanish era. Antoine Philippe's father, François, a chevalier of the Royal Order of Saint Louis and commandant at Mobile, fathered at least two métis daughters with enslaved Indian women. The first, Madeline-Renée, later described as "the natural [bâtard] daughter of Sr. de Mandeville begat of a sauvagesse slave," was born long before François' marriage, while the second was an adulterous daughter who was baptized in 1729, five months after François himself had died.[83] Although no extant sacramental records prove that Antoine Philippe fathered Luison, it is plausible that he followed in his father's footsteps, engaging in the relationship with María Juana a couple of years before he married in 1748, the year after Luison's likely birth. One of Antoine Philippe's sons, Pierre Philippe, testified on Clara's behalf, giving credence to her claim of being a Mandeville, which, in turn, linked her to one of Louisiana's few genuinely noble families.

These three generations of women symbolize the different constraints and choices that women of color faced when it came to forming families. María Juana was probably born into and died in slavery. Her daughter, Luison, was born a slave, but freed as a young woman. And her granddaughter, Clara, was born into freedom. For each woman, status as enslaved, emancipated, or free, combined with her racial categorization, shaped her ability to choose whom she established families with as well as the kind of recognition she would receive for those families. As an enslaved india or mestiza, María Juana had little choice: a relationship with her owner was probably not consensual, although she may have hoped that such a father would look kindly on his children. Emancipated as a young woman, Luison chose men of both European and African ancestry. Despite being the daughter of a prominent colonial official, as a woman born into slavery and one usually classified as a mulata, Luison would have found it difficult to establish a formally sanctioned relationship with a white man; hence her extramarital relationship with de la Peña followed by her marriage to pardo libre Durand.[84]

Two of Luison's daughters also chose white men as sexual partners, and both of them were able to have these relationships, and therefore their children, formally recognized by the state and the church, albeit belatedly in both cases.[85] Sometime before spring 1794, a sixteen-year-old Clara began a relationship with Louis Declouet, about ten years her senior, an officer in the Louisiana regiment and the son of a prominent St. Martinville family.[86] Their first child, Luisa (the one subject to "notorious prejudice"), was born at the end of 1794. They had two more daughters in 1796 and 1798. Both their baptisms were recorded in the book of blancos, as were all those of the couple's subsequent children, and in none of these records are Clara or her children identified with racial labels.[87] It was several months after the baptism of her third daughter that Clara filed her petition to have Luisa reclassified as white so that her racial identity would matching that ascribed to her other daughters.

Acting on Clara's petition, Bishop Luis accepted the testimonies of her witnesses that there was no "mixture of negro nor mulato" in Clara's lineage, nor therefore in her daughter's. He decreed that Luisa's baptism should be transferred to the registry of blancos, "where," he wrote, "it belongs." Luisa's baptism record was indeed changed. The original in the baptismal registry for negros and mulatos has marginal notations indicating that, "by judicial decree," the entry of Luisa Declouet, mestiza libre, had been moved to the current book of "solas Personas blancas." But the priests had the last word, transcribing the original record exactly and including the racial labels, although they changed Luisa to a "mestiza *or* mulata libre." Only then did they cross out both Luisa's and Clara's racial labels, as well as the designation of Luisa as "natural" rather than "legitimate," and add "doña" before Clara's name. And unlike some changed baptism records in which the previously designated racial label is impossible to read, Luisa's and Clara's are easy to make out. Finally, the priests noted in the margin the forced circumstances of the transposed baptism entry. Luisa could now claim to appear in the white registry, but she was still clearly a marked person.[88]

In changing Luisa's racial classification, Bishop Luis was probably as influenced by Clara's social status and connections to prominent Euro-Louisianan men as by her lack of "negro or mulato" blood. In many records, Clara was referred to as "doña," an honorific title that was given almost exclusively to Euro-Louisianan women and, even then, only to those of some social standing. All of the baptism records of Clara's children note her as "doña" except for Luisa's original entry in the book of negros and mulatos. Several of the records include the names of the child's paternal and maternal grandparents, and in none of these is Luison graced with the title "doña." Clara was also almost always noted with her surname. Although it was not usual for full names to be used with gens de couleur libre by the end of the eighteenth century, the fact that Clara's is consistently mentioned is another indication that she was perceived as having some social status.[89] She was probably granted this respect because of the men in her life: her husband, father, and maternal grandfather were all Euro-Louisianans who held colonial or military office and were themselves honored with the title "don" or "sieur." In addition, the five witnesses who testified about her ancestry were identified with "don." One of them—probably Clara's half uncle—was a knight of the Royal Order of St. Louis and a colonel in the New Orleans militia. The others were a perpetual regidor, an artillery captain in the militia, a retired warehouse guard (a position Clara's father had held earlier), and Don Alexo Lesassier, the former consort of her half sister Sofi.

Throughout her adult life and particularly in her petition to the bishop, Clara strategically used these connections, particularly her familial ones. Using Mandeville for her mother's surname and calling on her half uncle to testify on her behalf, she emphasized her connections to an old and prominent French creole family. Clara's husband, Louis, appears to have played no role in the reclassification of Luisa. The petition to the bishop was initiated and signed by Clara, and at the end of the case, it was Clara who was informed of the bishop's ruling. Yet the distinct possibility that Louis played a silent role should not be discounted. His family was not quite as distinguished as the Mandevilles, but his father had been commandant at Opelousas, and Louis and his brothers were officers in the Spanish military. By the early nineteenth century, Louis was a successful planter in the sugar parishes west of New Orleans and was worth almost 4,000 dollars.[90] So, although it was Clara who initiated the case and appears to be the one invested in having her daughter's racial designation changed, Louis' lineage and status was probably as important as Clara's connections to the Mandeville family in allowing Luisa to "become" white.

Clara may have convinced the bishop and won the right for her and her children to be racially unmarked, but her battle with the St. Louis priests continued. She and Louis had married in 1797 but not at the St. Louis Cathedral; the priests who baptized her daughter in 1798 and twin sons in 1800 refused to acknowledge the legality of her relationship with Louis, and the children were all noted as natural rather than legitimate. In 1801, Clara was forced to petition Bishop Luis once again to have her children noted as legitimate. In November of that year, her 1797 marriage was recorded, under judicial order, in the St. Louis registry and her previously baptized children were noted as legitimated by their parents' marriage.[91] Why the priests refused to recognize their marriage until forced to do so and why Clara and Louis had not married in the St. Louis Cathedral is unclear. Perhaps they married clandestinely, to avoid parental opposition, as Clara was only nineteen at the time. But of all their parents, only Luison was still alive, and Louis' family does not seem to have opposed his marriage to Clara, as two of his siblings served as godparents to their children. Perhaps the St. Louis priests had refused to marry them; unfortunately, the records do not reveal the full story of her antagonistic relationship with the priests.

The cases of Clara Lopez de la Peña and the mestizo slave petitioners of the 1790s reveal the mechanisms through which people of Indian ancestry been erased, as the individuals themselves or others who had much to gain selectively chose to emphasize certain aspects of their ancestry and downplay others. In order to free themselves, mestizo slaves emphasized, and perhaps occasionally created, maternal descent from Indian women, while their owners argued that what really mattered was their paternal, African ancestry. Lopez de la Peña also claimed descent from an Indian woman, acknowledging that she might be called a mestiza and yet denying that this made her ineligible for being unmarked by race and thus assumed to be white. New Orleans' social order, with its numerous racial classifications, allowed some people of color to renegotiate their identities even as priests policed the boundaries of whiteness, but the ambiguity regarding Indianness in particular made certain people of color better situated to manipulate their standing within New Orleans' racial order than others.

Despite the codification of New Orleans' tripartite racial system that occurred in the aftermath of the Louisiana Purchase with the arrival of Anglo-Americans and their own ideas about race, Lopez de la Peña was far from the last person to make a strategic claim of Indian ancestry in order to manipulate her racial identity. In 1916, the descendants of François Joubert filed suit, as Lopez de la Peña had, to have a baptismal record in the St. Louis Cathedral registries amended. Almost one hundred years earlier, two cousins, the children of Saint-Domingue refugees, were baptized. François Joubert was the natural son of Bazile Joubert and femme de couleur libre Eugenie Dorres, while Rose Joubert was the natural daughter of Noel Joubert and femme de couleur libre Charlotte Lapeye. Despite the same, albeit generic, racial labels given to their mothers, François was labeled a métis and Rose a quarteronné. The priest's decision to classify François as a métis enabled his descendants to claim Indianness and deny they had any African ancestry in an era when the Louisiana Supreme Court decreed that "any appreciable mixture of negro blood" subjected individuals to discriminatory laws. François' baptism record was, the rector noted in 1916, "hereby corrected in conformity with the judgment of the Civil District Court . . . and the status of François Joubert is hereby declared to be that of a white person."[92]

CHAPTER SEVEN

Codification of a Tripartite Racial System in Anglo-Louisiana

IN 1796, Eulalie Mandeville, a twenty-two-year-old femme de couleur libre, and Eugene Macarty, a twenty-eight-year-old blanco, began a relationship that would last almost fifty years, ending only with his death, and produce five children. Shortly after the relationship began, Mandeville received land and money from her family, "one of the most distinguished in Louisiana," and used them to develop a dry-goods business. By her mid-thirties, she had become a wealthy and respected businesswoman. At first conducting her business in Macarty's name, Mandeville increasingly made contracts in her own name after 1825 and was depositing large sums of money into her own bank account. A few weeks before he died, Macarty transferred more than 100,000 dollars into Mandeville's account, leaving himself with an estate of about 12,000 dollars at his death on October 25, 1845, at the age of seventy-seven.

Deprived of a substantial inheritance, Macarty's collateral white heirs sued Mandeville, arguing that she was "illegally in possession" of Macarty's estate, which they contended included real estate in New Orleans, several slaves, and additional cash that Mandeville claimed as her own personal property. They rested their case on the provision of Louisiana law that declared a concubine could not inherit more than 10 percent of her consort's estate. Drawing on both her familial ties to the Marigny family and her connections within the New Orleans business community, Mandeville easily demonstrated to the satisfaction of both the Jefferson Parish Probate Court and the Louisiana Supreme Court that the property in question, including the money Macarty had transferred to her shortly before his death, "belongs exclusively to her, and has been honestly acquired, and is the result of her industry and economy during half a century." In dismissing the plaintiffs' suit against her, Chief Justice George Eustis concluded that, given the impossibility of legalizing her relationship with Macarty, she "had, in all respects, rendered her condition as reputable and as useful as it could be made." In fact, their relationship was, in Eustis's words, "the nearest approach to marriage which the law recognized."[1] Beginning at the end of the Spanish era, Mandeville and Macarty's relationship survived, even thrived, during the Anglo-American era. And despite being denied the privileges of legal marriage, Mandeville and Macarty and many other couples like them formed families that continued to be tolerated as they had been in the eighteenth century. Yet circumstances had changed in the aftermath of the Louisiana Purchase, as the United States became the third and last government to take over the region that included New Orleans.[2]

Even before Louisiana became politically incorporated into the United States, changing economic conditions were bringing New Orleans' plantation society more in line with those of the surrounding southern states. With the reopening of the slave trade in the late 1770s, Euro-Louisianan planters could finally, after eighty years, purchase as many slaves as they needed or could afford. They then redoubled their efforts to find a profitable crop for their slaves to produce; their answer came in 1795 when Étienne Boré successfully crystallized Louisiana's local sugar cane. During the same time, liberalized Spanish immigration policies had encouraged Anglo-Americans to migrate into the lower Mississippi River Valley, bringing slaves and cotton cultivation with them. After a brief period of stagnation in the early 1790s, when tobacco and indigo prices declined, planters quickly converted their plantations to produce sugar and cotton on a large scale. By 1802, more than five thousand hogsheads of sugar and eighteen thousand bales of cotton were moving through the port of New Orleans; by 1810, these numbers had doubled.[3]

In addition to seeking to politically and economically incorporate New Orleans into the United States, Anglo-Americans who arrived after 1803 also sought to integrate the city into an Anglo-American racial hierarchy, one that radically differed from the order by then firmly entrenched there. As they attempted to transform the city's racial system into a binary one that equated blackness with enslavement and whiteness with freedom, authorities in Anglo-Louisiana began to undermine the legal and social position of gens de couleur libre by restricting manumission, limiting immigration, criminalizing racially exogamous marriages, and constraining the capacity of Euro-Louisianan men to transfer property to nonwhite consorts and children. In doing so, however, they codified enough elements of the colonial racial system so that sympathetic judges could rule in favor of gens de couleur libre who sought to protect their rights. Those already free were, to a great extent, able to secure their status, but those enslaved found it much harder to become free. Thus, what had been a more fluid casta system in the eighteenth century became truly codified as a tripartite racial order during the early decades of the nineteenth.

The Newness of the Scene

In 1819, sixteen years after the Louisiana Purchase and seven years after Louisiana had achieved statehood, Anglo-American architect Benjamin Latrobe and his family arrived in New Orleans. Mrs. Latrobe later explained her first reactions, writing she "had no language to describe [her] wonder on arriving at N. Orleans!" Everything astonished her, from oranges "as big as [her son] John's head almost" to the "jargon [that] assailed her equal to Babel its-self." She was, she concluded, "really confused by the newness of the scene."⁴ Her equally astonished husband was, fortunately for us, more descriptive than his wife. Arriving up the Mississippi, the Latrobes first saw, or rather heard, New Orleans from their boat as it docked in the fog. In his diary, Latrobe described "a sound more strange than any that is heard anywhere else in the world. . . . It is more incessant, loud, rapid, and various gabble of tongues of all tones than was ever heard at Babel." Latrobe compared the noises to those "that issue from an extensive marsh, the residence of a million or two frogs, from bull frogs up to whistlers." Suddenly the fog lifted and the Latrobes had their first glimpse of the city. It had "at first sight a very imposing, and handsome appearance, beyond any other city in the United States in which I have been." Latrobe now saw that "the strange and loud noise heard through the fog" emanated from the marketplace along the levee and that the sound was "not more extraordinary than the appearance of these noisy folks," the vendors and their customers. "Everything," he concluded, "had an *odd* look."

To its early nineteenth-century visitors, particularly those coming from Anglo-America, New Orleans did indeed have an "odd look." The city's physical appearance—its Spanish architecture, its central plaza with its grand Catholic cathedral—was strange to Anglo-American eyes but, most importantly, it was the city's people who struck visitors as "a sight wholly new even," confessed Latrobe, "to one who has traveled much in Europe and America." A few days after his arrival, Latrobe wandered through the city, passing "a couple of Choctaw Indian women and a stark naked Indian girl," before reaching the marketplace at the levee. There, he wrote, among the various wares spread on tables or Palmetto leaves on the ground, were "white men and women, and of all hues of brown, and of all classes of faces, from round Yankees, to grisly and lean Spaniards, black negroes and negresses, filthy Indians half naked, mulattoes, curly and straight-haired, quarterons of all shades, long haired and frizzled, the women dressed in the most flaring yellow and scarlet gowns, the men capped and hated. Their wares consisted of as many kinds as their faces."⁵

Amazement at this racial, ethnic, and linguistic diversity appears in almost

In addition to evocatively describing New Orleans, Latrobe sketched many city scenes, including this one foregrounding an elderly Indian woman selling fruit among the market's diverse participants. Benjamin Latrobe, *Market Folks*, [1819], in Sketchbook XIV. Maryland Historical Society, Baltimore, Md.

every description of the city from this period. More than anything else, nineteenth-century Anglo-American visitors struggled to understand New Orleans' racial order. The subtle racial nuances that New Orleanians took for granted confused Benjamin Latrobe's son John, who returned to the city as an adult in 1834. On his first day back, he strolled through the city with a local companion. Pointing to a nearby woman, he commented "Hah—what's that. A fine figure, a beautiful foot, an angle like an angels—an air quite distingué [*sic*], and then so strange, and characteristic—so Spanish, with that long black veil over the head." "Allons," his friend replied, "we will pass her." "Why she's a mulatto," Latrobe declared. "Fie—not at all—dont let her hear you—that's a quadroon." "A Quadroon!" Latrobe exclaimed. "Well, I'll know better next time." Despite this quick education in New Orleans' racial code, Latrobe mistook the next women he saw—ones "darker than we have just passed"—as quadroons, only to be told "Heavens no, they are Creoles—natives, whites—Spaniards and French mixed. . . . You must make the distinction." After this, Latrobe gave up, tiredly noting, "two . . . quadroons. No, those

are mulattoes. Well so be it." Reared within a two-caste racial system that designated all people of color as black, Latrobe "could not get it out of [his] mind that
those [quadroon] women that [he] saw were negroes nothing more or less."[6]

Frederick Law Olmsted, who visited the city in the 1850s, realized that his
Anglo-American readers would be similarly confused by the variety of racial classifications used in New Orleans. Therefore, he provided a genealogical chart to
explain each category, listing the parents on the right and their offspring on the
left.

scatra	griffe and negress
griffe	negro and mulatto
marabon	mulatto and griffe
quarteron	white and mulatto
metif	white and quarteron
meamelouc	white and metif
quarteron	white and meamelouc
sang-mêlé	white and quarteron

Olmsted did not define "mulatto," assuming that his readers would have been familiar with this one label for racial mixture, and he erased the Indian ancestry that was
an essential element of "metif" (métis). He also failed to clarify how one identified
particular individuals, whether such categories were determined strictly by knowledge of an individual's ancestry or whether that knowledge was presumed to be encoded in visual impressions, as John Latrobe's host implied. Indeed, he expressed
doubt at the "experts [who] pretend to be able to distinguish" among all these "sub-
varieties" (as he called them), although he was "certain they all exist in New Orleans."[7] On this point, however, Olmsted was wrong. Although most of his terms
do appear in the documentary record (though not always with the same meanings
as he attributes to them), a few—"marabon," "meamelouc," and "scatra"—do not.
Olmsted appears to have borrowed these additional terms from Médéric-Louis Élie
Moreau de Saint-Méry's description of Saint-Domingue's racial hierarchy. Precondi-
tioned to think of New Orleans as a foreign, specifically French-Caribbean-like place,
Olmsted appropriated Moreau's genealogy and mapped it onto New Orleans.[8]

Two Classes or One?

Olmsted's creative embellishments, however, do not undermine the differences
that did indeed exist between New Orleans' racial conceptions and those of Anglo-

America, disparities that are best represented in *State v. Harrison*. This 1856 Louisiana Supreme Court decision turned on the constitutionality of an 1855 Act Relative to Slaves and Free Colored Persons. Under the state constitution, legislative acts were required to embrace a single legal object; thus the question for the court was to determine whether or not "slaves" and "free colored persons" were a single class or two distinct classes. Writing for the court, Justice Alexander Buchanan argued "in the eyes of Louisiana law, there is, (with the exception of political rights, of certain social privileges, and of the obligations of jury and militia service,) all the difference between a free man of color and a slave, that there is between a white man and a slave." As he noted, gens de couleur libre could make contracts; possess, inherit, and transmit property; testify in civil and criminal cases; and were subject to trial "with the same formalities, and by the same tribunal, as the white man," all rights that were denied to slaves.

In a vigorously worded dissent, however, Justice Henry M. Spofford contended that far from being discrete legal classes, slaves and gens de couleur libre were, in fact, "a single, homogenous class of beings, distinguished from all others by nature, custom, and law, and never confounded with citizens of the State. No white person can be a slave; no colored person can be a citizen." Spofford suggested that a simple rewording of the act's title, calling it "an Act *relative to persons of color, whether bond or free*," would clarify that the two groups were indeed "one object" in law.[9] In these opinions, Buchanan and Spofford summarized the two systems of racial organization that competed for supremacy in Anglo-Louisiana. Despite Spofford's clear articulation that something like a one-drop rule should indeed be the law, the Louisiana Supreme Court was willing to recognize, as late as 1856, that Louisiana was governed by a tripartite racial system, one that officially recognized gens de couleur libre as a distinct legal category.

The willingness of justices Eustis and Buchanan to rule in favor of gens de couleur libre on the eve of the Civil War challenges the view that New Orleans' racial system was effortlessly Anglo-Americanized in the years following the Louisiana Purchase.[10] Some Franco-New Orleanian elites, such as those who had resisted the Spanish Código Negro of 1789, do appear to have easily reconciled themselves with Anglo-American racial ideology and perhaps were even happy to find themselves finally governed by those who shared their own views of race. Nevertheless, many New Orleanians continued to live socially, economically, and religiously intertwined lives. Most importantly, as they had at the beginning of the Spanish era, gens de couleur libre quickly learned what their legal rights were, demonstrated their readiness to resist further degradation of their status, and called on their intimate and patronage ties to Euro-New Orleanians when necessary.

At the time of the Louisiana Purchase, there were over thirteen hundred gens de couleur libre in New Orleans, almost one-fifth of the city's seven thousand residents.[11] Many were ex-slaves themselves but more were second- and third-generation libres born into freedom, and a few were the descendants of free people of African ancestry who had emigrated to New Orleans from Jamaica, Martinique, Havana, and France. Immigration of free people of African ancestry had been fairly negligible until the 1790s, when a small number of French-speaking gens de couleur libre arrived from Saint-Domingue despite the cabildo's best efforts to keep them out, and fellow refugees continued to trickle into the city during the first decade of the nineteenth century. This trickle became a flood in 1809, when 3,102 gens de couleur arrived within a single year. Along with just over three thousand slaves and just under three thousand whites, these Saint-Domingue refugees had fled to Cuba in 1803 after the expulsion of the Leclerc expedition but had been recently expelled by the Spanish government.[12] This influx of free, French-speaking, Catholic refugees tripled the size of New Orleans' gens de couleur libre population to almost five thousand in 1810. The gens de couleur libre population now made up just less than one-third of the city's inhabitants and almost one-half its free residents. The population continued to grow thereafter, peaking at fifteen thousand in 1840, mostly through natural increase, although manumission and migration continued to play minor roles.

The city's white population, however, grew at a faster rate. Anglo-Americans and then Irish and German immigrants poured into the expanding and increasingly diverse city, and, as a result, by 1840, the proportion of gens de couleur libre had declined from one-third back to one-fifth of the city's total population. In the following decade, gens de couleur libre began leaving the city, and the population dropped to just under ten thousand in 1850, less than one-tenth of the city's total.[13] Their exodus was a response to two related trends: increasing racial hostility engendered by new residents unfamiliar with the city's colonial race relations, who competed with gens de couleur libre for jobs, and to the growing hostility toward free people of African ancestry throughout the South after the emergence of proslavery ideologies in the 1830s. Although local conditions had clearly worsened for gens de couleur libre by the 1840s, this development was neither inevitable nor uncontested as, from the beginning of Anglo-Louisiana, gens de couleur libre fought to preserve their unique position within the city's racial order.

Will They Be Entitled to the Rights of Citizens or Not?

Immediately following the Louisiana Purchase, gens de couleur libre were briefly optimistic that they would be included among "the inhabitants of the ceded territory" to whom the Louisiana Purchase treaty promised "all these rights, advantages, and immunities of citizens of the United States."[14] In the summer of 1804, when they were not invited to a "meeting of citizens" gathering to write a memorial to Congress, an "influential" homme de couleur libre decided that they should hold their own meeting to "consult together as to *their* rights" and draft their own memorial. Fearful of what such a meeting might lead to, Governor William C. C. Claiborne reported that he would discourage any more meetings that might "publicly manifest . . . any disquietude."[15]

Yet another Anglo-American politician, Benjamin Morgan, was at least willing to consider "upon what footing . . . the free quadroon mulatto and black people [would] stand." Morgan, who had arrived in New Orleans before the purchase, described the gens de couleur libre as "a very numerous class in this city." Many, he noted, were "very respectable" and had "enjoy[ed] their rights in common with other subjects" under the Spanish government. Posing the question of whether, following the transfer of authority to the United States, they should "be entitled to the rights of citizens or not," Morgan suggested that "it is worth the consideration of government [whether] they may be made good citizens." He worried that if they were denied this opportunity, they could become the "formidable abettors of the black people [that is to] say slaves if they should ever be troublesome."[16]

It quickly became clear, however, that gens de couleur libre were not to become full citizens in Anglo-Louisiana, as Congress, the Territorial Legislature, and the State Constitution of 1812 all limited the privileges and obligations of citizenship to "free male white persons."[17] Before New Orleans' first election in the spring of 1805, one election official did question the precise French wording of the city's incorporation act and wondered whether "free colored inhabitants" could in fact vote. According to the English text of the act, "no person shall vote . . . who shall not be a free white male inhabitant of the said city," wording that clearly excluded slaves, nonwhites, and women from voting, but the French text read "habitant mâle, libre et blanc," which could be loosely read as granting suffrage to men who were either free or white. The city council acknowledged "there is ambiguity in these expressions" but stated that "the Legislative Council, without doubt, never had the intention of according the right to vote to free people of color."[18]

Although hommes de couleur libre never came close to gaining the right to vote or sit on juries, they were more successful in challenging their exclusion from militia service. Just one day after the transfer of Louisiana from France to the United States, James Wilkinson requested "a Garrison of 500 Regulars" to be dispatched to New Orleans. Despite declaring that "every thing in the City is still tranquil, and I feel no alarm," he was concerned that "difficulties" could emerge from various causes.

One cause that particularly concerned him was "the formidable aspect of the armed Blacks and Malattoes [*sic*], officered and organized"; such a sight was, he continued, "painful and perplexing."[19]

A week later, Claiborne "reflected with much anxiety" on the presence of "two large [Militia] Companies of people of Colour." Although he acknowledged they were "attached to the Service, and were esteemed a very Serviceable Corps under the Spanish Government," he worried about the consequences of either recommissioning or disbanding them: "To re-commission them might be considered an outrage on the feelings of the part of the Nation, and as opposed to those principles of Policy which the Safety of the Southern States has necessarily established; on the other hand not to be re-commissioned would disgust them, and might be productive of future mischief. To disband them would be to raise an armed enemy in the very heart of the Country, and to disarm them would favour too strongly of that desperate System of Government which Seldom succeeds."[20]

While Claiborne waited to hear from the federal government, he received a petition signed by about sixty hommes de couleur libre. Calling themselves "free Citizens of Louisiana," they declared their "respect and Esteem and sincere attachment to the Government of the United States" as well as their "lively Joy" that Louisiana had been "united with . . . the American Republic." They believed, rather wishfully, that their "personal and political freedom is thereby assured to us for ever." Then, asserting their loyalties to the new government and highlighting their "distinguished" service to the Spanish government, they requested the honor of organizing themselves "as a Corps of Volunteers," promising to "serve with fidelity and Zeal."[21] Assuring the petitioners of his own "confidences in their Military Zeal, and in the sincerity of their professions of attachment to the United States," Claiborne replied that he would leave the militias as currently organized until he "received particular instructions from the President."[22]

A month later, Secretary of War Henry Dearborn authorized Claiborne to organize "the corps of the Freeman of Colour." He was to choose "the principal officers . . . with caution," attending to their "respectability and integrity of character, as well as their popularity and influence among their associates."[23] Despite the militiamen's desire to be "commanded by people of their own Colour," Claiborne appointed two white majors to command the battalion, although the militiamen successfully opposed his attempt to appoint two additional "respectable White citizens as adjutants." At the same time that he held a "long conference" with "the most influential" militiamen to assuage their discontent, however, he duplicitously sent orders to Major Jean Michel Fortier to decrease the size of the battalion by not mustering anyone who resided outside of New Orleans and its suburbs and by not enrolling any new recruits. Fortier was to feign ignorance regarding the reason for these orders but to "presume, that the Battalion is deemed sufficiently numerous, and that the freemen of Colour not now attached thereto, may hereafter be formed into a separate corps."[24]

For the next few years, that status quo prevailed. The militia of hommes de couleur libre was neglected by the legislative council in a series of militia acts passed between 1804 and 1807 and by the state's first constitution of January 1812. "Ancient Louisianans" and Americans alike, according to Claiborne, opposed the reorganization and "thought it prudent to take no notice of the Mulatto Corps in the general Militia Law." But Claiborne realized that this refusal to recognize their willingness to serve "has soured them considerably with the American government," and he continued to urge the legislature to reconsider.[25] Finally, following the performance of New Orleans' hommes de couleur libre in defending the city against a slave insurrection in 1811, the legislature was forced into granting these militia companies formal status in September 1812. In doing so, however, it limited their size and membership. It ordered almost all adult white men to muster for the militia with no property requirements but restricted participation in the homme de couleur libre companies to under three hundred men, all of whom were required to be creoles, taxpayers, and the "owners, or sons of owners, of real estate worth at least three hundred dollars."[26]

As Justice Buchanan would note four decades later, hommes de couleur libre were indeed denied "political rights" and "the obligations of jury and militia service"; that is, they were excluded from exercising the formal aspects of political citizenship. Yet in many other respects, as "inhabitants of the ceded territory," they enjoyed most of the "rights, advantages, and immunities of citizens." They could possess property, make contracts, testify in all types of cases, even against whites, and enjoy the "right to trial by jury before the ordinary tribunal," in stark contrast to free people of African descent elsewhere in the South, as well as to slaves.[27] The civil code defined "freemen" as those "who have the right of doing whatever is not forbidden by law," while a slave was "one who is in the power of the master to whom he belongs. . . . [H]e can do nothing, possess nothing, nor acquire anything but what must belong to his master." Slaves were the objects of contracts, not legal parties to them; they could not possess, inherit, or distribute property; they could not testify in any civil case nor in most criminal ones; and, when on trial themselves, they were judged by special tribunals under which, in the opinion of Justice Buchanan, "the safeguards of the common law are unknown."[28] Politically and legally, gens de couleur libre did indeed occupy a position between slaves and whites.

Gens de couleur libre frequently defended challenges to their legal rights, and

the Louisiana Supreme Court consistently preserved these rights during the antebellum period. In an 1850 case upholding their right to testify against whites, Justice George Rogers King defended Louisiana's gens de couleur libre against the
charge that "free persons of color are incompetent to testify in cases in which
the rights of white persons are concerned" because "of the degraded condition
of the African in States where slavery exists." In Louisiana, he wrote, "Free persons
of color constituted a numerous class. In some districts they are respectable from
their intelligence, industry and habits of good order. Many of them are enlightened
by education, and the instances are by no means rare in which they are large property holders. So far from being in that degraded state which renders them unworthy of belief, they are such persons as courts and juries would not hesitate to believe
under oath." Although "certain classes of people are deemed incompetent to testify," he continued, the legislature's failure to include gens de couleur libre among
those classes was "recognition that they are *prima facie* worthy of credit, and that
their testimony may be safely received and weighed by courts and juries." More
importantly, King noted that without the right to testify against whites, "the gravest offences against their persons and property might be committed with impunity,
by white persons," and thus, "this numerous class is entitled to the protection of
our laws."[29]

Notwithstanding judicial affirmation of these important rights, throughout the
first half of the nineteenth century, the territorial and state legislatures as well as
the New Orleans' city council did systematically work to circumscribe the rights
of gens de couleur libre and to degrade their legal status.[30] Beginning with the 1806
Act Relative to Negroes and Other Slaves, the legislature distinguished between
gens de couleur libre and whites and increasingly aligned the former with slaves by
subjecting them to the same criminal statutes and punishments until, in 1855, it
passed a new black code whose very title—An Act Relative to Slaves and Free Colored Persons—equated the two classes.[31] The state's criminal laws distinguished
clearly between slaves and free persons but were more ambiguous in discriminating
between free whites and free people of color. Some crimes were defined as racially
specific. Rape, for instance, was a capital crime regardless of the status or race of
the perpetrator but only when perpetrated "on the body of any white woman or
girl." Other crimes resulted in different punishments depending on the race of the
perpetrator; gens de couleur libre received higher fines or longer prison sentences,
for example, than whites. Some punishments, especially whippings, were routinely
ordained for slaves, but not for free persons, whether white or of color, who were
more likely to be fined or imprisoned, although free persons were not exempt from

corporal punishments, and it was not until 1827 that whites were no longer subject to punishments of public shame.[32]

It is clear, however, that, in practice, physical chastisement became perceived as appropriate punishment for people of color alone. In the 1840s, the Louisiana Supreme Court heard two cases in which white men protested their physical mistreatment as unsuitable given their race. Both cases involved white slaveowners who whipped the victims for trespassing on their plantation and causing disorder among their slaves. In one case, the court recognized that slaveowners had a right to suppress any attempt to "excite [their] slaves to insubordination" but decreed that "whatever may be the character of a white person," that right did not extend to chastising such a person "in the manner in which they punish their slaves." In the other case, in which the slaveowner had his slave driver inflict "several blows with a heavy lash" on the trespasser, the court denounced the victim's assault as "the most ignominious to which a free man can be subjected."[33] These two cases pointed up the tension between slaveowners' desire for control over their slaves and white men's right not to be punished like slaves. Although both issues were central to the law's concern for racial order, the courts' rulings upheld the inviolability of whiteness to the detriment of slaveowners' authority.[34]

While Euro-Louisianans were increasingly protected from physical chastisement, whether judicially or informally enacted, slaves and gens de couleur libre were admonished "never to insult or strike white people." Slaves faced execution for assaulting their owners and could lose a limb for violence against "any white person." White violence against slaves was a different matter. Although whites, including owners, could be charged with "willfully killing" a slave and fined for "inflicting any cruel punishment," there were so many exceptions and circumstances under which white violence against slaves would be excused as to make the law almost meaningless.[35]

Both slaves and gens de couleur libre were required to subordinate themselves to whites. Gens de couleur libre in particular were admonished not to "presume to conceive themselves equal to the white" and "to yield to them in every occasion, and speak or answer to them but with respect." The conseil de ville, citing "the insolence" of mulâtres who "challenge whites to a duel," also tried to prohibit gens de couleur libre from taking fencing lessons. These laws to enforce deference toward whites were not only instruments of control over gens de couleur libre but also underwrote a racial hierarchy that placed all people of color beneath whites, regardless of other social attributes such as freedom, wealth, class, or education.[36]

Legislatures and councilmen did their best to create a "line of distinction . . .

between the several classes of this community."[37] They were particularly concerned that the presence of so many gens de couleur libre in New Orleans enabled slaves to pass as free. Fearing that slaves could easily "declare themselves free," the legislature required gens de couleur libre to carry proof of their freedom in certain circumstances. Similarly, slaves who sought to move about the city to hire themselves out were required to wear metal badges with their owners' names. Despite fears of permeable boundaries, native New Orleanian gens de couleur libre in general were not required to register their freedom until the 1840s, nor does it appear that these laws were regularly or effectively enforced in New Orleans.[38]

Legislating racial labeling was one more way in which authorities in Anglo-Louisiana tried to draw a firm boundary around gens de couleur libre and prevent them from passing, at least in legal documents, as white. Following Spanish practice, they decreed that their births and deaths were to be registered in separate books. But, in contrast to Spanish practice, they declared at the same time that they were uninterested in registering slave births or deaths. In addition, any personne de couleur libre was to be clearly identified as a "free man/woman of colour" whenever mentioned in legal documents. In the Spanish era, such marking was not a legal requirement, although it was common practice; now, however, if notaries and other clerks failed to properly mark gens de couleur libre with racial labels, they could be charged with a crime that carried a 100-dollar fine.[39]

The Anglo-American response to permeable boundaries may have been to equate African ancestry with enslavement, but this was difficult to do when between one-fifth and one-third of the city's population was both of African descent and free. When Anglo-American John Latrobe expressed his frustration at being unable to distinguish quadroons from French creoles, he dismissed the former as "negroes nothing more or less."[40] Many Anglo-Americans probably echoed Latrobe's sentiments; the territorial court, however, decided that there was a significant difference between quadroons and other sang-mêlé, on the one hand, and negroes, on the other, when it ruled in 1810 that the former should be presumed free.

The case arose in 1809 when Adéle Auger sued Frederick Beaurocher, claiming that he "pretends that your petitioner is his slave." Auger declared that she was a free woman of color, "born of a free family" in Guadeloupe. After her mother's death, then eleven-year-old Auger and her sister were taken in by Beaurocher, their mother's brother, and sent to boarding school in New York. A few years later, Auger moved to New Orleans at her uncle's request. Shortly after that she filed her petition asserting that her uncle was trying to sell her. Despite her inability to produce a written document or witnesses who could certify her freedom, Judge Louis

Moreau-Lislet ruled that, as a "person of colour" rather than a "negro," Auger should be presumed free. "Persons of colour," he continued, "may have descended from Indians on both sides, from a white parent, or mulatto parents in possession of their freedom. Considering how much probability there is in favor of the liberty of those persons, they ought not to be deprived of it upon mere presumption." Conversely, this presumption of freedom was not valid for "negroes." Reasoning that since "negroes [were] brought to this country generally being slaves, their descendants may perhaps fairly be presumed to have continued so, till they can show the contrary." Negroes who claimed to be free "would be required to establish [their] right [to freedom] by such evidence, as would destroy the force of presumption arising from colour."[41]

The presumption of freedom established by *Adéle v. Beauregard,* as the case mistakenly became known, starkly contrasts to how burden of proof was determined in the influential Virginia case of *Hudgins v. Wrights* decided just four years earlier (a case that one legal historian has called "probably the most influential Southern precedent in setting the presumption for slave/free status on the basis of race").[42] In *Hudgins,* several slaves successfully sued for freedom on the basis that they were descended through the maternal line from an Indian woman who had been illegally held in slavery. Much of the case revolved around whether or not the plaintiffs were visibly African, Indian, or European. Their lawyer argued they were "persons perfectly white," and the judges generally agreed. Opining that "nature has stampt upon the African and his descendants two characteristics, besides the mark of complexion, which often remain visible long after the characteristic of colour either disappears or becomes doubtful; a flat nose and woolly head of hair," Judge St. George Tucker ruled that only those who were "evidently white," "with a fair complexion, brown hair, not woolly nor inclining thereto," or "a copper-coloured person with long jetty black, straight hair" could, on visual characteristics alone, prove they had been falsely held in slavery. Judge Spencer Roane concurred that only "in the case of a person visibly appearing to be a white man, or an Indian" was "the presumption . . . that he is free, and it is necessary for his adversary to shew that he is a slave." Yet even in those cases, Roane implied that, with proper documentation, a putative owner could prove that such a person was truly a slave if she or he had some maternal African ancestry.[43] As outlined by the *Hudgins* opinion, anyone of identifiable African ancestry, however remote, was to be presumed a slave. This holding is the opposite of Moreau-Lislet's ruling in *Adéle* that, unless the person claiming false imprisonment appeared to have purely African ancestry, the burden to prove legal enslavement was on the putative owner.

Adéle influenced subsequent judicial and legislative decisions throughout the first half of the nineteenth century. Two years after *Adéle* was decided, the Louisiana Supreme Court upheld the testimony of one gen de couleur libre because "being [a woman] of colour, the presumption is that she was born free," and thus prohibitions against slaves giving testimony did not apply to her. In 1816, a negro named Jeffries Nash was able to overcome "the presumption which arises from [his] *color*" by proving that he had been purchased in a state where slavery was not lawful. Eleven years later, the legislature emancipated a slave woman in part because "her colour render[ed it] doubtful whether she is a slave or not."[44]

The decision in *Adéle v. Beauregard* privileged those of mixed ancestry by relieving them from the burden of establishing their own freedom, a burden the legislature had tried to place on them by requiring registration or freedom papers. The 1791 New Orleans census (the last to distinguish between sang-mêlé and negros among both the free and enslaved populations) demonstrates that there was a demographic basis for this presumption of freedom based on mixed ancestry. Out of almost 900 people identified as sang-mêlé, nearly 600 were free, while only 268 of those identified as negro were free out of a total negro population of 1,872. Put another way, while only one of every seven people identified as a negro was free, two of every three of those described as sang-mêlé were free.[45]

Limiting the Avenues to Freedom

At the same time that the legislature tried to circumscribe the legal status of gens de couleur libre, it also sought to limit their increasing numbers. Unable to stem natural increase, politicians focused on restricting the numbers of gens de couleur libre who migrated into Louisiana and on reducing the numbers of manumissions within the territory. Like Adéle Auger, many gens de couleur libre who arrived in New Orleans in the 1800s and 1810s originated in the French Caribbean, and their arrival continued to arouse concern among city officials. In one of the earliest sessions of conseil de ville, the new city council, members expressed apprehension over the abuses and dangers to "Public safety" that could occur if "colored people of all kinds and from all countries" were admitted into Louisiana. They sought a ban on all "black or colored persons" from entering "into this province under pretext of being servants or any other reason," allowing exceptions only for those "negroes decidedly recognized as uncivilized" who arrived directly from Africa and were uncontaminated by revolutionary ideologies emanating from the Caribbean.[46] In April 1804, the conseil received the governor's permission to inspect all incoming ships in order to prevent "the illicit entrance of negroes and colored people, coming from the Antilles, and particularly from San Domingo."[47]

In an attempt "to prevent the introduction of Free People of Colour," the legislature had passed an act in 1806 that required gens de couleur from Saint-Domingue to prove that they were free. The following year, it declared that "no free negro or mulatto shall emigrate or settle in this territory," but not long after, three thousand Saint-Domingue refugees were allowed to emigrate despite the law. Other violators were rarely prosecuted, leading the legislature to pass a new act in 1830 that declared that "all free negroes, mulattoes, or other free persons of colour" who had arrived in the state after January 1, 1825, were to be deported, while "free negroes, griffs, and mulattoes of the first degree" who had arrived between 1812 and 1825 were required to prove when they had first entered the state and to register with the parish judge.

Furthermore, native gens de couleur libre lost their entitlement to legal residence and were prohibited from returning to Louisiana if they traveled outside the United States, a proscription that especially targeted better-off gens de couleur libre, who went to France for education. A year later, in 1831, most likely in response to complaints from those gens de couleur libre, the legislature exempted "free negroes, mulattoes, or other persons of color" who were lawful residents of Louisiana, property owners, or permanent residents who "exercise a useful trade, and have always conducted themselves in an orderly and respectful manner" from the exclusion act. Such residents were then free to leave the country, "as their business may require," but they could not return to Louisiana if they visited the West Indies. Despite these restrictions on their mobility, free people of African ancestry continued to migrate into the state from elsewhere in the United States as, a decade later, the legislature passed yet another ban, this time entitled An Act to More Effectively Prevent Free Persons of Color from Entering into This State.[48]

In the 1830 and 1831 acts, the legislature also sought to restrict manumission under the same heading of "Prevent[ing] Free Persons of Color from Entering into This State," demonstrating that both immigration bans and manumission restrictions were efforts to limit the growth of the gens de couleur libre population. Unlike its attempts to restrict immigration, the legislature was far more successful in systematically restricting slaves' access to legal freedom, beginning with the 1807 Act to Regulate the Conditions and Forms of the Emancipation of Slaves and culminating in 1857 with An Act to Prohibit the Emancipation of Slaves.

These efforts began by attacking one of the most important Spanish contributions to the city's racial order. The very first article of the 1807 act declared that "no person shall be compelled, either directly or indirectly, to emancipate his or her slave or slaves," thus nullifying the most important provision of coartación. Slaves could still purchase their own freedom, but only if their owner consented. The 1807 act also limited manumission to slaves who were at least thirty years old and who had carried themselves with "an honest conduct" for the previous four years. Exceptions could be made for slaves who had "saved the life of their master, his wife, or any of his children." Further, the act required that all manumissions include "the tacit but formal obligation on the part of the donor, to nourish and maintain" manumitted slaves in cases of "sickness, old age, insanity, or other proved infirmity," thus preventing owners from using manumission to rid themselves of the burden of caring for elderly or sickly slaves, a policy that had been a part of both the French Code Noir of 1724 and the Spanish Código Negro of 1789.[49]

Finally, the legislature more formally systematized manumission procedures. Whereas during the Spanish era an owner could free slaves by notarial act, baptism, or testament, after September 1807, he had to first appear before a parish judge to declare his intention to manumit his slave. The slave's name and age then had to be posted; after forty days, the owner had to return to the courthouse where, on certification by a court official that no opposition had been made, the judge could authorize the manumission. Only then could the owner appear before a notary, who would draw up an act manumitting the slave or slaves named in the judge's authorization. Both owners and notaries were threatened with a 100-dollar fine if they attempted to pass a manumission act without following these procedures.[50]

Twenty years later the 1827 legislature declared that only slaves born in Louisiana could be manumitted, thus excluding the vast number of slaves who had arrived in the state via the internal slave trade. At the same time, however, it amended its earlier restriction on manumitting slaves under thirty by allowing owners to petition their local police juries, which were authorized to determine if the owners' "motives are sufficient to allow the said emancipation." In 1830, the legislature required emancipated slaves to leave the state and owners to post a 1,000-dollar bond to guarantee their departure; in 1852, it condemned emancipated slaves to a life in exile in Liberia and required owners to pay 150 dollars for their transportation. Ex-slaves who failed to emigrate or who later returned to the state would "forfeit their freedom and become slaves and revert to their former owners." Finally, in 1857, the legislature categorically decreed "no slave shall be emancipated in this State."[51]

The restriction and elimination of manumission was neither a constant progression nor consistently enforced. The legislature at times backtracked from making it more difficult for slaves to gain their freedom, granting exemptions to earlier laws. Just one year after requiring manumitted slaves to leave the state, parish juries were given the power to allow slaves who had been manumitted "for long, faithful or important service" to remain in Louisiana.[52] Similarly, three years after mandating exile to Liberia, the legislature allowed owners to include requests in their petitions for manumitted slaves to remain in the state.[53]

The legislature was also receptive to passing individual acts of emancipation that exempted slaves from age and exile requirements. Between 1823 and 1827, it passed a total of seventy-four such acts, and in a single month in 1853, it passed nine acts manumitting twenty slaves who were allowed "to remain in this State, all the laws to the contrary notwithstanding."[54] Burdened by such appeals, the legislature delegated authority to make exceptions to the local courts in 1827 and in 1855, which granted almost all the petitions they heard.[55] The willingness of the legislature and the courts to undermine legislative intent regarding manumission demonstrates that the codification of the tripartite racial order was not a smooth one. On the one hand, access to freedom did become increasingly restricted in Anglo-Louisiana, especially after 1827; on the other, it is clear that Euro-Louisianans—as property owners, judges, and as members of juries and legislatures—continually sought to make exceptions to the restrictions on traditional grounds.

Even with these exceptions, restrictive legislation had an immediate impact on the number and types of manumissions passed, as is apparent in the years surrounding passage of the March 1807 act and its enactment in September of that year. In the three years following the Louisiana Purchase, about sixty slaves (half of whom were under thirty) were freed annually in Orleans Parish, roughly the same rate as during the final years of Spanish Louisiana.[56] Only twenty-three slaves were manumitted in 1808, and the annual numbers subsequently fluctuated from a low of sixteen manumissions in 1816 to a high of seventy-three in 1818, the only year in which manumissions exceeded the pre-1807 average. Unsurprisingly, given the act's age restriction, just fifty-six slaves under thirty were manumitted between 1808 and 1820, far fewer than the almost one hundred who were manumitted in the three years before 1807 and even fewer than the seventy-six manumitted in 1807 alone.

Manumissions during the year the act was passed further illustrate the impact of Anglo-Louisiana's restrictive policy toward emancipation. A total of 117 slaves were manumitted in 1807, almost twice as many as in previous years. Before March 9, when the act was passed, slaves were freed at about the same rate as in the previous three years. Between the passage of the act and the day it became law on September 1, slaves were manumitted at more than three times the previous rate and two-thirds of them were under thirty, as slaves and their owners clearly acted to beat the deadline. And in the four months following September 1, only three slaves were manumitted, one of whom was under thirty.

Some would-be manumitters found ways around the new restrictions after September 1807. One month after the new act went into effect, Narcisse Broutin recorded an act for a fellow notary, the Irish-born John Lynd, who claimed that he had purchased the freedom of a one-year-old quadroon two months earlier, thus before the law was implemented. A classic scenario that suggests paternal involvement, professional connections probably enabled Lynd to convince Broutin to issue the carta without following the new formalities and restrictions.[57] The following year, négresse libre Marie Louise Conway purchased the freedom of her daughter from William Conway for 1,000 piastres. The act recording this coartación makes no mention that either party had received permission to manumit the ten-year-old, but perhaps the fact that Conway was a representative in the territorial legislature led the notary to forget to ask.[58]

For those without connections or political standing, subterfuge was a more common approach. Manumitters could declare their slaves older than they were, but that only worked for slaves who were at least in their twenties. When Sebastien Ferrer promised his mulâtresse Catherine her freedom in his will, she was described as about twenty, but the following year, when Ferrer's testamentary executor freed her, she was described as thirty.[59] Francisco Delille Dupard freed four mulatico children in 1808, ranging from between eight and seventeen years old, by swearing to the notary he had actually freed them privately in 1801. Immediately after making this declaration, he freed their mother, negra María Nard.[60] Another ploy was to involve priests, both knowingly and unknowingly, in the deception by persuading them to baptize infant slaves as free. Before 1807, when manumission at baptism was legal, just over one-quarter of manumitted slaves under thirty were freed this way, but after 1807, it jumped to almost one-half. Portuguese-born Manuel Danse appeared before Father Antonio de Sedella in October 1808 to have his seventeen-day-old son Manuel baptized. Although Manuel's mother was Danse's negra slave María, Manuel was marked as a mulato libre. Over the next couple of years, Sedella and his colleague C. Thomas baptized several other children as free, noting that they had received either a verbal or written declaration of freedom from the mother's owner.[61] François Mato's evasion of Louisiana law to manumit his namesake and probable son, François, a six-year-old mulâtre, was among the most convoluted. First, he sold François to Gaspar Borras for 300 piastres. A week later, Borras manumitted the boy in Pensacola, which was still under Spanish rule, before returning François to Mato, who registered him as free before a New Orleans notary.[62]

Some slaves were merely declared free, perhaps in the hope that no one would check for a formal manumission act, although this left them in a precarious position if they were ever challenged. Other owners simply renounced ownership in a certain slave, perhaps hoping that act did not technically qualify as manumission. Jacques Desvignes and Pierre Eliot Lamaignère engaged in both of these strategies in a single sale in 1816, when Desvignes sold Hélène, a twenty-two-year-old mulâtresse, to Lamaignère for 1,000 piastres. Desvignes then declared that Hélène's two quarteron children, four-and-a-half-year-old Marguerite and two-and-a-half-year-old Agalie, were free and therefore not part of the sale, despite the fact that they had been born after 1807 to an enslaved mother. To further stress their liberty, Lamaignère renounced any ownership in the two children.[63] As with gens de couleur libre who purchased their slave relatives but could not free them because of legislative requirements, it is possible that regardless of their ability to prove their status as free, Marguerite and Agalie grew up being treated as such.

Several other sales of young slaves that occurred after September 1807 included explicit promises by the buyers to free the slaves as soon as they attained legal age and to treat them well before then. Dominique Dussac promised to free two-year-old mulâtresse Justine Marie as soon as legally possible when he purchased her for 150 piastres from femme de couleur libre Magdeleine Carpentier. He also agreed to let the child remain with her mother, Fanny, until she was ten years old and to treat her as if she were already free.[64] When Joseph Rey sold two young slaves to their mother, Cerine, described as a négresse or griffon libre, she obligated herself to treat them as a good mother would and "to consider them as free until the moment of their legal enfranchisement" as they were "the natural children of the purchaser." A few days earlier, Rey had purchased a two-and-a-half-year-old cuarteróna with the promise to free her. In the margin, where notaries classified acts, these sales were described as a "slave sale, but conditional," suggesting that such transactions had become routine enough for notaries to treat them as a separate category.[65]

The Louisiana Supreme Court ruled these promises of freedom were legally binding in a remarkable case from 1855. A couple of decades earlier, M. C. Hardesty had purchased Sukey Wormley and her child Adeline. At the sale, he stipulated that he would manumit them when Wormley repaid him their purchase price. In 1834, he successfully petitioned the St. Tammany Police Jury for permission to free them, noting that Wormley had already repaid half the price. Wormley continued to live with Hardesty until his death in 1853. After Hardesty's death, his heirs tried to claim Wormley as their slave, claiming that her emancipation was a disguised donation to a concubine. In an opinion striking for its sympathy to a woman of color, Chief Justice Thomas Slidell ruled that evidence presented at trial had not proved concubinage and that even if it had, this would not have "discharged [the master] . . . from the fulfillment of his promise of emancipation." Having promised to free Wormley when he purchased her, Hardesty was "legally bound to fulfill the obligation" regardless of their prior or subsequent relationship. Slidell praised Wormley for her "unusual industry, economy, and good character" in "laboring day and night for the purpose of purchasing her offspring" while condemning Hardesty's heirs, calling their lawsuit "a monstrous injustice" and "a cruel experiment upon the liberty and hard earnings of an humble and deserving woman."[66]

Many owners did go through legal channels and petitioned the courts or the legislature to request an exemption. In March 1820, the Orleans Parish sheriff, George W. Morgan, petitioned the legislature on behalf of the deceased George Moreau, who had set aside 500 dollars to be invested until it was sufficient to purchase the freedom of Catherine Moreau. Passing An Act for the Relief of Catherine Moreau the legislature authorized "Morgan to emancipate the said Catherine Moreau . . . even if she has not attained the age of thirty years, any law to the contrary notwithstanding." Six years later, Julia Avart, owner of Catherine's young son, Theodule, petitioned to emancipate him despite his age. Again the legislature authorized the act and further directed Avart to take control of the original 500 dollars and any accrued interest to use "for the best interests of the said Theodule" until he reached the age of majority, when she was to give him all remaining sums.[67] In addition to Theodule, the legislature authorized the emancipation of thirty-six other underage slaves in February and March 1826, more than half of whom were manumitted by their free relatives, often their parents or grandparents.[68] That gens de couleur libre sought to free their relatives who were not yet thirty should not be surprising; that the legislature fulfilled these desires is somewhat more so.

Slaves under thirty and forced coartaciòns were the two main targets of the 1807 legislative restrictions on manumission. Just as the number of young slaves manumitted dropped dramatically after 1807, the number of coartaciòns also fell, although less precipitously. This suggests that during the late Spanish and early Anglo periods, at least some owners were receptive to coartaciòn only because the courts could force them to free their slaves for a price. Once they could no longer be forced to do so, they became less willing. One-third of manumissions before 1807 involved some form of payment, but between 1808 and 1820 less than one-quarter did. 1807 was once again exceptional: more than one-half of all manumissions that year involved payment, as family members—white, gen de couleur libre, and enslaved alike—tried to free their kin, two-thirds of them under thirty.[69] Although a few Euro-Louisianans used these manumission acts to formally recognize their children, far more white men manumitted mothers and children without explicitly acknowledging their ties to them, as they had done during the Spanish period.[70]

Slaves continued to use the courts when promised manumissions did not materialize, but they found them far less friendly than Spanish ones had been. Before 1807, at least one coartación agreement was upheld against an owner's wishes by the Superior Court, which ordered the manumission of nègre Paul upon his payment of 450 piastres.[71] Once the legislature decreed that an owner's consent was required, the courts could have, but did not, dismiss coartación suits out of hand, yet they did make success more difficult. Prince Matthews's coartación was upheld by the Louisiana Supreme Court in 1843 against Michael Boland, his resistant owner, but only because he had a notarized act in which Boland acknowledged having "received, at sundry times . . . six hundred and fifty dollars, in full for his purchase." The court ruled, however, that Matthews was not "entitled to an absolute and unconditional decree for his freedom" and required him to undergo the usual formalities, emphasizing in particular his need to prove his good conduct and character.[72] Others were less successful. In 1816, Victoire sued her owner Dussuau, claiming that he had "agreed to emancipate her on condition of obtaining the reimbursement of [her] price." After the parish court ruled against her, Victoire appealed to the state supreme court, which upheld Victoire's right "to maintain an action for her emancipation and freedom," asserting that, as a legacy of Spanish law, slaves were "incapable of making any contract for themselves, *except* for their freedom." But where Spanish law had allowed for oral testimony as evidence of such contracts, the court decreed that Anglo-Louisiana's civil code required all contracts involving the disposal of property to be written. As Victoire offered no written evidence of her contract with Dussuau, she lost her suit for freedom.[73] The following year, negro Marie Cuffy was able to produce a written contract and yet still lost her case. In this three-generation coartación case spanning over thirty years, Marie Cuffy's claim to have paid in full the agreed freedom price was ignored by the Louisiana Supreme Court. Justice George Mathews Jr., who had written the opinion in Victoire's case, again upheld coartación in principle but ruled that an owner could not "be compelled to free [a slave] after he has received a partial payment only." Marie and her family were left in slavery.[74]

Victoire, Marie Cuffy, and other slaves were often thwarted when they sought manumission through the courts, but gens de couleur tended to be more successful when they, like Adéle Auger, claimed that they were being illegally held in slavery in the first place. Native-born gens de couleur libre could rely on local knowledge to demonstrate their liberty if challenged, so most of the cases that reached the superior or supreme courts involved immigrant gens de couleur. Negro Betsey Seves, born in New Jersey, accompanied her godmother to Nova Scotia at the end of the Revolutionary War. Becoming a lady's maid, she traveled with a variety of employers to Jamaica, Saint-Domingue, and Cuba, where she was hired by Marianne Delongy's mother, a free woman of color. In 1809, Delogny brought Seves to New Orleans, and since then, according to Seves, Delogny "hath pretended and given out that your petitioner was her slave." When Delogny tried to sell Seves and her nine-year-old mulatto daughter to Jean Mayat, Seves sued both putative owners, seeking 1,000 dollars in "damages for the injury she has sustained in being . . . fraudulently . . . deprived of her liberty." Supported by a white man who testified that he knew her mother as free in New Jersey, Seves successfully gained freedom for herself and her daughter, but she received only 24 dollars "for her unlawful detention in slavery."[75]

Adelaide Metayer, a mulâtresse immigrant, also won her freedom in a series of cases that dragged on from 1810 to 1819. Born in Saint-Domingue, Adelaide claimed to have bought her freedom for 325 dollars from her owner, Charles Metayer, in 1801. Whether or not she was legally free, she moved without her owner to St. Yago, Cuba, in 1803 and then to New Orleans in 1809. In 1810, Louis Noret seized her and her two children "under a false pretence" that she was "a slave." She petitioned Judge Moreau-Lislet, who ordered her released. In 1816, Noret acted to seize her again, this time having been deputized by Jean Pierre Metayer, the son of Adelaide's former owner. By this time, Adelaide and Noret were, according to Adelaide, "living in concubinage," and she accused Noret of "fraudulently obtaining her confidence and under the pretence of friendship and safekeeping" taking the receipt that proved she had purchased her freedom in 1801. She sued Noret, and after a brief deliberation, the jury returned a favorable verdict, although it declined to award her the 600 dollars in damages she sought.

Ruling on Noret's appeal, Justice (and future governor) Pierre Dérbigny narrowed the case to a single issue: Adelaide's "enjoyment of her freedom during a number of years." If Adelaide had enjoyed her freedom—if her owner had made no claim on her as a slave—for at least twenty years, she would be free, according to Dérbigny's reading of Spanish precedents. Pointing to Adelaide's 1803 move to St. Yago as signaling the beginning of her freedom, Judge Dérbigny thus ruled that she had enjoyed her freedom for five years short of the required twenty years. Adelaide immediately filed suit again, this time against Jean Pierre Metayer, now claiming that she had been freed by the declaration of general emancipation in Saint-Domingue in August 1793. When Judge James Pitot of the parish court ruled in her favor, Metayer appealed, and Dérbigny once again heard the case. This time he agreed with Adelaide that she had effectively enjoyed her freedom from 1793 to 1816, when Metayer first tried to reclaim her, and ruled that she should indeed be free by prescription.[76]

Despite the courts' commitment to upholding Spanish precedents where they had not been directly countermanded by legislative actions, the tide had clearly turned against slaves seeking legal freedom. Nonetheless, the presumption of freedom for those of perceived mixed ancestry, as decreed in the *Adéle* decision, made it somewhat easier for sang-mêlé, especially when they claimed unlawful enslavement rather than a desire to free themselves from slavery. Petitioners also tended to be successful when their claims were supported by sympathetic white witnesses, such as the man who testified he had known Betsy Seves's mother in New Jersey. Although gens de couleur libre owners appear to have been overrepresented in those cases that reached the state's higher courts, slaves were not always successful when their owner was a person of color, nor did they always fail to win their freedom when their owners were white. But, unlike Spanish judges, who could be fairly reliably counted on to rule in favor of slaves seeking freedom, Anglo-Louisiana judges were not so consistent.

Nor did legislators act consistently in regard to manumission; on the one hand, they enacted more stringent laws limiting access to legal freedom but, on the other, they granted almost every request for extraordinary emancipation of an underage slave or permission for a freed slave to remain in the state.[77] Exceptions notwithstanding, freedom did become increasingly difficult to acquire after the Louisiana Purchase. However, Anglo-Americanization of New Orleans' racial order was neither smooth nor hegemonic. Slaves and gens de couleur libre continued to fight for freedom and to protect what rights they had, and they continued to find, albeit far less often, jurymen, judges, and legislators sympathetic to their causes.

Unnatural Alliances

By severely restricting the ability of slaves to become free, authorities in Anglo-Louisiana took great strides toward rigidifying New Orleans' racial order. This same rigidity guided their efforts to undermine the formation of interracial families. In 1808, the legislature banned marriages between "free white persons" and "free people of colour" as well as those between "free persons and slaves." Identifying three groups defined by race and status, the act required members of those groups—free whites, free people of color, and slaves—to marry endogamously, thus attempting to perpetuate the separate and segregated existence of each group. At the same time that the legislature declared exogamous marriages void, however, it failed to specify criminal or fiscal penalties, and nonmarital sex went unmentioned.[78] As usual, legislation did not describe social practice, and a few marriages were performed after 1803.[79]

Mulata libre Sofi Esteves and blanco Lazare Balthasar Latill married in 1829, having already spent three and a half decades together. Esteves was the half sister of Clara Lopez de La Peña, whose story was told in chapter 6. Despite sharing the same mother, through whom Lopez claimed Indian rather than African ancestry, Esteves was never marked as a mestiza. Like Lopez, however, eventually Esteves passed through the documentary records unmarked by a racial label. Esteves had her first child in 1789 with blanco Alexo Lesassier, who recognized his daughter Sofia, noted as a mulata libre, at her baptism. Three years later at the baptism of their second daughter, neither mother nor daughter were labeled, and the entry was recorded in the book of blancos.

Shortly thereafter Esteves began her relationship with Latill. Their first child was born in 1793, and Latill appeared at the baptism of each of their four children, all of whom were recorded in the white registry. When their six-day-old daughter died, however, her funeral was recorded in the book of libres and slaves; only her mother was named, and, instead of Latill, she was given the surname of Brunet, her maternal grandmother's occasional surname. Like Lopez, Esteves usually had her mother noted as Luison Mandeville, a far more prominent surname in New Orleans than Brunet or Brouner.

Neither of Esteves's partners could have been ignorant of her ancestry. Lesassier had testified on Lopez's behalf in her suit to reclassify her daughter's racial identity, and Latill certainly knew Esteves's mother, who served as godmother to their oldest child. Nor had Latill been cut off from his family because of his relationship with Esteves, as his mother was godmother to another of their children. Within just this single family, at least six individuals whose ancestries should have labeled them as mulata (Esteves) or quarterons (her children) were entered into the sacramental records unmarked by race, and four of the children (including the only one who had been identified as a mulata at birth) went on to acquire spouses who were similarly unmarked, entering into marriages that were recorded in the white registries.[80]

Between 1821 and 1830, Father Antonio Sedella and his fellow priests mistakenly recorded four marriages between gens de couleur libre, including one of Jacqueline Lemelle's granddaughters in 1817, in the white registry, where the spouses appeared unmarked by a racial label. A fifth may have been a racially exogamous marriage as, in the amended entry, the groom was not raced whereas the bride was noted as a "femme de couleur libre." Three of the couples were natives of New Orleans and

Sedella, who had presided over Orleans Parish for several decades, should have known their genealogies; the other two marriages involved immigrants from Saint-Domingue and Cuba. When rectifying these errors, Sedella usually noted that the record properly belonged in the registry "for only gente de color" because "the two parties are both of color."[81] He uncovered another mistake after marrying Pedro Dupre and María Theresa Journe in 1826. They must have told Sedella that they had had a son baptized in 1811, and when he went to note that the son was legitimated by the subsequent marriage of his parents, he discovered that the baptism was in the gente de color registry, where son and parents were all marked with racial labels. He duly noted the now legitimated status of the son and added his usual comment to the parents' marriage entry.[82] One of the reasons behind keeping separate registries for blancs and gente de color was to prevent unsuspecting whites from marrying someone with nonwhite ancestry, and Sedella seems to have taken his role in policing the racial identities of marriage partners and baptized infants very seriously.[83] But, illustrating the fallibility of the recording priests, and thus of the registries, he failed to catch the fact that Esteves was unraced and that her marriage was recorded in the white registry. Almost certainly additional exogamous marriages are, in fact, recorded in the sacramental records, but without an intimate knowledge of the genealogies of the partners involved, they are difficult to find.

Other couples evaded Louisiana law by marrying in France, as Pierre Heno and femme de couleur libre Agathe Fanchon did in 1830. Like Esteves and Latill, the couple had been together for some time and already had several children before they decided to legalize their relationship. Heno had been born in New Orleans in 1770 to a French father and a French-Canadian mother. At eighteen, he married a fellow Franco-New Orleanian, sixteen-year-old Marguerite Tonnelier, the daughter of a master mason. They quickly began having children, and Heno set about supporting his family as a butcher.[84] In the early 1800s, however, Heno began a relationship with Fanchon. As is usually the case, Fanchon's history is harder to trace. She first appears in the sacramental records at the baptism of her son Pedro in 1808, although she had at least one child already. She was probably born in the early 1780s, making her a decade or so younger than Heno, and was, in all probability, born free. Although Pedro's father was not identified at his baptism, given their shared name (which was also the name of Heno's first-born son with Tonnelier), it is mostly likely that Heno was indeed Pedro's father. Heno had either not yet left Tonnelier by the time of Pedro's birth or he returned to her afterward, as their last child together was born in October 1813, four months after he appeared for the first time at the baptism of one of Fanchon's children, three-and-a-half-month-old Juan Andres, to declare his paternity and give the boy his surname.[85]

By the time Tonnelier died in 1818, Heno had, according to his legitimate children, "for a long time lived apart" from his wife. Following their mother's death, the three youngest children, aged from five to twenty, remained living in her house, supported by their eldest brother, Pierre Jr., and in 1820, Pierre Jr. and the younger children sued their father for alimony. Heno, however, denied that he had the means to support them in a separate household, and he insisted that they move into "the house where he resides" so he could "provide for them in the best manner which his scanty means will permit." The "house where he resides" in fact belonged to Fanchon, where, according to several witnesses at the trial, they "lived in open concubinage" with their children.

In upholding the First District Court's judgment for the children, the Louisiana Supreme Court denounced Pierre Heno for insisting that his legitimate white children live with him and his second family. As Justice François Xavier Martin declared, Heno's relationship with Fanchon was "certainly a good reason why the court should not compel his [eight-year-old] daughter, a white girl, to return to his house; neither can there by any propriety, though the reasons are not equally strong, in ordering the sons to return there, when it is shewn that their father made them associate and eat with the woman with whom he lives, and her children." Denying Heno's efforts to desegregate his two families, the court ordered him to pay at least 125 dollars per month toward his white children's support.[86] Fanchon and Heno continued living together and finally decided to marry when Heno was almost sixty and Fanchon about forty-five.[87] For a white butcher who had struggled with his finances in earlier years and a woman of color who, after March 1830, could be refused reentry into Louisiana, such a decision could not have been made lightly.

There was also no guarantee that a French marriage would be recognized in Louisiana, and in 1855 the Louisiana Supreme Court invalidated another marriage that had been performed in France twenty years earlier, taking the opportunity to denounce racially exogamous marriage as an "unnatural alliance." Praising the "wisdom" of the civil code in its ban on marriages between free white persons and persons of color, Justice Henry Spofford ruled "the Courts of Louisiana cannot give effect to these acts, without sanctioning an evasion of the laws and, setting at naught the deliberate policy of the State." With that, the court nullified the couple's marriage.[88]

A racially exogamous marriage was at issue in another Louisiana Supreme Court decision a few years later. Like Spofford, Chief Justice Edwin Thomas Merrick heartedly endorsed the state's ban, stating that it was "one eminently affecting the public order." Quoting the lower court judge, he declared that marriages "between persons of the two difference races" could not be permitted "to exist . . . for a moment." Cora Lalande and Raimond Domec had married in March 1847 at Annunciation Church in New Orleans. At the time, however, Domec, according to his later testimony, was unaware that his new bride was a woman of color. When he discovered "the mystery of her birth" in November 1855, he placed a notice in the New Orleans *Bee* announcing his separation from Lalande. She was, he declared "a colored woman" who had "no right whatever to assume the name of Madame Domec." As his notice makes clear, Domec was fully aware that racially exogamous marriage was "considered, in the eyes of the law, as having no existence."

A few years later, however, Lalande was awarded just over 1,000 dollars in a suit she had filed against the estate of Jean Michel Minvielle, and Domec reconsidered his earlier rejection of his wife. Approaching the estate's executor, he claimed that, as "head of the matrimonial community," he should receive the money from the judgment. When both the executor and Lalande refused to turn the money over to him, he sued. At trial, Lalande denied "that she is, or ever was the wife" of Domec, although she did acknowledge that they had lived together. When Domec produced the marriage certificate, Lalande countered by offering to prove that Domec was "a white man, and she a coloured woman," and that therefore, no legal marriage could have existed, introducing the *Bee* notice into evidence to support her contention. Witnesses testified that Lalande was "a woman of color, or what is generally called a mulatress" and that Domec was a Frenchman. In his handwritten opinion, Judge H. P. Morgan of the New Orleans Second District Court declared: "The celebration of such marriages is forbidden and the marriage is void." Morgan, or perhaps Merrick as he read the case files before writing the Louisiana Supreme Court's decision, underlined the entire passage to emphasize the point. With their marriage nullified, Domec's attempt to assert himself as the head of the marital community failed, and Lalande retained possession of the money.[89]

The Louisiana Supreme Court did not, however, nullify or denounce every interracial marriage that came before it. When Franco-creole François Bernoudy died in 1816, he left a will that included 5,000-dollar bequest to his daughter Adelaide Jung and her four children.[90] But Bernoudy also left forced heirs—his legitimate children from his marriage to Anna Dreux and their children—who refused to pay Jung her share of his estate, forcing Jung to sue Françoise Bernoudy, veuve Doriocourt.[91] The case turned on whether Jung, as Bernoudy's adulterous daughter and a woman of color, could inherit from her father. In its ruling, the court highlighted the double bind that offspring like Jung found themselves in during the antebellum era.[92] Adulterous children did "not enjoy the right of inheriting the estates of their natural father or mother" and were entitled to "nothing more than a mere alimony." But, in order to claim alimony, Jung would have had to prove that Bernoudy was her father, as he had never formally acknowledged her. Under the 1825 civil code, "illegitimate children, who have not been legally acknowledged" were permitted to prove their paternity but only if they were "free and white" or, for "free illegitimate children of colour, . . . from a father of color only."[93] Thus Jung could not—as an adulterine—inherit a share of Bernoudy's estate nor—as the nonwhite child of a white man—prove her paternity in order to claim alimony.[94]

One issue that was raised in this case of a contested testamentary bequest was Adelaide Jung's marriage to a Franco-New Orleanian. Two months before Bernoudy died, Jung, the daughter of a *mulata libre* and a *blanco*, married Joseph Le Blanc de Villanueva, a former military officer and city official. They already had four children together, born between 1792 and 1802.[95] At the trial, Doriocourt's lawyers claimed that Jung was "not, as is alleged, married to Villeneuve Leblanc," hoping to prove that she was not the same Adelaide Jung mentioned in Bernoudy's will. The court thus had the opportunity to interrogate the circumstances of her marriage, but it declined to do so, dismissing the question as "irrelevant." In addition to setting aside any investigation of Jung and Le Blanc's marriage, the court also failed to look into that of one of their daughters, who had married a French-born *blanc* in 1817. The judges' lack of interest in these two interracial marriages stands in contrast to their overriding concern with illegitimate children of color. "Cases of bastardy," Justice François Xavier Martin complained, were far too "frequent among us" and thus required the courts to strictly observe "the laws relative to illegitimate children, especially those of color."[96]

An Incapacity to Inherit

Disputes over property generated most of the cases about nonmarital relationships that reached the courts, which were far more numerous those disputing marriages. By denying their parents the right to marry, the legislature defined all children born from racially exogamous relationships after 1808 as illegitimate and, as a consequence, restricted their ability to inherit from their parents. Continuing Spanish-era practice, however, white men who formed families with women of color often made bequests to their consorts and children. Now, however, they faced new legal restrictions on just how much and what kind of property they could bequeath. Participants in extramarital relationships were strictly limited in what they could leave to each other. The civil code stated: "Those who have lived together in open concubinage are respectively incapable of making to each other . . . any donation of immoveables [including slaves]; and if they make a donation of movables, it cannot exceed one tenth part of the whole value of their estate."[97]

As for children of extramarital relationships, Anglo-Louisianan law, like Spanish law, distinguished among legitimate and "two sorts of illegitimate children." Children who were born outside of marriage but "from two persons, who, at the moment when the said children were conceived, might have been duly married together" could be legitimated by the subsequent marriage of their parents, which then granted them "the same rights as if they were born during marriage." Children whose parents could, but did not, marry could still be acknowledged by their parents at baptism or before a notary and thus be transformed from "bastards" into "natural children." But children who were "born from persons to whose marriage there existed at the time, some legal impediment" could not be later legitimated or acknowledged. In this, Anglo-Louisiana law went beyond Spanish precedents that had only mentioned canonical impediments; theoretically, children born of a racially exogamous relationship—to which there was a legal impediment—could not be acknowledged.

Yet, in defining children who could not be legitimated or acknowledged, the legislature specified only "adulterous and incestuous bastards" and in fact did allow white parents to acknowledge their nonwhite children. Despite its interests in preventing interracial family formation, then, the legislature allowed fathers to determine whether or not to acknowledge their children. It did, however, discriminate between white and nonwhite children who had "not been legally acknowledged" by their fathers, as Adelaide Jung learned to her detriment. Only "free and white" children were allowed to "prove their paternal descent" from a white father.[98] Constructed in this way, the civil code granted white fathers the power to voluntarily recognize their sang-mêlé children, but it did not allow such children to legally establish their white paternity against unwilling or deceased fathers.

Although most cases that reached the Louisiana Supreme Court involved transfers of property from white fathers to their nonwhite children, one of the earliest cases it heard on these matters was initiated by a white father who sought to prove his paternity of a cuarteróna libre in order to inherit her estate. In 1815, Philippe Pijeaux, a white man, sued Francis Duvernay, a free man of color, for possession of the estate of Marie Françoise dit Therese Pijeaux, who had died intestate. Pijeaux claimed that Marie Françoise was his natural daughter, and he produced a copy of her baptism certificate naming him as her father. But Duvernay, Marie Françoise's half brother, denied that Pijeaux was her father, arguing that he had not signed the baptismal register. Although Judge James Pitot acknowledged Pijeaux's failure to sign, he ruled in favor of the father, in part because Pijeaux claimed to be raising three other children, full siblings to Marie Françoise.[99]

Duvernay appealed the decision to the Louisiana Supreme Court, this time arguing that Pijeaux had failed to properly legally acknowledge Marie Françoise as his natural daughter, and the court agreed. The civil code allowed for two forms of paternal acknowledgment: a father could claim paternity while "registering . . . the birth or baptism of the child" or he could make "a declaration executed before a notary public, in presence of two witnesses." The court denied that Pijeaux's name in Maria Françoise's baptismal certificate qualified, since without his signature, "it does not appear to have been done with his consent or knowledge." The court ruled her estate should pass to Duvernay. The court went so far as to ask whether the child of "a white man and . . . a woman of colour . . . could be the object of a legal acknowledgement," but it sidestepped this problem in declaring that Pijeaux had never formally acknowledged his daughter.[100] Three decades later, in 1845, the court would acknowledge that "illegitimate children of color, not the offspring of an incestuous or adulterous connection," could indeed by legally acknowledged "by a white father." It reiterated the legality of acknowledgement in 1851, only to condemn "the parent [who] has been so lost to shame as to make an authentic act of his degradation" before reversing course in 1857, when it called such actions "offensive to morality" and "without any . . . effect in law."[101]

Another aspect of the codification of New Orleans' racial order was inheritance rights. The civil code strictly regulated the rights to inherit of duly recognized natural children, whether white or not. These rights greatly depended on the existence of "legal heirs" (lawful descendants, lawful ascendants, and collateral kindred).[102] If the deceased had any legitimate descendants, natural children could only receive "what is strictly necessary to procure them sustenance, or an occupation or profession which may maintain them." If there were no legitimate descendants, mothers could leave their entire estate to natural children, while fathers could bequeath between one-fourth and one-third, depending on what other legitimate relations he left. But recognized natural children were better off than "bastard [that is, unacknowledged], adulterous or incestuous children," who were only entitled to receive "a mere alimony."[103]

It was disputes over inheritances that led to the legal action in most racially exogamous relationships that came to the courts' attention, as white relatives contested the transmission of property to nonwhite consorts and children.[104] When such bequests exceeded the legal limits, the courts usually reduced them accordingly. Before J. Elisha Crocker's 1854 death, he decreed that his property should be divided among Sofa, "his housekeeper, who is a colored woman and was once his slave," and their three children, whom he had "legally acknowledged . . . previous to his death." Although he died without legal descendants or ascendants, he was survived by a brother and several nieces and nephews. One of the nephews, William Reed, sued to have the will annulled on the grounds that it distributed more than one-fourth of the property to Crocker's natural children. Rejecting legislative control of inheritance, several of Crocker's white relatives opposed Reed's suit and renounced any claims they might have to Crocker's estate out of "love and affection for the deceased, and from regard to the children of the deceased and of their mother." Further, they declared that "any legal proceedings to defeat the benevolent intentions of [Crocker], and to prevent the property by him left at his decease from being distributed and disposed of as the testator has desired and expressed in his said last will, is entirely contrary to our wishes."

The court, however, ignored these relatives and ruled in favor of Reed, taking the opportunity to interpret the legislature's intention in restricting the amount of property natural children could inherit. "The design of the Legislature," Justice Cole wrote, was "to stamp its disapprobation on illicit intercourse, by depriving the natural parent . . . of the liberty of bequeathing his estate according to his volition." In this way, "the parent has been punished, for he has been deprived in his death of the consolidation of knowing that his fortune will be enjoyed by those who are still precious in his sight." The court did grant Crocker's children the one-quarter of his estate they were legally allowed to inherit and divided the rest between his nieces and nephews.[105]

Despite its condescension toward white men, like Crocker, who chose women of color as their life partners and the mothers of their children, the court consistently upheld their bequests within the legal limits. In 1856, Justice Spofford (the same justice who argued that gens de couleur libre were no different from slaves and elsewhere referred to a racially exogamous marriage as an "unnatural alliance") upheld a donation of 2,000 dollars made by Jean Baptiste Décuir to Margaret Bush ("f.w.c."), declaring that having "lived in a state of concubinage" was not sufficient reason to deny the donation of moveables that did not exceed 10 percent of Décuir's entire estate.[106]

Some consorts and children successfully defended themselves against white heirs who sought to have them disinherited. Mulâtresse libre Magdelaine Cabaret had lived for many years with Joseph Carrel before he died in 1806, and his will named her as his universal heir. Eleven years later, Carrel's brother and four sisters filed suit, arguing that Carrel and Cabaret had "lived in open and notorious concubinage"; that as his concubine, Cabaret was "infamous and unworthy to be instituted heir"; and that as Carrel's "nearest relations," they should inherit his estate rather than Cabaret. At trial in the First District Court, witnesses testified that Cabaret "lived under the same roof as Mr. Joseph Carrel, ate at the same table as he, and slept in the same bed" both at his Plaquemines habitation and in her New Orleans house. The jury concluded that Cabaret and Carrel had indeed "lived together for many years . . . in a state of open concubinage," but it ultimately decided the case against her on the technicality that Carrel's will had not been properly written. Cabaret appealed to the Louisiana Supreme Court, which overturned the lower court's decision. Its opinion, written by Justice Dérbigny, dismissed the question of concubinage, declaring her "capable of inheriting," and found that the plaintiffs had let too many years pass after Carrel's death to have the right to contest Cabaret's possession of the estate.[107]

Later nonwhite consorts and children of white men argued for their bequests differently by denying their relationships to the deceased. Shortly before he died in 1843, Maurice Prévost bequeathed "a certain portion of his immoveable property" to Florestine Cecile and "all of his entire moveable estate" to Clarisse, both free women of color. The remainder of his estate was left to his sister, Emilie Prévost, widow Majastre. A second sister and his brother contested the will, claiming that Clarisse "was notoriously the concubine of the deceased" and Florestine his "bastard daughter . . . begotten by him from his said concubine" and arguing that they, along with Majastre, were the "only legitimate heirs." Florestine denied that she was Prévost's daughter; for her part, Majastre, who stood to benefit most if Prévost's bequests were invalidated, argued that, as her brother's named heir, she was the only one with a legitimate interest to contest the bequests, which she declined to do. Majastre then joined Florestine in her denial of Prévost's paternity and requested that the testator's wishes be upheld. Ultimately the court did not rule on whether Florestine was Prévost's daughter nor whether his donations to her and Clarisse exceeded the amounts allowable by law. Rather, in upholding Clarisse and Florestine's inheritances, it accepted Majastre's contention that her siblings did not have the right to contest Prévost's will.[108] In the disputes over Carrel's and Prévost's estates, the court was willing to accept (or in Prévost's case, to studiously ignore) white men's extramarital relationships with women of color because there were no competing legitimate white families. In each of these cases, the contesting relatives were collateral heirs with less legal claim to the deceased's property than that of either legitimate children or parents.

Some white men realized that, ironically, by not acknowledging their natural children they could leave larger bequests to them. The Louisiana Supreme Court too became aware of this and in 1840 sought to end this method of evading the law. Before Alexander Verdun died, he sold several plots of land to Jean-Baptiste

Gregoire and "six or seven other colored persons." Verdun's heirs alleged that these were "disguised donations to [Verdun's unacknowledged] illegitimate colored bastard children," and they sued to have the sales annulled and the properties added to their inheritances. Using a law designed to work against children of color, Gregoire's lawyer argued that, since "the proof of the descent of free illegitimate children of color from a white father is prohibited by law," Verdun's heirs could not offer evidence in support of his paternity. The court accused the defense of "pretend[ing] that the absence of legal acknowledgement ought to afford them a greater advantage, and more extensive rights than if they had been duly acknowledged." It ruled that such evidence was permissible but only when it was "made against" children of color, not when it was in their favor. Under this judicial interpretation, fathers who failed to acknowledge their children, like Verdun, left them vulnerable to having all donations and bequests nullified, not just those over the legal limit.[109]

As these cases illustrate, white relatives weighed in on both sides in some inheritance cases that went to court.[110] Far more relationships never came to the attention of the judicial system, arguably because white heirs, like Prévost's sister and Crocker's relatives, did not oppose their relatives' choices about family formation. When Jean Baptiste François Macarty (brother of Mandeville's lifelong consort) died in 1808, he was survived by three legitimate children, ages nineteen to twenty-five, and one acknowledged natural child, Theophile, the nine-year-old son of *mulâtresse libre* Rosette Beaulieu. He left the bulk of his estate to his legitimate children but made a bequest of 4,000 piastres to Theophile and 2,000 piastres to Beaulieu, requesting that his testamentary executor invest Theophile's inheritance and have him educated.[111] Joseph Dauphine, a sixty-seven-year-old native of New Orleans, named *mulâtresse libre* Marie Therese his universal heir for his estate, which included a habitation at Chapitoulas and five slaves, for having "served me [for forty years] without receiving any compensation or salary."[112] French-born Jean Dubreuil acknowledged his natural daughter, Manette Dubreuil, daughter of *négresse libre* Marie Jeanne Dubourg, and named her as his universal heir as well as leaving a small bequest to *cuarteróna libre* Marie Louise Leonais without identifying his relationship to her.[113] Louisiana native Jean Baptiste Picou recognized ten natural children with *femme de couleur libre* Victoire Deslonde and left his estate to be divided between his children and his brother.[114] Few white wives were as generous as Marie Jeanne Gaudais, *veuve* Perou, however. In her will, the Saint-Domingue native not only manumitted her husband's *mulâtresse* "natural daughter" but also gave her three slaves.[115] In these and many other cases, there is no evidence that white relatives contested the bequests, suggesting that not all white

Louisianans supported the legislature and the courts in their effort to eradicate interracial families.[116]

Interracial relationships were certainly common enough during the first few decades of the nineteenth century for most visitors to the city to comment on them. In his travels up and down the Mississippi River, French consul Pierre Laussat noted several habitations at which the planters had mulatto children. In particular, he mentioned the Hazeur de Lorme brothers, "real French knights from whom I had received many marks of kind attention." Praising them for their honor, loyalty, and faithfulness to France as well as for their good company, Laussat acknowledged they had one failing: "They were not married. That was their shameful side, their colonial weakness; they were surrounded by offspring whose color betrayed their origin." The Hazeur de Lorme family had been in Louisiana ever since the early eighteenth century and had held prominent government positions. By the early nineteenth century, they had two "well-kept" habitations at Chapitoulas, among other properties. One of the brothers, Louis, acknowledged at baptism several children he had with mulâtresse libre Felicite Hazeur, his sister's former slave, whom he had manumitted in 1793. Another, Louis François Xavier, participated in the baptisms of at least five children and recognized a total of six with Jalinette or Marguerite Duval in his 1816 will, in which he left them small bequests.[117]

Laussat observed these families in the privacy of their homes, but other visitors encountered them on the public streets of New Orleans. Benjamin Latrobe described "a white man, and a bright quadroon woman" riding through town together in 1819; twenty-five years later, his son John observed "a most handsome barouche in which rode a white planter . . . with his mulatto wife or mistress, a mulatto friend of hers and his mulatto children."[118] Though many observers dismissed relationships between white men and women of color as concubinage, evidence from wills demonstrates that they were often de facto marriages. Such extralegal families coexisted alongside the more public face of interracial sex displayed at the quadroon balls, which, despite the best efforts of city politicians, flourished in the antebellum era.[119]

THE LOUISIANA PURCHASE TREATY had initially held out the promise of civic incorporation to gens de couleur libre, but ultimately they were in fact excluded from some of its most important privileges, such as voting and jury service. Gens de couleur libre and enslaved persons of African descent together faced a legislature that attempted to restrict access to the most basic right: freedom. Yet, despite those efforts, local juries, judges, and even legislators themselves were inclined to be sympathetic to slaves' desire for freedom when confronted with individual petitions for emancipation. Similarly, courts were sometimes sympathetic to families that were prevented by law from being recognized; it generally allowed extralegal family members to inherit when those donations were within the letter of the law. Yet these were exceptions that elided the strict racial and status boundaries that were written into law. Precisely because they could not have their relationships legally recognized, the families of femmes de couleur libre and white men were necessarily restricted and denied many legal, as well as social, privileges. And as hommes de couleur libre protested their exclusion, claiming a public voice through petitions and their militia battalion, some femmes de couleur libre quietly continued to form families with white men and sought to protect their families and property as best they could.

A few women of color were able to parlay their relationships with white men into freedom, if enslaved, and even into wealth. Connections to white consorts and kin were central to these women's efforts to successfully navigate New Orleans' racial order. Even those like Eulalie Mandeville, who cited her own industriousness in building up her assets, began with the support, financial and otherwise, of her white father's family. According to the 1850 federal census, there were more than 10,000 free adult women of color living in the lower South (from Georgia to Texas); just over one-third of them resided in the city of New Orleans. Of the 561 throughout the region who were noted as heads of households and owners of real property, almost one-half lived in New Orleans, with another quarter residing elsewhere in Louisiana. The property holdings of Louisiana's free women of color averaged 3,602 dollars, 20 percent more than the regional average for this group. Their combined total wealth was more than 1.5 million dollars, a staggering 92 percent of the total property held by free women of color in the lower South. New Orleans' 257 free women of color property holders were, however, just a tiny minority of the city's gens de couleur libre, comprising just under 3 percent.[120] Most gens de couleur libre, men and women alike, were not so fortunate, and it is important not to exaggerate their general condition as "privileged" or "elite."[121] But this economic snapshot of New Orleans' free women of color (and the contrast between their situation and that of free women of color elsewhere in the lower South) illustrates the continuing legacies of the city's colonial history. Yet even these fortunate few faced increasing hostility and erosion of their rights in the years leading up to the Civil War and beyond.

Despite their very best efforts to undermine New Orleans' racial order, Anglo-Louisiana authorities, in the legislature and the courts, had instead codified it, albeit in a simplified form. Forced to accept the presence of gens de couleur libre, they sought to more clearly set this third racial group apart, making it both more

difficult for slaves to enter it and for gens de couleur libre to leave it through passing as white. The Louisiana Supreme Court, in its 1810 *Adéle* decision, ruled that
people of perceived mixed ancestries were to be presumed free and that those of
perceived unmitigated African ancestry were to be presumed slaves; these pre-
sumptions were prompted by frequent racial exogamy and the manumission of
sang-mêlé children that had created an association between mixed ancestry and
free status. At the same time, distinctions among gens de couleur collapsed and the
range of racial labels that had been used in the colonial era slowly faded from legal
and sacramental records. Following the legislature's designation of "f.m.c." and
"f.w.c." as required legal identities in 1808, the priests at the St. Louis Cathedral
belatedly followed suit in the late 1810s, when they generally stopped distinguishing among negros, mulatos, and quarterons.[122]

The legislature and the city council also denigrated gens de couleur libre, requiring that they, like slaves, act subordinately and with respect toward all whites
and further lumping them with slaves in various criminal statutes. They prohibited
racially exogamous marriage and made it much harder for white men to bequeath
patrimonies to their nonwhite consorts and children. Nevertheless, some slaveowners continued to manumit their slaves, sometimes relying on sympathetic notaries, jury men, judges, and even legislators to help them overcome legal disabilities,
and some white men continued to form families with women of color while seeking
ways to evade laws banning marriages and restricting inheritances. New Orleans'
social order had indeed become organized around race at its core, but some New
Orleanians still refused to let the racialized dictates of political elites determine
their everyday lives.

Epilogue

ON JANUARY 1, 1832, Alexis de Tocqueville was in New Orleans. He included the city on his tour of the United States in 1831–32 precisely to contrast its racial order with Anglo-America's, although perhaps a desire "to enjoy the pleasures so celebrated of New Orleans" tempted him as well. Like most European and Euro-American male visitors during the antebellum era, Tocqueville attended a "ball of the quadroons" during his short stay. It was, he noted, a "strange sight: all the men white, all the women colored or at least with African blood. . . . A sort of bazaar." Feeling as if he were "a thousand miles from the United States," Tocqueville observed "faces with every shade of colour" and voices speaking "French, English, Spanish, Creole," all together composing a population "just as mixed" as the city's architecture with its Spanish roofs, English bricks, and French carriage entrances. Focusing in particular on the gens de couleur libre, Tocqueville noted there was a "multitude of coloured people at New Orleans. Small number in the North. Why?"

The answer for Tocqueville lay in both "national character and temperament" and the material circumstances of colonization. Whereas he was struck by "incredible laxity of morals" in New Orleans, at least among "colored women" and their white consorts, he repeatedly characterized (Anglo-)Americans as "very chaste" and even credited this characteristic as one of the reasons for the success of democratic governance in the United States. The English, he believed, were "the one [race] that has most preserved the purity of its blood," in part because "they belong to a Northern race." In contrast, "immorality between the races" prevailed in New Orleans. His assumption that the southern "races" of Europeans who colonized New Orleans were less virtuous, and therefore engaged in more interracial sex, goes unstated.

Although Tocqueville asserted that these contrasting traits were "strong reasons" for the different rates of racially exogamous sex, he also credited demography:

"Spanish America was peopled by adventurers drawn by thirst for gold, who, transplanted along to the other side of the Atlantic, found themselves in some sort forced to contract unions with the women of the land where they were living. The English colonies were peopled by men who escaped from their country for reasons of religious zeal, and whose object in coming to the New World, was to live there cultivating the land. They came with wives and children, and could form a complete society on the spot."[1] Leaving aside for a moment Tocqueville's selective presentation of the history of New England as that of colonial Anglo-America writ large, he did presciently expound the cultural and materialist interpretations of sex and racial formation that would be put forward by later generations of historians.[2]

But neither of these explanations, alone or together, accounts for the rise and decline of racially exogamous relationships in early New Orleans. Although demography played its part, economic and pragmatic considerations promoted relationships between Indian women and French men during the first decades of the eighteenth century. Those between women of African ancestry and European men were few during the French era but greatly increased in number during the last third of the eighteenth century for reasons that do not fit the usual demographic and cultural explanations. Sex ratios, which earlier in the century had been skewed heavily toward Euro-Louisianan men and slightly toward Afro-Louisianan women, slave and free, leveled out somewhat at the same time that relationships between Euro-Louisianan men and women of color became more frequent.[3] They also became more public and apparently more acceptable. Increasing numbers of Euro-Louisianans, from wealthy merchants and government officials to lowly soldiers and laborers, openly acknowledged their nonwhite families. Although some of this might have been due to the arrival, after 1763, of Spanish immigrants, whom Gilberto Freyre and others have described as being more open to intimate relations with women of color, the men who formed families with women of color included second- and third-generation French creoles as well as the occasional immigrant from Anglo-America and elsewhere. A better explanation for the growing numbers of these relationships lies in the creolization of both Franco- and Afro-Louisianans whose parents and grandparents had arrived in the colony mostly in the 1710s and 1720s. By the mid- to late eighteenth century, many of those born locally shared, to a great extent, a culture, a language, and a religion.[4] Thus relationships between Euro- and Afro-Louisianans during the latter half of the century were culturally endogamous even if they may have been perceived as racially exogamous.

The Louisiana Purchase ushered in a new era, and the number of stable, openly acknowledged interracial unions declined, although not until the late 1820s. Franco-

Louisianan men who came of age before the Louisiana Purchase continued to form families with women of color. Those who came of age after 1803 (as well as more recent Anglo-American, German, and Irish immigrants) were far less likely to do so, as younger Franco-Louisianans and non-Anglo immigrants seem to have emulated Anglo-Americans' public scorn for interracial unions. Equally important, free women of color themselves appear to have increasingly rejected extramarital liaisons with white men in preference to racially endogamous marriages.[5]

Very few interracial unions in any era received legal or religious sanction. Laws prohibiting racially exogamous relationships were not an exact reflection of social practices, but they were significant racial projects in their own right. Officials used them to define racial categories and encode them into the social order. The question of incorporating cultural or racial "others" into the colony through marriage came up almost as soon as the French established themselves on the Gulf Coast in 1699. Although some officials, mostly missionaries, argued that marriages between Indian women and French men would serve many useful purposes, others opposed such unions, in great part because they perceived the differences between the region's native peoples and its colonial newcomers—differences in gender roles, marital and inheritance practices, and sexual mores—as innate and fixed. The Crown ultimately decreed that such marriages should be strongly discouraged, but it never prohibited them outright, which suggests an ambivalence in its attitude on the matter of whether the differences between Indians and the French were cultural, and therefore malleable, or racial, and therefore fixed.

French officials had no hesitancy, on the other hand, in prohibiting all sexual relationships between Afro- and Euro-Louisianans. The Code Noir, promulgated by the French Crown in 1724, defined noirs and blancs as people who were incapable of marrying each other. It also prohibited both blancs and free noirs from engaging in extramarital relationships with slaves. After 1769, Spanish slave law replaced the Code Noir. Local officials did not, however, pass any new laws regarding racially exogamous marriage, although the Crown did decree that all marriages should ideally be between social equals. This premise theoretically opened the possibility for marriage between a wealthy woman of color and a poorer Euro-Louisianan man. The Anglo-American regime eliminated this opportunity three years after the Louisiana Purchase. The territory's first civil digest, compiled in 1808, unambiguously required "free white persons," "free persons of colour," and slaves to marry endogamously, thus using the regulation of sex to define the tripartite system's three castes.[6]

Bans on interracial marriages did not, of course, prevent the birth of sang-mêlé children, although they did condemn them to illegitimacy and limited their ability to inherit wealth and status from their parents. Over the course of the eighteenth century, New Orleanians developed an elaborate vocabulary to define these children. "Mulâtre" and "métis" appeared fairly early in the eighteenth century, supplemented by "quarteron" around midcentury. But French census takers, priests, and other official record takers were inconsistent about how they used these terms and sometimes failed to mark people of color at all, particularly if they were free. The increasing numbers of sang-mêlé born during the last third of the century as well as the arrival of Spanish secular and religious officials resulted in a more consistent use of racial labels to identify people of color. Using the language of castas, developed elsewhere in the Spanish Americas, priests in particular tried to fix an individual's identity under a simplistic label that supposedly summarized his or her genealogy and character. But ancestry was not the only criterion used to determine calidad, and it was sometimes contradicted by legal and socioeconomic status as well as appearance. The existence of competing criteria meant that different record takers could attribute different racial labels to the same individual, providing some small room for individuals to try to define their own identity.[7]

This was particularly true for New Orleanians who claimed Indian ancestry. By the 1790s, the frontier exchange economy that had done so much to make Indians integral participants in the colony's development had been fully supplanted by plantation slavery, thus making Indians seemingly irrelevant to colonial society, unlike those of African descent, who were deemed essential even as they were relegated to the lowest rungs of the hierarchy. Written out of the colonial order, people of Indian descent sought to remake themselves as free or even white. Their efforts to do so offer a unique opportunity to analyze how some nonelite people sought to define their own racial identities and also reveal how the racialization of Indians and Africans differed at the end of the eighteenth century.

The more elaborate racial hierarchy of the colonial era was greatly simplified during the first few decades of the nineteenth century. Following a legislative decree in 1808, notaries and legal officials were required to record all free mulattos, quadroons, and other sang-mêlé simply as free men and women of color, a practice priests began emulating a few years later. By restricting manumission (thus making the boundary between slavery and freedom much harder to cross), by requiring marital endogamy among whites, free people of color, and slaves, and by lumping all free people of color into a single legal category, authorities in Anglo Louisiana transformed what had been a relatively more fluid casta system into a rigid tripartite one. But this was just the most recent in a long line of elite efforts to use race and sex to impose social order, efforts that were often frustrated by New Orleanians' everyday practices. Indeed, Anglo-Louisianan officials were forced to codify a tripartite system because of the legacies of actions taken by New Orleanians during the eighteenth century as some sought freedom and others formed racially exogamous families. In this way, the tripartite system was the consequence of the politics and practices of race and sex in early New Orleans.

AND SO IT WAS THAT visitors to New Orleans in the early nineteenth century, whether Europeans like Tocqueville, or Anglo-Americans like the Latrobes and Fredrick Law Olmsted, were struck by the differences between New Orleans' racial order and that of the rest of the United States. Those differences, however, blinded them, and subsequent historians, to the similarities.[8] New Orleans was indeed in many ways sui generis. It had an African American majority almost immediately, and it was governed by three different regimes in relatively quick succession. Yet it shared these traits with other regions in North America. South Carolina too had a black majority within a generation of colonization as did certain plantation districts of Tidewater Virginia. Nor was New Orleans alone in being subjected to multiple colonial regimes. Roughly two-thirds of the North American continent—from Quebec to St. Augustine, New Netherlands to Santa Fe—were first colonized by a nation other than England and, on incorporation into the United States, brought with them their own colonial histories and legacies. Residents of those regions, as well as the continent's indigenous inhabitants, would have sympathized with New Orleanians, who had to live under foreign rule and negotiate new political and legal systems.

But more importantly, other Americans would have recognized New Orleanians' refusal to allow their lives to be determined by the racialized dictates of colonial elites. Recent studies that go beyond analyzing race at the level of discourse and ideology, that, in Philip Morgan's words, "differentiate . . . private practice from public opinion," demonstrate that racially exogamous relationships were not so uncommon in the Anglo-American colonies and the states they became. Although the eighteenth century saw an increase in the hostility directed toward racially exogamous relationships, these relationships—including those between white women and black men—continued to receive a measure of toleration, and perhaps even at times acceptance, well into the nineteenth century.[9]

When Tocqueville contrasted New Orleans with the rest of the United States, he represented New England as typical of all of English North America. As we know now, New England was the exception rather than the rule.[10] And, as we heed Gary Nash's call to find those "who conducted their lives, formed families, raised children, and created their own identities in ways that defied the official racial ideology," to uncover what he calls the "Hidden History of Mestizo America," we may find that New Orleanians were indeed far more like their Anglo neighbors than previously thought.[11] But this is not because New Orleanians lived within a fully developed racialized slave system that had emerged within a generation of colonization and was governed by a stable and confident white elite who successfully kept the city's multiracial population socially and sexually segregated.[12] Rather, it is because other colonial Americans behaved more like New Orleanians.

Abbreviations

AHR	*American Historical Review*
AC	Archives des Colonies, Archives nationales de France (series A, B, C11, C13, F, and G)
AGI, PC	Archivo General de Indias, Papeles Procedentes de Cuba
AGI, SD	Archivo General de Indias, Audiencia de Santo Domingo
Cabildo Records	Records and Deliberations of the Cabildo
Carondelet Dispatches	El Baron de Carondelet, 1789–97, Spanish Governors of Louisiana Dispatches, Manuscripts Division, Howard-Tilton Memorial Library, Tulane University
Census Tables	*The Census Tables for the French Colony of Louisiana from 1699 through 1732,* ed. Charles R. Maduell Jr.
CVOP	Conseil de Ville, Official Proceedings, 1803–29
First Families	*The First Families of Louisiana,* comp. and trans. Glenn R. Conrad
General Digest	*A General Digest of the Acts of the Legislature of Louisiana, Passed from the Year 1804 to 1827 Inclusive, and in Force at This Last Period with an Appendix and General Index,* ed. Louis Moreau-Lislet (1828)
HT	Special Collections, Manuscripts Department, Howard Tilton Memorial Library, Tulane University
JAH	*Journal of American History*
JR	*The Jesuits Relations and Allied Documents: Travels and Explorations of the Jesuit Missionaries in New France, 1610–1719,* ed. Reuben Gold Thwaites
Letter Books	*Official Letter Books of W. C. C. Claiborne,* ed. Dunbar Rowland
LH	*Louisiana History*
LHQ	*Louisiana Historical Quarterly*

Loix et constitutions	*Loix et constitutions des colonies françoises de l'Amérique sous le vent*, ed. Médéric-Louis Élie Moreau de Saint-Méry
Louisiana Acts	Louisiana, *Acts of the Legislature*, 1812–1857
MPAFD	*Mississippi Provincial Archives: French Dominion*, ed. Dunbar Rowland, A. G. Sanders, and Patricia Galloway
NONA	New Orleans Notarial Archives (notarial acts are cited by the name of the notary, volume [if available], and folio numbers)
NOPL	City Archives and Special Collections, Louisiana Division, New Orleans Public Library
Records of the Diocese	Records of the Diocese of Louisiana and the Floridas, University of Notre Dame
RSC	Records of the Superior Council, Louisiana State Museum
RSC, *LHQ*	Index to the Records of the Superior Council, published in the *Louisiana Historical Quarterly* (1917–1943)
SCLHA, UNO	Supreme Court of Louisiana Historical Archives, Earl K. Long Library, University of New Orleans
SJR	Spanish Judicial Records, Louisiana State Museum
SJR, *LHQ*	Index to the Spanish Judicial Records, published in the *Louisiana Historical Quarterly* (1923–1948)
SLC	Sacramental records of the St. Louis Cathedral, Archives of the Archdiocese of New Orleans
SMV	*Spain in the Mississippi Valley, 1765–1794*, ed. Lawrence Kinnaird
SR	*Sacramental Records of the Roman Catholic Church of the Archdiocese of New Orleans*, eds. Earl C. Woods, Charles E. Nolan, and Dorenda Dupont
Vaudreuil Letterbooks	Vaudreuil Letterbooks, 1743–47, Loudoun Collection, Manuscripts Department, Huntington Library
Vaudreuil Papers	Vaudreuil Papers, French Colonial Manuscripts, 1743–53, Loudoun Collection, Manuscripts Department, Huntington Library
WMQ	*William and Mary Quarterly*

Introduction

1. [André] Pénicaut, "Établissements des Français aux cotes du Golfe du Mexique et dans la vallée du Mississipi, 1698–1722," *Découvertes et établissements des français dans l'ouest et dans le sud de l'Amérique Septentrionale (1614–1754): Mémoires et documents originaux recueillis,* ed. Pierre Margry, 6 vols. (Paris, 1876–86), 5:394; André Pénicaut, *Fleur de Lys and Calumet: Being the Pénicaut Narrative of French Adventure in Louisiana,* trans. Richebourg Gaillard McWilliams (Tuscaloosa, Ala., 1988), 23–24.

2. Instructions pour le Sieur d'Iberville, capitaine de fregate Legere, pour le voyage qu'il va faire au Mississippy, August 27, 1701, AC, B, 1:161v–62, cited in Guillaume Aubert, "'Français, Nègres et Sauvages': Constructing Race in Colonial Louisiana" (PhD diss., Tulane University, 2002), 148.

3. The literature on the transformation from ethnocentrism to racism is vast. For an especially nuanced interpretation, see George M. Frederickson, *Racism: A Short History* (Princeton, N.J., 2002), chapter 1. For one that pays particular attention to the contradictory nature of these ideologies, see Joyce Chaplin, "Race," in *The British Atlantic World, 1500–1800,* ed. David Armitage and Michael J. Braddick (Basingstoke, England, 2002), 154–72. Among the classics and more recent works are: David Brion Davis, *The Problem of Slavery in Western Culture* (Ithaca, N.Y., 1966); Winthrop Jordan, *White Over Black: American Attitudes Toward the Negro, 1550–1812* (Chapel Hill, N.C., 1968); William B. Cohen, *The French Encounter with Africans: White Response to Blacks, 1530–1880* (Bloomington, Ind., 1980), 1–99; Anthony Pagden, *The Fall of Natural Man: The American Indian and the Origins of Comparative Ethnology* (Cambridge, England, 1982); special issue on "Constructing Race," *WMQ,* 3rd ser., 54 (1997): 3–252; Kathleen M. Brown, "Native Americans and Early Modern Concepts of Race," in *Empire and Others: British Encounters with Indigenous Peoples, 1600–1850,* ed. Martin Daunton and Rick Halpern (Philadelphia, 1999), 79–100; Guillaume Aubert, "'The Blood of France': Race and Purity of Blood in the French Atlantic World," *WMQ,* 3rd ser., 61 (2004): 439–78; David Brion Davis, *Inhuman Bondage: The Rise and Fall of Slavery in the New World* (New York, 2006).

For British North America, the search for the origins of racism has dominated much of this discussion. For summaries and opposing critiques, see Alden Vaughan, "The Origins Debate: Slavery and Racism in Seventeenth-Century Virginia," in *Roots of American Racism: Essays on the Colonial Experience* (New York, 1995), 136–74, and Theodore W. Allen, *The Invention of the White Race,* vol. 1, *Racial Oppressions and Social Control* (New York, 1994), introduction. The debate was revived in 1997 by James H. Sweet, who argued that the roots of American racism can be found in fifteenth-century Iberia ("The Iberian Roots of American Racist Thought," *WMQ,* 3rd ser., 54 [1997]: 143–66).

4. The phrase "image archive" comes from Sue Peabody, "'A Nation Born to Slavery': Missionaries and Racial Discourse in Seventeenth-Century French Antilles," *Journal of Social History* 38 (2004): 113. On the mobility of images across linguistic borders, see Janet Whatley, introduction, in *History of a Voyage to the Land of Brazil, Otherwise Called America,* ed. Jean de Léry (Berkeley, Calif., 1990), xxiv, and Jennifer L. Morgan, *Laboring Women: Reproduction and Gender in New World Slavery* (Philadelphia, 2004), 49.

5. For analyses of French and Spanish racial ideologies that Louisiana colonists could draw on, see Sue Peabody, *"There Are No Slaves in France": The Political Culture of Race and Slavery in the Ancien Régime* (New York, 1996); Peabody, "'A Nation Born to Slavery,'" 113–26; Malick Walid Ghachem, "Sovereignty and Slavery in the Age of Revolution: Haitian Variations on a Metropolitan Theme" (PhD diss., Stanford University, 2001); Aubert, "'Français, Nègres et Sauvages'"; Ann Twinam, *Public Lives, Private Secrets: Gender, Honor, Sexuality, and Illegitimacy in Colonial Spanish America* (Stanford, Calif., 1999); Patricia Seed, *To Love, Honor, and Obey in Colonial Mexico: Conflicts over Marriage Choice, 1574–1821* (Stanford, Calif., 1988); Ramón A. Gutiérrez, *When Jesus Came, the Corn Mothers Went*

Away: Marriage, Sexuality, and Power in New Mexico, 1500–1846 (Stanford, Calif., 1991). For an analysis of various lines of European thought that Anglo-Americans drew upon, see Chaplin, "Race."

6. Christopher Columbus, *La carta de Colon anunciando el descubrimiento del Nuevo Mundo, 15 febrero–14 marzo 1493* (rpt., Madrid, 1962); Richard Hakluyt, *The Principall Navigations, Voiages, and Disoveries of the English Nation,* 3 vols. (London, 1598–1600); Denis Diderot and Jean le Rond d'Alembert, *Encyclopédie; ou, Dictionnaire raisonné des sciences, des arts et des métiers,* 35 vols. (Paris, 1751–77).

Many of the authors cited in note 3 pay do pay attention to how race was written into colonial law but for specific analyses of codification, see A. Leon Higginbotham Jr., *In the Matter of Color: The Colonial Period* (New York, 1978); Ian F. Haney López, *White by Law: The Legal Construction of Race* (New York, 1996); Kathleen M. Brown, *Good Wives, Nasty Wenches, and Anxious Patriarchs: Gender, Race, and Power in Colonial Virginia* (Chapel Hill, N.C., 1996); Kirsten Fischer, *Suspect Relations: Sex, Race, and Resistance in Colonial North Carolina* (Ithaca, N.Y., 2002).

7. My simultaneous top-down and bottom-up approach is clearly indebted to Karl Marx's dictum that "man makes his own history" but not "out of conditions chosen by himself" (*The Eighteenth Brumaire of Louis Bonaparte* [New York, 1963], 15). For a theoretical overview of this approach (called "practice theory" by anthropologists), see Pierre Bourdieu, *Outline of a Theory of Practice,* trans. Richard Nice (Cambridge, England, 1978), and Sherry B. Ortner, "Making Gender: Toward a Feminist, Minority, Postcolonial, Subaltern, etc., Theory of Practice," in *Making Gender: The Politics and Erotics of Culture* (Boston, 1996), 1–20.

8. The concept of racial formation as articulated by sociologists Michael Omi and Howard Winant emphasizes "the sociohistorical processes by which racial categories are created, inhabited, transformed, and destroyed" (*Racial Formation in the United States: From the 1960s to the 1990s,* 2nd ed. [New York, 1994], chapter 4, quotation on 55).

9. For an analysis of just how New Orleans' exoticism became enshrined in the writing of U.S. history, see Daniel H. Usner Jr., "Between Creoles and Yankees: The Discursive Representations of Colonial Louisiana in American History," in *French Colonial Louisiana and the Atlantic World,* ed. Bradley G. Bond (Baton Rouge, La., 2005), 1–21.

10. To represent slavery and racism as exceptions to the national narrative, New Englanders also had to erase their own histories of slavery. See Joanne Pope Melish, *Disowning Slavery: Gradual Emancipation and "Race" in New England, 1780–1860* (Ithaca, N.Y., 1998), and John D. Seelye, *Memory's Nation: The Place of Plymouth Rock* (Chapel Hill, N.C., 1998).

11. Jack P. Greene, *Pursuits of Happiness: The Social Development of Early Modern British Colonies and the Formation of American Culture* (Chapel Hill, N.C., 1988).

12. For a recent overview of the Atlantic World approach, see Alison Games, "Atlantic Histories: Definitions, Challenges, and Opportunities," *AHR* 111 (2006): 741–57.

13. Frank Tannenbaum, *Slave and Citizen* (New York, 1947).

14. On the risk of Atlantic history merely becoming "boiled-over imperial history," see David Hancock, "The British Atlantic World: Co-ordination, Complexity, and the Emer-

gence of an Atlantic Market Economy, 1651–1815," *Itinerario* 23 (1999): 107–26. On the significance of Indian-made decisions, see Fred Anderson and Andrew Cayton, *The Dominion of War: Empire and Liberty in North America, 1500–2000* (New York, 2005); Juliana Barr, *Peace Came in the Form of a Woman: Indians and Spaniards in the Texas Borderlands* (Chapel Hill, N.C., 2007); and Kathleen DuVal, *The Native Ground: Indians and Colonists in the Heart of the Continent* (Philadelphia, 2006). For an exception to the inability to incorporate Indians, see Stephen Saunders Webb, *1676: The End of American Independence* (New York, 1984). April Lee Hatfield also keeps Indians as an integral part of her history of Atlantic Virginia (rather than just as backdrop in the first chapter, as is so often the case) precisely because she situates Virginia not just within the English Atlantic but also within the continent (*Atlantic Virginia: Intercolonial Relations in the Seventeenth Century* [Philadelphia, 2004]). For a rare attempt to analyze the impact of Spanish-American systems of slavery on the institution's development in an English colony, see Michael Joseph Guasco, "Encounters, Identities, and Human Bondage: The Foundations of Racial Slavery in the Anglo-Atlantic World" (PhD diss., College of William and Mary, 2000).

15. See Alan Taylor, *American Colonies* (New York, 2001); Elizabeth A. Fenn, *Pox Americana: The Great Smallpox Epidemic of 1775–82* (New York, 2001); James F. Brooks, *Captives and Cousins: Slavery, Kinship, and Community in the Southwest Borderlands* (Chapel Hill, N.C., 2002). Indian historians have, to a great extent, always been continentalists, attentive as they have been to connections among Indian groups and with competing European colonies, even as many have also heeded trans-Atlantic events as Indians became increasingly caught up in the market economy.

16. For this critique, see Emily Clark, "Moving from Periphery to Center: Scholarship on the Non-British in Colonial North America," *Historical Journal* 42 (1999): 903–10.

17. Daniel H. Usner Jr., *Indians, Settlers, and Slaves in a Frontier Exchange Economy: The Lower Mississippi Valley before 1783* (Chapel Hill, N.C., 1992); Gwendolyn Midlo Hall, *Africans in Colonial Louisiana: The Development of Afro-Creole Culture in the Eighteenth Century* (Baton Rouge, La., 1992). See also Thomas N. Ingersoll, *Mammon and Manon in Early New Orleans: The First Slave Society in the Deep South, 1718–1819* (Knoxville, Tenn., 1999), and Emily Clark, *Masterless Mistresses: The New Orleans Ursulines and the Development of a New World Society, 1727–1834* (Chapel Hill, N.C., 2007).

18. Although most Louisiana historians agree that the 1780s and 1790s were the pivotal decades in this transition, Ira Berlin and Thomas Ingersoll have drawn different depictions of the chronology. Berlin argues that the lower Mississippi River Valley devolved from a slave society (brought about in the 1720s by the rapid importation of thousands of slaves directly from Africa) to a slaveowning society after 1730. It did not reemerge as a slave society until after the reopening of the slave trade in the late 1770s and Étienne Boré's successful experimentations with sugar cane in 1795 (*Many Thousands Gone: The First Two Centuries of Slavery in North America* [Cambridge, Mass., 1998], chapters 4, 8, and 12). Thomas Ingersoll, conversely, argues that New Orleans became a full-fledged slave society in 1731, although his principal criterion is simply the presence of a slave majority rather than slavery's centrality to the economy, politics, and culture (*Mammon and Manon*). Guillaume Aubert concurs with Ingersoll, arguing that French officials had a fully developed racist

ideology by the early eighteenth century, one that allowed for no social fluidity, although he acknowledges that his focus on "the evolution of French colonial elite discourse" cannot stand in for "the views of the French colonial population at large" ("'Français, Nègres et Sauvages,'" quotations on 264). What I highlight is precisely the disconnect between elite and popular conceptions of race and the persistence of less rigid ideas outside elite discourse. See also Clark, *Masterless Mistresses,* 5, who argues that the Ursuline nuns also continued to practice racial integration into the nineteenth century.

19. For an introduction to a well-developed colonial Latin American literature analyzing the continuing intersecting influences of race, class, and gender, see John K. Chance and William B. Taylor, "Estate and Class in a Colonial City: Oaxaca in 1792," *Comparative Studies in Society and History* 19 (1977): 454–87; Robert McCaa, Stuart B. Schwartz, and Arturo Grubessich, "Race and Class in Colonial Latin America: A Critique," *Comparative Studies in Society and History* 21 (1979): 421–33; John K. Chance and William B. Taylor, "Estate and Class: A Reply," *Comparative Studies in Society and History* 21 (1979): 434–42; Elizabeth Anne Kuznesof, "Ethnic and Gender Influences on 'Spanish' Creole Society in Colonial Spanish America," *Colonial Latin American Review* 4 (1995): 153–76; and Susan Kellog, "Depicting *Mestizaje*: Gendered Images of Ethnorace in Colonial Mexican Texts," *Journal of Women's History* 12 (2000): 69–92.

20. See, for example, Thomas E. Buckley, "Unfixing Race: Class, Power, and Identity in an Interracial Family," *Virginia Magazine of History and Biography* 102 (1994): 349–80; Martha Hodes, *White Women, Black Men: Illicit Sex in the Nineteenth-Century South* (New York, 1997); Timothy J. Lockley, "Crossing the Race Divide: Interracial Sex in Antebellum Savannah," *Slavery and Abolition* 18 (1997): 159–73; Joshua D. Rothman, *Notorious in the Neighborhood: Sex and Families across the Color Line in Virginia, 1787–1861* (Chapel Hill, N.C., 2003).

21. Philip D. Morgan, "Interracial Sex in the Chesapeake and the British Atlantic World, 1700–1820," in *Sally Hemings and Thomas Jefferson: History, Memory, and Civil Culture,* ed. Jan Lewis and Peter Onuf (Charlottesville, Va., 1999), 52–84. Rothman describes relationships between white men and black women in Virginia as "open secrets" (*Notorious in the Neighborhood,* 31).

22. *Census of the City of New Orleans, Exclusive of Seamen and the Garrison,* 1803, *American State Papers: Miscellaneous* (Washington, D.C., 1832–34), 10:384. This census enumerates only the city proper. Of the larger New Orleans region, free people of color were just over 10 percent of the population (*Census of the Districts or Posts of Louisiana and West Florida,* [1803], *American State Papers: Miscellaneous,* 10:384).

23. Leonard P. Curry, *The Free Black in Urban America, 1800–1850: The Shadow of the Dream* (Chicago, 1981), 244–46; Berlin, *Many Thousands Gone,* 316–24. The 1791 census of New Orleans, which is the last one to distinguish between sang-mêlé (mixed blood) and negros, identified almost 70 percent of free people of color as sang-mêlé (*Census of New Orleans,* November 6, 1791, NOPL).

24. Louisiana historiography is particularly rich on this point not just because of its multiple colonial regimes but also because it brings together historians trained in Latin American, French colonial, Spanish borderlands, and colonial U.S. history.

25. David J. Weber argues that we should understand U.S. history as the incorporation

of diverse cultures rather than in terms of the idea of Anglo-American westward expansion ("John Francis Bannon and the Historiography of the Spanish Borderlands: Retrospect and Prospect," *Journal of the Southwest* 29 [1987]: 331–63).

26. It is important to note, however, that manumission per se did not have to be an antislavery act; indeed, it was often an integral part of the institution of slavery to the extent that owners used it to offer freedom as a reward to those who, in their view, worked hard and compliantly. See Ira Berlin, *Slaves Without Masters: The Free Negro in the Antebellum South* (New York, 1974), 149, and Orlando Patterson, *Slavery and Social Death: A Comparative Study* (Cambridge, Mass., 1982), 217.

27. A. Leon Higginbotham Jr. and Barbara K. Kopytoff, "Racial Purity and Interracial Sex in the Law of Colonial and Antebellum Virginia," *Georgetown Law Journal* 77 (1989): 1967–2029; Verena Martinez-Alier, *Marriage, Class and Colour in Nineteenth-Century Cuba: A Study of Racial Attitudes and Sexual Values in a Slave Society* (Ann Arbor, Mich., 1989); Barbara J. Fields, "Slavery, Race and Ideology in the United States of America," *New Left Review* 181 (1990): 107–8; Ann L. Stoler, "Carnal Knowledge and Imperial Power: Gender, Race, and Morality in Colonial Asia," in *Gender at the Crossroads of Knowledge: Feminist Anthropology in the Postmodern Era,* ed. Micaela di Leonardo (Berkeley, Calif., 1991), 51–101; Tessie Liu, "Teaching the Differences among Women from a Historical Perspective: Rethinking Race and Gender as Social Categories," *Women's Studies International Forum* 14 (1991): 265–76; Gutiérrez, *When Jesus Came;* Ann L. Stoler, "Sexual Affronts and Racial Frontiers: European Identities and the Cultural Politics of Exclusion in Colonial Southeast Asia," *Comparative Studies in Society and History* 34 (1992): 514–51; Brown, *Good Wives;* Peter W. Bardaglio, "'Shamefull Matches': The Regulation of Interracial Sex and Marriage in the South before 1900," in *Sex, Love, Race: Crossing Boundaries in North American History,* ed. Martha Hodes (New York, 1999), 112–38; Fischer, *Suspect Relations;* Randall Kennedy, *Interracial Intimacies: Sex, Marriage, Identity, and Adoption* (New York, 2003), especially chapter 2.

28. Sharon Block, *Rape and Sexual Power in Early America* (Chapel Hill, N.C., 2006); Brown, *Good Wives,* 355–56; Ann L. Stoler, *Carnal Knowledge and Imperial Power: Race and the Intimate in Colonial Rule* (Berkeley, Calif., 2002).

29. Angela Y. Davis, *Women, Race and Class* (New York, 1983), 25–29; Ann duCille, "'Othered Matters': Reconceptualizing Dominance and Difference in the History of Sexuality in America," *Journal of the History of Sexuality* 1 (1990): 102–27; Adele Logan Alexander, *Ambiguous Lives: Free Women of Color in Rural Georgia, 1789–1879* (Fayetteville, Ark., 1991), 64–66; Antonia I. Castañeda, "Sexual Violence in the Politics and Policies of Conquest: Amerindian Women and the Spanish Conquest of Alta California," in *Building with Our Hands: New Directions in Chicana Studies,* ed. Adela de la Torre and Beatríz M. Pesquera (Berkeley, Calif., 1993), 15–33; Saidiya Hartman, *Scenes of Subjection: Terror, Slavery, and Self-Making in Nineteenth-Century America* (New York, 1997), 81–85; Trevor Burnard, "The Sexual Life of an Eighteenth-Century Jamaican Slave Overseer," in *Sex and Sexuality in Early America,* ed. Merrill D. Smith (New York, 1998), 176. For a penetrating critique of the agency granted to Sally Hemings by recent historians, see Mia Bay, "In Search of Sally Hemings in the Post-DNA Era," *Reviews in American History* 34 (2006): 407–26.

30. Patterson, *Slavery and Social Death,* 173; Thelma Jennings, "'Us Colored Women

Had to Go through a Plenty': Sexual Exploitation of African-American Slave Women,"
Journal of Women's History 1 (1990): 45–74; Virginia Meacham Gould, "In Full Enjoyment
of Their Liberty: The Free Women of Color of the Gulf Ports of New Orleans, Mobile
and Pensacola, 1769–1860" (PhD diss., Emory University, 1991), 3–5; Brown, *Good Wives,*
237–38; Morgan, "Interracial Sex in the Chesapeake and the British Atlantic World," 52–84;
Eileen J. Suárez Findlay, *Imposing Decency: The Politics of Sexuality and Race in Puerto Rico,
1870–1920* (Durham, N.C., 1999), 31–33; Adrienne Davis, "The Private Law of Race and Sex:
An Antebellum Perspective," *Stanford Law Review* 51 (1999): 227n12, 229–30; Rothman,
Notorious in the Neighborhood, 2–3; Trevor Burnard, "'Do Thou in Gentle Phibia Smile':
Scenes from an Interracial Marriage, Jamaica, 1754–86," in *Beyond Bondage: Free Women of
Color in the Americas,* ed. David Barry Gaspar and Darlene Clark Hine (Urbana, Ill., 2004),
82–105. Sharon Block and Tiya Miles both note that white women, especially but not ex-
clusively servant women, were also subject to sexual coercion and had limited sexual
choices, although both are careful to note the differences between them and enslaved
women (Block, "Limits of Color, Sex, and Service: Comparative Sexual Coercion in Early
America," in *Sex, Love, Race: Crossing Boundaries in North American History,* ed. Martha
Hodes [New York, 1999], 141–63; Miles, *Ties That Bind: The Story of an Afro-Cherokee Family in Slavery and Freedom* [Berkeley, Calif., 2005], 45–48, 233n13).

31. On the importance of marriage in defining social boundaries, see Kingsley Davis,
"Intermarriage in Caste Societies," *American Anthropologist,* n.s., 43 (1941): 376–95, and
Gerald D. Berreman et al., "Discussion: Characterization of Caste and Class Systems," in
Caste and Race: Comparative Approaches, ed. Anthony De Reuck and Julie Knight (Boston,
1967), 18–19. On the role of the state in defining legitimate and illegitimate marriage part-
ners, see Nancy F. Cott, *Public Vows: A History of Marriage and the Nation* (Cambridge,
Mass., 2000), 1–7.

32. For the life story of one twentieth-century Cuban woman who chose to marry a
white man in order to improve the possibilities for her children, see María de los Reyes
Castillo Bueno, as told to her daughter Daisy Rubiera Castillo, *Reyita: The Life of a Black
Cuban Woman in the Twentieth Century* (Durham, N.C., 2000), 21–22, 166.

33. Jennifer M. Spear, "Revolutionary Revelry? Disorder among New Orleans' 'Lower
Orders,'" *Atlantic Studies: Literary, Cultural, and Historical Perspectives* (forthcoming).

34. This was also true in the British North American colonies and the antebellum U.S.
South; even when relationships involved Euro-American women and African American
men, authorities did not always prosecute them (Hodes, *White Women, Black Men;* Rothman, *Notorious in the Neighborhood*).

35. Patricia Galloway, *Choctaw Genesis, 1500–1700* (Lincoln, Nebr., 1996).

36. Usner, *Indians, Settlers, and Slaves.*

37. [*Summary of Census of Louisiana*], 1785, *American State Papers: Miscellaneous,* 10:381.
In greater New Orleans, 62 percent of the inhabitants were slaves, 6 percent free people of
color, and 32 percent white. Almost 60 percent of the entire colony's slave population lived
within this region as did over three-quarters of its free people of color. Today, this region
includes the eastern half of Jefferson Parish, Orleans Parish, the western half of St. Bernard
Parish, and the northern third or so of Plaquemines Parish.

38. Paul Lachance, "The Growth of the Free and Slave Populations of French Colonial Louisiana," in *French Colonial Louisiana and the Atlantic World,* 204–43.

39. Paul Lachance, "The Formation of a Three-Caste Society: Evidence from Wills in Antebellum New Orleans," *Social Science History* 18 (1994): 226–27. In 1769, for every 100 Euro-Louisianan women, there were 135 Euro-Louisiana men; for every 100 free women of color, there were 48 free men of color; and for every 100 enslaved women, there were 81 enslaved men.

40. Usner, *Indians, Settlers, and Slaves;* Lachance, "Growth of the Free and Slave Populations." On the variety of slave work, see, for example, "Case of Slaves of Sr. Dubreuil Held for Theft," June 9–24, 1748, RSC, *LHQ* 19 (1936): 1089–94, and Thomas N. Ingersoll, "A View from the Parish Jail: New Orleans," *Common-place* 3 (2003), www.common-place .org/vol-03/no-04/new-orleans (accessed June 7, 2007).

41. On the importance of distinguishing between slaveowning and slave societies, see Berlin, *Many Thousands Gone,* 8–9, and Philip D. Morgan, "British Encounters with Africans and African-Americans, circa 1600–1780," in *Strangers Within the Realm: Cultural Margins of the First British Empire,* ed. Bernard Bailyn and Morgan (Chapel Hill, N.C., 1991), 157–219.

42. Virginia's situation in the nineteenth century was clearly quite different, yet face to face relations also had a mitigating effect on race relations there. See Marvin Patrick Ely, *Israel on the Appomattox: A Southern Experiment in Black Freedom from the 1790s through the Civil War* (New York, 2004), and Eva Sheppard Wolf, *Race and Liberty in the New Nation: Emancipation in Virginia from the Revolution to Nat Turner's Rebellion* (Baton Rouge, La., 2006), chapter 4.

43. Clark, *Masterless Mistresses,* 166–68.

44. Tannenbaum, *Slave and Citizen.*

45. Kimberly S. Hanger, *Bounded Lives, Bounded Places: Free Black Society in Colonial New Orleans, 1769–1803* (Durham, N.C., 1997), 111.

46. Stoler, "Carnal Knowledge and Imperial Power," 86; Hodes, *White Women, Black Men.*

47. For similar cautions, see Chaplin, "Race," 154, and Barbara Y. Welke, "When All the Women Were White, and All the Blacks Were Men: Gender, Class, Race, and the Road to *Plessy,* 1855–1914," *Law and History Review* 13 (1995): 315–16. For an exceptional analysis that treats race as influencing but not determining the behavior and experiences of nonelite Mexicans, see R. Douglas Cope, *The Limits of Racial Domination: Plebeian Society in Colonial Mexico City, 1660–1720* (Madison, Wisc. 1994).

48. As Greg Dening has argued, "cross-cultural history should be written in such a way that the reader is always reminded of strangeness by leaving key words untranslated" (*Performances* [Chicago, 1996], 77).

49. David Goodman Croly, George Wakenman, and E. C. Howell, *Miscegenation: The Theory of the Blending of the Races, Applied to the American White Man and Negro* (New York, 1863), ii, 25. On the history of the word "miscegenation," see David Roediger, *The Wages of Whiteness: Race and the Making of the American Working Class* (New York, 1991), 155–56, and Hodes, *White Women, Black Men,* 9, 264n49.

50. According to nineteenth-century travel accounts, "plaçage" developed as just such a term. However, the word rarely appears in the archival record and, when it does, it is more likely to be used to describe a racially endogamous couple. See Diana Williams, " 'They Call It Marriage': The Interracial Louisiana Family and the Making of American Legitimacy" (PhD diss., Harvard University, 2007), 188–91. Ken Aslakson, in a conversation with the author in February 2004, also suggested that this is how the term is used in the records.

51. "De color libre" appears in the nonwhite marriage registers for the first time in 1816 (St. Louis Cathedral, marriages of negros and mulatos, 1777–1830, SLC, M3, 51v). My thanks to Emily Clark for bringing this to my attention. On the wide range of racial categories used throughout the Americas and the multiplicity of their meanings, see Thomas Mack Stephens, *Dictionary of Latin American Racial and Ethnic Terminology,* 2nd ed. (Gainesville, Fla., 1999).

52. In addition, as Ramon Gutiérrez notes, "we have little information concerning what racial classifications may or may not have meant in the routine of daily life" (*When Jesus Came,* 196).

Chapter 1. Indian Women, French Women, and the Regulation of Sex

1. Nuncupative will of Charles Hegron, surnamed Lamothe, March 18, 1745, Cabildo Archives, *LHQ* 3 (1920): 564–66; [succession of Charles Egron], March 18, May 7–8, 1745, RSC; baptism of Marie Magdelaine Egron, April 20, 1728, *Sacramental Records of the Roman Catholic Church of the Archdiocese of Mobile,* ed. Michael L. Farmer (Mobile, Ala., 2002), 206; baptism of Charles Aigron, December 3, 1736, *Love's Legacy: The Mobile Marriages Recorded in French, Transcribed, with Annotated Abstracts in English, 1724–1786,* ed. Jacqueline Olivier Vidrine (Lafayette, La., 1985), 126–27; marriage of Mathieu Threisnek and Magdeleine Sabourdin, August 26, 1760, *Love's Legacy,* 306–7. On Françoise's status as a slave, see Vidrine, *Love's Legacy,* xiii. On the precariousness of families that united enslaved and free, see Tiya Miles, *Ties That Bind: The Story of an Afro-Cherokee Family in Slavery and Freedom* (Berkeley, Calif., 2005).

2. D'Artaguiette to Pontchartrain, February 12, 1710, AC, C13a, 2:533–34. The commissaire ordonnateur was second in command after the governor.

3. Bienville was governor for twenty-two of the sixty-seven years between 1699 and 1766: 1701–13, 1716–17, 1718–25, 1733–43 (Joseph G. Dawson III, ed., *The Louisiana Governors: From Iberville to Edwards* [Baton Rouge, La., 1990], 7–13).

4. D'Artaguiette, "Libertinage manifeste de la population et moyen d'y remédier," September 8, 1712, AC, C13a, 2:799. Priests in the *pays d'en haut* were similarly more equivocal on the question of Indian-French marriages than secular officials, who "were much more consistent in their opposition" (Richard White, *The Middle Ground: Indians, Empires, and Republics in the Great Lakes Region, 1650–1815* [New York, 1991], 69–70).

5. Light Townsend Cummins, "Exploration and Settlement, 1519–1715," in *Louisiana: A History,* ed. Bennett H. Wall (Arlington Heights, Ill., 1984), 13–16.

6. Robert S. Weddle, introduction, in *La Salle, the Mississippi, and the Gulf: Three Primary Documents,* ed. Robert S. Weddle, Mary Christine Morkovsky, and Patricia Galloway (College Station, Tex., 1987), 3–7; Robert S. Weddle, *Wilderness Manhunt: The Spanish*

Search for La Salle (College Station, Tex., 1999), 10–11; Henri Joutel, *The La Salle Expedition to Texas: The Journal of Henri Joutel, 1684–1687*, trans. Johanna S. Warren (Austin, Tex., 1998).

7. James S. Pritchard, *In Search of Empire: The French in the Americas, 1670–1730* (New York, 2004); Marcel Giraud, "France and Louisiana in the Early Eighteenth Century," *Mississippi Valley Historical Review* 36 (1950): 657–74.

8. Jean-Baptiste Bérnard de La Harpe, *The Historical Journal of the Establishment of the French in Louisiana,* trans. Joan Cain and Virginia Koenig (Lafayette, La., 1971), 75–76; Daniel H. Usner Jr., *Indians, Settlers, and Slaves in a Frontier Exchange Economy: The Lower Mississippi Valley before 1783* (Chapel Hill, N.C., 1992), 63.

9. *Census of the Inhabitants of the First Settlement on the Gulf Coast, Fort Maurepas,* December 1699, *Census Tables,* 1–3.

10. *Census of the Officers, Petty Officers, Sailors, Canadians, Freebooters, and Others Located at Biloxi,* May 25, 1700, *Census Tables,* 4–7.

11. [Nicolas de La Salle], *Census of Louisiana,* August 12, 1708, AC, C13a, 2:225–27.

12. M. de Rémonville, "Memoir, Addressed to Count de Pontchartrain, on the Importance of Establishing a Colony in Louisiana," December 10, 1697, *Historical Collections of Louisiana and Florida, including Translations of Original Manuscripts Relating to Their Discovery and Settlements, with Numerous Historical and Biographical Notes,* ed. B. F. French (New York, 1869), 15–16.

13. *List of the Marriageable Girls Who Arrived Aboard the Pelican at Biloxi,* 1704, *Census Tables,* 8; Nicolas de La Salle, "Dénombrement dechaque chose et l'estate où se trouve à présent la colonie de la Louisiane," August 31, 1704, AC, C13a, 1:468–70; André Pénicaut, *Fleur de Lys and Calumet: Being the Pénicaut Narrative of French Adventure in Louisiana,* trans. Richebourg Gaillard McWilliams (Tuscaloosa, Ala., 1988), 96.

14. M. Thomas Hatley, *The Dividing Paths: Cherokees and South Carolinians through the Revolutionary War* (Oxford, 1995), 34, 44, 96–97; James Merrell, *The Indians' New World: Catawbas and Their Neighbors from European Contact through the Era of Removal* (New York, 1989); Sylvia Van Kirk, *Many Tender Ties: Women in Fur-Trade Society, 1670–1870* (Norman, Okla., 1983); White, *Middle Ground,* 69; Joshua Aaron Piker, *Okfuskee: A Creek Indian Town in Colonial America* (Cambridge, Mass., 2004), 167–71.

15. Father Le Petit to Father d'Avaugour, July 12, 1730, *JR,* 68:201.

16. Antoine Simon Le Page du Pratz, *Histoire de Louisiane, contenant la découverte de ce vaste pays,* 3 vols. (Paris, 1758), 2:397–405. Le Page du Pratz may have fathered a child with a Natchez woman (Marcel Giraud, *A History of French Louisiana,* vol. 5, *The Company of the Indies, 1723–1731,* trans. Brian Pearce [Baton Rouge, La., 1991], 393). On Indian woman as "cultural mediators," see Clara Sue Kidwell, "Indian Women as Cultural Mediators," *Ethnohistory* 39 (1992): 97–107.

17. Giraud, "France and Louisiana in the Early Eighteenth Century," 657–74.

18. Pénicaut, *Fleur de Lys,* 105–7. Natchitoches, like Hasinais, one of the other Caddo confederacies, probably used physical gestures to welcome visitors in ways that Europeans misunderstood as sexual invitations. See Juliana Barr, "A Diplomacy of Gender: Rituals of First Contact in the 'Land of the Tejas,'" *WMQ,* 3rd ser., 61 (2004): 425–27, and; George Sabo, III, "Reordering their World: A Caddoan Ethnohistory," in *Visions and Revisions:*

Ethnohistoric Perspectives on Southern Cultures, ed. George Sabo III and William M. Schneider (Athens, Ga., 1987), 34–35.

19. Pénicaut, *Fleur de Lys,* 107, 108, 115–16; Jean François Benjamin Dumont de Montigny, *Mémoires historiques sur la Louisiane, contenant ce qui y est arrivé de plus mémorable depuis l'année 1687 jusqu'à présent,* ed. Jean Baptiste Le Mascrier, 2 vols. (Paris, 1743), 2:41–42, 35–36. See also "Mémoire sur la Louisiane," [after July 28], 1710, AC, C13a, 2:564. As late as 1726, post commandants bemoaned the necessity of sending soldiers to live "among the Indian nations" (Drouot de Valdeterre, ["Mémoire"], 1726, AC, C13a, 10:10v.

20. Le Page du Pratz, *Histoire de Louisiane,* 2:324–25.

21. Kathleen M. Brown, "The Anglo-Algonquian Gender Frontier," in *Negotiators of Change: Historical Perspectives on Native American Women,* ed. Nancy Shoemaker (New York, 1995), 26–48.

22. Duclos to Pontchartrain, July 10, 1713, *MPAFD,* 2:75; Cadillac to Pontchartrain, October 26, 1713, *MPAFD,* 2:168–69.

23. D'Artaguiette to Pontchartrain, June 20, 1710, *MPAFD,* 2:56.

24. Pontchartrain to Bienville, January 30, 1704, *MPAFD,* 3:17.

25. Pénicaut, *Fleur de Lys,* 68–69, 101–2.

26. Le Page du Pratz, *Histoire de Louisiane,* 1:82–83, 114–16.

27. *General Census of Inhabitants in the Area of Biloxi and Mobile, as Reported by Le Sieur Diron, Habitants of Fort Louis de la Mobile,* June 26, 1721, *Census Tables,* 23–27; *General Census of All Inhabitants of New Orleans and Environs, as Reported by Le Sieur Diron,* November 24, 1721, *Census Tables,* 17–22.

28. Giraud, *History of French Louisiana,* 5:316; James T. McGowan, "Planters without Slaves: Origins of a New World Labor System," *Southern Studies* 16 (1977): 18.

29. Cadillac to Pontchartrain, October 26, 1713, *MPAFD,* 2:169.

30. Father Henry de La Vente, "Mémoire sur la conduite des françois dans la Louisiane," 1713 or 1714, AC, C13a, 3:390; Cadillac to Superior Council, January 2, 1716, AC, C13a, 4:530–32.

31. Cadillac to Superior Council, January 2, 1716, AC, C13a, 4:531–32; Cadillac to Pontchartrain, October 26, 1713, *MPAFD,* 2:169.

32. La Vente to Pontchartrain, March 2, 1708, *MPAFD,* 2:31; superiors of the Foreign Missions to minister, [1708], AC, C13a, 2:161–64.

33. Bienville to Pontchartrain, February 25, 1708, *MPAFD,* 3:124; Bienville to Pontchartrain, October 12, 1708, *MPAFD,* 2:43.

34. Cadillac to Superior Council, January 2, 1716, AC, C13a, 4:531–32.

35. Gabriel Marest to Père Germon, November 9, 1712, *JR,* 66:293.

36. La Vente, "Mémoire sur la conduite des françois dans la Louisiane," 393–95; [La Salle], *Census of Louisiana,* August 12, 1708, AC, C13a, 2:226.

37. La Vente, "Mémoire sur la conduite des françois dans la Louisiane," 393–95; "Mémoire sur la Louisiane," 2:565.

38. La Vente, "Mémoire sur la conduite des françois dans la Louisiane," 392–93; Father Raphaël to Abbé Raguet, May 15, 1725, *MPAFD,* 2:478. Karen Anderson argues that Catholic missionaries in New France saw "the institution of Christian marriages" as "the key to

control of the entire [native] society" (*Chain Her by One Foot: The Subjugation of Native Women in Seventeenth-Century New France* [New York, 1991], 79).

39. Pénicaut, *Fleur de Lys,* 97.

40. Colbert to Talon, April 5, 1666, AC, CII, 2:205–5v; Colbert to St. Germain, April 6, 1667, AC, CII, 2:297; Mack Eastman, *Church and State in Early Canada* (Edinburgh, 1915), 119. On the pragmatism of Colbert's policies "despite his personal revulsion for indigenous peoples," see Alisa V. Petrovich, "Perception and Reality: Colbert's Native American Policy," *LH* 39 (1998): 73–83. On Colbert's promarriage and pronatalist policies in France itself, see Jean-Louis Flandrin, *Sex in the Western World: The Development of Attitudes and Behavior,* trans. Sue Collins (Philadelphia, 1991), 5.

41. Cadillac to minister, October 18, 1700, *Michigan Historical Collections* 33 (1903): 99; Cadillac to Maurepas, [between 1693 and 1704], *Découvertes et établissements des français dans l'ouest et dans le sud de l'Amérique Septentrionale (1614–1754): Mémoires et documents originaux recueillis,* ed. Pierre Margry, 6 vols. (Paris, 1876–86), 5:146–47. On New France, see Honorius Provost, "Mariages entre Canadiens et sauvages," *Bulletin de Recherches historiques* 54 (1948): 46–57, and Cornelius J. Jaenen, "Miscegenation in Eighteenth-Century New France," in *New Dimensions in Ethnohistory: Papers of the Second Laurier Conference on Ethnohistory and Ethnology,* ed. Barry Gough and Laird Christie (Hull, Quebec, 1991), 79–115. On the impact that Indian resistance to conversion had on missionaries' representations of them, see Masarah Van Eyck, "'We Shall Be One People': Early Modern French Perceptions of the Amerindian Body" (PhD diss., McGill University, 2001), 175, and Sue Peabody, "'A Nation Born to Slavery': Missionaries and Racial Discourse in Seventeenth-Century French Antilles," *Journal of Social History* 38 (2004): 113–26.

42. Cadillac likely supported La Vente's proposal not only because it built on his own past policies but also because he and Bienville, who remained in the colony as military commander while Cadillac was governor, had disagreements and because he perceived the colony to be a particularly disordered, indeed detestable, place. See Cadillac to Superior Council, January 2, 1716, AC, C13a, 4:530–32. For his part, Bienville's opposition may have, in part, stemmed from his dislike of La Vente and the latter's challenge to his secular authority. See Jean Delanglez, *The French Jesuits in Lower Louisiana (1700–1763)* (Washington, D.C., 1935), 396.

43. Bienville to minister, October 10, 1706, AC, C13b1, 1:13v–14.

44. Duclos to Pontchartrain, December 25, 1715, AC, C13a, 3:820–21.

45. Diron d'Artaguiette, "Journal of Diron d'Artaguiette," 1722–23, *Travels in the American Colonies,* ed. Newton Dennison Mereness (New York, 1916), 48, 73. On French misunderstandings of native sexual practices, see White, *Middle Ground,* 61–65.

46. Joutel, *The La Salle Expedition to Texas,* 219.

47. Pénicaut, *Fleur de Lys,* 85–86, 18.

48. Iberville, "The Iberville Journal," 1699, *A Comparative View of French Louisiana, 1699 and 1762: The Journals of Pierre Le Moyne d'Iberville and Jean-Jacques-Blaise d'Abbadie,* ed. and trans. Carl A. Brasseaux (Lafayette, La., 1979), 50.

49. Vaughan Baker, Amos Simpson, and Mathé Allain, "*Le Mari Est Seigneur:* Marital Laws Governing Women in French Louisiana," in *Louisiana's Legal Heritage,* ed. Edward F.

Haas, *Studies in Louisiana Culture* (Pensacola, Fla., 1983), 7–17; Vaughan B. Baker, "Cherchez les Femmes: Some Glimpses of Women in Early Eighteenth-Century Louisiana," *LH* 31 (1990): 21–37; Roderick Phillips, "Women and Family Breakdown in Eighteenth-Century France: Rouen, 1780–1800," *Social History* 2 (1976): 197–218; Amos E. Simpson, "Women and the Law in French Colonial Louisiana," in *Proceedings of the Fifth Meeting of the French Colonial Historical Society, March 29–April 1, 1979,* ed. James J. Cooke (Washington, D.C., 1980), 16–17.

50. Diron d'Artaguiette, "Journal of Diron d'Artaguiette," 48. See also Pierre François Xavier de Charlevoix, *Journal of a Voyage to North America,* 2 vols. (London, 1761), 264–65.

51. John R. Swanton, *The Indians of the Southeastern United States* (Washington, D.C., 1946), 707–8.

52. Patricia Galloway, "'The Chief Who Is Your Father': Choctaw and French Views of the Diplomatic Relation," in *Powhatan's Mantle: Indians in the Colonial Southeast,* ed. Peter H. Wood, Gregory A. Waselkov, and M. Thomas Hatley (Lincoln, Nebr., 1989), 254–56; Fred B. Kniffen, Hiram F. Gregory, and George A. Stokes, *The Historic Indian Tribes of Louisiana: From 1542 to the Present* (Baton Rouge, La., 1987), 223–25, 231–32.

53. Jean Bernard Bossu, *Nouveaux voyages aux Indes Occidentales, contenant une relation des différens peuples qui habitent les environs du grand fleuve Saint-Louis appelé vulgairement le Mississipi,* 2 vols. (Paris, 1768), 2:21; Le Petit to Father d'Avaugour, July 12, 1730, *JR,* 68:135; "Relation du Sieur de Lamothe Cadillac," [1718], *Découvertes et établissements,* 5:101–2.

54. Le Petit to Father d'Avaugour, July 12, 1730, *JR,* 68:143.

55. Diron d'Artaguiette, "Journal of Diron d'Artaguiette," 48; d'Artaguiette to Pontchartrain, June 20, 1710, *MPAFD,* 2:58; Duclos to Pontchartrain, December 25, 1715, AC, C13a, 3:820–21.

56. François Le Marie [to minister], January 15, 1714, ed. Jean Delangez, *Mid-America,* n.s. 8, 19 (1937), 143–44.

57. Robert Morrissey, "'Contrary to Good Order': Negotiating Authority and Subjection in Eighteenth Century Illinois Country" (paper presented at the eleventh annual conference of the Omohundro Institute of Early American History and Culture, University of California, Santa Barbara, June 2005).

58. D'Artaguiette, "Libertinage manifeste de la population et moyen d'y remédier," 799.

59. Tivas de Gourville, "On the Establishment of Louisiana," June 1712, *MPAFD,* 2:69.

60. Cadillac to Pontchartrain, October 26, 1713, *MPAFD,* 2:167, 171.

61. In another context, Vaudreuil defended a French soldier who had been accused of rape, claiming that "young men are subject to such weaknesses" (Vaudreuil to Father Baudouin, October 13, 1745, Vaudreuil Letterbooks, 3:181).

62. La Vente, "Mémoire sur la conduite des françois dans la Louisiane," 392.

63. "Relation de la Louisianne, ou Mississipi, écrite à une dame, par un officer de marine," *Relations de la Louisiane, et du fleuve Mississipi,* ed. Jean Frédéric Bernard (Amsterdam, 1720), 13.

64. Périer to Count de Maurepas, July 25, 1732, AC, C13a, 14:69–69v.

65. Ann Stoler argues that "it was through the policing of sex that subordinate European military and civil servants were kept in line and that racial boundaries were thus maintained" ("Carnal Knowledge and Imperial Power: Gender, Race, and Morality in Colonial Asia," in *Gender at the Crossroads of Knowledge: Feminist Anthropology in the Postmodern Era,* ed. Micaela di Leonardo [Berkeley, Calif., 1991], 55).

66. Southeastern Indian women, as the principal farmers within their own communities, in fact had much they could offer the struggling French colonizers, who often failed to grow enough to feed themselves.

67. Duclos to Pontchartrain, December 25, 1715, AC, C13a, 3:819–24; Procès-verbal du Conseil [de Marine], September 1, 1716, French Provincial Records (1678–1762), Mississippi Department of Archives and History, 8:30–32; d'Artaguiette to Pontchartrain, June 20, 1710, *MPAFD,* 2:58.

68. Sarah Hanley, "Family and State in Early Modern France: The Marital Law Compact," in *Connecting Spheres: European Women in a Globalizing World, 1500 to the Present,* ed. Marilyn J. Boxer and Jean H. Quataert (New York, 2000), 61–72.

69. Baker, Simpson, and Allain, *"Le Mari Est Seigneur,"* 7–17; Barbara B. Diefendorf, "Widowhood and Remarriage in Sixteenth-Century Paris," *Journal of Family History* 7 (1982): 379–95.

70. All of the quotations in this and the next two paragraphs come from the following sources: Fleuriau to Superior Council, [before December 18, 1728], transcribed in Charles Gayarré, *Histoire de la Louisiane,* 2 vols. (New Orleans, 1846–47), 1:239–41; La Chaise to Company of the Indies, February 15, 1729, *Histoire de la Louisiane,* 1:238–39; "Arrêt du Conseil Supérieur de la Louisiane concernant le mariage des Français avec les sauvagesses," December 18, 1728, AC, A, 23:102–3. Additional information comes from Jaenen, "Miscegenation in Eighteenth-Century New France," 101–2.

71. See Lettres patentes pour l'établissement d'une compagnie de commerce, sous le nom de "Compagnie d'Occident," August 1717, *Édits, ordonnances royaux, declarations et arrêts du Conseil d'État du Roi concernant le Canada,* 3 vols. (Quebec, 1854–56), 1:381, article 23. Earlier patents had explicitly granted régnicole status to Indians who converted to Catholicism (Acte pour l'établissement de la compagnies des cent associés pour le commerce du Canada, contenant les articles accordés à ladite compagnis par M. Le Cardinal de Richelieu, April 29, 1627, *Édits,* 1:5–11, article 17; Contrat de rétablissement de la Compagnie des Isles de l'Amérique, avec les articles accordés par sa majesté aux associés, February 12, 1635, *Loix et constitutions,* 1:29–33, article 11; Édit concernant la Compagnie des Isles de l'Amérique, March 1642, *Loix et constitutions,* 1:51–55, article 13). On changing conceptions of citizenship in eighteenth-century France, see David Avrom Bell, *The Cult of the Nation in France: Inventing Nationalism, 1680–1800* (Cambridge, Mass., 2001), and Peter Sahlins, "Fictions of a Catholic France: The Naturalization of Foreigners, 1685–1787," *Representations* 47 (1994): 85–110. Fleuriau's distinction between Indian women who lived under French laws (and presumably within the French church) and those "who always remained in their villages" echoes a practice visible in the Mobile sacramental registries of the early eighteenth century. Priests described as "Indienne" those women who had become Catholics,

married French men, and settled at the French post while using "sauvagesse" for all others. See, for instance, marriage of Pierre Paquet and Magdelaine Baudrau, August 26, 1726, *Love's Legacy,* 52–53, as well as Vidrine's introduction, xvi.

72. In early modern France, mothers were not as a matter of law automatically appointed guardians of their minor children on the death of their husbands but, in practice, they most often were unless they were also minors (Julie Hardwick, *The Practice of Patriarchy: Gender and the Politics of Household Authority in Early Modern France* [University Park, Penn., 1998], 120–24, and Diefendorf, "Widowhood and Remarriage in Sixteenth-Century Paris," 386).

73. "Arrêt du Conseil Supérieur de la Louisiane concernant le mariage des français avec les sauvagesses," 23:102–3; Jaenen, "Miscegenation in Eighteenth-Century New France," 101.

74. La Chaise to Company of the Indies, February 15, 1729, *Histoire de la Louisiane,* 1:238–39.

75. [Succession of Charles Egron], March 18, May 7–8, 1745, RSC; petition of Thomas Desercy, July 22, 1746, RSC.

76. Decree of Superior Council, December 18, 1728, AC, F3, 11.2:292–96, cited in Jaenen, "Miscegenation in Eighteenth-Century New France," 101.

77. Cadillac to Minister, January 2, 1716, AC, C13a, 4:530.

78. Procès-verbal du Conseil [de Marine], September 1, 1716, French Provincial Records, 8:30–32; Duclos to Pontchartrain, December 25, 1715, AC, C13a, 3:819–24.

79. Although the Spanish term "mulato" had come to mean mixed European-African ancestry by Duclos' time, in the sixteenth century it referred to mixed Spanish-Muslim ancestry (Thomas Stephens, *Dictionary of Latin American Racial and Ethnic Terminology,* 2nd ed. [Gainesville, Fla., 1999], 352–54). According to a 1701 French dictionary, the Spanish word could refer more generally to children "born of parents from different religions" (Abbé Antoine Furetière, *Dictionnaire universel, contenant generalement tous les mots françois tant vieux que modernes, et les termes des sciences et des arts . . . ,* 2nd ed., rev., corr., and aug. Basnage de Bauval, 3 vols. [La Haye and Rotterdam, 1701], entry for "mulat").

80. Vaudreuil and Raudot to minister, November 14, 1709, AC, C11a, 30:453–54. As Catherine Desbarats notes, Vaudreuil's rhetoric of "bad blood" emerged precisely at the time that Indian slavery was being legalized in New France; thus it operated as a justificatory discourse ("Following *The Middle Ground,*" *WMQ,* 3rd ser., 63 [2006]: 91–92).

81. Procès-verbal du Conseil [de Marine], September 1, 1716, French Provincial Records, 8:31, quoting La Vente's metropolitan supervisors, the superiors of the Foreign Missions.

82. Le Page du Pratz, *Histoire de Louisiane,* 3:238. Le Page du Pratz's knowledge of this speech, at which there were no European observers, probably came from the Natchez noblewoman, La Bras-Piqué (Stung Arm), who, after the Natchez uprising, was captured and sent as a slave to work on the concession that Le Page du Pratz was managing (Shannon Lee Dawdy, "Enlightenment from the Ground: Le Page du Pratz's *Histoire de la Louisiane,*" *French Colonial History* 3 [2003]: 21).

83. La Vente to l'abbé Jacques de Brisacier, July 4, 1708, Séminaire de Québec, État general des fonds, Lettres R., no. 83, 20, le Centre de reference de l'Amérique Française, maf.mcq.org/anq/fiches/fiche-453.html?p=113 (accessed August 31, 2008). See also "Mé-

moire sur la Louisiane," 2:565, based on La Vente's reporting, in which he argued the children's "blood is not corrupted."

84. Bishop of Quebec to the directors of the Company of the Indies, October 15, 1725, 422–23.

85. Pénicaut, *Fleur de Lys,* 24.

86. Procès-verbal du Conseil [de Marine], September 1, 1716, French Provincial Records, 8:30.

87. Pénicaut, *Fleur de Lys,* 110; [Bourgmont], "Exact Description of Louisiana, of Its Harbors, Lands, and Rivers, and Names of the Indian Tribes That Occupy It, and the Commerce and Advantages to be Derived Therefrom for the Establishment of a Colony," [1710s?], in Frank Norall, *Bourgmont, Explorer of the Missouri, 1698–1735* (Lincoln, Nebr., 1988), 109. On the crucial role of aesthetic judgments in eighteenth- and nineteenth-century French racialist ideologies, see Tzevtan Todorov, *On Human Diversity: Nationalism, Racism and Exoticism in French Thought* (Cambridge, 1993), 103–5.

88. "Relation de la Louisianne, ou Mississipi, ecrite à une dame, par un officer de marine," 13 ("olive complexion"); Chevalier de Bonrepos, *Description du Mississipi, le nombre des villes et colonies établies par les françois, les isles, rivières, et territoires qui le bordent depuis le levant jusqu'au couchant et du nord au sud, les moeurs et négoces des sauvages que y habitent, le manière de se faire la guerre et la paix, la fertilité du pays, et la chasse aux diférens animaux que s'y trouvant* (Paris, 1720), 14 ("of a swarthy complexion"); Le Marie [to minister], January 15, 1714, 143 ("reddish rather than olivastre").

89. Bossu, *Nouveaux voyages aux Indes Occidentales,* 2:187–88. On the belief that pregnant women's thoughts could influence their children's physical appearance, see Mary E. Fissell, "Gender and Generation: Representing Reproduction in Early Modern England," *Gender and History* 7 (1995): 433–56. For a rare author who suggested malleability in considering Africans' skin color, which he attributed to maternal impression, see Jean Mocquet, *Voyages en Afrique, Asie, Indes Orientales, et Occidentales* (Rouen, 1645), 254–55.

90. Le Page du Pratz, *Histoire de Louisiane,* 2:311.

91. On color-coded discourses of race, see Nancy Shoemaker, "How Indians Got to Be Red," *AHR* 102 (1997): 625–44.

92. Jaenen, "Miscegenation in Eighteenth-Century New France," argues that there was no consistent overarching policy either for or against Indian-French marriages. Giraud, *History of French Louisiana,* 5:463–65, contends that prohibitory decrees were ineffective, while Delanglez, *French Jesuits in Lower Louisiana,* 402, finds no evidence that the December 1728 decree was ratified and that overall "the French Government never issued any positive prohibition," although it did wish "to make these marriages more difficult." Even the white supremacist nineteenth-century historian Charles Gayarré, *History of Louisiana,* vols. 1–2, *The French Domination* (New York, 1867), 1:393, argued that the government "neither sanctioned . . . nor actually prohibited" French-Indian marriage. Cf. Guillaume Aubert, "'Français, Nègres et Sauvages': Constructing Race in Colonial Louisiana" (PhD diss., Tulane University, 2002), 133–76, who insists that the 1716 instructions imposed a generally effective ban on Indian-French marriages.

93. Instructions pour le Sieur d'Iberville, capitaine de fregate Legere, pour le voyage

qu'il va faire au Mississippy, August 27, 1701, AC, B, 1:161v–62, cited in Aubert, "'Français, Nègres et Sauvages,'" 148. See also "Mémoire donné par le sieur d'Iberville des costes, qu'occupe l'Angleterre dans l'Amérique septentrionales, depuis la rivière Saint-Mathieu jusqu'à la rivière Saint-Georges," 1701, *Découvertes et établissements,* 4:550n1.

94. Pontchartrain to Cadillac, July 6, 1709, AC, B, 30:164. For Vaudreuil's opposition, see Vaudreuil and Raudot to minister, November 14, 1709, AC CIIa, 30:4–22v.

95. "Mémoire du roi pour servir d'instructions à La Mothe-Cadillac, gouverneur de Louisiane," December 27, 1710, AC, C13a, 3:716; "Memoir . . . to Sieur de Muy, Governor of Louisiana, to Serve Him When He Arrives in That Country," June 30, 1707, *MPAFD,* 3:56; Pontchartrain to Bienville, May 10, 1710, *MPAFD,* 3:140.

96. Remarks on letters of Cadillac, September 15, 1708, *Michigan Historical Collections* 33 (1903): 391; Pontchartrain to Bienville, May 10, 1710, *MPAFD,* 3:140–41; "Mémoire du roi pour servir d'instructions à La Mothe-Cadillac," 716. For similar fears among New France officials, see White, *Middle Ground,* 58.

97. Périer to Count de Maurepas, January 25, 1733, AC, C13a, 16:184v–85. See also Vaudreuil to Maurepas, December 6, 1744, Vaudreuil Letterbooks, 1:39v. Complaints about the independence of Illinois' habitants may have reflected various governors' frustration at their inability to govern as they thought appropriate rather than actual (mis)behavior of the region's residents.

98. "Declaration du roi, qui supprime et déclare nuls tous les Congez et permissions qui ont esté et seront expediez pour aller en traite chez les sauvages du Canada," May 21, 1696, *Acts of French Royal Administration Concerning Canada, Guiana, the West Indies and Louisiana, Prior to 1791,* comp. Lawrence C. Wroth and Gertrude L. Annan (New York, 1930), 34; "Instructions pour le sieur chevalier de callières, gouverneur et lieutenant general pour le roy," May 25, 1699, *Collection de manuscrits contenant lettres, mémoires, et autres documents historiques relatifs a la Nouvelle-France, recueillis aux Archives de la province de Québec, ou copiés a l'étranger,* 4 vols. (Quebec, 1883–1885), 2:319–26.

99. Procès-verbal du Conseil [de Marine], September 1, 1716, French Provincial Records, 8:31–32; "Mémoire du roi pour servir d'instruction à Lespinay, gouverneur, et à Hubert, ordonnateur," [1716], AC, C13a, 4:977–78.

100. See the discussion of the 1724 Code Noir in chapter 2.

101. "Arrêt du Conseil Supérieur de la Louisiane concernant le mariage des français avec les sauvagesses, 23:102–3; Fleuriau to Superior Council, [before December 18, 1728], 1:239–41. An unknown commentator, perhaps La Chaise, noted in the margins that "despite this prohibition, there are already several of these marriages in the Colony." See also Périer and La Chaise to the directors of the Company of the Indies, March 25, 1729, *MPAFD,* 2:636–37, in which Périer and La Chaise claim they were doing "everything in our power to prevent alliances of Frenchmen with Indian women."

102. La Chaise to Company of the Indies, February 15, 1729, *Histoire de la Louisiane,* 1:238–39.

103. Salmon to minister, July 17, 1732, AC, C13a, 15:167–68; Périer to Maurepas, July 25, 1732, AC, C13a, 14:69–69v. Salmon speculated that "these alliances should reinforce the union and that the sauvages should consider as us brothers, and that they should keep for us an inviolable fidelity." But, he continued, their "nature is stronger," and their attach-

ments were driven by who could offer them the most, regardless of marital ties. He also complained that English traders were convincing Illinois Indians to oppose French efforts to take their lands.

104. Maurepas to Father Joseph François Lafitau, 1735, AC, B, 62:88v. In an interesting reversal of the usual impact of New France policies on Louisiana, in 1749, the commandant general of New France considered requesting "a prohibition from the Court similar to the one it issued for the Government of Louisiana" but decided instead to apply pressure on the bishop of Quebec to reduce the numbers of French-Indian marriages (Marquis de La Galissonière to Bishop Pontbriand, May 14, 1749, Archives de l'archevêché de Québec, registre G, 3:102, cited in Jaenen, "Miscegenation in Eighteenth-Century New France," 103).

105. André Lachance and Sylvie Savoie found only 180 sanctified Indian-French marriages between 1640 and 1780 throughout French North America ("Les Amérindiens sous le régime français," in *Les Marginaux, les exclus et l'Autre au Canada aux 17e et 18e siècles,* ed. André Lachance [Ville Saint-Laurent, Quebec, 1996], 190). Clearly marriages celebrated according to native customs as well as relationships that were never celebrated in the church but were long term and stable account for far more.

106. "Natchitoches and the Trail to the Rio Grande: Two Early Eighteenth Century Accounts by the Sieur Derbanne," trans. and ed. Katherine Bridges and Winston De Ville, *LH* 8 (1967): 241–42.

107. See, for instance, marriage of Jean Baptiste Brevel and Anne, July 27, 1736, *Natchitoches, 1729–1803: Abstracts of the Catholic Church Registers of the French and Spanish Post of St. Jean Baptiste des Natchitoches in Louisiana,* comp. Elizabeth Shown Mills (New Orleans, 1977), 4; baptism of Jean Baptiste, May 20, 1736, *Natchitoches, 1729–1803,* 7; baptism of Marie Louise, June 19, 1739, *Natchitoches, 1729–1803,* 16; funeral of Marie Thérèse Nantios, November 20, 1740, *Natchitoches, 1729–1803,* 28; marriage of Joseph Duc dit Ville Franche and Marie Anne Guedon, April 23, 1743, *Natchitoches, 1729–1803,* 42–43; marriage of Pierre Raimond and Françoise, March 20, 1774, *Natchitoches, 1729–1803,* 126–27.

108. F. Émile Audet, *Les premiers établissements français au pays des Illinois* (Paris, 1938), 43–44.

109. Petition of new marriage contract, February 15–23, 1725, RSC.

110. *Thibierge v. Marin de La Marque,* January 8, February 24, 1746, RSC, *LHQ* 15 (1932): 125, 146–151; Natalia Maree Belting, *Kaskaskia under the French Regime* (Urbana, Ill., 1948), 93; Superior Council, minutes, May 31, 1724, to February 3, 1725, *MPAFD,* 3:476.

111. Dumont de Montigny, *Mémoires historiques sur la Louisiane,* 2:75–78. Additional information comes from William Beer, "The Visit of Illinois Indians to France in 1725," *LHQ* 6 (1923): 189–93, and Frank Norall, *Bourgmont, Explorer of the Missouri,* 81–88. Dumont failed to make any mention Françoise Missoury in either his epic poem about Louisiana or the manuscript version of his history (entitled "Établissements du Mississippi"), which was heavily edited by Abbé Le Mascrier before being published as *Mémoires historiques sur la Louisiane.* Villiers du Terrage argues that it is highly improbable that the supposed massacre ever took place and suggests that Le Mascrier molded Dumont's more generalized portrayal of Indians as barbarous and treacherous using Françoise because she would have been well known in contemporary France (*La découverte du Missouri et l'histoire*

du Fort d'Orleans (1673–1728) [Paris, 1925], 115–24; "L'établissement de la province de la Louisiane: Poème composé de 1728 à 1742, par Dumont de Montigny," *Journal de la Société des Américanistes de Paris*, n.s., 23 [1931]: 285).

The creole nationalist historian Charles Gayarré repeated Dumont's story, in equally derisive terms, in his mid-nineteenth century *History of Louisiana*, although he changed some of the details, making Dubois the governor of the Illinois post, making Françoise an Illinois "princess," and claiming she helped her people "butcher" her husband and other French colonizers (1:394–96). Jean Bernard Bossu, who lived in Louisiana in the 1740s and visited later in the century, also related the story of the Missouri "Indian Princess" and her trip to France. His account makes it clear that Françoise Dubois was the same woman, as he notes that she later married Dubois and then Marin. According to Bossu, at the time of the trip to France (which he misdates as 1720), she was the Missouri commander M. de Bourgmont's "mistress" but married Dubois. For him, the story ends with the "Missourian lady" spreading word of the glories of France and Catholicism among her countrymen rather than abandoning French ways (*Nouveaux voyages aux Indes Occidentales*, 1:161–62, 166). Le Page du Pratz briefly mentions that the garrison at Fort d'Orléans "was slaughtered" but was not willing to simply blame Indian "treachery" as it could also have been, he points out, "the fault of the French" (*Histoire de Louisiane*, 1:325).

The trip of the Illinois, Missouri, Osage, and Oto chiefs to Paris had been organized by Bourgmont, who was continually in trouble with metropolitan officials for his "scandalous" and "infamous life" (for example, he deserted his post at Detroit with a married métis woman and fathered a son with a Missouri woman, perhaps Françoise). Officials attempted to have him arrested, but nonetheless they recognized that his knowledge and relationships with Illinois country nations made him useful. In 1722 he received a commission from the Company of the Indies to open a trade route to the Padoucas (Plains Apaches) and, on successfully completing this mission, was rewarded with elevation to the nobility. See Norall, *Bourgmont, Explorer of the Missouri.*

112. An emigrant from Montreal, Raphael Beauvais may have been unusual in that his first wife, whom he married in 1737, was Illinois métis Marie Catherine Alaric or Alarc, while his second (whom he married in 1762) was Marie Françoise, an Indian woman and the widow of Joseph Seguin (Belting, *Kaskaskia under the French Regime*, 91). In her study of the Illinois country, Cecilé Vidal argues that mixed marriages were "very numerous" in the early period and declined with the arrival of more European women after 1720. Most marriages after 1720 involved "lesser-well-off habitants" except where the bride was "a rich Amerindian widow of a deceased white habitant" and therefore a desirable marriage partner even for "the richest habitants" ("Africains et européens au pays des Illinois durant la période française (1699–1765)," *French Colonial History* 3 (2003): 62.

113. Belting, *Kaskaskia under the French Regime*, 10–12, 86–112.

114. Bienville and Salmon to minister, April 15, 1734, AC, C13a, 18:98–103. Bienville's decision was determined by a desire to keep relationships between Illinois Indians and the French colony peaceful.

115. Marriage of Angelique Girardy and Alain Dugue, June 25, 1727, SLC, M1, 131–32; marriage of Angelique Girardy and Jean Baptiste Rejas dit Laprade, June 26, 1730, SLC,

MI, 213–14. Angelique is noted as legitimate, indicating that her parents had been married before the church.

116. Marriage of Mathurin L'Horo and Marie, July 3, 1731, SLC, B6, 97. Marie, who was not given a last name, was identified as from the "Cauitta Village." She was the widow of a drummer who had died in the Natchez uprising of 1729.

117. Marriage of Joseph Turpin and Hyppolite, November 7, 1731, SLC, B1, 52.

118. Baptism of Pierre Ignace, October 20, 1720, *Sacramental Records of the Roman Catholic Church of the Archdiocese of Mobile,* 97.

119. Baptism, March 10, 1729, Mobile, parish register, cited in Marcel Giraud, *Histoire de la Louisiane française,* vol. 4, *La Louisiane après le système de law (1721–1723)* (Paris, 1974), 431–32; marriage of Etienne Teyssier and Madeline Renée de Mandeville, September 18, 1725, *Love's Legacy,* 20–21. For more on the Mandeville family and their relationships with Indian women, see chapter 5. Although Mandeville's fathering Madeline Renée did his career no harm, her husband, Sergeant Etienne Teyssier, was denied a promotion in 1726, despite a recommendation from Abbé Raguet, at least in part because of his recent marriage to "the natural daughter of Sr. de Mandeville, begat with a sauvagesse" ("État des éclaircissementes que la compagnie demande . . . ," [ca. October 1726], AC, G1, 412; "Mémoire concernant les demandes particulieres au sujet de différentes personnes qui sont à la Louisianne," [ca. October 1726], AC, G1, 412. See also Aubert, " 'Français, Nègres et Sauvages,' " 161.

120. Raphaël to Abbé Raguet, May 18, 1726, AC, C13a, 10:46v.

121. François Le Marie, "Mémoire sur la Louisiane, pour ester presente avec le carte de ce pais au Conseil souverain de la Marine," March 1, 1717, Bibliothèque nationale, Paris, Manuscrits, Fonds français, 12105:17, Library of Congress and Bibliothèque nationale de France, *France in America/La France en Amérique,* gallica.bnf.fr/ark:/12148/bpt6k1094680 (accessed July 26, 2008).

122. Tartarin's words here and in the next two paragraphs come from the following sources: Tartarin, "Mémoire sur les mariages des sauvagesses avec les françois," 1738, AC, C13a, 23:241–42; Tartarin to [unknown], 1738, AC, C13a, 23:243–43v.

123. La Vente, "Mémoire sur la conduite des françois dans la Louisiane," 392.

124. Giraud, "France and Louisiana in the Early Eighteenth Century," 668; Marcel Giraud, *A History of French Louisiana,* vol. 1, *The Reign of Louis XIV, 1698–1715,* trans. Joseph C. Lambert (Baton Rouge, La., 1974), 303–11.

125. Jennifer M. Spear, "Colonial Intimacies: Legislating Sex in French Louisiana," *WMQ,* 3rd ser., 60 (2003): 75–98.

126. Procès-verbal du Conseil [de Marine], September 1, 1716, French Provincial Records, 8:31.

127. D'Artaguiette, "Libertinage manifeste de la population et moyen d'y remédier," 799; d'Artaguiette to minister, February 26, 1708, AC, C13a, 2:137.

128. La Salle to minister, May 12, 1709, AC, C13a, 2:399–400.

129. D'Artaguiette, "Libertinage manifeste de la population et moyen d'y remédier," 799.

130. Mandeville, "Memoir on the Colony of Louisiana," April 29, 1709, *MPAFD,* 2:49. Just as La Vente's proposal to support French-Indian marriages followed on northern

precedents, so too did the calls for importing French brides. Colbert arranged for more than seven hundred women to be sent as brides to New France between 1663 and 1673; they were known as the "filles du roi" because the king supported them until their marriages and paid their dowries. Colbert also required his subordinate officers in New France to do all they could to encourage habitants and soldiers to marry (Colbert to Talon, February 11, 1671, *Collection de manuscrits,* 1:206–7; Yves Landry, "Gender Imbalance, Les Filles du Roi and Choice of Spouse in New France," in *Canadian Family History: Selected Readings,* ed. Bettina Bradbury [Toronto, 1992], 14–32).

131. Populating the "huge country" was one of the most vexing problems that faced French, and later Spanish, authorities. As one anonymous memoir reported, "This country is too extensive to preserve it with so few people" ("État de la Louisiane . . . ," AC, C13c, 1:384v; see also [Crozat], "Mémoire sur la nécessité de peupler la Louisiane," September 4, 1714, AC, C13a, 3:505–6).

132. The following paragraphs are drawn from Marcel Giraud, *A History of French Louisiana,* 1:256–89; Marcel Giraud, *A History of French Louisiana,* vol. 2, *Years of Transition, 1715–1717,* trans. Brian Pearce (Baton Rouge, La., 1993), 115–31; Carl A. Brasseaux, "The Image of Louisiana and the Failure of Voluntary Immigration, 1683–1731," in *Proceedings of the Fourth Annual Meeting of the French Colonial Historical Society,* ed. Andrew Alf Heggory and James J. Cooke (Washington, D.C., 1979), 47–56; Mathé Allain, "French Emigration Policies: Louisiana, 1699–1715," in *Proceedings of the Fourth Annual Meeting of the French Colonial Historical Society,* 106–14; Philip P. Boucher, *Les Nouvelles Frances: France in America, 1500–1815, an Imperial Perspective* (Providence, R.I., 1989), 69–76; Emily Clark, *Masterless Mistresses: The New Orleans Ursulines and the Development of a New World Society, 1727–1834* (Chapel Hill, 2007), 36–39.

133. "Memoir to Make Known the Necessity of Sending Settlers to the Colony of Louisiana," 1714, AC, C13a, 3:655–64, translated in *The French Tradition in America,* ed. Yves F. Zoltvany (Columbia, S.C., 1969), 138.

134. Arrest du Conseil d'État du Roi, qui ordonne qu'il ne sera plus envoyé de vagabonds, gens sans aveu, fraudeurs et criminels à la Louisianne; que les ordres que sa majesté auroit pu donner a ce sujet seront changez, et la destination desdits vagabonds faite pour les autres colonies françoises, May 9, 1720, *Recueils de réglemens, édits, déclarations et arrests, concernant le commerce, l'administration de la justice, et la police des colonies françaises de l'Amérique, et les engagés* (Paris, 1745), 68–70; see also Glenn R. Conrad, "Émigration Forcée: A French Attempt to Populate Louisiana, 1716–1720," in *Proceedings of the Fourth Annual Meeting of the French Colonial Historical Society,* 57–66. The company further complained that such migrants "corrupt[ed] the other Colonists and even the natives of the Country." For contemporary metropolitan descriptions of these state-supported "kidnappings to populate the country called Mississippi," see *Mémoires de Saint-Simon,* ed. A. de Boislisle (Paris, 1925), 256, and Jean Buvat, *Journal de la Régence (1715–1723),* 2 vols. (Paris, 1865), 1:422, 438–39, 441, 465, 2:40. For a popular fictional account, see Abbé Antoine-François Prévost, *Manon Lescaut,* trans. Steve Larkin (Sawtry, England, 2001).

135. According to one (perhaps slightly exaggerated) report, just over seven thousand Europeans arrived between late 1717 and mid-1721: 18 percent were "illicit salt dealers,

smugglers, and exiles," and a similar proportion were women. Engagés made up the single largest group, at 35 percent ("Mémoire sur l'état actuel où est la colonie de la Louisiane pour juger de ce que l'on peur en espérer," [after 1721], AC, C13c, 1:329–31v, excerpts translated in Charles Le Gac, *Immigration and War: Louisiana, 1718–1721: From the Memoir of Charles Le Gac,* trans. Glenn R. Conrad [Lafayette, La., 1970], 42–43).

136. Jean Bochart, chevalier de Champigny, *État-present de la Louisiana: Avec toutes les particularités de cette province d'Amerique* (1776), cited in J. Hanno Deiler, *The Settlement of the German Coast of Louisiana and the Creoles of German Descent* (Philadelphia, 1909), 17.

137. Bienville, "Report on Each Indian Nation," May 15, 1733, *MPAFD,* 1:193; Brasseaux, "Image of Louisiana," 50–52; Boucher, *Les Nouvelles Frances,* 76; Villiers du Terrage, *The Last Years of French Louisiana,* x, 12–20, 84.

138. Rémonville, "Memoir," 16; Pontchartrain to Bienville, January 30, 1704, AC, B, 25:4v–5; Hubert, "Compte rendu de sa traversée . . . ," [after 1717], AC, C13a, 1:57–58.

139. Gourville, "On the Establishment of Louisiana," 2:70–71.

140. D'Artaguiette, "Mémoire sur la situation présente de la colonie de la Louisiane," May 12, 1712, French Provincial Records, 3:175; d'Artaguiette, "Memoir to Prevent Libertinism in Louisiana as Far as Possible," September 8, 1712, *MPAFD,* 2:62, 73; "Mémoire du roi à La Mothe-Cadillac, gouverneur de Louisiane, pour servir de supplement au mémoire du 13 mai 1710," December 18, 1712, AC, C13a:723.

141. Pontchartrain to Bienville, January 30, 1704, *MPAFD,* 3:15–16. In order to protect their virtue during the Atlantic crossing, the ship's captain was ordered to prevent any contact between the "girls and women" and the officers and crew (instructions to Coudray January 30, 1704, AC, B, 25:7v).

142. Pénicaut, *Fleur de Lys,* 77; Bienville to Pontchartrain, September 6, 1704, *MPAFD,* 3:24; Bienville to minister, October 10, 1706, AC, C13b1, 1:18v–19; Bienville to Pontchartrain, July 28 [and October 10], 1706, *MPAFD,* 2:28; *List of the Marriageable Girls Who Arrived Aboard the Pelican at Biloxi,* 1704, *Census Tables,* 8; *Census of Families and Habitants of Louisiana,* 1706, *Census Tables,* 10; "Memoir . . . to Sieur de Muy," 3:58–59.

143. "Mémoire du roi à La Mothe-Cadillac, gouverneur de Louisiane, pour servir de supplément au mémoire du 13 mail 1710," 3:723.

144. Cadillac to Pontchartrain, October 26, 1713, *MPAFD,* 2:184–85. See also Pontchartrain to Clairambault, December 20, 1712, AC, B, 34:157.

145. Duclos to minister, July 15, 1713, AC, C13a, 3:139–40.

146. Cadillac to Pontchartrain, October 26, 1713, *MPAFD,* 2:185; La Mothe Cadillac to Crozat, [1713], AC, C13a, 3:356. The following year, Father Le Marie reported that most of "the last batch of girls" remained unmarried; those who had married wed "soldiers who can not even support themselves" ([to minister], January 15, 1714, 150).

147. "List of Private Passengers and Girls Embarked on the *Mutine* Commanded by M. de Marlonne and Bound for Louisiana," 1719, *First Families,* 1:26–28; "List of Company Employees, Concessionaries, Private Passengers, Tobacco Smugglers, Illicit Salt Dealers, Vagabonds, Deserters and Others Embarked on the *Deux Frères* Commanded by M. Ferret Bound for Louisiana from La Rochelle," 1719, *First Families,* 1:60–65; "List of Concessionaries

and Their People, Workers for the Company, Private Passengers, Soldiers, Illicit Salt Dealers, Tobacco Smugglers, Vagabonds, Deserters and Others Embarked on the *Duc de Noailles* Commanded by Monsieur Couttant Departing from the Roadstead of Chef de Baye Bound for Louisiana," September 12, 1719, *First Families,* 1:66–70.

148. Pénicaut, *Fleur de Lys,* 96, 144, 249–50; directors of the Company of the Indies, "Brevet de directeur des filles de l'hôpital général de Paris portant volontairement pour la Louisiane, pour la Soeur Gertrude," June 12, 1720, AC, B, 42bis; directors of Company of the Indies, "Brevet de conductrice des filles de l'hôpital général de Paris portant pour la Louisiane, pour la Soeur Louise [et Bergere]," June 12, 1720, AC, B, 42bis; Pontchartrain to Crozat, November 30, 1712, AC, B, 34:136.

149. Dumont de Montigny, *Mémoires historiques sur la Louisiane,* 2:30–31. Dumont's tale of the battle over the unattractive Hélène became local lore and was repeated in early nineteenth century accounts of the city (C. C. Robin, *Voyage to Louisiana, 1803–1805: An Abridged Translation from the Original French,* trans. Stuart Landry Jr. [New Orleans, 1966], 35–36, and Georges J. Joyaux, "Forest's Voyage aux États-Unis de l'Amérique en 1831," *LHQ* 39 [1956]: 464).

Dumont himself married an épouseuse. Marie Baron was among the "girls sent from Paris" in 1719 aboard the *Mutine.* After her first husband, Jean Roussin, was killed at Natchez in 1729, she married Dumont in 1730 and they had at least two children ("List of Private Passengers and Girls Embarked on the *Mutine, First Families,*" 1:28; marriage of François Binjamin Dumont dit Montigny and Marie Baron, April 19, 1730, *SR,* 1:12, 91; baptism of Marie Françoisse Dumont Demartigny, November 23, 1731, *SR,* 1:91; baptism of Jean François Dumont Demartigny, ca. January 5, 1733, *SR,* 1:91).

150. Dumont de Montigny, *Mémoires historiques sur la Louisiane,* 2:50–51. Calls for more immigrants, including potential brides, continued ("État de la Louisiane de ses productions et des avantages qu'on peut en retirer," [ca. 1740], AC, C13c, 1:375–85v).

151. Rémonville, "Memoir," 16.

152. Father du Poisson to Father ———, October 3, 1727, *JR,* 67:285.

153. Chassin to Father Bobé, July 1, 1722, *MPAFD,* 2:274–75.

154. Jesuit Jacques Gravier praised Marie Rouensa as "thoroughly . . . imbued with the spirit of God." She successfully reformed her first husband, coureur de bois Michel Accault, who was renowned for "his debaucheries," and threatened to disinherit her son, also called Michel, if he refused to return to live amongst the French (as a youth, he had returned to her natal village). It was the younger Michel to whom Tartarin referred to when he claimed that only one "legitimate métis" had "retired among the sauvages" (Jacques Gravier to R. P. Jacques Bruyas, superior of the mission, February 15, 1694, *JR,* 64:193–95, 213; Belting, *Kaskaskia under the French Regime,* 13–14; Tartarin to [unknown], 1738, AC, C13a, 23:243–43v). On Marie Rouensa, see Eric Hinderaker, *Elusive Empires: Constructing Colonialism in the Ohio Valley, 1673–1800* (New York, 1997), 62–63, 114–15, and Susan Sleeper-Smith, *Indian Women and French Men: Rethinking Cultural Encounter in the Western Great Lakes* (Amherst, Mass., 2001), 23–37.

In 1725, the Company of the Indies revoked Chassin's commission as clerk and storekeeper for mismanagement of funds and a vague reference to "evil conduct." He died sometime before July 1737, the month his métis widow married surgeon René Roy, and probably before

1730 when his wife "renounced their marital community of property" (ordre de révocation pour le S. Chassin Commis, November 28, 1725, AC, B, 43:555; Belting, *Kaskaskia under the French Regime*, 19, 73; *Census of Illinois*, January 1, 1732, AC, G1, 464:151; Carl J. Ekberg, *French Roots in the Illinois Country: The Mississippi Frontier in Colonial Times* [Urbana, Ill., 1998], 34, 41). Cf. Aubert, "'Français, Nègres et Sauvages,'" 173, who argues that Chassin's marriage to Philippe was the reason for his recall. Yet other French-Indian or métis marriages of the time were well regarded: surgeon Roy's career does not appear to have been damaged by his marriage to the same woman (in 1740, he was earning 1,000 livres per year for his services at Fort Chartres) while Joseph Lorrain's marriage to Marie Philippe (Agnès' mother or sister) was witnessed by the commandant of the Oubache post and the future commandant of the Illinois post (Audet, *Les premiers établissements des français au pays des Illinois*, 44–45).

155. Carl A. Brasseaux, "The Moral Climate of French Colonial Louisiana, 1699–1763," *LH* 27 (1986): 31. On the support promised to immigrating women and on the flourishing of prostitution in New Orleans, see Giraud, *History of French Louisiana*, 5:261, 269–70, and Mathé Allain, *"Not Worth a Straw": French Colonial Policy and the Early Years of Louisiana* (Lafayette, La., 1988), 86.

156. Cadillac to the [Navy] Council, January 2, 1716, AC, C13a, 4:530–31; minutes of the [Navy] Council, August 29, 1716, *MPAFD*, 2:211; La Chaise and the counselors of Louisiana to the council of the Company of the Indies, April 26 to June 3, 1725, *MPAFD*, 2:462; Superior Council to the directors of the Company of the Indies, August 28, 1725, to April 4, 1726, *MPAFD*, 2:494. Besides La Chaise's suggestion that forced male migrants be returned to France, no other colonial official recommended that male Euro-Louisianans be exiled. Indeed, officials were more concerned with their desertion and worked hard to keep these men in the colony. See, for example, Bienville to Pontchartrain, October 12, 1708, *MPAFD*, 2:38; d'Artaguiette, "Mémoire sur la situation présente de la colonie de la Louisiane," May 12, 1712, French Provincial Records, 3:172.

157. Périer and La Chaise to the directors of the Company of the Indies, November 2, 1727, *MPAFD*, 2:558–60; Sister Mary Magdeleine Hachard to her father, January 1, 1728, *The Ursulines in New Orleans*, ed. Henry Churchill Semple (New York, 1925), 199.

158. Périer and Salmon to Maurepas, March 29, 1732, *MPAFD*, 4:118. The Crown approved a pension fund of 4,500 livres for supporting the orphaned girls and praised colonial administrators for their "attention . . . to banishing disorder and scandal." See Maurepas to Bienville and Salmon, September 2, 1732, AC, B, 57:810–11v. Despite all of the complaints about sexual immorality and prostitution, the extant records reveal no prosecutions for either, although individuals may have been exiled for their misconduct. For instance, a Dame Tessoneau was forced to leave the colony by d'Abbadie in 1764 for "her indecent and scandalous conduct" (d'Abbadie, ["Journal"], 1763–1764, *A Comparative View of French Louisiana*, 131; Shannon Lee Dawdy, "La Ville Sauvage: 'Enlightened' Colonialism and Creole Improvisation in New Orleans, 1699–1769" [PhD diss., University of Michigan, 2003]).

159. La Chaise to the directors of the Company of the Indies, September 6 and 10, 1723, *MPAFD*, 2:315.

160. Mandeville, "Memoir on the Colony of Louisiana," 2:49–50. Complaints to metropolitan officials about the quality and quantity of immigrants, and not just the female

ones, were frequent. See, for instance, company director Charles Le Gac, who repeatedly noted that "there were no knowledgeable workers among them" and that most immigrants "were unsuitable," even "utterly useless" (*Immigration and War,* 6–7, 26, 29–32).

161. Vaudreuil to Jean Jacques de Macarty-Mactique, August 8, 1751, Vaudreuil Papers, LO 325, 8, cited in Jaenen, "Miscegenation in Eighteenth-Century New France," 104.

162. Delanglez was unable to find any more references to Indian-French marriages in official correspondence after Tartarin's 1738 letter, although Mary Borgias Palm claims that one Indian-French marriage took place in 1747 with the permission of the Illinois commandant (*French Jesuits in Lower Louisiana,* 402; Palm, "Jesuit Missions of the Illinois Country, 1673–1763" [PhD diss., St. Louis University, 1931], 84–85).

163. In a stark example of defiance of secular authority, in 1774 the bishop of Quebec permitted the parish curé at St. Joseph de Beauce to celebrate a particular marriage even though, he noted, "marriage of the French with the sauvages is not at all authorized by the government" (cited in Provost, "Mariages entre Canadiens et sauvages," 53–54).

Chapter 2. Legislating Slavery in French New Orleans

1. Declaration in registry, September 18 and 29, 1736, RSC, *LHQ* 8 (1925): 497–98.

2. Petition to hire out slaves, October 30, 1737, RSC, *LHQ* 5 (1922): 418, 420; declaration in registry, September 18 and 29, 1736, RSC, *LHQ* 8 (1925): 497–98; declaration in registry, September 8, 1737, RSC, *LHQ* 9 (1926): 513–14.

3. Petition for open road, September 13, 1725, RSC, *LHQ* 2 (1919): 472; complaint in assault case, May 2, 1729, RSC, *LHQ* 4 (1921): 332; Brosset déclaration, August 23, 1746, RSC. Chaperon also filed his own complaints against others for abusing his slaves (report on disabled slaves, December 20, 1739, RSC, *LHQ* 7 [1924]: 519–20; declaration, March 15, 1745, RSC, *LHQ* 14 [1931]: 97).

4. Jean Bernard Bossu, *Nouveaux voyages aux Indes Occidentales, contenant une relation des différens peuples qui habitent les environs du grand fleuve Saint-Louis appelé vulgairement le Mississipi,* 2 vols. (Paris, 1768), 1:18.

5. Further explored in chapter 4.

6. Peter H. Wood, *Black Majority: Negroes in Colonial South Carolina from 1670 through the Stono Rebellion* (New York, 1974), 196.

7. Father du Poisson described the differences between concessionaries and habitants thusly: the former were the "gentlemen of this country" who employed many engagés and slaves to work their large land grants, while the latter received smaller grants that they worked on with a "wife or [a] partner" (Father du Poisson to Father ——, October 3, 1727, *JR,* 67:281–83).

8. Petition for fair treatment, September 1, 1725, RSC, *LHQ* 2 (1919): 468; decision in labor suit, October 22, 1725, RSC, *LHQ* 2 (1919): 479; colonial jurisprudence, November 5, 1725, RSC, *LHQ* 2 (1919): 481. On Louisiana's unfavorable reputation, see Philip P. Boucher, *Les Nouvelles Frances: France in America, 1500–1815, an Imperial Perspective* (Providence, R.I., 1989), 69, 76; Carl A. Brasseaux, "The Image of Louisiana and the Failure of Voluntary Immigration, 1683–1731," in *Proceedings of the Fourth Annual Meeting of the French Colonial*

Historical Society, ed. Andrew Alf Heggory and James J. Cooke (Washington, D.C., 1979), 47; Carl A. Brasseaux, "The Administration of Slave Regulations in French Louisiana, 1724–1766," *LH* 21 (1980): 139–58; W. J. Eccles, *France in America,* rev. ed. (East Lansing, Mich., 1990), 174; James T. McGowan, "Planters without Slaves: Origins of a New World Labor System," *Southern Studies* 16 (1977): 5–26.

9. Pierre-François-Xavier de Charlevoix, *Histoire et description general de la Nouvelle France: Avec le journal historique d'un voyage fait par ordre du roi dans l'Amérique Septentrionale,* 3 vols. (1744; rpt., Montreal, 1976), 3:415.

10. Hubert to the Superior Council, October 26, 1717, *MPAFD,* 2:247; Robert to Pontchartrain, November 26, 1708, *MPAFD,* 2:45.

11. Bienville to Pontchartrain, October 27, 1711, *MPAFD,* 3:160.

12. Périer to [Abbé Raguet], May 12, 1728, *MPAFD,* 2:573–74.

13. [Jean Bochart Chevalier de Champigny], *The Present State of the Country and Inhabitants, Europeans and Indians, of Louisiana, on the North Continent of America,* 2nd ed. (London, 1744), 26.

14. Bienville to Pontchartrain, October 12, 1708, *MPAFD,* 2:37.

15. Pontchartrain to Muy, June 30, 1707, *MPAFD,* 3:47; Pontchartrain to Bienville, May 10, 1710, *MPAFD,* 3:141; Robert to Pontchartrain, November 26, 1708, *MPAFD,* 2:45.

16. Hurson to minister, September 1752, AC, F3, 90:70–71, cited in Gwendolyn Midlo Hall, *Africans in Colonial Louisiana: The Development of Afro-Creole Culture in the Eighteenth Century* (Baton Rouge, La., 1992), 181–82.

17. [Champigny], *Present State of the Country,* 26; Hall, *Africans in Colonial Louisiana,* 57; James T. McGowan, "Creation of a Slave Society: Louisiana Plantations in the Eighteenth Century" (PhD diss., University of Rochester, 1976), 23.

18. McGowan, "Creation of a Slave Society," 125; Hall, *Africans in Colonial Louisiana,* 182–83; Daniel H. Usner Jr., *Indians, Settlers, and Slaves in a Frontier Exchange Economy: The Lower Mississippi Valley before 1783* (Chapel Hill, N.C., 1992), 47. Slave majorities were unusual in the North American mainland colonies. Besides Louisiana, only South Carolina had a black majority population and not until almost forty years after its colonization by the British in 1670 (Wood, *Black Majority,* 144, 146–47, 152).

19. *General Census of All Inhabitants of the Colony of Louisiana,* January 1, 1726, *Census Tables,* 51–76; André Pénicaut, *Fleur de Lys and Calumet: Being the Pénicaut Narrative of French Adventure in Louisiana,* trans. Richebourg Gaillard McWilliams (Tuscaloosa, Ala., 1988), 244; "Carte particuliere du fleuve St. Louis dix lieües au dessus et dessous de la Nouvelle Orleans ou sont marqué les habitations et les terrains concedés à plusieurs particuliers au Mississipy," ca. 1723, Edward Ayers Manuscripts, Newberry Library, Chicago; Poisson to Father ——, October 3, 1727, *JR,* 67:281–83, 287; Henry P. Dart, "The Career of Dubreuil in French Louisiana," *LHQ* 18 (1935): 330–31; Usner, *Indians, Settlers, and Slaves,* 51; James Pritchard, "Population in French America, 1670–1730: The Demographic Context of Colonial Louisiana," in *French Colonial Louisiana and the Atlantic World,* ed. Bradley G. Bond (Baton Rouge, La., 2005), 185.

20. On slaveowning versus slave societies, see Philip D. Morgan, "British Encounters with Africans and African-Americans, circa 1600–1780," in *Strangers Within the Realm:*

Cultural Margins of the First British Empire, ed. Bernard Bailyn and Morgan (Chapel Hill, N.C., 1991), 163; Ira Berlin, *Many Thousands Gone: The First Two Centuries of Slavery in North America* (Cambridge, Mass., 1998), 8–9.

21. On South Carolina, see Wood, *Black Majority;* Berlin, *Many Thousands Gone,* chapters 3, 6, 11.

22. Usner, *Indians, Settlers, and Slaves,* 276–86.

23. On frontier slave societies, see Morgan, "British Encounters with Africans and African-Americans," 181, 184.

24. Eccles, *France in America.*

25. Tivas de Gourville, "On the Establishment of Louisiana," June 1712, *MPAFD,* 2:71.

26. D'Artaguiette, "Memoir on the Present Situation of the Colony of Louisiana," May 12, 1712, *MPAFD,* 2:61.

27. Périer and La Chaise to the directors of the Company of the Indies, April 22, 1727, *MPAFD,* 2:532.

28. Cadillac to Pontchartrain, October 26, 1713, *MPAFD,* 2:166–69, 177.

29. Bienville to Pontchartrain, July 28 [and October 10], 1706, *MPAFD,* 2:23.

30. "État de la Louisiane de ses productions et des avantages qu'on peut en retirer," [ca. 1740], AC, C13c, 1:375; Michel to Rouillé, September 23, 1752, *MPAFD,* 5:116.

31. Périer and La Chaise to the directors of the Company of the Indies, November 3, 1728, *MPAFD,* 2:592; John G. Clark, *New Orleans, 1718–1812: An Economic History* (Baton Rouge, La., 1970), 40. On slave prices, see Marcel Giraud, *A History of French Louisiana,* vol. 5, *The Company of the Indies, 1723–1731,* trans. Brian Pearce (Baton Rouge, La., 1991), 125.

32. Pénicaut, *Fleur de Lys,* 229–30.

33. La Chaise to the directors of the Company of the Indies, October 18, 1723, *MPAFD,* 2:372–73; Hall, *Africans in Colonial Louisiana,* 126–27.

34. Pénicaut, *Fleur de Lys,* 251.

35. Michel to Rouillé, September 23, 1752, *MPAFD,* 5:115.

36. Captain Harry Gordon, "Extract from Journal of an Expedition along the Ohio and Mississippi," 1766, *LHQ* 6 (1923): 19–20.

37. Ann Patton Malone, *Sweet Chariot: Slave Family and Household Structure in Nineteenth-Century Louisiana* (Chapel Hill, N.C., 1992), 21. In 1803, there were eighty-one sugar plantations, and by 1815, Louisiana was producing ten million pounds of sugar a year, a figure that then doubled in the next three years.

38. Hall, *Africans in Colonial Louisiana,* 10; Malone, *Sweet Chariot,* 21.

39. Michel to Rouillé, January 22, 1750, *MPAFD,* 5:39–40; Superior Council of Louisiana to the general directors of the Company of the Indies, February 27, 1725, *MPAFD,* 2:402, 404; Lauren C. Post, "The Domestic Animals and Plants of French Louisiana as Mentioned in the Literature," *LHQ* 16 (1933): 576. See also Usner, *Indians, Settlers, and Slaves,* 278; Virginia R. Dominguez, *White by Definition: Social Classification in Creole Louisiana* (1986; rpt., New Brunswick, N.J., 1994), 104; Ingersoll, *Mammon and Manon in Early New Orleans: The First Slave Society in the Deep South, 1718–1819* (Knoxville, Tenn., 1999), 127–30.

40. Gordon, "Extract from Journal of an Expedition along the Ohio and Mississippi," 19.

41. Usner, *Indians, Settlers, and Slaves,* 277–78. Louisiana's history in this respect was again similar to that of South Carolina, which began with a fairly diverse economy. It traded deerskins and slaves with Indians and exported forest products (lumber, tar, pitch, rosin, and turpentine) and livestock to the West Indies (Wood, *Black Majority,* 33–34).

42. Vaudreuil and Michel to Rouillé, May 19, 1751, *MPAFD,* 5:80. See also Usner, *Indians, Settlers, and Slaves,* 277–78.

43. Louis Sala-Molins, *Le code noir; ou, Le calvaire de Canaan* (Paris, 1987), reprints both codes side by side. Thirty-two articles of the 1724 code are identical to the 1685 code, although the article numbers are often different because some of the 1685 articles were deleted and others condensed into a single article. Another twenty are very similar, often with minor changes generally in the fines prescribed or in references to the colony's governing structure. The most important and distinct changes made to the 1685 code are in articles 9 (1724, article 6), 39 (34), and 55 (50). Articles 32 (26), 57 (52), and 59 (54) contain significant additions.

Vernon Valentin Palmer argues that the 1685 code was principally authored by Caribbean officials with "firsthand experience" of slavery in the colonies and that it incorporated locally authored decrees from the previous fifty years. He acknowledges, however, that the metropole rearranged the submitted draft code in ways that suggest its own agenda against those of the colonists. As an example of this rearrangement, Palmer notes that the draft's authors included the anticoncubinage article under criminal offenses; the Crown moved it to the section of the code dealing with religion, "as if to subscribe to the view that [extramarital sex] with slaves was not so much a public order question as a serious religious dereliction" ("The Origins and Authors of the Code Noir," *Louisiana Law Review* 56 [1995]: 364–66, 379–80n56). Palmer's analysis is convincing regarding local authorship of the 1685 code; however, the duplication of most of its articles in the 1724 code, as well as the important differences I discuss in this chapter, suggests that the later code was amended by the metropole with little input from Louisiana officials.

44. Articles 1, 3, and 4.

45. Kathleen M. Brown, *Good Wives, Nasty Wenches, and Anxious Patriarchs: Gender, Race, and Power in Colonial Virginia* (Chapel Hill, N.C., 1996), 135, 223. For a concise description of how "white" replaced "Christian" as a group identity and for an account of its relationship to African slavery in the English colonies, see Nancy Shoemaker, *A Strange Likeness: Becoming Red and White in Eighteenth-Century North America* (New York, 2004), 129–30.

46. Charles E. O'Neill, *Church and State in French Colonial Louisiana: Policy and Politics to 1732* (New Haven, Conn., 1966), 270; Sue Peabody, *"There Are No Slaves in France": The Political Culture of Race and Slavery in the Ancien Régime* (New York, 1996), 13. On the Ursuline nuns and their commitment to a "universalist vision" that led them to make "their convent a space that resolutely welcomed women of all races, classes, and nationalities," see Emily Clark, *Masterless Mistresses: The New Orleans Ursulines and the Development of a New World Society, 1727–1834* (Chapel Hill, N.C., 2007), 61. On the importance of Christianity

to early modern European conceptions of identity, see James Muldoon, *Identity on the Medieval Irish Frontier: Degenerate Englishmen, Wild Irishmen, Middle Nations* (Gainesville, Fla., 2003).

47. Articles 40–42 and 44–49.

48. Articles 6 and 12–16.

49. In 1774 Jean Villeneuve successfully defended himself in a civil suit over the death of a hired slave by arguing that it was "the custom of this country [for] the negroes [to] work where it seems suitable to them on Sunday without permission from anyone" (*Don Joseph Loppinot v. Juan Villeneuve,* April 15, 1774, *LHQ* 12 [1929]: 48–120). This custom became so well entrenched that the otherwise restrictive Black Code of 1806 required owners to pay their slaves fifty cents a day if they made them to work on Sundays (An Act Prescribing the Rules and Conduct to Be Observed with Respect to Negroes and Other Slaves of this Territory, June 7, 1806, *General Digest,* §1; see also *Rice v. Cade,* 10 La. 288 [1836]).

50. Articles 2, 5, 7–8, 11, 18–21, and 43.

51. Articles 38 and 39.

52. Articles 27 and 32–33. On the frequency of executions, see Giraud, *History of French Louisiana,* 5:322. On whether the French Code Noir indicates a more or less benevolent slave system (à la Frank Tannenbaum), see David C. Rankin, "The Tannenbaum Thesis Reconsidered: Slavery and Race Relations in Antebellum Louisiana," *Southern Studies* 18 (1979): 5–31; Thomas N. Ingersoll, "Slave Codes and Judicial Practice in New Orleans, 1718–1807," *Law and History Review* 13 (1995): 23–62; Hans W. Baade, "The *Gens de Couleur* of Louisiana: Comparative Slave Law in Microcosm," *Cardozo Law Review* 18 (1996): 535–86. Ingersoll rightfully stresses that, in considering this question, we need to examine the behavior of slaveowners rather than rely on legal codes that "reveal very little about actual slave treatment" (23), especially when those codes are written by the metropole and not the planters themselves. In conclusion, he states, "if the slaves had been asked to choose among [the successive legal regimes] they would have regarded it as an empty privilege indeed" (62).

53. 1685 Code Noir, article 9. The Spanish Las Siete Partidas had a similar clause: it argued that "so great is the force of matrimony" that if an enslaved women married her master she immediately became free, as did any children of the relationships (*The Laws of Las Siete Partidas, Which Are Still in Force in Louisiana,* trans. Louis Moreau-Lislet and Henry Carlton, 2 vols. [New Orleans, 1820], 1:545–46, partida 4, title 13, law 1).

54. Article 6.

55. Peggy Pascoe, "Race, Gender, and Intercultural Relations: The Case of Interracial Marriage," *Frontiers* 12 (1991): 7.

56. An Act Concerning Negroes and Other Slaves, 1664, *Archives of Maryland,* ed. William Brown (Baltimore, Md., 1883–1912), 1:533–34; Martha Hodes, *White Women, Black Men: Illicit Sex in the Nineteenth-Century South* (New Haven, Conn., 1997), 1, 4, 222n27. It is important to note, however, that Hodes argues that relationships between Euro-American women and African-American men did not always engender hysteria and were sometimes tolerated by local communities. Hodes's formulation does not account for the free mixed ancestry of children born to free African or African American women. For an overview of legislation on interracial relationships, see Peter W. Bardaglio, " 'Shamefull Matches': The Regulation of Interracial Sex and Marriage in the South before 1900," in *Sex, Love, Race:*

Crossing Boundaries in North American History, ed. Martha Hodes (New York, 1999), 112–38.

57. An Act Concerning Negroes and Other Slaves, 1664, *Archives of Maryland,* 1:533–34; [case of Hugh Davis], 1630, *The Statutes at Large, Being a Collection of All the Laws of Virginia, from the First Session of the Legislature in the Year 1619,* ed. William Hening (Richmond, Va., 1809–23), 1:479; An Act for Suppressing Outlying Slaves, April 1681, *The Statutes at Large,* 3:87; An Act for the Better Preventing of a Spurious and Mixt Issue, October 24, 1705, *Acts and Resolves, Public and Private, of the Province of the Massachusetts Bay* (Boston, 1869), §§1–2, 4.

58. Cited in Paul Leroy-Beaulieu, *De la colonisation chez les peuples modernes,* 2 vols. (Paris, 1902), 1:165.

59. Pierre H. Boulle, "In Defense of Slavery: Eighteenth-Century Opposition to Abolition and the Origins of a Racist Ideology in France," in *History from Below: Studies in Popular Protest and Popular Ideology in Honour of George Rudé,* ed. Frederick Krantz (Oxford, 1988), 227. Cf. McGowan, "Creation of a Slave Society," 49.

60. 1685 Code Noir, article 55. It is significant that parental consent was not required because persons under the age of twenty-five were ordinarily considered minors.

61. 1724 Code Noir, article 50. See also Mathé Allain, "Slave Policies in French Louisiana," *LH* 21 (1980): 136.

62. 1685 Code Noir, article 56; 1724 Code Noir, article 51.

63. Gwendolyn Midlo Hall, "Saint Domingue," in *Neither Slave Nor Free: The Freedmen of African Descent in the Slave Societies of the New World,* ed. David W. Cohen and Jack P. Greene (Baltimore, Md., 1972), 172–73; Declaration . . . qui régle la manière d'elire des tuteurs et des curateurs aux enfants dont les peres possédaient des biens, tant dans le royaume, que dans les colonies, et qui défend à ceux qui seront émancipés de disposer de leurs nègres," November 21, 1721, *Recueils de réglemens, édits, déclarations et arrests* (1765), 2:6–12. See Pritchard, "Population in French America, 1670–1730," 177, for Saint-Domingue population numbers.

64. Ordonnance du roi, concernant l'affranchissement des esclaves des isles; et ordonnance des administrateurs en conséquence, June 15, 1736, *Loix et constitutions,* 3:453–54.

65. Elsa V. Goveia, *The West Indian Slave Laws of the Eighteenth Century* (Barbados, 1970), 42.

66. Emilien Petit, *Traité sur le gouvernement des esclaves,* 2 vols. (Paris, 1777), 2:69. On the 1685 code and its manumission provisions, see Malick Walid Ghachem, "Sovereignty and Slavery in the Age of Revolution: Haitian Variations on a Metropolitan Theme" (PhD diss., Stanford University, 2001), chapter 1.

67. 1724 Code Noir, article 21.

68. 1724 Code Noir, articles 54 and 52; 1685 Code Noir, articles 59 and 57. The 1685 code's intent that affranchis enjoy "the same privileges as persons born free" was used to exempt gens de couleur libre in the French Antilles from a head tax in 1686 and 1712, although they had been subjected to it before 1686 and were again after 1730 (Auguste Lebeau, *De la condition des gens de couleur libres sous l'ancien régime: D'après des documents des Archives Coloniales* [Paris, 1903], 48–54).

69. 1724 Code Noir, article 54; 1685 Code Noir, article 59.

70. 1724 Code Noir, article 53; 1685 Code Noir, article 58.

71. On the increasing reliance on race rather than status in metropolitan legislation and official rhetoric, see Peabody, *"There Are No Slaves in France"*; Boulle, "In Defense of Slavery."

72. 1724 Code Noir, article 22; 1685 Code Noir, article 28.

73. 1724 Code Noir, articles 24, 151; 1685 Code Noir, articles 25, 153.

74. 1724 Code Noir, articles 26 and 28–31.

75. 1724 Code Noir, article 34; 1685 Code Noir, article 39. The French codes were not unique in distinguishing between freeborn and freed persons of African ancestry. In Dutch Surinam, the freeborn were entitled to vote, if they met certain economic requirements but the freed were not. This limitation did not apply to the free persons of mixed ancestry, who were eligible to vote, again having met the economic requirements, whether or not they were freeborn or freed. See H. Hoetink, "Surinam and Curaçao," in *Neither Slave Nor Free*, 75.

76. Mithon to Pontchartrain, November 20, 1704, AC, C8a, 15, cited in Peabody, *"There Are No Slaves in France,"* 13–14.

77. Although I agree with Ingersoll's contention that "there is no indication that free blacks enjoyed all rights and privileges of free people," I disagree with his forceful, but ultimately unconvincing, argument that "it is not true that free blacks in this period [in Ira Berlin's words] 'enjoyed a considerably higher status' than their counterparts in the English colonies" ("Slave Codes and Judicial Practice," 33, quoting Ira Berlin, *Slaves Without Masters: The Free Negro in the Antebellum South* [New York, 1974], 110).

78. Preamble. Article 2 in both codes refers to buying "newly arrived nègres." Article 7 of the 1685 code refers to the "market of nègres," which probably means the slave market, and article 40 in the 1685 code and article 36 in the 1724 code place a tax on "each nègre head" to compensate owners for executed slaves. In legislation emerging from the French West Indies, "nègre" was often used alone to indicate enslaved persons. See, for example, Règlement de M. de Tracy, lieutenant général de l'Amérique, touchant les blasphémateurs et la police des isles, June 19, 1664, *Loix et constitutions*, 1:117–22; Réglemens du Conseil de la Martinique, touchant la police des esclaves, October 4, 1677, *Loix et constitutions*, 1:306–7.

Early eighteenth-century editions of Richelet's *Dictionnaire françois* equate nègres with slaves in defining the former as "black slaves [esclaves noirs] who are drawn from the coast of Africa and who are sold in the Isles of America for the cultivation of the country, and in the mainland [Terra Firma] to work at the mines and the sugar refineries." By 1772, the *Dictionnaire des arts et des sciences* confirmed the conflation, noting that "to treat someone as a Nègre" is "to treat someone as a slave." Both are quoted in Simone Delesalle and Lucette Valensi, "Le Mot 'nègre' dans les dictionnaires français d'ancien régime: Histoire et lexicographie," *Langue française* 15 (1972): 86, 87.

79. The 1685 code refers once to "persons born free" but clearly in an inclusive manner, as the context is granting the manumitted "the same rights, privileges and immunities enjoyed by persons born free" (article 59/54).

80. 1685 Code Noir, article 10 (article 7 in 1724 code); 1724 Code Noir, articles 6, 24, and 52.

81. Cadillac and Duclos, Ordinance . . . qui deffend de rien achepter des esclaves, May 20, 1714, AC, A, 23:4v; Superior Council of Louisiana, Arrêt . . . contre ceux qui débauchent les esclaves, October 17, 1725, AC, A, 23:63v–64; Superior Council of Louisiana, Arrêt . . . qui défend de vendre des boissons aux esclaves, March 29, 1727, AC, A, 23:84–84v.

82. [Nicolas de La Salle], *Census of Louisiana*, August 12, 1708, AC, C13a, 2:225–27; *General Census of All Inhabitants of the Colony of Louisiana*, January 1, 1726, *Census Tables*, 51–76.

83. Such a penalty was present in West Indian legislation as early as 1677 (Réglemens du Conseil de la Martinique, touchant la police des esclaves, October 4, 1677, *Loix et constitutions*, 1:306, article 4). Article 33 of the 1685 Code Noir (article 27 of the 1724) limited the application of the death penalty to those slaves whose assault bruised or drew blood from their owners.

84. Règlements du Conseil Supérieur de la Louisiane, concernant les esclaves, November 12, 1714, AC, A, 23:5–6.

85. Vaudreuil and Michel, Règlement sur la police des cabarets, des esclaves, des marchés en Louisiane, February 18 to March 1, 1751, AC, C13a, 35:46v, 49v, 51, 44–44v.

86. Regulations issued by the Company of the Indies in 1725, on "being informed of the bad usage that has been made in Louisiana of its nègres," did require company slaves to be baptized and supplied with sufficient clothes and provisions. Although the company's primary concern was for its own profits, it does suggest that it thought better treatment of its slaves would achieve that end (Company of the Indies, Ordonnance pour les Nègres domestiques de la compagnie, July 25, 1725, AC, B, 43:535–37v).

87. Petition for emancipation of Indian slave, October 22, 1729, RSC; Clark, *Masterless Mistresses*, 81. The prohibition on donations and legacies to free and enslaved Afro-Louisianans did not stop Euro-Louisianans from trying to bestow them. See, for example, Pierre Clermont's donation of 2,000 livres to his freed mulâtre Victoire (manumission of Pierre, Marguerite, Michel, George, and Victoire, July 30, 1766, RSC).

88. *D'Ernville v. Battard*, June 15, 1751, RSC, *LHQ* 20 (1937): 1122–26, 1129–31. See chapter 3 for a discussion of this case.

89. *D'Ausseville v. Aufrère*, July 1–13, 1737, RSC, *LHQ* 5 (1922): 401–3.

90. [*Boyer v. Senet*], October 8, 1738, RSC; *Louboey v. François Melisan*, April 21, 1745, RSC, *LHQ* 14 (1931): 104–8.

91. [*Crown v. Baron*], August 12–October 5, 1753, RSC, *LHQ* 22 (1939): 861–87.

92. Father Raphaël to Abbé Raguet, May 15, 1725, *MPAFD*, 2:482; Father Raphaël to Abbé Raguet, April 18, 1727, AC, C13a, 10:326v; Cirillo to Echevarria, August 6, 1772, AGI, SD, leg. 2594, 427v; [*Crown v. Sieur Loquet de La Pommeraye*], June 14 and July 5, 1738, Cabildo Archives, *LHQ* 3 (1920): 291–94; petition for cemetery burial of baptized slave, June 14, 1738, RSC, *LHQ* 5 (1922): 599; Mary Veronica Miceli, "The Influence of the Roman Catholic Church on Slavery in Colonial Louisiana" (PhD diss., Tulane University, 1979), 73, 78–81, 91.

93. Father Raphaël to Abbé Raguet, May 18, 1726, AC, C13a, 10:46v.

94. Petition, July 11, 1737, RSC, *LHQ* 9 (1926): 303.

95. Petition to sell slave, February 28, 1738, RSC, *LHQ* 5 (1922): 588.

96. Articles of partnership, February 24, 1736, RSC.

97. *D'Ausseville v. Le Roy* is discussed in several Superior Council documents dating from January 17, 1730, to January 16, 1731. See the following RSC summaries published in *LHQ* 4 (1922), 510, 521, and *LHQ* 5 (1922), 87, 89, 91, 92, 94, 102, 103–4, 107. Another accusation of abortion caused by violence against a slave woman can be found in court summons, November 6, 1737, RSC, *LHQ* 5 (1922): 420.

98. For summaries of *Merveilleux v. Gaullas* (June 18, 1727–January 10, 1728), see *LHQ* 4 (1921): 221, 226–29, 231–32, 239–40.

99. On violence and race in eighteenth-century North Carolina, see Kirsten Fischer, *Suspect Relations: Sex, Race, and Resistance in Colonial North Carolina* (Ithaca, N.Y., 2002), 159–90.

100. Declaration in registry, June 3, 1737, RSC, *LHQ* 9 (1926): 290; [*Widow La Croix v. Dupre Terrebonne, Junior*], May 24, 1763, Cabildo Archives, *LHQ* 3 (1920): 93–95; *La Pommeraye v. Dubois*, January 31, February 10, 1763, RSC, *LHQ* 24 (1941): 800, 813–14. See also "Suit for Damages for Personal Injuries to a Slave," June 11, 1764, *LHQ* 5 (1922): 58–62.

101. *La Sonde v. Coupart*, August 14, 1724, RSC, *LHQ* 1 (1917): 242–43.

102. *Prat v. Dautir*, September 6–7, 1737, RSC, *LHQ* 5 (1922): 412.

103. Examination of a delinquent steward, January 17, 1730, RSC, *LHQ* 4 (1921): 510; report of supposed cruelty to horse, September 23, 1724, RSC, *LHQ* 1 (1917): 246.

104. Salmon to minister, February 10, 1737, AC, C13a, 22:124–25v.

105. *Procureur Général v. Pierre Antoine Dochenet*, June 12–28, 1752, RSC, *LHQ* 21 (1938): 567–73.

106. Declaration, May 30, 1745, RSC, *LHQ* 14 (1931): 118; succession of Terrebonne, March 10, 1764, RSC.

107. *Raguet v. Bayou and Mamourou*, June 9, 1748, RSC, *LHQ* 19 (1936): 1094–96.

108. [*Crown v. Guela*], January 4, 10, and 12, 1737, RSC, *LHQ* 5 (1922): 386–88.

109. McGowan, "Creation of a Slave Society," 131–32; Ingersoll, "Slave Codes and Judicial Practice," 24.

110. [*Pierre Claveau v. Ignace Broutin*] and [*Ignace Broutin v. Pierre Claveau*], February 4, 1741, RSC, *LHQ* 10 (1927): 568–69.

111. Capuchins of Louisiana to the directors of the company, May 16, 1724, AC, C13a, 8:418v; Father Raphaël to Abbé Raguet, May 18, 1726, AC, C13a, 10:46v.

112. *General Census of All Inhabitants of the Colony of Louisiana*, January 1, 1726, *Census Tables*, 51–76; [*Census of Inhabitants along the River Mississippi*], 1731. Shannon Lee Dawdy argues that Le Page du Pratz believed in a "paternalistic approach" to slave management as a matter of "moral and practical necessity," while Patricia Galloway analyzes his "self-fashioning as a humane and competent manager" (Dawdy, "Enlightenment from the Ground: Le Page du Pratz's *Histoire de la Louisiane*," *French Colonial History* 3 [2003]: 26; Galloway, "Rhetoric of Difference: Le Page du Pratz on African Slave Management in Eighteenth-Century Louisiana," *French Colonial History* 3 [2003]: 1).

113. Le Page du Pratz, *Histoire de Louisiane, contenant la découverte de ce vaste pays*, 3 vols. (Paris, 1758), 1:333, 341–44. The most accessible translation, but one that unfortunately is much abridged, is a facsimile reproduction of the 1774 English edition (*The History of*

Louisiana: Translated from the French of M. Le Page du Pratz, ed. Joseph G. Tregle Jr. [1774; rpt., Baton Rouge, La., 1975]).

114. Bossu, *Nouveaux voyages aux Indes Occidentales,* 1:201.

115. Cited in Marilyn Yalom, *A History of the Breast* (New York, 1997), 70, 85. On attitudes toward wet nursing in France and the British Caribbean, see Dorinda Outram, *The Body and the French Revolution: Sex, Class, and Political Culture* (New Haven, Conn., 1989), 187–88n46, and Barbara Bush, *Slave Women in Caribbean Society, 1650–1838* (Bloomington, Ind., 1990), 15.

116. Thomas Walter Laqueur, *Making Sex: Body and Gender from the Greeks to Freud* (Cambridge, Mass., 1990), 38–40.

117. Le Page du Pratz, *Histoire de Louisiane,* 1:343–45.

118. Diderot, d'Alembert, et al., *Encyclopedia: Selections,* trans. Nelly S. Hoyt and Thomas Cassirer (Indianapolis, Ind., 1965), 263.

119. John D. Hargreaves, "Assimilation in Eighteenth-Century Senegal," *Journal of African History* 6 (1965): 177–84.

120. Bienville to Maurepas, February 4, 1743, *MPAFD,* 3:776; Bienville et al. to [Lagac?], October 28, 1719, AC, C13a, 5:212.

121. Diron d'Artaguiette, [*Report on the Census of Louisiana*], November 24, 1721, AC, G1, 464:n.p., *Louisiana Historical Society Publications* 5 (1911): 93–103, quotation on 99. Diron went on to admit that colonial actions, rather than Euro-Louisianans' less robust constitutions or Louisiana's climate, greatly contributed to their demise and reduced productivity (101). See also "Procès-verbal du conseil de commerce tenu à l'Ile Dauphine," April 10, 1719, AC, C13a, 5:331.

122. Vaudreuil and Michel to Rouillé, May 20, 1751, *MPAFD,* 5:81–83. James McGowan argues that Euro-Louisianans refused to participate in agricultural labor, thus bringing about the development of African slavery ("Planters without Slaves," 5–26).

123. "Attribution d'une négresse à Fazende, conseiller," November 4, 1724, AC, C13a, 8:139; Giraud, *History of French Louisiana,* 5:325.

124. McGowan, "Creation of a Slave Society," 180–81; Brasseaux, "Administration of Slave Regulations," 143.

125. Le Page du Pratz, *Histoire de Louisiane,* 1:348–49.

Chapter 3. Affranchis and Sang-Mêlé

1. Marriage of Jean Baptiste Raphael and Marie Gaspart, August 4, 1725, SLC, M1, 89–90.

2. The change was most likely made in the early nineteenth century when Father Antonio de Sedella had indexes constructed for all of the extant registries.

3. Baptism of Marie [Raphael], January 4, 1731, SLC, B1, 1.

4. Baptism of Marie [Raphael], January 4, 1731, SLC, B1, 1. For marriages of free persons of African descent, see marriage of Thomas Hos and Jeanne Marie, June 5, 1730, SLC, M1, 207, and marriage of Simon Vanon and Marie Anne, March 19, 1731, SLC, B1, 48. Stanley L. Guerin, a twentieth-century translator of the archdiocesan's sacramental records

and thus someone intimately knowledgeable of their internal workings, was the first to suggest that Gaspart was misidentified as négresse in the marginal notation. See also Emily J. Clark, "A New World Community: The New Orleans Ursulines and Colonial Society, 1727–1803" (PhD diss., Tulane University, 1998), 91. Cf. Thomas N. Ingersoll, *Mammon and Manon in Early New Orleans: The First Slave Society in the Deep South, 1718–1819* (Knoxville, Tenn., 1999), 402n97, and Guillaume Aubert, "'The Blood of France': Race and Purity of Blood in the French Atlantic World," *WMQ,* 3rd ser., 61 (2004): 473–74, who both note that just because Gaspart was born in Europe does not mean that she was not of African descent. However, the omission of racial labels for Gaspart and both her parents in the marriage entry as well as the continuing failure to mark Gaspart as other than white in other records, in addition to the other circumstances mentioned, strongly suggests that she was not.

5. Robbery reported, July 13–14, 1723, RSC, *LHQ* 1 (1917): 110–11. In a moment of histori-cal revisionism, in 1917 the *LHQ's* translator noted, this was "evidently a slander" since "mar-riage between whites and blacks was not sanctioned by the church nor permitted by the government in Louisiana." However, this case occurred in 1723, one year *before* the Code Noir's proscription of racial exogamy. See also Marcel Giraud, *History of French Louisiana,* vol. 5, *The Company of the Indies, 1723–1731,* trans. Brian Pearce (Baton Rouge, La., 1991), 326.

6. "*Le Galathée,* voyage du Sénégal et de la Louisiane, et de St. Domingue Isle de la Merique," 1727, Section Marine, Archives nationales de France, 4JJ, 16:13, cited in Gwen-dolyn Midlo Hall, *Africans in Colonial Louisiana: The Development of Afro-Creole Culture in the Eighteenth Century* (Baton Rouge, La., 1992), 128; Peter Caron, "'Of a Nation Which the Others Do Not Understand': Bambara Slaves and African Ethnicity in Colonial Loui-siana," *Slavery and Abolition* 18 (1997): 107. The 1732 census of New Orleans identifies a Pinet, occupation gunsmith, living on Rue St. Pierre with an unnamed and unraced woman. As my discussion of census taking demonstrates, this does not indicate that his wife was Euro-pean (*Recensement general de la ville de la Nlle. Orleans,* January 1732, AC, G1, 464:n.p.).

7. Marriage of Jean Lafrance and Marie Charles, ca. April 23, 1767, SLC, M2, 56; bap-tism of Charlotte Lafrance, April 2, 1769, SLC, B6, 45; baptism of Catherine Lafrance, October 18, 1771, SLC, B6, 121; baptism of Juan Lafrance, August 1, 1774, SLC, B7, 39; baptism of François Lafrance, October 29, 1776, SLC, B7, 66; baptism of Antonio Lafrance, March 15, 1779, SLC, B8, 106; baptism of María Lafrance, January 1, 1785, SLC, B9, 352; baptism of Francisco Lafrance, March 21, 1787, *SR,* 4:175; Bartlomé Bta. grifo libre, contra Juan Lafrance sobre impedir este el matrimonio de su hija con el dicho Bartólome, Septem-ber 6, 1788, SJR. Two mulâtresses named Marie were baptized in 1752, making them about the right age for a woman who married in 1767 and had her first child two years later; both had godfathers who first names were Charles, which Lafrance's wife could have adopted as her surname (baptism of Marie, January 6, 1752, SLC, B2, 242; baptism of Marie Rose, September 10, 1752, SLC, B2, 264).

8. Marriage of Juan Bautista [Charrayse] and Mariana [Barco], January 20, 1777, SLC, M3, 2.

9. Marriage of Pedro [Langliche] and Carlota Adelaida, January 10, 1779, SLC, M3, 3.

10. Marriage of Christoval De Armas and Mari Duplessi, February 23, 1783, *SR,* 3:74, 110.

11. In 1816, Langliche declared he was eighty-four; two years later he claimed to be about eighty-seven, indicating that he was born in 1731–32. My calculation of Charrayse's

and Barco's birthdates are based on the assumptions that the marriage was the first for both and that they were of typical marriage age.

12. Funeral records, which in general are less useful as they often contain very terse entries, are the most scanty: complete and incomplete records cover only the years 1724–34. See Earl C. Woods and Charles E. Nolan, eds., *Sacramental Records of the Roman Catholic Church of the Archdiocese of New Orleans* (New Orleans, 1987–92), 1:viii, 2:viii.

13. *D'Ernville v. Battard,* June 15, 1751, RSC, *LHQ* 20 (1937): 1122–26, 1129–31; Michel to minister, July 15, 1751, AC, C13a, 35:287v.

14. Michel to minister, July 15, 1751, AC, C13a, 35:287–96; Carlota d'Erneville, will, September 9, 1801, Pedesclaux, NONA, 39:513.

15. Baptism of Charles Jean Baptiste Fleuriau, January 8, 1752, *SR,* 2:88; *Census of the Militias and of the Inhabitants of the Colony of Louisiana, 1766, Some Late Eighteenth-Century Louisianians: Census Records 1758–1796,* comp. and trans. Jacqueline K. Voorhies (Lafayette, La., 1973), 106–63; manumission of Carlota [d'Erneville], February 22, 1771, Garic, NONA, 2:78; manumission of Carlota d'Erneville, October 27, 1773, Almonester, NONA, 268v–70; obligation, February 16, 1775, Almonester, 85–86; manumission of Carlos, February 13, 1775, Almonester, NONA, 72; "Rolle des mulâtre libre de la Nouvelle Orleans," [ca. 1770?], AGI, PC, leg. 188A, expediente 2, doc. 6; d'Erneville, will, September 9, 1801, Pedesclaux, NONA, 39:513–15v; Kimberly S. Hanger, *Bounded Lives, Bounded Places: Free Black Society in Colonial New Orleans, 1769–1803* (Durham, N.C., 1997), 65. Charlotte may have also helped to free her mother, whom she described as "the deceased negra libre" in her will.

16. Pedro Henrique d'Erneville, will, August 8, 1781, Mazange, NONA, 645–50; "Relación de la pérdida que cada individuo ha padecido en el incendio de esta cuidad . . . ," September 30, 1788, AGI, SD, leg. 2576; d'Erneville, will, September 9, 1801, Pedesclaux, NONA, 39:514–14v.

17. Certificat de liberté pour Marie Louise, November 14, 1745, RSC. La Porche freed Marie Louise just a few days before he married Marie Françoise Panque. Marie Louise may have continued to live with her father and his new wife ("Census of the Parish of Point Coupée," December 20, 1745, Vaudreuil Papers).

18. [Manumission of Jeanneton], July 11, 1737, RSC, *LHQ* 5 (1922): 403.

19. Regarding manumission policy, I have determined the end of the French era to be November 25, 1769, the date that O'Reilly instituted Spanish law and dramatically changed the colony's manumission policies (see chapter 4). It is not always possible to verify whether or not a manumission was ratified; however, in the discussion that follows, I use "manumission" and "manumitted" to mean a promise of freedom that was in some way followed up on even if it did not result in freedom. My analysis is based on Gwendolyn Midlo Hall, "Louisiana Free Database, 1719–1820," in *Databases for the Study of Afro-Louisiana History and Genealogy, 1699–1860: Computerized Information from Original Manuscript Sources,* ed. Gwendolyn Midlo Hall (Baton Rouge, La., 2000), as well as my own reading of a variety of sources, the most important being the RSC.

20. Manumission of Caton, Manon, and Felicite, April 20, 1758, RSC.

21. Manumission of Adrienne, August 22, 1767, RSC.

22. Manumission of La Mirre, March 5, 1763, RSC.

23. Power of attorney, August 23, 1736, RSC, *LHQ* 5 (1922): 384; declaration in the

registry of Superior Council, June 29, 1737, RSC, *LHQ* 9 (1926): 299. For other possible consorts, see donation by François Noyon, December 26, 1744, RSC; manumission of Fanchon, October 16, 1758, RSC; manumission of Mimi, April 8 and 10, 1762, RSC, *LHQ* 23 (1940): 924.

24. Pierre Boyer, will, February 23, 1745, RSC; Claude Vignon dit La Combe, will, August 16, 1747, RSC; ["État des mulâtres et negres libres de la ville"], [ca. 1770?], AGI, PC, leg. 188A, expediente 5, doc. 5.

25. Manumission, July 20, 1767, RSC.

26. Sale, July 10, 1767, SJR; Joseph Dusuau de La Croix, will, June 14, 1794, F. Broutin, NONA, 30:143–50.

27. Manumission of Rosette, July 7, 1757, RSC; manumission of Françoise, January 1, 1761, RSC.

28. Manumission of Marie Charlotte and Louise, October 9, 1735, RSC, *LHQ* 8 (1925): 143–44; petition, July 29, 1737, RSC, *LHQ* 9 (1926): 310–11; petition, November 23, 1743, RSC; petition, November 29, 1743, RSC, *LHQ* 12 (1929): 485; *Marion [Marie Charlotte] v. Aufrère,* February 6, 1745, RSC.

29. La Chaise, "Proposal to Free Negroes," May 16, 1730, in Heloise Hulse Cruzat, "New Orleans Under Bienville: Sidelights on New Orleans in Bienville's Time," *LHQ* 1 (1917): 132–33; "Proposition to Free Negroes for Military Merit," May 13, 1730, RSC, *LHQ* 4 (1921): 524.

30. "Copie des délibérations du Conseil supérieur de la Louisiane," November 21, 1725, AC, C13a, 9:268–68v.

31. Manumission of Jean Baptiste Poulierdon, December 15, 1758, RSC; manumission of Jacques, August 7, 1764, RSC. See also Jean Baptiste Senet, will, July 7, 1739, RSC; Jean Joseph Delfaut de Pontalba, will, July 9, 1760, RSC, *LHQ* 23 (1940): 281–83.

32. Jacques de Coustilhas, will, August 26, 1738, RSC; petition for copy of will, March 4, 1739, RSC, *LHQ* 6 (1923): 303; [manumission of Louis Connard et al.], March 6, 1739, RSC, *LHQ* 6 (1923): 304. See also excerpt, May 10, 1747, RSC, *LHQ* 18 (1935): 440; manumission of Pierre, Jeanne, and their children, March 17, 1756, RSC; manumission of Pierre, Marguerite, Michel, George, and Victoire; manumission of Joseph Marie Baptiste, Catoche, and their children, May 9, 1767, RSC.

33. Three of the male-female couples manumitted together were described as husband and wife; in the other three manumissions, no relationship was mentioned. See emancipation paper, October 1, 1733, RSC, *LHQ* 5 (1922): 250; manumission of Caton, Manon, and Felicite; manumission of Pierrot and Genevieve, June 16, 1761, RSC; judgment rendered in case of Roussin and his wife, July 21, 1728, RSC, *LHQ* 7 (1924): 688; succession of d'Auberville, November 16, 1758, RSC; manumission of Françoise and Laplante, January 22, 1762, RSC, *LHQ* 23 (1940): 603. For "veille Marie," see manumission of Zacarie dit Jacob, July 16, 1743, RSC, *LHQ* 11 (1928): 633.

34. 1724 Code Noir, article 21.

35. Sale of estate of Joseph Duport (Dupard), February 16, 1770, SJR, *LHQ* 6 (1923): 706–8.

36. Manumission of Hypolite and Isidore, February 8, 1762, RSC, *LHQ* 23 (1940): 613.

37. Dame Ste. Hermaine, will, October 21, 1765, RSC.

38. Manumission of Spadille, November 8, 1768, RSC.

39. Manumission of Marie Angelique, February 15, 1738, RSC. For a reference to Marie Angelique as free, see sale of real property, March 20, 1739, RSC, *LHQ* 6 (1923): 310.

40. [Succession of Jaffre dit La Liberté], February 24 to August 24, 1740, RSC, *LHQ* 10 (1927): 261, 412, 423, 426; [manumission of Jeanneton and Marie Jeanne], October 27, 1762, RSC, *LHQ* 24 (1941): 557–59. At least one other widow challenged bequests made to a probable consort and child (réquisition de Marie Claude Bernard, veuve comte Pechon, July 6, 1769, RSC).

41. Emancipation paper, October 1, 1733, RSC, *LHQ* 5 (1922): 250; petition to ratify freedom, June 4, 1735, RSC, *LHQ* 5 (1922): 265. That the Superior Council used this particular case to restrict its own authority is somewhat ironic because it involved Marie, an elderly nègresse who had been freed in 1733, along with her husband Jorge, by Bienville, who was governor at the time of the act in 1733 and also at the time in 1735 when the council refused to confirm Marie's freedom. Given these circumstances, the council could easily have asserted its own legitimate authority to ratify his act and have assumed that, as governor, he would have ratified his own request.

42. Baptism of Louis François [Rançon], June 19, 1751, SLC, B2, 223.

43. Baptism of Agathe [Lemelle], May 5, 1760, SLC, B4, 30; baptism of Jeanne Françoise [Lemelle], September 7, 1769, SLC, B6, 58. For more on Jacqueline Lemelle and her efforts to free herself and her children, see chapter 5, and Virginia Meacham Gould, "Urban Slavery—Urban Freedom: The Manumission of Jacqueline Lemelle," in *More Than Chattel: Black Women and Slavery in the Americas,* ed. David Barry Gaspar and Darlene Clark Hine (Bloomington, Ind., 1996), 298–314. Although no local or metropolitan legislation addressed the issue of baptizing the children of enslaved mothers as free in Louisiana, it was addressed in the French islands where priests were prohibited "from baptizing as free any children, unless the manumission of the mothers is proven to them beforehand" (Ordonnance du roi, concernant l'affranchissement des esclaves des isles; et ordonnance des administrateurs en consequence, June 15, 1736, *Loix et constitutions,* 3:453–54; Arrêt du Conseil du Cap, touchant les libertés, et la qualification de libre donnée aux enfans des gens de couleur, November 25, 1777, *Loix et constitutions,* 5:802–3).

44. Baptism of Françoise, March 11, 1745, SLC, B2, 34; baptism of Claude, October 21, 1765, SLC, B5, 105; baptism of Marie Joseph, May 7, 1766, SLC, B5, 129.

45. Manumission of Charlotte and Louis, February 1, 1746, RSC; manumission of Charlotte and her children, February 12, 1767, RSC.

46. Pradel to his brother, April 10, 1755, *Le chevalier de Pradel: Vie d'un colon français en Louisiane au XVIII° siécle d'après sa correspondance et celle de sa famille,* ed. A. Baillardel and A. Prioult (Paris, 1928), 257–59; Pradel to his brother, October 29, 1763, *Le chevalier de Pradel,* 298; Mme. de Pradel to her brother, July 12, 1765, *Le chevalier de Pradel,* 380–81. Sometime before 1774, St. Louis, now calling himself San Luis Lanuitte, purchased eight arpents of land along the Bayou St. Jean road (sale of property, April 8, 1777, Garic, NONA, 8:156; sale of property, December 15, 1777, Garic, NONA, 8:489.

47. Marriage of Thomas Hos and Jeanne Marie, June 5, 1730, SLC, M1, 207; marriage of Simon Vanon and Marie Anne, March 19, 1731, SLC, B1, 48, entry 7; Ingersoll, *Mammon and Manon,* 77–78.

48. "Rolle des passagers embarquez sur le vaisseau le comte de Toulouz commandé par

Monsieur le chevalier de Grieu, pour aller a la Louissianne," November 15, 1718, AC, G1, 464:n.p.; "Ship Lists of Passengers Leaving France for Louisiana," 1718–1724 (fourth installment), trans. Albert Laplace Dart, *LHQ* 21 (1938): 965; "List of Workers for the Ste. Catherine Concession Embarked on the Ship of the Company of the Indies, the *Loire*, Bound for Louisiana from Lorient," August 20, 1720, *First Families*, 1:113–17; "List of Persons Who Embarked on the *l'Aurore*, *Driade*, and *Aventurier* Bound for Louisiana," January 4, 1720, to January 24, 1721, *First Families*, 1:71–72.

49. Marriage license, free negro and slave, November 28, 1727, RSC, *LHQ* 4 (1921): 236; Ingersoll, *Mammon and Manon*, 78.

50. Marriage license, free negro and slave, November 28, 1727, RSC, *LHQ* 4 (1921): 236; agreement for hire of free negroes, October 21, 1729, RSC, *LHQ* 4 (1921): 355; petition for adjusted account, November 21, 1730, RSC, *LHQ* 5 (1922): 102; remonstrance, November 25, 1730, RSC, *LHQ* 5 (1922): 103; decision between Mingo and Darby, November 25, 1730, RSC, *LHQ* 5 (1922): 103; ["Account of Jonathas Darby"], [ca. 1751–53], *Records of the American Catholic Historical Society of Philadelphia*, 10 (1899): 201–7.

51. Tiocou's name was also rendered "Dicou" and "Diocou."

52. Emancipation of Marie Aram, a slave, July 15, 1737, Cabildo Archives, *LHQ* 4 (1921): 366–68; petition to redeem slave wife, June 28, July 6, and October 29 1737, RSC, *LHQ* 5 (1922): 401–2, 418; emancipation of Marie Aram, a slave, redeemed by her husband's labor during seven years, March 6–10, 1744, Cabildo Archives, *LHQ* 3 (1920): 551–53.

53. Jean Baptiste Marly, free negro, agrees to serve Mr. Jean Jose Delfaut de Pontalba, November 9, 1745, RSC, *LHQ* 14 (1931): 594. See also manumission of Jean Baptiste Poulierdon, and manumission of Marie, February 22, 1764, RSC. Marly was literate and had been in the colony since at least 1733, as indicated by his signature at the baptism of his godchild Marthe (Baptism of Marthe, March 16, 1733, SLC, B1, 36).

54. Stuart B. Schwartz, "The Manumission of Slaves in Colonial Brazil: Bahia, 1684–1745," *Hispanic American Historical Review* 54 (1974): 603–35; Frederick P. Bowser, "The Free Person of Color in Mexico City and Lima: Manumission and Opportunity, 1580–1650," in *Race and Slavery in the Western Hemisphere: Quantitative Studies*, ed. Stanley L. Engerman and Eugene D. Genovese (Princeton, N.J., 1975), 331–68; B. W. Higman, *Slave Populations of the British Caribbean, 1807–1834* (Baltimore, Md., 1984), 383–85; David Barry Gaspar, "'To Be Free Is Very Sweet': The Manumission of Female Slaves in Antigua, 1817–26," in *Beyond Bondage: Free Women of Color in the Americas*, ed. David Barry Gaspar and Darlene Clark Hine (Urbana, Ill., 2004), 64. This contrasts with Eva Sheppard Wolf's findings for post-Revolutionary Virginia where men were freed in slightly more numbers than women (*Race and Liberty in the New Nation: Emancipation in Virginia from the Revolution to Nat Turner's Rebellion* [Baton Rouge, La., 2006], chapter 2).

55. *Census of Louisiana*, September 2, 1771, *SMV*, 1:196.

56. Ira Berlin, *Slaves Without Masters: The Free Negro in the Antebellum South* (New York, 1974), 108–9; Virginia R. Dominguez, *White by Definition: Social Classification in Creole Louisiana*. (1986; rpt., New Brunswick, N.J., 1994), 23; cf. Ingersoll, *Mammon and Manon;* James T. McGowan, "Creation of a Slave Society: Louisiana Plantations in the Eighteenth Century," (PhD diss., University of Rochester, 1976), 176–77.

57. The links among status, wealth, and race have been well established for Spanish America. See John K. Chance, *Race and Class in Colonial Oaxaca* (Stanford, Calif., 1978); Patricia Seed, "Social Dimensions of Race: Mexico City, 1753," *Hispanic American Historical Review* 62 (1982): 569–606; Elizabeth Anne Kuznesof, "Ethnic and Gender Influences on 'Spanish' Creole Society in Colonial Spanish America," *Colonial Latin American Review* 4 (1995): 153–76.

58. *Raphael v. Cadot,* May 9–10, 1724, RSC, *LHQ* 1 (1917): 238; Périer and La Chaise to the directors of the Company of the Indies, November 2, 1727, *MPAFD,* 2:557; internment of Paulin Cadot, June 16, 1727, *SR,* 1:38.

59. *Raphael v. Dumanoir,* July 26 and September 20, 1724, RSC, *LHQ* 1 (1917): 242, 245–46. See also *Isabelle v. Succession of Jean-Baptiste Gon de Chavannes,* December 2, 1752, RSC, *LHQ* 21 (1938): 1245, in which négresse libre Isabelle successfully sued the estate of Jean Baptiste de Chavannes for her wages and ended up receiving all his goods, although they were noted as being of little value.

60. [Manumission of Louis Connard et al.], March 6, 1739, RSC, *LHQ* 6 (1923): 304; *Raguet v. Jean Baptiste and Pantalon,* August 14–September 14, 1743, RSC, *LHQ* 11 (1928): 649–50, 652–53; 12 (1929): 145–47.

61. *Procureur Général v. Jeanette,* April 8–11, 1747, RSC, *LHQ* 18 (1935): 168. Shannon Lee Dawdy suggests that the reenslavements of Jean Baptiste and Jeanette were "actually a shady legal maneuver to settle" the Coustilhas estate, which was still being contested in the decade after his death ("La Ville Sauvage: 'Enlightened' Colonialism and Creole Improvisation in New Orleans, 1699–1769" [PhD diss., University of Michigan, 2003], 250n44).

62. Petition, September 3, 1763, RSC, *LHQ* 25 (1942): 1135–36.

63. Conviction and sentence of flogging and incarceration, September 13, 1722, RSC, *LHQ* 7 (1924): 678.

64. Superior Council's reprimand of a free negress for holding assemblies of slaves and servants at night, September 3, 1746, RSC, *LHQ* 17 (1934): 187.

65. Sala-Molins, *Le code noir; ou, Le calvaire de Canaan* (Paris, 1987), 1724, article 54.

66. James C. Scott, *Seeing Like a State: How Certain Schemes to Improve the Human Condition Have Failed* (New Haven, Conn., 1998), 64–71, 76–83. See also Melissa Nobles, *Shades of Citizenship: Race and the Census in Modern Politics* (Stanford, Calif., 2000), and Ipek K. Yosmaoglu, "Counting Bodies, Shaping Souls: The 1903 Census and National Identity in Ottoman Macedonia," *International Journal of Middle Eastern Studies* 38 (2006): 55–77. On the caution required in interpreting French colonial censuses, see Paul Lachance, "The Growth of the Free and Slave Populations of French Colonial Louisiana," in *French Colonial Louisiana and the Atlantic World,* ed. Bradley G. Bond (Baton Rouge, La., 2005), 205; James Pritchard, "Population in French America, 1670–1730: The Demographic Context of Colonial Louisiana," in *French Colonial Louisiana and the Atlantic World,* 176.

67. [Nicolas de La Salle], *Census of Louisiana,* August 12, 1708, AC, C13a, 2:225–27.

68. *Recensement des habitans et concessionaries de la Nouvelle Orleans et lieux circonvoisins avec le nombre des enfans, domestiques blancs, hommes et femmes de force, esclaves nègres, esclaves sauvages, bestes a corne et chevaux,* November 24, 1721, Louisiana Historical Society *Publications,* 5 (1911): 87–93. The Biloxi and Mobile census for the same year includes the

same categories, suggesting that census takers were told what categories to include (*General Census of Inhabitants in the Area of Biloxi and Mobile, as Reported by Le Sieur Diron, Habitants of Fort Louis de la Mobile,* June 26, 1721, *Census Tables,* 23–27). Périer and Salmon issued such an order in December 1732 when they requested a tally of "all the families, blancs, nègres, sauvages, livestock, and weapons" (Ordonnance . . . pour faire faire la déclaration des maisons, blancs, sauvages, nègres, bestiaux et armes des habitants, December 24, 1732, AC, A, 23:111).

69. *Recensement general . . . de la Nouvelle Orleans,* July 1, 1727, AC, G1, 464:n.p.; [*Census of Inhabitants along the River Mississippi*], 1731, AC, G1, 464:n.p.; *Recensement general de la ville de la Nlle. Orleans,* January 1732, AC, G1, 464:n.p. A 1724 census does distinguish between adult nègres and negrillons or negrittes (boys and girls) (*Recensement des habitants depuis la ville de la Nouvelle Orleans jusqu'aux Ouacha ou le village des allemands a dix lieues au dessus de la dite ville,* November 15, 1724, AC, G1, 464:n.p).

70. *Recensement general . . . de la Nouvelle Orleans,* July 1, 1727, AC, G1, 464:n.p.

71. [*Census of Inhabitants along the River Mississippi*], 1731, AC, G1, 464:n.p.

72. *Recensement general de la ville de la Nlle. Orleans,* January 1732, AC, G1, 464:n.p.

73. *État récapitulatif du recensement général de la Louisiane,* 1737, AC, C13c, 4:197. Its categories were "men and boys capable of carrying arms," "women," "boys," "girls," "nègres," "négresses," "negrillons," "negrittes," "sauvages," and "sauvagesses," along with the various categories of domesticated animals. The columns "nègres" through "sauvagesses" were not explicitly identified as slaves.

74. *Recapitulation général des recensements ci-joints faits à la Nouvelle Orléans et dans tous les quartiers qui en dependent depuis le bas du fleuve jusqu'à la jurisdiction de la Pointe Coupée, inclusivement . . . ,* September 1763, AGI, SD, leg. 2595.

75. *Estado general de todos los habitantes de la colonia de la Louisiana segun los padrones que se han hecho el año de 1766,* 1766, AGI, SD, leg. 2595.

76. "Rolle des mulâtre libre de la Nouvelle Orleans," [ca. 1770?], AGI, PC, leg. 188A, expediente 2, doc. 6; "Liste des nègres libres établir tant à 4 lieues de cette ville en remontée le fleuve, que ceux de la ville de nommés ci-après comme suit," [ca. 1770?], AGI, PC, leg. 188A, expediente 5, doc. 8; ["État des mulâtres et negres libres de la ville"], [ca. 1770?], AGI, PC, leg. 188A, expediente 5, doc. 5. Even being quite generous in matching names across the lists there are at least fifty mulâtres and forty nègres for a total of ninety men.

77. "Liste de la quantité des naigres libres de la Nouvelle Orléans," February 22, 1770, AGI, PC, leg. 188A, expediente 2, 5–9. When O'Reilly arrived to assert Spanish control over the colony in 1769, there were 160 Cuban pardo and moreno militiamen among his two thousand troops. It is possible that Bacus' list includes some of these men, although Dawdy argues that the lack of identifiable Spanish surnames suggests this was not the case ("La Ville Sauvage," 218). See also Hanger, *Bounded Lives, Bounded Places,* 118.

78. Historians have relied upon the 1763 and 1771 censuses to demonstrate the small number of mulâtres and affranchis, thus proving, in their minds, that French Louisianans neither engaged in racially exogamous relationships nor freed their slaves in any great numbers. Even those who have acknowledged that the census numbers might not be accurate have assumed that all those with European and African ancestry were identified as mulâtres

and that all free people of color were clearly identified as such. See, for instance, McGowan, "Creation of a Slave Society," 132. On the undercounting of free people of color in the French censuses, see Virginia Meacham Gould, "In Full Enjoyment of Their Liberty: The Free Women of Color of the Gulf Ports of New Orleans, Mobile and Pensacola, 1769–1860" (PhD diss., Emory University, 1991), 81, and Hanger, *Bounded Lives, Bounded Places*, 11–12.

79. Funeral of Catherine, July 13, 1732, SLC, B1, 76. One mulâtre, four-year-old slave Pierre, appears in an earlier list compiled by Father Raphaël of people who died in 1726 ("List of Those Persons Whose Death Was Recorded from January 8, 1726, to January 10, 1727," *First Families*, 2:96).

80. Baptism of Marie, July 6, 1733, SLC, B1, 40; SLC, B2, passim.

81. Baptism of Charlotte, April 13, 1748, SLC, B2, 122.

82. Baptism of Etienne, April 9, 1752, SLC, B2, 251. Etienne's baptism was unusual for another reason as well as godparents were usually from the same or higher social status than their godchild; the freeborn Etienne's godparents were slaves. For an earlier reference to "an unknown white" father, see baptism of Françoise, June 9, 1748, SLC, B2, 128.

83. Baptism of Nicholas Rohedeng, January 20, 1750, SLC, B2, 174.

84. Baptism of Louis François [Rançon], June 19, 1751, SLC, B2, 223. The priest noted that Rançon had "procured emancipation for" Louis from his owner, Monsieur Volant, the commandant of the Swiss troops. Rançon may have had a second child with Marie, also baptized as free, in 1760. A year and a half later, like many Euro-Louisianan men who had relationships with women of color, he married a Franco-Louisianan woman (Baptism of Marguerite, November 9, 1760, SLC, B4, 42; marriage of Louis Rançon and Marie Françoise Gallot, February 1, 1762, *SR*, 2:133, 234).

85. Abbé Antoine Furetière, *Dictionnaire universel, contenant generalement tous les mots françois tant vieux que modernes, et les termes des sciences et des arts . . .* , 2nd ed., rev., corr., and aug. Basnage de Bauval, 3 vols. (La Haye, 1701), entries for "mulat," "mestif," "metif," and "metis."

86. Baptism of Françoise Coussot, January 26, 1748, SLC, B2, 117; baptism of Marie Magdelaine Coussot, July 23, 1747, SCB, B1, 85; baptism of Pierre Coussot, November 22, 1756, SLC, B3, 67.

87. Baptism of Pierre, October 30, 1747, SLC, B2, 110.

88. Baptism of François, November 26, 1750, SLC, B2, 203; baptism of Marthe, March 16, 1733, SLC, B1, 36; baptism of Philbertin, January 25, 1746, SLC, B2, 60. Neither of François' parents were identified; Philbertin and Marthe's mothers were both négresses slaves.

89. Baptism of Cecile, December 31, 1744, SLC, B2, 29.

90. Baptism of Marie, December 30, 1751, SLC, B2, 239. "Quarteron" does not appear again in the baptism registries until 1767. See baptism of Augustin, September 16, 1767, SLC, B6, 6, and baptism of Marie Françoise, January 22, 1769, SLC, B6, 39. Both Augustin and Marie Françoise were enslaved, indicating that the label was not reserved for the free.

91. Baptism of Simon, September 18, 1744, SLC, B2, 23; baptism of Marthe, December 8, 1748, SLC, B2, 139; baptism of Charlotte, April 6, 1749, SLC, B2, 149; baptism of Marie

Jeanne, March 2, 1749, SLC, B2, 146; baptism of François, May 20, 1747, SLC, B2, 101; baptism of Etienne, 254.

92. Baptism of Marie, August 21, 1745, SLC, B2, 48; baptism of Anne, February 28, 1753, SLC, B2, 283.

93. Baptism of Jean Paul Leflot, December 17, 1747, SLC, B2, 114. I have not been able to find any additional baptisms for children of Jean Leflot that might indicate whether they were born in "legitimate marriage," nor have I been able to locate a marriage entry, although this is the era of the missing marriage registers (1734–58).

Chapter 4. Slavery and Freedom in Spanish New Orleans

1. [*Catherina v. Estate of Juan Bautista Destrehan*], June 25, 1773, SJR, *LHQ* 9 (1926): 556–59; manumission of Catalina and Felicité, November 6, 1773, Almonester, 287v–90.

2. Paul F. Lachance, "The Politics of Fear: French Louisianians and the Slave Trade, 1786–1809," *Plantation Societies in the Americas* 1 (1979): 162–97.

3. Thomas N. Ingersoll, *Mammon and Manon in Early New Orleans: The First Slave Society in the Deep South, 1718–1819* (Knoxville, Tenn., 1999), 181. The same conditions prevailed in late eighteenth-century and early nineteenth-century Cuba with similar consequences (Matt D. Childs, *The 1812 Aponte Rebellion in Cuba and the Struggle against Atlantic Slavery* [Chapel Hill, N.C., 2006], chapter 2).

4. Captain Campbell to George Johnstone, December 12, 1764, *Mississippi Provincial Archives: English Dominion*, ed. Dunbar Rowland (Nashville, Tenn., 1911), 267.

5. Royal Decree Commissioning Don Antonio de Ulloa Governor of Louisiana, May 21, 1765, *SMV*, 1:1; Gilbert C. Din and John E. Harkins, *The New Orleans Cabildo: Colonial Louisiana's First City Government, 1769–1803* (Baton Rouge, La., 1996), 38–48; Kimberly S. Hanger, *Bounded Lives, Bounded Places: Free Black Society in Colonial New Orleans, 1769–1803* (Durham, N.C., 1997), 7–8; Jack D. L. Holmes, *A Guide to Spanish Louisiana, 1762–1806* (New Orleans, 1970), 1–4. O'Reilly (1723–94) was an Irishman who enlisted in the Spanish military as a young man and served in campaigns throughout Europe. He also had a brief stint in the French army. In the mid-1760s, he was sent to Puerto Rico and then Cuba to oversee improvement of the defenses and militias there (Joseph G. Dawson III, ed. *The Louisiana Governors: From Iberville to Edwards* [Baton Rouge, La., 1990], 49–52).

6. Some historians have argued that Spanish officials sought to bolster the numbers of free people of color to create an intermediate class or buffer between the minority Euro-Louisianans and majority slaves as well as between themselves and discontent Franco-Louisianan elites. See Gilbert C. Din, "Proposals and Plans for Colonization in Spanish Louisiana," *LH* 11 (1970): 197–213; Laura Foner, "The Free People of Color in Louisiana and St. Domingue: A Comparative Portrait of Two Three-Caste Slave Societies," *Journal of Social History* 3 (1970): 406–30; Virginia Meacham Gould, "In Full Enjoyment of Their Liberty: The Free Women of Color of the Gulf Ports of New Orleans, Mobile and Pensacola, 1769–1860" (PhD diss., Emory University, 1991), 80; Hanger, *Bounded Lives, Bounded Places,* 11, 21, 24. Cf. Ingersoll, *Mammon and Manon.* Regardless of whether or not this was a conscious goal, slaves and free people of color took advantage of the opportunities offered by Spanish officials to pursue their own goals of freedom and security.

7. Royal Order to Don Pedro Gurcia, Mayoral, January 28, 1771, *Historical Collections of Louisiana, Embracing Translations of Many Rare and Valuable Documents Relating to the Natural, Civil and Political History of that State,* ed. Benjamin F. French, 5 vols. (New York, 1846–53), 5:246–47; Royal Decree Commissioning Don Antonio de Ulloa Governor of Louisiana, 1:1; "O'Reilly's 1769 Commission: A Personal View," trans. Jack D. L. Holmes, *LH* 24 (1983): 307.

8. Ordinances and Instructions of Don Alexander O'Reilly, November 25, 1769, *Historical Collections of Louisiana,* 5:254–58. The cabildo finally received a copy of the recopilación in 1778 (cabildo, minutes, July 31, 1778, Cabildo Records [Spanish transcriptions], 147b–48). On the cabildo, see Henry P. Dart, "Courts and Law in Colonial Louisiana," *LHQ* 4 (1921): 255–89; Hans W. Baade, "The Law of Slavery in Spanish *Luisiana,* 1769–1803," in *Louisiana's Legal Heritage,* ed. Edward F. Haas (Pensacola, Fla., 1983), 43–86, especially 56–58; Din and Harkins, *New Orleans Cabildo;* Ingersoll, *Mammon and Manon,* 149.

9. Ordonnance de Don A. O'Reilly chargeant Fleauriau et Ducros de l'exécution de l'édit de mars 1724, August 27, 1769, AC, C13a, 49:69. After 1803, Anglo-Louisiana jurists tried to determine what laws had been enforce during the Spanish period. At least one court ruled that, despite Governor O'Reilly's proclamation reinstating the 1724 Code Noir, his actions clearly indicated that Spanish law had supplanted the French Code Noir (*Beard v. Poydras,* 4 Mart. [O.S.] 348 [1816], docket no. 72, 367–68). Historians have disagreed over the extent to which Spanish law superseded French law in Louisiana. Ingersoll, for instance, contends that the French Code Noir of 1724 continued to govern race relations in Spanish Louisiana "except in minor details," although he admits that coartación indeed marked a significant change in the law (*Mammon and Manon,* 149, 158, 221). In his detailed analysis of judicial practice, however, Hans W. Baade convincingly argues that Spanish systems of governance, justice, and law were operative in Louisiana after 1769, particularly in New Orleans where Spanish power was most clearly established. He does acknowledge that where Spanish bureaucracy was limited, such as in frontier outposts, a "dual state" emerged in which French "legal folkways" remained even as they operated with a Spanish structure ("Law of Slavery," 44; Hans W. Baade, "Marriage Contracts in French and Spanish Louisiana: A Study in 'Notarial' Jurisprudence," *Tulane Law Review* 53 [1979]: 1–93).

10. Nicolás María Vidal to the cabildo, October 24, 1800, Cabildo Records, 4:28; [appeal of the cabildo], July 23, 1790, published in Charles Gayarré, *The History of Louisiana,* vol. 4, *The American Domination* (New York, 1854–66), 301–5.

11. "L'arrêt de la Cour supérieur rieure de la province," October 29, 1768, published in Philip Pittman, *The Present State of the European Settlements on the Mississippi with a Geographical Description of that River* (Cleveland, Ohio, 1906), 123, 147.

12. Unzaga to Don Antonio Bucarely y Ursua, June 22, 1771, Spanish Governors of Louisiana Dispatches, 1766–91, HT, 3:43.

13. Testimony of Pierre La Violeta, June 12, 1795, Carondelet Dispatches, 267–69; *Criminales seguidos de oficio contra el pardo libre Pedro Bahy,* October 7, 1791, SJR; *Paul Macarty's Case,* 2 Mart (O.S.) 279 (1812).

14. Real cédula sobre la educación, trato y occupaciones de los esclavos, May 31, 1789, *Colección de documentos para la historia de la formación social de Hispanoamérica, 1493–1810,*

ed. Richard Konetzke, 3 vols. (Madrid, 1958–62), 3:643–52, quotations from articles 1, 8; Code Noir ou Loi Municipale, February 12, 1778 (New Orleans, 1778).

15. Real cédula sobre la educación, trato y occupaciones de los esclavos, article 7; Code Noir ou Loi Municipale, articles 7–8, 10.

16. Real cédula sobre la educación, trato y occupaciones de los esclavos, articles 8–11, 13; Code Noir ou Loi Municipale, articles 12–15.

17. *Manuel de Lanzos v. Pedro Francisco Santilly,* December 11, 1779, SJR, *LHQ* 14 (1931): 150. See also succession of Pelagia Lorreins, wife of Andres Jung, September 7, 1781, SJR, *LHQ* 17 (1934): 213–18; *Crown v. Madame Bara Alias Le Blond,* July 31, 1792, Point Coupée Parish Records; *Marie Louise v. Don Carlos La Chiapella,* June 18 and July 8, 1794, Point Coupée Parish Records, indexed in Derek Noel Kerr, *Petty Felony, Slave Defiance and Frontier Villainy: Crime and Criminal Justice in Spanish Louisiana, 1770–1803* (New York, 1993), 358.

18. *Francisco Pechon v. Don Juan Antonio Lugar,* June 18, 1803, N. Broutin Court Proceedings, NONA, 59; *Francisco Broutin v. Joseph Touton (aka Forstall),* September 6, 1782, SJR, *LHQ* 19 (1936): 515; *Basilio Ximenes v. Francisco Broutin,* June 3, 1786, SJR; *Crown v. Guy Dreux,* November 2, 1796, SJR. See also *Porte v. Delery,* June 17, 1786, SJR.

19. Joseph Xavier Pontalba to Jeanne Françoise de Breton de Charmaux, November 4, 1796, Letters of Baron Joseph X. Pontalba to His Wife, 1796, HT, 395–97; *State v. Vincent Lesassier,* September 27, 1793, SJR; *State v. Claude Tremé,* December 21, 1787, SJR; *Don Antonio Ramos v. Don Claude Tremé,* May 31, 1796, SJR; Ingersoll, *Mammon and Manon,* 239; Kerr, *Petty Felony,* 95–96, 123.

20. Real cédula sobre la educación, trato y occupaciones de los esclavos, preamble; Baron de Carondelet, A Regulation Concerning the General Police; the Keeping Bridge, Roads and Bridges and Causeys in Repair, and the Government of Slaves—For the Use of the Commandants and Syndics of the Posts, and the Coasts in the Province of Louisiana, June 1, 1795, in "A Decree for Louisiana," ed. and trans. James A. Padget, *LHQ* 20 (1937): 600; confidential instructions issued by Joseph de Gálvez, acting for Charles III, to Bernardo de Gálvez, November 25, 1776, Rosemonde E. and Emile Kuntz Collection, 1655–1878, HT, article 22; Vidal to the cabildo, October 24, 1800, Cabildo Records, 4:23–29.

21. Childs, *The 1812 Aponte Rebellion in Cuba,* 35–38.

22. Cabildo, minutes, February 13, 1778, Cabildo Records, 1:279–80; cabildo, minutes, February 19, 1779, Cabildo Records, 1:306; cabildo, minutes, February 26, 1779, Cabildo Records, 1:306–7; cabildo, minutes, March 1, 1779, Cabildo Records, 1:307–9.

23. Cabildo, minutes, June 11, 1784, Cabildo Records, 225–27; Gilbert C. Din, *Spaniards, Planters, and Slaves: The Spanish Regulation of Slavery in Louisiana, 1763–1803* (College Station, Tex., 1999), 101–2; Baade, "Law of Slavery," 66–67.

24. Cabildo, minutes, February 26, 1790, Cabildo Records, 2:96; cabildo, minutes, July 23, 1790, Cabildo Records, 2:115; [appeal of the cabildo], July 23, 1790, *History of Louisiana,* 4:301–5.

25. Consulta del consejo de las Indias sobre el reglamento expedido en 31 de mayo de 1789 para la mejor educación, buen trato y ocupación de los negros esclavos de America, March 17, 1794, *Colección de documentos,* 3:726–32; Juan Ignacio de Urriza, Francisco de

Saavedra, and Sr. Don Antonio Ventura de Taranco, Informe del consejo de Indias acerca de la observancia de la real cédula de 31 de Mayo de 1789 sobre la educación, trato y ocupaciones de los esclavos, January 3, 1792, *Historia de la esclavitud de la raza Africana en el Nuevo Mundo y en especial en los países Americo-Hispanos,* ed. José Antonio Saco (Havana, 1938), 3:247–78; Howard Prince, "The Spanish Slave Code of 1789," in *Columbia Essays in International Affairs 1966,* ed. Andrew W. Cordier (New York, 1967), 2:163–65.

26. [Appeal of the cabildo], July 23, 1790, *History of Louisiana,* 4:301–5; Urriza et al., Informe del consejo de Indias.

27. Real cédula sobre la educación, trato y occupaciones de los esclavos, article 3.

28. Code Noir ou Loi Municipale, articles 36, 44, 59, 28, 6, 9–10, 68, 11.

29. Code Noir ou Loi Municipale, article 72.

30. Code Noir ou Loi Municipale, article 68.

31. See chapter 2.

32. Code Noir ou Loi Municipale, article 72.

33. Real cédula sobre la educación, trato y occupaciones de los esclavos, article 6.

34. *The Laws of Las Siete Partidas, Which Are Still in Force in Louisiana,* trans. Louis Moreau-Lislet and Henry Carlton, 2 vols. (New Orleans, 1820), 1:232–33, partida 3, title 22, law 18.

35. Real cédula al gobernador de la Habana, ordenandole haga observar el metodo y reglas que se expresan, en la exacción del derecho de alcabala de la venta de los negros esclavos coartados de aquella isla, June 21, 1768, *Colección de documentos,* 3:339. On the development of coartación in Cuba, see Herbert S. Klein, *Slavery in the Americas: A Comparative Study of Virginia and Cuba* (Chicago, 1967), 62–65, 78n62, 195–200; Rebecca J. Scott, *Slave Emancipation in Cuba: The Transition to Free Labor, 1860–1899* (Princeton, N.J., 1985), 13–14, 74–75; and Alejandro de la Fuente, "Slave Law and Claims-Making in Cuba: The Tannenbaum Debate Revisited," *Law and History Review* 22 (2004): 339–69.

36. Hanger, *Bounded Lives, Bounded Places,* 25.

37. Of course, there were also extralegal means to freedom. Slaves could runaway and try pass as free.

38. Louis Claude Lechert, will, November 18, 1769, RSC; sale of a negress, ratification of the sale and emancipation of a slave, December 23, 1769, SJR, *LHQ* 6 (1923): 162; baptism of Pierre Joseph, December 17, 1769, SLC, B6, 71.

39. Hanger, *Bounded Lives, Bounded Places;* Gwendolyn Midlo Hall, "Louisiana Free Database, 1719–1820," in *Databases for the Study of Afro-Louisiana History and Genealogy, 1699–1860: Computerized Information from Original Manuscript Sources,* ed. Gwendolyn Midlo Hall (Baton Rouge, La., 2000).

40. Hanger, *Bounded Lives, Bounded Places,* 21.

41. Lachance, "Politics of Fear," 196.

42. Eva Sheppard Wolf, *Race and Liberty in the New Nation: Emancipation in Virginia from the Revolution to Nat Turner's Rebellion* (Baton Rouge, La., 2006), chapter 2. In early nineteenth-century Antigua, slaves had a roughly one in 450 chance of receiving freedom (David Barry Gaspar, "'To Be Free Is Very Sweet': The Manumission of Female Slaves in Antigua, 1817–26," in *Beyond Bondage: Free Women of Color in the Americas,* ed. David

Barry Gaspar and Darlene Clark Hine [Urbana, Ill., 2004], 62). Slaves in Louisiana continued to be manumitted at a far greater rate than those in the rest of the South as late as 1860 (Shawn Cole, "Capitalism and Freedom: Manumissions and the Slave Market in Louisiana, 1725–1820," *Journal of Economic History* 65 [2005]: 1013).

43. Lachance, "Politics of Fear."

44. Hanger, *Bounded Lives, Bounded Places,* 20, figure 1.1.

45. Code Noir ou Loi Municipale, articles 70–71.

46. Code Noir ou Loi Municipale, articles 22, 24.

47. Hanger, *Bounded Lives, Bounded Places,* 21–34, especially tables 1.2 and 1.4.

48. *Census of New Orleans,* June 1778, *Louisiana Census and Militia Lists, 1770–1789,* ed. Albert J. Robichaux, 2 vols. (Harvey, La., 1973–74), 1:23–68; *Resumen general del padron hecho en la provincia de la Luisiana, distrito de la Movila, y plaza de Panzacola,* 1788, Records of the Diocese, 2:403–4; *Census of New Orleans,* November 6, 1791, NOPL; Hall, "Louisiana Free Database"; Hanger, *Bounded Lives, Bounded Places,* 23–30. Studies of Latin American manumission practices have found similar patterns: women outnumbered men about two to one, even in regions where the enslaved population was predominately male; women were more likely to be freed unconditionally than men; and blacks and Africans were more likely to purchase freedom while graciosa manumissions favored creoles and mulatos (Stuart B. Schwartz, "The Manumission of Slaves in Colonial Brazil: Bahia, 1684–1745," *Hispanic American Historical Review* 54 [1974]: 611–12; Frederick P. Bowser, "The Free Person of Color in Mexico City and Lima: Manumission and Opportunity, 1580–1650," in *Race and Slavery in the Western Hemisphere: Quantitative Studies,* ed. Stanley L. Engerman and Eugene D. Genovese [Princeton, 1975], 331–68; Herbert S. Klein, *African Slavery in Latin America and the Caribbean* [New York, 1986], 228; Mary C. Karasch, *Slave Life in Rio de Janero, 1808–1850* [Princeton, N.J., 1987]). Trevor Burnard found a similar pattern in mid-eighteenth-century Jamaica (55 percent of all manumissions were children; of adult manumissions, 65 percent were women) ("'Do Thou in Gentle Phibia Smile': Scenes from an Interracial Marriage, Jamaica, 1754–86," in *Beyond Bondage,* 100n10).

49. Baptism of Pierre Joseph, December 17, 1769, SLC, B6, 71; baptism of María Manuela, March 17, 1799, SLC, B15, 85–86; manumission of María de la Merced, September 26 1798, Pedesclaux, NONA, 758v; baptism of María de la Merced, November 15, 1798, SLC, B15, 56. See also manumission of María Luisa, September 20, 1783, Rodríguez, NONA, 836; baptism of María Luisa, October 5, 1783, SLC, B10, 17; baptism of Juan Francisco and Juan Pedro, March 27, 1799, SLC, B15, 91–92.

50. Baptism of Gaspar, June 29 1773, SLC, B7, 25. See also baptism of Francisco Jacobo, December 2, 1781, SLC, B8, 239; baptism of Margarita, March 18, 1781, SLC, B8, 198; baptism of Miguel, September 23, 1781, SLC, B8, 231.

51. Baptism of Thomas, January 3, 1798, SLC, B13, 436; proceedings brought by Pedro Jeanty to annotate the baptismal entry of one of his slaves who had been recorded as free, [February 1], 1800, Records of the Diocese, 9:82–88.

52. Manumission of Marie [Bodaille?] and her son, February 12, 1772, Garic, 13:35–36v, NONA; Marcos de Olivares, will, December 18, 1791, Pedesclaux, NONA, 13:764v–69; manumission of Margarita and María Luisa, June 5, 1771, Garic, 2:187v–89, NONA; manumission of Margarita and her daughters, October 7, 1772, Almonester, NONA, 266v–68.

Brazilian manumitters also rarely cited "expressions of religious motivation" (Schwartz, "The Manumission of Slaves in Colonial Brazil," 619).

53. *Mariano Murè v. Henrique Roche,* February 16, 1782, SJR, *LHQ* 17 (1934): 596; *Manuel de Lanzos v. Pedro Francisco Santilly,* December 11, 1779, SJR, *LHQ* 14 (1931): 150.

54. [Manumission of Francisco], October 16, 1770, SJR, *LHQ* 6 (1923): 530.

55. Manumission of María Estenne, December 28, 1775, Garic, NONA, 6:324–25.

56. Manumission of Carlota, January 12, 1778, Almonester, NONA, 18–19v; manumission of María, January 19, 1791, F. Broutin, NONA, 7:101v–2.

57. Manumission of Fanchon, December 30, 1773, Garic, NONA, 4:366–66v; [*Pierre Fauché v. François Demazilière*], February 5, 1783, SJR, *LHQ* 20 (1937): 519–21. After ten years in St. Domingue, Fanchon was finally able to prove that she was free; see the discussion in the text.

58. See, for example, manumission of Elizabeth, María Luisa, and Adelaida, October 4, 1775, Garic, NONA, 6:237v–38v; manumission of Catarina and her daughter, Holineta, September 4, 1773, Garic, NONA, 4:245v–46.

59. On notarial practices, see Julie Hardwick, *The Practice of Patriarchy: Gender and the Politics of Household Authority in Early Modern France* (University Park, Penn., 1998); Kathryn Burns, "Notaries, Truth, and Consequences," *AHR* 110 (2005): 350–79.

60. Manumission of Basilio, August 2, 1794, Pedesclaux, NONA, 21:734; manumission of Francisca, February 19, 1801, Pedesclaux, NONA, 38:118v–19; manumission of Honorato, July 21, 1798, Ximénez, NONA, 15:526v–27v; manumission of Carlos, August 16, 1801, Pedesclaux, NONA, 39:523v–24; manumission of Juana, December 22, 1792, F. Broutin, NONA, 15:381v–82; emancipation of Angelica, July 12, 1770, SJR, *LHQ* 6 (1923): 515.

61. Mothers also freed their enslaved children but most often through third-party purchases or coartación proceedings against their owners.

62. [*Antonio Guichard v. Francisco Daniel Dupain*], December 18, 1782, SJR, *LHQ* 19 (1936): 1124–25; manumission of Carlos, October 30, 1793, Pedesclaux, NONA, 19:904v–5v; manumission of Eugenia, January 31, 1793, Pedesclaux, NONA, 16:79v–80.

63. Manumission of Juaneton, March 14, 1796, Pedesclaux, NONA, 27:127v–28; sale of slave, March 14, 1796, Pedesclaux, NONA, 27:127–27v; manumission of Rozeta, February 25, 1799, Ximénez, NONA, 16:28v–29v. Bonne may have freed Rozeta's mother a few months later (manumission of Catalina, October 29, 1799, Ximénez, NONA, 16:259).

64. Manumission of Juan, July 29, 1771, Almonester, 154–54v; sale of slave, July 29, 1771, Almonester, NONA, 152–53v.

65. Manumission of María and Juan Luis, September 17–18, 1793, Pedesclaux, NONA, 18:746v–48v.

66. Emancipation of Luis, November 15, 1770, SJR. Jousson may also have not immediately freed the younger Luis if he was unsure about how the recent change in sovereignty would affect the process of manumission. Other manumissions that followed shortly after purchases include manumission of Antonio Domingo, January 22, 1788, Rodríguez, NONA, 2:76v–78v; sale of negress and child, February 20, 1770, SJR, *LHQ* 6 (1923): 313; manumission of Margueritte and Françoise, March 8, 1770, SJR. For those including negra or mulata mothers and mulato or cuarterón children, see manumission of Luisa and her children, January 10, 1772, Garic, NONA, 13:5v–6v; manumission of Jacqueline, Agata,

María Francisca [alias Tonton], and Adelaida, November 10, 1772, Almonester, NONA, 291v–93.

67. Manumission of François, December 12, 1779, Mazange, NONA, 12:564–65.

68. Another, less likely, possibility is that Louisiana slaves learned about coartación from two slaves who were returned from Havana, having spent almost ten years there as runaways (procuration, September 1, 1744, RSC, *LHQ* 13 [1930]: 156; Vaudreuil to Maurepas, March 20, 1748, AC, C13a, 32:31–34v; declaration by fugitive negroes, Manuel and John, belonging to M. de Benac, March 22, 1748, RSC). On the legal acuity of slaves and free people of color in Havana, see de la Fuente, "Slave Law and Claims-Making in Cuba," 339–69, Childs, *The 1812 Aponte Rebellion in Cuba,* 63–66.

69. Manumission of Bautista, March 30, 1771, Garic, NONA, 2:112–12v.

70. Manumission of Juana Catalina, December 14, 1771, Almonester, NONA, 242–44v.

71. [*María Theresa v. Marie-Françoise Girardy, Widow Desruisseau*], September 4, 1782, SJR, *LHQ* 19 (1936): 512–15; *Michel v. Françoise Girardy,* October 9, 1783, SJR, *LHQ* 22 (1939): 269–71; *María v. Succession of Francisca Plazan,* May 10, 1782, SJR, *LHQ* 18 (1935): 749–50; *María Theresa v. Estefania de Guyon,* February 24, 1785, SJR, *LHQ* 26 (1943): 1197–99.

72. Manumission of Mariana, January 8, 1778, Almonester, NONA, 14–15.

73. Succession of Francisco Muñoz, August 23, 1784, SJR, *LHQ* 24 (1941): 894–900.

74. Hall's database codes 1,058 manumissions as purchases, of which only 114 involved litigation (67 by the slaves themselves and another 47 by third parties). These calculations are slightly different from Hanger's: she identified 897 cases involving purchase plus another 154 that required court actions; however her category of "tribunal" manumissions includes litigation filed for reasons other than to initiate or enforce coartación agreements (Hanger, *Bounded Lives, Bounded Places,* 27, table 1.4).

75. *Michel v. Françoise Girardy,* October 9, 1783, SJR, *LHQ* 22 (1939): 269–71.

76. *Juan Bautista Blaquet v. Francisco Maney,* January 14, 1773, SJR, *LHQ* 9 (1926): 149–50.

77. *Luis Canela, Negro, v. Heirs of María Luisa Carmouche,* November 19, 1784, SJR, *LHQ* 25 (1942): 594–96; *Juaneta v. Mr. Moroteau,* August 21, 1783, SJR.

78. *María Theresa v. Estefania de Guyon,* February 24, 1785, SJR, *LHQ* 26 (1943): 1197–99.

79. *Nicolas v. Mr. Mercier,* October 27, 1780, SJR, *LHQ* 15 (1932): 164–65 (freed for 800 pesos despite a higher valuation of 1,200 pesos); *Michel v. Françoise Girardy,* October 9, 1783, SJR, *LHQ* 22 (1939): 269–71 (freed for 500 pesos instead of 700).

80. *Bernarda Arciny, Negress Slave, [v. Francisco Daniel Dupain],* January 14, 1783, SJR, *LHQ* 20 (1937): 266–68. This was the second time Daniel Dupain had been ordered to issue a carta on behalf of his absent son ([*Antonio Guichard v. Francisco Daniel Dupain*], December 18, 1782, SJR, *LHQ* 19 [1936]: 1124–25).

81. [*María Juana, a Negress Slave, v. Juan Suriray de la Rue*], February 28, 1776, SJR, *LHQ* 11 (1928): 338–40. I offer a further discussion of María Juana's case later in this chapter.

82. *Bernarda Arciny, Negress Slave, [v. Francisco Daniel Dupain]*, January 14, 1783, SJR, *LHQ* 20 (1937): 266–68.

83. [*María Theresa v. Marie-Françoise Girardy, Veuve Desruisseau*], September 4, 1782, SJR, *LHQ* 19 (1936): 512–15; manumission of María Theresa, November 7, 1782, Perdomo, NONA, 409–9v.

84. Courts in Spanish New Orleans consisted of the governor or an alcalde (there were two alcaldes at any given time), an escribano, and a letrado. The last was a "learned lawyer" whose responsibility was to interpret Spanish law for the presiding judge, who was often uneducated in the law. Appeals could be made from an alcade's court to the governor's and from both of those to the cabildo as well as to Havana, either for further advice from a letrado or for a hearing by an appeals court that was created for cases originating out of Louisiana. See Henry P. Dart, "Civil Procedure in Louisiana under the Spanish Regime as Illustrated in Loppinot's Case, 1774," trans. and comp. Laura L. Porteus, *LHQ* 12 (1929): 34–35.

85. Succession of Renato Chouteau, April 21, 1776, SJR, *LHQ* 11 (1928): 513–19.

86. *María v. Succession of Francisca Plazan,* May 10, 1782, SJR, *LHQ* 18 (1935): 749–50.

87. [*Catherina v. Estate of Juan Bautista Destrehan*], June 25, 1773, SJR, *LHQ* 9 (1926): 556–59.

88. Succession of Andres Juen, inventory and appraisement of his estate, September 14, 1784, SJR, *LHQ* 24 (1941): 1258–74; *Valentin v. Succession of Andres Juen,* September 23, 1784, SJR, *LHQ* 24 (1941): 1274–80.

89. *Valentin v. Succession of Andres Juen,* September 23, 1784, SJR, *LHQ* 24 (1941): 1274–80.

90. [*Catherina v. Estate of Juan Bautista Destrehan*], June 25, 1773, SJR, *LHQ* 9 (1926): 556–59.

91. *Elena v. Henrique Desprez,* August 12, 1780, SJR, *LHQ* 14 (1931): 619–21; manumission of Nata Andres, March 8, 1779, Almonester, NONA, 262.

92. *Nicolas v. Mr. Mercier,* October 27, 1780, SJR, *LHQ* 15 (1932): 164–65.

93. [*Catherina v. Estate of Juan Bautista Destrehan*], June 25, 1773, SJR, *LHQ* 9 (1926): 556–59.

94. [*María Theresa v. Marie-Françoise Girardy, Widow Desruisseau*], September 4, 1782, SJR, *LHQ* 19 (1936): 512–15.

95. [*Antonio Guichard v. Francisco Daniel Dupain*], December 18, 1782, SJR, *LHQ* 19 (1936): 1124–25.

96. Intestate succession of Marie Eva LaBranche, wife of Alexandro Baure, September 14, 1779, SJR, *LHQ* 14 (1931): 119–32.

97. Gwendolyn Midlo Hall, "Mean Prices by Gender, Origin and Decade," August 21, 2001, *Afro-Louisiana History and Genealogy, 1718–1820,* www.ibiblio.org/laslave/calcs/prices .html (accessed August 17, 2006); Hanger, *Bounded Lives, Bounded Places,* 31, table 1.6.

98. *María Theresa v. Estefania de Guyon,* February 24, 1785, SJR, *LHQ* 26 (1943): 1197–99.

99. [Marguerite], will, March 1, 1770, SJR, *LHQ* 6 (1923): 316.

100. *María Theresa v. Estefania de Guyon,* February 24, 1785, SJR, *LHQ* 26 (1943): 1197–99; *Valentin v. Succession of Andres Juen,* September 23, 1784, SJR, *LHQ* 24 (1941): 1274–80;

Angelica, Negra Slave, v. Santiago Porta, July 29, 1779, SJR, *LHQ* 13 (1930): 700–701. Five hundred and thirty manumissions involved third-party purchases. In 52 percent of these cases, the money came from libres, in 28 percent from whites, and in 18 percent from other slaves. Of the 430 cases in which the benefactor's relationship to the manumitted is noted, the overwhelming majority—nearly three-quarters—were parents. Grandparents and siblings were each involved in about 7 percent of the cases, followed by spouses or consorts (5.8 percent), children (2.8 percent), collateral relatives (2.6 percent), and godparents (1.9 percent) (Hanger, *Bounded Lives, Bounded Places,* 45).

101. [*Catherina v. Estate of Juan Bautista Destrehan*], June 25, 1773, SJR, *LHQ* 9 (1926): 556–59.

102. *Elena v. Henrique Desprez,* August 12, 1780, SJR, *LHQ* 14 (1931): 619–21.

103. *Margarita v. Mariana Lerable,* May 22, 1782, SJR, *LHQ* 18 (1935): 757–58.

104. *Luis Dor, negro esclavo de Dn. Joseph Dusuau, contra la sucesión de Estevan Lalande, mulato libre,* January 10, 1794, F. Broutin Court Proceedings, NONA, 31A:1–43, cited in Kimberley S. Hanger, "Greedy French Masters and Color-Conscious, Legal-Minded Spaniards in Colonial Louisiana," in *Slavery in the Caribbean Francophone World: Distant Voices, Forgotten Acts, Forged Identities,* ed. Doris Y. Kadish (Athens, Ga., 2000), 110–12; manumission of Luis [Dor], May 26, 1794, F. Broutin, NONA, 30:119.

105. Succession of Pelagia Lorreins, wife of Andres Jung, September 7, 1781, SJR, *LHQ* 17: 213–18.

106. Manumission of Jose Ginefry, May 12, 1798, Pedesclaux, NONA, 31:359–61.

107. *María Luisa Saly v. Matheo Parin Called Canon, Her Owner,* January 23, 1781, SJR, *LHQ* 15 (1932): 546–48. For cases upheld by Panis, see, for example, manumission of [Juan Bautista?], November 6, 1781, Almonester, NONA, 449v–51; manumission of Gabriel, June 25, 1781, Almonester, NONA, 236v–38; [*María Theresa v. Marie-Françoise Girardy, Veuve Desruisseau*], September 4, 1782, SJR, *LHQ* 19 (1936): 512–15; *Claude Guillory v. Michel Barre and Margarita,* January 20, 1781, SJR, *LHQ* 15 (1932): 545–46; *Margarita, a free negress, v. Guillory Heirs,* March 9, 1782, SJR, *LHQ* 18 (1935): 204–12. For Panis' manumission, see sale of slave, January 10, 1775, Almonester, NONA, 9, and manumission of Miguel, May 30, 1776, Garic, NONA, 7:171–72. For other cases denied for lack of documentation, see testimonio de las diligencia obradas por María Josepha, negra esclava, del Pe. Fr. Josef de Xerez, July 30, 1792, Records of the Diocese, 3:119–38, and *Antonio, Mulatto, v. Deshotels Succession,* March 7, 1774, SJR, *LHQ* 10 (1927): 300–301. Antonio's case failed despite his having six blancos who testified on his behalf that his owner had indeed intended to free him.

108. [*Joseph v. Degout Succession*], August 8, 1783, SJR, *LHQ* 21 (1938): 939–40, 947–50.

109. [*María Juana, a Negress Slave, v. Juan Suriray de la Rue*], February 28, 1776, SJR, *LHQ* 11 (1928): 338–40.

110. *Juan Suriray de la Rue v. Edward Jenkins,* February 28, 1776, SJR, *LHQ* 11 (1928): 340–52; [*María Juana, a Negress Slave, v. Juan Suriray de la Rue*], February 28, 1776, SJR, *LHQ* 11 (1928): 338–40.

111. [*Catherina v. Estate of Juan Bautista Destrehan*], June 25, 1773, SJR, *LHQ* 9 (1926): 556–59.

112. Baade suggests that Gálvez's hostility stemmed from his own ownership of slaves and his marriage into one of the largest slaveowning families in the colony ("Law of Slavery," 64–66). Yet Unzaga had married into the very same family and continued to support coartación (Dawson, ed., *Louisiana Governors,* 52–61).

113. Hall, "Louisiana Free Database."

114. *María called Mariquine v. Pedro Methode,* November 8, 1780, SJR, *LHQ* 15 (1932): 165–66. Methode may have been slow to act, as María petitioned the court the following June to have a copy of Gálvez's ruling sent to the commander at Pointe Coupée.

115. Emancipation of Margarita and her children, September 27, 1771, Almonester, NONA, 207–8v; [*Claude Guillory v. Michel Barre and Margarita*], January 20, 1781, SJR, *LHQ* 15 (1932): 545–46; *Margarita, Negra Libre, v. Guillory Heirs,* March 9, 1782, SJR, *LHQ* 18 (1935): 204–12. It is possible that Gregoire Guillory was the father of Margarita's children (Carl A. Brasseaux, Keith P. Fontenot, and Claude F. Oubre, *Creoles of Color in the Bayou Country* [Jackson, Miss., 1994], 14–15).

116. [*Pierre Fauché v. François Demazillière*], February 5, 1783, SJR, *LHQ* 20 (1937): 519–21.

117. Hanger, *Bounded Lives, Bounded Places,* 22.

118. Virginia Meacham Gould similarly argues that Spanish rule benefited free people of color without necessarily improving the lot of slaves ("In Full Enjoyment of Their Liberty," 7).

Chapter 5. Limpieza de Sangre and Family Formation

1. Don Bernardo de Gálvez to Don Joseph de Gálvez, May 27, 1779, Confidential Despatches of Don Bernardo de Gálvez, Fourth Spanish Governor of Louisiana, Sent to his Uncle, Don José de Gálvez, Secretary of State and Ranking Official of the Council of the Indies, 1770–82, HT, 98.

2. Carlota Fazende, widow of Francisco Xavier Delino, March 3, 1782, SJR, *LHQ* 18 (1935): 200; documentation presented to authenticate the purity of blood and good character of Marie-Françoise Gerard, November 25, 1781, to February 20, 1782, *The Favrot Family Papers: A Documentary Chronicle of Early Louisiana,* ed. Guillermo Náñez Falcón, 5 vols. ([New Orleans], 1988–2001), 1:289; [petition requesting royal permission for marriage between Martin Palao and Martina Josefa Preito y Laronde], 1796, Carondelet Dispatches, 237.

3. On limpieza de sangre in Spain and its transformation in Spanish America, see Henry Kamen, *Inquisition and Society in Spain in the Sixteenth and Seventeenth Centuries* (Bloomington, Ind., 1985), 114–17; Albert A. Sicroff, *Les controverses des statuts de "pureté de sang" en Espagne du 15e au 17e siècle* (Paris, 1960); Deborah Root, "Speaking Christian: Orthodoxy and Difference in Sixteenth-Century Spain," *Representations* 23 (1988): 132; María Elena Martínez, "Limpieza de Sangre," in *Encyclopedia of Mexico: History, Society, and Culture,* ed. Michael Werner (Chicago, 1997), 1:749–52; Verena Stolcke, "Conquered Women," *Report on the Americas* 24 (1991): 25; María Elena Martínez, "The Black Blood of New Spain: *Limpieza de Sangre,* Racial Violence, and Gendered Power in Early Colonial

Mexico," *WMQ*, 3rd ser., 61 (2004): 483–84; Ann Twinam, *Public Lives, Private Secrets: Gender, Honor, Sexuality, and Illegitimacy in Colonial Spanish America* (Stanford, Calif., 1999), 41–47.

4. Petition [by Don Nicolas Daunoy for his son, Carlos Favre Daunoy, to join the Spanish company of the royal guard corps], ca. October 26, 1793, Carondelet Dispatches, 155.

5. Jean-Baptiste Macarty, will, November 21, 1808, N. Broutin, NONA, 18:491v–92; baptism of Ysidro Macarty, February 11, 1797, *SR*, 6:183; baptism of Eulalia Macarty, July 15, 1799, *SR*, 6:182; baptism of Bernardo Theodulo Macarty, April 26, 1806, SLC, B19, 56; *Marie L. Badillo v. Francisco Tio*, 6 La. Ann. 129 (1851), 611–13.

6. Blancas possessed a mere 3 percent, while blancos possessed the overwhelming majority of the city's wealth (conversation with Virginia Meacham Gould, February 2004). Ironically, it was precisely because free women of color did not marry their blanco consorts that they are so visible among property owners. Wealthy blancas had their property subsumed into that of their husbands (Kenneth R. Aslakson, "Free Women of African Descent in the New Orleans Courts, 1803–1813," paper presented at the Society for Historians of the Early American Republic, Montreal, July 2006).

7. In contrast, Charleston's 951 free African Americans comprised just 5 percent of the city's population in 1800. The two U.S. cities at that time with the largest percentages of free African-Americans were Baltimore (a total of 2,771) and Philadelphia (4,210), both with about 10 percent (Leonard P. Curry, *The Free Black in Urban America, 1800–1850: The Shadow of the Dream* [Chicago, 1981], table A-8).

8. *Recensement general . . . de la Nouvelle Orleans,* July 1, 1727, AC, G1, 464; *Census of Louisiana,* September 2, 1771, *SMV*, 1:196; [*Summary of Census of Louisiana*], 1785, *American State Papers: Miscellaneous* (Washington, D.C., 1832–34), 10:381; *Census of New Orleans,* November 6, 1791, NOPL; Daniel H. Usner Jr., *Indians, Settlers, and Slaves in a Frontier Exchange Economy: The Lower Mississippi Valley before 1783* (Chapel Hill, N.C., 1992), 114–15; John E. Harkins, "The Regulatory Function of the New Orleans Cabildo, 1769–1803" (M.A., Louisiana State University, 1971), 6–7.

9. During the French era, men appointed to positions on the Superior Council were required to undergo an "inquiry of life and morals," but it appears to have been fairly perfunctory, focusing on their behavior as good Catholics rather than on investigating their ancestries. See, for instance, information de vie et moeurs du Sieur Paquier, March 22, 1737, RSC, *LHQ* 10 (1927): 73–74, and Henry Plauché Dart, "Politics in Louisiana in 1724," *LHQ* 5 (1922): 302.

10. The twenty or so limpieza de sangre petitions I found were scattered throughout various document collections, including SJR, NONA, AGI, SD, and AGI, PC. One case turned up in a collection of family papers. My thanks to Mary Williams for bringing several of the SJR cases to my attention.

11. Remite las adjuntas diligencias por las que pretende contraher matrimonio el capitan graduado y ayudante maior de esta plaza Don Jacinto Panis con Doña Margarita Wiltz, 1776, AGI, SD, leg. 2547, doc. 151, [2]; información producia por D. Franco. Riado pa. hacer contrar su legitimidad y limpieza de sangre, March 15, 1785, Quiñones Court Proceedings, NONA, 4:26–35.

12. Remite las adjuntas diligencias por las que pretende el theniente Don Manuel Perez contraher matrimonio con Doña Juana Catalina Dubois, February 16, 1776, AGI, SD, leg. 2547, doc. 153, 327.

13. *The Laws of Las Siete Partidas, Which Are Still in Force in Louisiana,* trans. Louis Moreau-Lislet and Henry Carleton, 2 vols. (New Orleans, 1820), 1:547, partida 4, title 13, law 2; Juana Catalina Dubois, January 31, 1776, SJR, *LHQ* 11 (1928): 326–30; información producia por D. Franco. Riado pa. hacer contrar su legitimidad y limpieza de sangre, March 15, 1785, Quiñones Court Proceedings, NONA, 4:27.

14. María Catarina Grifon, May 14, 1782, SJR, *LHQ* 18 (1935): 751–53; [petition requesting royal permission for marriage between Martin Palao and Martina Josefa Preito y Laronde], 1796, Carondelet Dispatches, 229–30; información producia por D. Franco. Riado pa. hacer contrar su legitimidad y limpieza de sangre, March 15, 1785, Quiñones Court Proceedings, NONA, 4:28v. Despite the increasing racialization of limpieza de sangre in the colonies, religion continued to play an important role (Martínez, "Black Blood of New Spain," 484).

15. Petition [by Don Nicolas Daunoy for his son, Carlos Favre Daunoy, to join the Spanish company of the royal guard corps], ca. October 26, 1793, Carondelet Dispatches, 154–55, 163; [petition requesting royal permission for marriage between Martin Palao and Martina Josefa Preito y Laronde], 1796, Carondelet Dispatches, 229–38.

16. On the importance of honor in Spanish America, see Ann Twinam, "Honor, Sexuality and Illegitimacy in Colonial Spanish America," in *Sexuality and Marriage in Colonial Latin America,* ed. Asunción Lavrin (Lincoln, Nebr., 1989), 118–55, and Ramón A. Gutiérrez, *When Jesus Came, the Corn Mothers Went Away: Marriage, Sexuality and Power in New Mexico, 1500–1846* (Stanford, Calif., 1991), 176–240.

17. Sobre limpieza de sangre de Doña Adelaida d'Estrehan, 1795–97, AGI, SD, leg. 2588, 768–69; petition [by Don Nicolas Daunoy for his son, Carlos Favre Daunoy, to join the Spanish company of the royal guard corps], ca. October 26, 1793, Carondelet Dispatches, 135; [petition requesting royal permission for marriage between Martin Palao and Martina Josefa Preito y Laronde], 1796, Carondelet Dispatches, 241–42; documentation presented to authenticate the purity of blood and good character of Marie-Françoise Gerard, *Favrot Family Papers,* 1:291; información de legitimidad, vida y conumbres de Dn. Joaquin de Lisa, vecino de Nueva Orleans, August 22, 1785, Quiñones Court Proceedings, NONA, 4:106v–7.

18. Margarita Wiltz, February 7, 1776, SJR, *LHQ* 11 (1928): 330–32; [petition of Pedro de La Ronde], 1778, Carondelet Dispatches, 247–48; [petition requesting royal permission for marriage between Martin Palao and Martina Josefa Preito y Laronde], 1796, Carondelet Dispatches, 241–42, 250–51.

19. María Catarina Grifon, May 14, 1782, SJR, *LHQ* 18 (1935): 753; [petition requesting royal permission for marriage between Martin Palao and Martina Josefa Preito y Laronde], Carondelet Dispatches, 219–20; petition [by Don Nicolas Daunoy for his son, Carlos Favre Daunoy, to join the Spanish company of the royal guard corps], ca. October 26, 1793, Carondelet Dispatches, 133.

20. Pragmática sanción para evitar el abuso de contraer matrimonios desiguales, March

23, 1776, *Colección de documentos para la historia de la formación social de Hispanoamérica, 1493–1810,* ed. Richard Konetzke, 3 vols. (Madrid, 1958–62), 3:406–13.

21. Real cédula declarando la forma en que se ha de guardar y cumplir en las Indias la pragmática sanción de 23 de marzo de 1776 sobre contraer matrimonios, April 7, 1778, *Colección de documentos,* 3:438–42. Many New Orleanians noted that their parents were deceased or did not live in the colony when they applied for marriage licenses. See, for example, diligencias practicadas por Antonio Hernandez para contraer matrimonio con Antonia Rodriguez, January 10, 1793, SJR; licencia de matrimonio a Don Claudio Treme, March 21, 1793, SJR.

22. Twinam, *Public Lives, Private Secrets,* 308–12.

23. Similarly, Martínez argues that, while people of African descent were denied as a group the privileges of colonial membership in early colonial Mexico, individuals could earn belonging through particular acts of loyalty, bravery, and the like ("Black Blood of New Spain," 488–89).

24. For alternative readings of the 1778 cédula and its implementation, see Patricia Seed, *To Love, Honor, and Obey in Colonial Mexico: Conflicts over Marriage Choice, 1574–1821* (Stanford, Calif., 1988), 205–25 (the cédula was intended to prevent interracial marriages but most Mexican parents objected on other grounds); Robert McCaa, *"Calidad, Clase,* and Marriage in Colonial Mexico: The Case of Parral, 1788–90," *Hispanic American Historical Review* 64 (1984): 491 (Mexican authorities generally ignored the cédula, except with regard to elites, and formal parental opposition was rare as most marriages were class and race endogamous); and Twinam, *Public Lives, Private Secrets,* 309–10 (both elites and lower-status whites throughout Spanish America filed objections and most centered on racial rather than socioeconomic disparities). It was not until 1805 that the Crown explicitly discouraged interracial marriages (Real cédula . . . acerca de los matrimonios que personas de conocida noleza pretendan contrear con las de castas de negros y mulatos, October 15, 1805, *Biblioteca de legislación ultramarina: en forma de diccionario alfabético,* ed. José María Zamora y Coronado [Madrid, 1845], translated in Verena Martinez-Alier, *Marriage, Class and Colour in Nineteenth-Century Cuba: A Study of Racial Attitudes and Sexual Values in a Slave Society* [Ann Arbor, Mich., 1989], 12–13).

25. Louis Sala-Molins, *Le code noir; ou, Le calvaire de Canaan* (Paris, 1987), article 6; Code Noir ou Loi Municipale, February 12, 1778 (New Orleans, 1778), articles 6–11.

26. Real cédula sobre la educación, trato y occupaciones de los esclavos, May 31, 1789, *Colección de documentos,* 3:645–47, articles 6, 3.

27. Luis Peñalver y Cárdenas, bishop of Louisiana, to the pastors of the diocese of Louisiana, December 21, 1795, Records of the Diocese, 4:581–82.

28. [Proceedings over the clandestine marriage of Jose Fafar and Isavel Olivo in Ovachita, Carmel Parish], May 6, 1799, to May 24, 1800, Records of the Diocese, 9:262–89. Filhiol was later acquitted of illegally officiating at marriage ceremonies (diligencia contra D. Juan Filhiol, comandante que fue de el puesto de el Ouchitas sobre haber presenciado como párroco aivirros [*sic*] matrimonios, March 4, 1802, Records of the Diocese, 10:716–88). Most marriage dispensations sought, and granted, were for consanguinity, particularly among the highly ethnically endogamous community of Acadians. See, for example, documents concerning the petition of Theofilo Brousard for a dispensation from the diriment

impediment . . . , October 12, 1795, Records of the Diocese, 4:418–30. At least one petitioner played on the church's concern for concubinage when requesting his dispensation, claiming that "unless their marriage is confirmed, they will be exposed to human frailty" ([documents concerning the petition of Dionisio Landry for a dispensation from the diriment impediment . . .], August 24, 1795, Records of the Diocese, 4:107–201).

29. Almost every documentable relationship was between a Euro-Louisianan man and a woman of color. For an extremely rare mention of a relationship between a "mujer blanco" and a negro, see proceedings against Father Carlos Burk [Charles Burke], pastor of Baton Rouge, over a quarrel with his parishioner, [Armand] Duplantier, November 20, 1799, Records of the Diocese, 8:880, in which negra María Theresa testifies that she lived with another negra and "a mulatica, the daughter of a mujer blanca and a negro."

30. According to one "resident," the situation was similar in 1850 (*New Orleans As It Is: Its Manners and Customs—Morals—Fashionable Life—Profanation of the Sabbath—Prostitution—Licentiousness—Slave Markets and Slavery* [(New Orleans?), 1850], 35). Failure to marry was not unusual in the Spanish Americas or Brazil and was not restricted to racially exogamous relationships. See Kimberly S. Hanger, *Bounded Lives, Bounded Places: Free Black Society in Colonial New Orleans, 1769–1803* (Durham, N.C., 1997), 90–92, 97; Kathy Waldron, "The Sinners and the Bishop in Colonial Veracruz: The *Vista* of Bishop Mariano Martí, 1771–1784," in *Sexuality and Marriage in Colonial Latin America,* 163; Elizabeth Kuznesof, "Sexual Politics, Race and Bastard-Bearing in Nineteenth-Century Brazil: A Question of Culture of Power?" *Journal of Family History* 16 (1991): 241, 248; William Taylor, *Magistrates of the Sacred: Priests and Parishioners in Eighteenth-Century Mexico* (Stanford, Calif., 1996), 244, 660n43; and Twinam, *Public Lives, Private Secrets,* 9–10. For an argument that it also may have been more common in Anglo-America than previously considered, see Richard Godbeer, *The Sexual Revolution in Early America* (Baltimore, Md., 2002).

31. Luis Peñalver y Cárdenas, "General Proceedings of the Visit of the Diocese of Louisiana and in Particular of New Orleans by Don Luis Peñalver y Cárdenas, Its First Bishop, and the Notary Dr. Jose María de Rivas, His Private and Official Secretary," July 29 to December 22, 1795, Records of the Diocese, 4:531–46, 577; Luis Penalvery y Cardenas, ["On the State of Religion and Morals in the Colony"], 1799, translated in Charles Gayarré, *The History of Louisiana,* vol. 4, *The American Domination* (New York, 1854–66), 408. See also Luis Peñalver y Cárdenas to Eugenio Llaguno y Amirola, November 1, 1795, AGI, SD, leg. 2673.

32. Peñalver y Cárdenas, instructions, December 22, 1795, "General Proceedings of the Visit of the Diocese of Louisiana," 4:589.

33. Baptismal ceremonies provided for Luisa Declouet, January 25, 1795, SLC, B13, 177; baptism of María del Carmen Declouet, January 21, 1797, SLC, B14, 22; marriage of Luis Declouet and Clara [Lopez] de la Peña recorded November 20, 1801, SLC, M5, 156; marriage of Juan Peralta an d María de los D[*] Formayor, [December 9], 1787, *SR,* 4:241, 131; testimony produced by Juan Peralta to prove that his son Manuel was baptized, November 18, 1797, Records of the Diocese, 7:60–73.

34. Seed, *To Love, Honor, and Obey,* 205–25; Gilbert C. Din, *Spaniards, Planters, and Slaves: The Spanish Regulation of Slavery in Louisiana, 1763–1803* (College Station, Tex., 1999), 71.

35. Baptism of Carolina María Salome Hinard, January 24, 1793, SLC, B13, 23; baptism

of María Josefa de las Mercedes Hinard, February 6, 1795, *SR,* 5:209; donation of slave, February 21, 1798, Pedesclaux, NONA, 31:112–13; Nicolás María Vidal, will, May 4, 1798, Pedesclaux, NONA, 31:323v–26v; testamentaria de Don Francisco Hisnard que falleción en el puesto de Opellousas, August 27, 1798, SJR, 6v–9v.

36. Grimaldi to Ulloa, September 1768, *SMV,* 1:9.

37. Baptism of Fernando Gayoso de Lemos, December 10, 1797, *SR,* 6:133–34; Hans W. Baade, "The Form of Marriage in Spanish North America," *Cornell Law Review* 61 (1975): 73–74. Governor Bernardo de Gálvez married the creole Marie Felicite Maxent without seeking royal permission. He claimed to be "gravely ill," although he lived for another nine years (marriage of Bernardo de Gálvez and Feliciana Maxent, November 2, 1777, *SR,* 3:77, 206; Joseph G. Dawson III, ed. *The Louisiana Governors: From Iberville to Edwards* [Baton Rouge, La., 1990], 57, 59).

38. Marriage contract of Pierre-Joseph Favrot and Marie-François Gérard, December 11, 1784, *Favrot Family Papers,* 2:18–20; baptismal certificate of Victoire-Stephanie-Fortunee Favrot, December 8, 1784, *Favrot Family Papers,* 2:18.

39. Legal recognition of natural children seems to have similarly encouraged high rates of illegitimacy in nineteenth-century Brazil as well (Kuznesof, "Sexual Politics, Race and Bastard-Bearing in Nineteenth-Century Brazil," 257n8, citing Katia M. de Queirós Mattoso, *Bahia: A Cidade do Salvador e seu mercado no século XIX* [São Paulo, 1978], 205–6).

40. It was not just blancos whose children were legitimated by their parents' marriages. See, for example, marriage of Pedro Demouy and Juana, August 20, 1802, SLC, M3, 21v–22, and Pedro Demouy, will, August 20, 1802, Pedesclaux, NONA, 41:578v–81v.

41. Ordinances and Instructions of Don Alexandro O'Reilly, November 25, 1769, *Historical Collections of Louisiana, Embracing Translations of Many Rare and Valuable Documents Relating to the Natural, Civil and Political History of that State,* ed. Benjamin F. French, 5 vols. (New York, 1846–53), 5:284–85. On the legal distinctions among types of children, their rights to inheritance, and the impact of these distinctions on the state, see Linda Lewin, *Surprise Heirs: Illegitimacy, Patrimonial Rights, and Legal Nationalism in Luso-Brazilian Inheritance, 1750–1821,* 2 vols. (Stanford, Calif., 2003). Although the English church recognized a distinction between children born of parents who eventually married each other and those who never did so, English common law courts did not and treated all out-of-wedlock children the same. Anglo-American governments began to allow for the postnatal legitimation of children through marriage as early as 1785 (Alan Macfarlane, "Illegitimacy and Illegitimates in English History," in *Bastardy and Its Comparative History: Studies in the History of Illegitimacy and Marital Nonconformism in Britain, France, Germany, Sweden, North America, Jamaica and Japan,* ed. Peter Laslett, Karla Oosterveen, and Richard M. Smith [Cambridge, Mass., 1980], 73–74; Michael Grossberg, *Governing the Hearth: Law and the Family in Nineteenth-Century America* [Chapel Hill, N.C., 1985], 197–98, 204–5).

42. In colonial New Mexico, those without property, status, or honor to protect tended not to marry (Gutiérrez, *When Jesus Came,* 201).

43. [Nicolas Chauvin de Lafrénière or Julien Jérome Doucet], *Mémoire des habitans et négocians de la Louisianne, sur l'événement du 29 Octobre 1768* (New Orleans, 1768), 17.

44. On literacy rates in French New Orleans, see Emily Clark, *Masterless Mistresses: The New Orleans Ursulines and the Development of a New World Society, 1727–1834* (Chapel Hill, N.C., 2007), 113–21.

45. Marriage contract of Jean Paillet and Catiche or Catherine Villeray, November 16, 1769, RSC; "Census of New Orleans," June 1778, *Census and Militia Lists, 1770–1789,* ed. Albert J. Robichaux (Harvey, La., 1973–74), 1:23–68; baptism of François Paillet, October 14, 1770, SLC, B6, 91; baptism of Manuel Tusant Paillet, June 27, 1785, SLC, B9, 374; baptism of Josef Beronic Julia and Eugenia Emé Paillet, June 26, 1787, SLC, B11, 33; "Census of New Orleans," November 6, 1791, NOPL.

46. Marriage of Bautista Rafael Fancon and María Andrea Gotié, May 1, 1779, SLC, M3, 3v.

47. *María Theresa Cheval v. Phelipe Lafarga,* April 12, 1779, Quiñones Court Proceedings, NONA, 1:30–44.

48. Cited in Hanger, *Bounded Lives, Bounded Places,* 93.

49. Ursuline Convent, minutes, October 31, 1797, déliberations du conseil, 1727–1902, Archives of the Ursuline Convent of New Orleans; Clark, *Masterless Mistresses,* 134–35. My thanks to the Archives of the Ursuline Convent for sharing this document with me and to Emily Clark and Charles Nolan for first bringing it to my attention and sharing their interpretations with me.

50. Marriage of Juan Bautista Toupard and Carlota Lafrance, June 19, 1785, SLC, M5, 39; baptism of María Clara Toupart, March 4, 1793, SLC, B11, 248; marriage of Bartolomé Bautista and Catarina Lafrance, September 12, 1788, SLC, M3, 7; Bartolomé Bta. grifo libre, contra Juan Lafrance sobre impedir este el matrimonio de su hija con el dicho Bartólome, September 6, 1788, SJR; Hanger, *Bounded Lives, Bounded Places,* 95–96. Charlotte's whitening at her marriage to a blanco is an example of what Robert McCaa calls "racial drift, or the tendency to change *calidad* at marriage." In his study of marriages in Parral, Mexico, between 1788 and 1790, McCaa found that women were twice as likely as men to experience racial drift ("*Calidad, Clase,* and Marriage," 497).

51. Manumission of Miguel Alard, María Felicite, and María Emea, July 28, 1785, Rodríguez, NONA, 594; baptism of Agata Girodeau, December 3, 1791, SLC, B12, 279; baptism of Luisa Pellerin, November 4, 1791, SLC, B12, 274.

52. It was this open acknowledgment of children, whether at baptisms or in wills, that most distinguished racially exogamous relationships in New Orleans from elsewhere in the North American South where, though relationships between white men and women of color might be tolerated, they were rarely openly acknowledged (Virginia Kent Anderson Leslie, *Woman of Color, Daughter of Privilege: Amanda America Dickson, 1849–1893* [Athens, Ga., 1995]; Joshua D. Rothman, *Notorious in the Neighborhood: Sex and Families across the Color Line in Virginia, 1787–1861* [Chapel Hill, N.C., 2003]; Tiya Miles, *Ties That Bind: The Story of an Afro-Cherokee Family in Slavery and Freedom* [Berkeley, Calif., 2005], 138–39).

53. Marion Dubreuil, will, June 16, 1802, Pedesclaux, NONA, 41:445–46v; Marion Dubreuil, codicil, December 20, 1802, Pedesclaux, NONA, 42:923–23v.

54. Baptism of Domingo Gallard, May 29, 1797, *SR,* 6:130.

55. On the influence of notaries on their clients, see Kathryn Burns, "Notaries, Truth, and Consequences," *AHR* 110 (2005): 366.

56. Peñalver y Cárdenas, ["On the State of Religion and Morals in the Colony"], *History of Louisiana,* 4:408.

57. Mary Veronica Miceli, "The Influence of the Roman Catholic Church on Slavery in Colonial Louisiana" (PhD diss., Tulane University, 1979), 83, 88, 92.

58. Baptism of María Luisa Marta Cazelar, April 2, 1793, SLC, B13, 42; Pierre Cazelar, will, June 17, 1797, F. Broutin, NONA, 46:118v–22.

59. Baptism of Pedro [Daniau Rousseau], September 28, 1782, SLC, B8, 306; baptism of Francisco de Paula Tribuño, July 15, 1793, SLC, B13, 68. For baptisms that record an unknown white father, see baptism of Pedro Luis Lalande, May 6, 1795, SLC, B13, 200, and baptism of Francisco, May 5, 1794, SLC, B13, 129. For records in which the fathers are named and labeled as white, see baptism of Federico Plats Toutant, June 29, 1795, SLC, B13, 212, and baptism of Brigida Adelaida Raby, October 12, 1795, SLC, B13, 236.

60. Baptism of Helena Hazeur, October 25, 1792, SLC, B13, 5; manumission of Helena, January 14, 1793, Pedesclaux, NONA, 16:24v–26; manumission of Feliciana, January 31, 1793, Pedesclaux, NONA, 16:77v–78; baptism of Antonita Hazeur, December 2, 1796, SLC, B13, 333; baptism of Luisa Hazeur, July 16, 1798, SLC, B15, 23; baptism of Susana Hazeur, March 10, 1803, SLC, B16, 112.

61. Baptism of Ramon Juan Antonio Perdomo, September 5, 1791, *SR,* 5:301; baptism of Rita Josefa Lugar, June 24, 1793, SLC, B13, 65; baptism of Petronilda Lugar, March 3, 1795, SLC, B13, 183; marriage contract of Joseph Cabaret and María Juana Prudhome, March 5, 1801, N. Broutin, NONA, 3:78–79v; marriage of María Juana Prudhome and Joseph Cabaret, March 10, 1801, SLC, M3, 20; Hanger, *Bounded Lives, Bounded Places,* 51, 76, 141–42.

62. Pedro Dauphin, will, April 3, 1800, N. Broutin, NONA, 2:93v–96.

63. Bartolomé Toutant Beauregard, will, February 27, 1792, F. Broutin, NONA, 15:39v–42v. On Luisa Toutant and the Ursulines school, see Clark, *Masterless Mistresses,* 140–41n20.

64. Manumission of María and Pedro, January 7, 1782, Mazange, NONA, 5:12v–13v; Francisco Emanuel Demazilière, will, December 6, 1787, Rodríguez, NONA, 13:1143v–51v; manumission of Clemencia, March 11, 1788, Pedesclaux, NONA, 2:335; Marie Demazilière [Bienvenu], will, June 30, 1791, Pedesclaux, NONA, 13:436v–39; manumission of María Iris, August 18, 1794, Ximénez, NONA, 7:325–26v; manumission of Rosalía, April 22, 1801, N. Broutin, NONA, 3:131v–39v; manumission of Basilio, February 18, 1803, Ximénez, NONA, 19:118. Basilio, who was freed in 1803, apparently bore no ill will towards his former owner/half brother as he served as godfather to Pedro Baltazar's son several months after being manumitted (baptism of Francisco Manuel Demazilière, November 26, 1803, *SR,* 7:95). Although Demazilière did not claim his paternity of Pedro Baltazar and Pedro Agusto in his will, his testamentary executor and nephew Don Joseph Dusuau de La Croix (who, as we will see, had several nonwhite children of his own), described them as Demazilière's "natural sons" in María Iris' 1794 manumission.

65. Don Juan Antonio Lugar, will, July 20, 1801, Pedesclaux, NONA, 39:444v–47v.

66. Marcos de Olivares, will, December 18, 1791, Pedesclaux, NONA, 13:764v–69;

burial of Marcos de Olivares, December 20, 1791, *SR*, 5:288; receipt, October 7, 1794, Pedesclaux, NONA, 22:884v–85v.

67. "Census of New Orleans," June 1778, *Louisiana Census and Militia Lists, 1770–1789*, 1:23–68.

68. Succession of Andres Juen, inventory and appraisement of his estate, September 14, 1784, SJR, *LHQ* 24 (1941): 1258–74.

69. Donation of property, June 2, 1794, Pedesclaux, NONA, 21:614–15v; marriage of Bertrand Gravier and María Joseph Delande, December 20, 1786, *SR*, 4:82, 153.

70. Baptism of Marie Joseph Modeste Deverges, March 6, 1770, *SR*, 2:93; baptism of Marie Louise Prudence Duverges, June 6, 1771, *SR*, 2:114; baptism of Marguerite Françoise Constance Duverges, April 23, 1773, *SR*, 3; manumission of Mariana, December 24, 1785, Rodríguez, NONA, 6:1156; manumission of Mariana and her children, September 4 1790, F. Broutin, NONA, 7:8v–9v; Pedro Devergé, will, September 9, 1790, F. Broutin, NONA, 7:9v–12v.

71. Antoine Demouy, will, April 24, 1778, Garic, NONA, 9:247–49; succession of Antonio Jaillot Demuy or Demouy, May 21, 1778, SJR, *LHQ* 13 (1930): 348–49. Antonio Demouy was the uncle of Joseph Duval Demouy, who manumitted his consort Catalina and their children in 1788.

72. Baptism of Joseph Forneret, March 26, 1786, *SR*, 4:131; Louis Forneret, will, April 19, 1791, F. Broutin, NONA, 7:203v–6.

73. Jacqueline's son Louis had already been promised a habitation at English Turn from Dusuau's uncle, perhaps explaining why his father left him no bequest of his own (Francisco Emanuel Demazilière, will, December 6, 1787, Rodríguez, NONA, 13:1143v–51v).

74. Joseph Dusuau de La Croix, will, June 14, 1794, F. Broutin, NONA, 30:143–50; baptism of María Josefa De Gruy, July 20, 1794, *SR*, 5:105; baptism of Jose Dusuau de La Croix, September 13, 1800, *SR*, 7:120–21; sale, July 10, 1767, SJR; Clark, *Masterless Mistresses*, 137–38, 268. Dusuau, who died in 1804 at the age of seventy-two, freely manumitted two mulata women and their children in 1802: twenty-two-year-old Ortanza with her unraced four-year-old son and twenty-one-year-old María Rosa Eulalia with her two cuarteróna daughters, ages five and two. Given Dusuau's polygynous sexual history, it is possible that these two women were his daughters, born during the seven-year gap between his first and second children with María Dusuau, or perhaps his much younger consorts (internment of Joseph Dusuau de La Croix, October 22, 1804, *SR*, 8:122; manumission of Ortanza and Francisco, August 17, 1802, Pedesclaux, NONA, 41:567–67v; manumission of María Rosa Eulalia and her two daughters, November 16, 1802, N. Broutin, NONA, 4:473–74).

75. Donation of a house, June 30, 1770, SJR; succession of Juan Perret, May 3, 1774, SJR, *LHQ* 10 (1927): 440–43; [*Angélica, Negra Libre, v. Heirs of Juan Perret*], May 25, 1774, SJR, *LHQ* 10 (1927): 445.

76. Pedro Darby, will, June 18, 1803, N. Broutin, NONA, 5:291–93v; *Marie Corbin (Baschemin Darby) v. François Darby*, June 9, 1804, Records of the Superior Court, NOPL; *Francis Darby v. Marie Corbin, Veuve Jonatas Darby, and Edward Forstall* (1805), docket no. 532, Records of the Superior Court, NOPL; *Petition of Francis Darby* (1807), docket no. 1251, Records of the Superior Court, NOPL. See also promovido por María Cofiny parda libre

sobre que se estime su hermano Antonio esclavo de Doña Francisca Monget para su libertad, June 23, 1795, SJR, in which the widow of Don Claudio Cofignie opposed the manumission of one of her husband's children by a grifa slave.

77. *Marie Baschemin v. Louis Darby Danicant* (1805), docket no. 458, Records of the Superior Court, NOPL; *Joanna Dessales Danicant v. Louis Darby Danicant* (1805), docket no. 271, Records of the Superior Court, NOPL.

78. Baptism of María Francisca Foucher y Bernoudy, November 8, 1781, SLC, B8, 238; baptism of Juana Margarita Foucher, March 9, 1788, *SR,* 4:133; marriage of Antoine Foucher and Felicite Badon, January 30, 1787, *SR,* 4:133.

79. Baptism of Susana Hazeur, March 10, 1803, SLC, B16, 112; baptism of María Macarty, February 13, 1792, SLC, B12, 287–88; baptism of Bernardo Theodulo Macarty, April 26, 1806, SLC, B19, 56; baptism of María Hazeur de le Lorme, March 10, 1797, *SR,* 6:148; baptism of Eulalia Hazeur de le Lorme, April 30, 1800, *SR,* 7:165; baptism of François Paillet, October 14, 1770, SLC, B6, 91. On the functions of godparenting in France and Spanish America, see Julie Hardwick, *The Practice of Patriarchy: Gender and the Politics of Household Authority in Early Modern France* (University Park, 1998), 165–81; Sidney W. Mintz and Eric Wolf, "An Analysis of Ritual Co-Parenthood (Compadrazgo)," *Southwestern Journal of Anthropology* 6 (1950): 341–68; Herbert S. Klein, *Slavery in the Americas: A Comparative Study of Virginia and Cuba* (Chicago, 1967), 173–74, 231; and Stephen Gudeman and Stuart B. Schwartz, "Cleansing Original Sin: Godparenthood and the Baptism of Slaves in Eighteenth-Century Bahia," in *Kinship Ideology and Practice in Latin America,* ed. Raymond T. Smith (Chapel Hill, N.C., 1984), 35–58.

80. On the caution needed in relying on lawsuits challenging white men's bequests to nonwhite families, see Paul F. Lachance, "The Formation of a Three-Caste Society: Evidence from Wills in Antebellum New Orleans," *Social Science History* 18 (1994): 217–18.

81. Donation of property, December 4, 1788, Pedesclaux, NONA, 4:1255–56; donation of slave, May 3, 1790, Pedesclaux, NONA, 10:357–57v; donation of property, May 3, 1790, Pedesclaux, NONA, 10:357v–58v; donation of slaves, January 8, 1796, Pedesclaux, NONA, 27:10–10v.

82. For a nuanced analysis of one enslaved woman's dilemma, see Trevor Burnard, " 'Do Thou in Gentle Phibia Smile': Scenes from an Interracial Marriage, Jamaica, 1754–86," in *Beyond Bondage: Free Women of Color in the Americas,* ed. David Barry Gaspar and Darlene Clark Hine (Urbana, Ill., 2004), 82–105. Burnard concludes that "neither victim nor heroine [Phibbia] shows how effectively a resourceful, intelligent, and determined woman could become the agent of her own fortune" (98–99).

83. Manumission of Catalina, her children, and grandchildren, April 15–16, 1788, Pedesclaux, NONA, 3:505v–10, 511–17, 520–20v. Unlike many manumission acts involving multiple parties, Demouy insisted on writing a separate act for each manumitted slave, a process that took two days.

84. Joseph Meunier, will, July 26, 1775, Garic, NONA, 6:182–84; Joseph Meunier, will, September 15, 1777, Garic, NONA, 8:338v–40.

85. Manumission of Gabriela, Luison, and Juan Bautista, December 22, 1779, Almonester, NONA, 683–84; Henrique Mentzinger, will, December 23, 1779, Almonester, NONA, 684–87.

86. Juan Garro, will and codicil, May 5 and 6, 1802, N. Broutin, NONA, 4:203–5v, 206–6v; manumission of Rosa and Juan Jose, July 19, 1802, N. Broutin, NONA, 4:298v–99v. Rosa and Garro may have also had a daughter (baptism of Josefina Garo, June 22, 1800, *SR,* 7:146).

87. Manumission of María Josefa, February 27, 1778, Garic, NONA, 9:91v–92v; manumission of Mariana, February 15, 1781, Mazange, NONA, 3:109.

88. Louis Laumonier, will, November 8, 1798, F. Broutin, NONA, 47:243v–247v; internment of Luis Laumonier, November 12, 1797 [*sic*], *SR,* 6:167.

89. Baptiste Trenier, will, August 3, 1792, F. Broutin, NONA, 15:251v–55v; Bautista Trenier, will, October 12, 1799, N. Broutin, NONA, 1:238–41.

90. Manumission of María Serafina and Rosa, January 26, 1776, Almonester, NONA, 49–50v; manumission of Juan Bautista, November 25, 1791, Ximénez, NONA, 1:497v–501.

91. Following her manumission, María Juana had a son, Louis, who, at the time of his 1798 marriage, claimed François Lemelle as his father. Thus Jacqueline (mother) and María Juana (daughter) were the consorts of two brothers (Jacques and François Lemelle respectively) making for a tangled family genealogy, in which, for instance, Jacqueline was Louis' grandmother and his common-law aunt (marriage of Louis Lemelle and Celeste Olimpie Grandpres, October 16, 1798, *Marriage Contracts of the Opelousas Post, 1766–1803,* trans. and abstracted by Jacqueline Olivier Vidrine and Winston De Ville [Ville Platte, La., 1960], 49).

92. Jacques Lemelle to Aubry and Foucault, January 10, 1767, James Brown Papers, 1765–1867, 5 vols., Manuscript Division, Library of Congress, 1:[1]; sale, July 10, 1767, SJR; sale of property, October 23, 1794, F. Broutin, NONA, 30:286v–89; sale of slaves, October 23, 1794, F. Broutin, NONA, 30:289–90.

93. Lemelle to Aubry and Foucault, January 10, 1767, James Brown Papers, 1765–1867, 5 vols., Manuscript Division, Library of Congress, 1:[1]; manumission of Jacqueline, Agata, María Francisca [alias Tonton], and Adelaida, November 10, 1772, Almonester, NONA, 291v–93; manumission of María Juana and Julia, December 5, 1772, Garic, NONA, 3:366–67; succession of Santiago Lemelle, March 21, 1784, SJR, *LHQ* 23 (1940): 314–37; Virginia Meacham Gould, "In Full Enjoyment of Their Liberty: The Free Women of Color of the Gulf Ports of New Orleans, Mobile and Pensacola, 1769–1860" (PhD diss., Emory University, 1991), 161, 301–2, 332–33.

94. *Janeta v. Marcos Darby,* December 21, 1778, SJR, *LHQ* 13 (1930): 525.

95. *Fancon v. Pedro Bonne,* September 3, 1783, SJR, *LHQ* 21 (1938): 1260–61; obligation, September 21, 1792, Pedesclaux, NONA, 15:537. For another suit, see *Mariana San Juan v. Estate of Santiago Constant,* September 23, 1793, F. Broutin Court Proceedings, NONA, 22:518–27.

96. *Magdalena Canella v. Luis Beaurepos,* January 20, 1777, SJR, *LHQ* 12 (1929): 341–48. Beaurepos may have had children by two other women of color. In 1771, he freely manumitted mulata Margarita and her young daughter and in 1779 he started to manumit, but then voided the act, a young mulatica, the daughter of his former slave Adelaida, perhaps the same woman he had given to Canella (manumission of Margarita and María Luisa, June 5, 1771, Garic, NONA, 2:187v–89; manumission of Felicite, April 5, 1779, Almonester, NONA, 1:184v–85v).

97. *Rosa, parda libre, contra Don Josef Bonneville,* July 27, 1791, SJR.

98. [*María Juana, a Negress Slave, v. Juan Suriray de la Rue*], February 28, 1776, SJR, *LHQ* 11 (1928): 338–40.

99. *María Luisa Saly v. Matheo Parin Called Canon, Her Owner,* January 23, 1781, SJR, *LHQ* 15 (1932): 546–48.

100. "Proceedings to Discover the Criminals and Accomplices Who Started the Fire in Mr. Meuillon's House . . . ," April 5, 1781, SJR, *LHQ* 16 (1933): 345–48; criminal prosecution of Joseph Leon, Joseph Pivoto, and Manuel, soldier of dragoons, February 16, 1781, SJR, *LHQ* 15 (1932): 687–706; [*Pablo Collot v. Geronimo Roig*], July 8, 1785, SJR, *LHQ* 29 (1946): 813–47; *Francisco Labrada v. Felipe Silva,* September 11, 1802, N. Broutin Court Proceedings, 55:265–303.

101. Criminal prosecution of Pedro La Cabanne and the mulatress, Madelon, belonging to Nicolas Perthuis, March 28, 1778, SJR, *LHQ* 13 (1930): 339–43.

102. [Francisco Bouligny], memorandum regarding the instructions for the governor-general of Louisiana, September 1, 1776, Rosemonde E. and Emile Kuntz Collection, 1655–1878, HT, article 32. Although Bouligny's proposal was adopted, there is no evidence that any mulatas were in fact exiled (confidential instructions, November 25, 1776, Kuntz, article 24).

103. Miró, Bando de buen gobierno, June 1, 1786, cabildo records, 1:106–7.

104. *Don Pedro Fabrot v. Marion Cofinie,* June 8, 1795, SJR.

105. Manumission of María [Cofignie], September 7, 1781, Mazange, NONA, 4:708; promovido por María Cofiny parda libre sobre que se estime su hermano Antonio esclavo de Doña Francisca Monget para su libertad, June 23, 1795, SJR; Hanger, *Bounded Lives, Bounded Places,* 215–16n46.

106. [Pierre-Joseph Favrot], "List of Suggested Changes with Regard to the Black Population of New Orleans," [June 1795], *Favrot Family Papers,* 2:169–70. Favrot recommended that "all the gens de Couleur and Nègres-Libres" be exiled from the city so that blanc workmen would marry young girls of their own race, thus "increas[ing] the blanc population."

107. Marques de Casa Calvo to Nicolás María Vidal, October 24, 1800, Cabildo Records (Spanish transcriptions), 4:20–21.

108. [Petition requesting royal permission for marriage between Martin Palao and Martina Josefa Preito y Laronde], 1796, Carondelet Dispatches, 243.

Chapter 6. Negotiating Racial Identities in the 1790s

1. [Diligencias promovidar por Clara Lopez de (la) Peña para justificar su descendencia de India y que la partida de su hija Luisa se traslade del libro de negros al de blancos], September 14, 1799, Records of the Diocese, 8:677–78; baptismal ceremonies provided for Luisa Declouet, January 25, 1795, SLC, B13, 177.

2. Ruth Wallis Herndon and Ella Wilcox Sekatau, "The Right to a Name: The Narragansett People and Rhode Island Officials in the Revolutionary Era," in *After King Philip's War: Presence and Persistence in Indian New England,* ed. Colin G. Calloway (Hanover, N.H., 1997), 114–43.

3. Minutes of the [Navy] Council, September 1, 1716, *MPAFD*, 2:218–19n2; Louis Sala-Molins, *Le code noir; ou, Le calvaire de Canaan* (Paris, 1987), 109.

4. Jennifer M. Spear, "Colonial Intimacies: Legislating Sex in French Louisiana," *WMQ*, 3rd ser., 60 (2003): 75–98.

5. Berquin-Duvallon, *Vue de la colonie espagnole du Mississipi ou des provinces de Louisiane et Floride Occidentale, en l'année 1802* (Paris, 1803), 191–92; Paul Alliot, "Historical and Political Reflections on Louisiana," July 1, 1803–April 13, 1804, in *Louisiana Under the Rule of Spain, France and the United States, 1785–1807: Social, Economic, and Political Conditions of the Territory Represented in the Louisiana Purchase,* ed. James Alexander Robertson, 2 vols. (Cleveland, 1911), 1:81; Fortescue Cuming, *Early Western Travels, 1748–1846,* vol. 4, *Cuming's Tour to the Western Country, 1807–1809,* ed. Reuben G. Thwaites (Cleveland, 1904), 351–52.

6. Benjamin Henry Boneval Latrobe, *Impressions Respecting New Orleans: Diary and Sketches, 1818–1820* (New York, 1951), 76–77; [Baron de Montlezun], *Voyage fait dans les années 1816 et 1817, de New-Yorck a la Nouvelle-Orléans, et de l'Orénoque au Mississipi, par les Petites et les Grandes-Antilles,* 2 vols. (Paris, 1818), 1:244, 247; Édouard de Montulé, *Voyage en Amérique, en Italie, en Sicile et en Égypte, pendant les années 1816, 1817, 1818 et 1819,* 2 vols. (Paris, 1821), 1:123, 141; Timothy Flint, *Recollections of the Last Ten Years, Passed in Occasional Residences and Journeyings in the Valley of the Mississippi from Pittsburg and the Missouri to the Gulf of Mexico, and from Florida to the Spanish Frontier; in a Series of Letters to the Rev. James Flint, of Salem, Massachusetts* (Boston, 1826), 135.

7. James Merrell, "'The Customes of Our Countrey': Indians and Colonists in Early America," in *Strangers within the Realm: Cultural Margins of the First British Empire,* ed. Bernard Bailyn and Philip D. Morgan (Chapel Hill, N.C., 1991), 154. On neighboring Indians in New Orleans and elsewhere in North America, see Daniel H. Usner Jr., "American Indians in Colonial New Orleans," in *Powhatan's Mantle: Indians in the Colonial Southeast,* ed. Peter H. Wood, Gregory A. Waselkov, and M. Thomas Hatley (Lincoln, Nebr., 1989), 104–27; Daniel J. Usner Jr., "Indian-Black Relations in Colonial and Antebellum Louisiana," in *Slave Cultures and the Cultures of Slavery,* ed. Stephan Palmié (Knoxville, Tenn., 1995), 145–61; Helen C. Rountree, *Pocahontas's People: The Powhatan Indians of Virginia through Four Centuries* (Norman, Okla., 1990); Jean M. O'Brien, *Dispossession by Degrees: Indian Land and Identity in Natick, Massachusetts, 1650–1790* (New York, 1997); Herndon and Sekatau, "The Right to a Name"; Thomas L. Doughton, "Unseen Neighbors: Native Americans of Central Massachusetts, a People Who Had 'Vanished,'" in *After King Philip's War,* 207–30; John Wood Sweet, *Bodies Politic: Negotiating Race in the American North, 1730–1830* (Baltimore, Md., 2003).

8. Daniel H. Usner Jr., *Indians, Settlers, and Slaves in a Frontier Exchange Economy: The Lower Mississippi Valley before 1783* (Chapel Hill, N.C., 1992), 284–85.

9. John K. Chance, *Race and Class in Colonial Oaxaca* (Stanford, Calif., 1978), 94–97. See also Jorge Klor de Alva, "*Mestizaje* from New Spain to Aztlán: On the Control and Classification of Collective Identities," in *New World Orders: Casta Painting and Colonial Latin America,* ed. John A. Farmer and Ilona Katzew (New York, 1996), 58–71, who argues that the labels "mestizo" and "mulato" took on their specific racial, and usually disparaging, meanings during the second half of the seventeenth century (61).

10. The great majority of extant casta paintings were produced in Mexico (fifty out of fifty-nine series); the remainder came from Peru, Ecuador, and Spain (Abby Sue Fisher, "Mestizaje and the Cuadros de Castas: Visual Representations of Race, Status, and Dress in Eighteenth Century Mexico" [PhD diss., University of Minnesota, 1992], 2). For the social and political contexts that produced the casta paintings, see James Lockhart and Stuart B. Schwartz, *Early Latin America: A History of Colonial Spanish America and Brazil* (Cambridge, England, 1983), 346–68, and Klor de Alva, *"Mestizaje* from New Spain to Aztlán," 64. For reproductions of the paintings, see María Concepción García Sáiz, *Las castas mexicanas: Un género pictórico americano* (Milan, 1989); *New World Orders;* Gary B. Nash, "The Hidden History of Mestizo America," *JAH* 82 (1995): 941–64.

11. Patricia Seed, "Social Dimensions of Race: Mexico City, 1753," *Hispanic American Historical Review* 62 (1982): 599–600.

12. Luis Peñalver y Cárdenas, "General Proceedings of the Visit of the Diocese of Louisiana and in Particular of New Orleans by Don Luis Peñalver y Cárdenas, Its First Bishop, and the Notary Dr. Jose María de Rivas, His Private and Official Secretary," July 29 to December 22, 1795, Records of the Diocese, 4:582. A cursory examination of parish registries from outside New Orleans held at the Archdiocesan Archives of New Orleans suggests that rural priests were not following Spanish practice in keeping separate books, thus confirming Hans W. Baade's finding that Spanish law and practice was weak outside of the colonial capital, although a contributory factor could be the difficulty in obtaining extra books ("The Law of Slavery in Spanish *Luisiana,* 1769–1803," in *Louisiana's Legal Heritage,* ed. Edward F. Haas [Pensacola, Fla., 1983], 44).

13. Real cédula previniendo medios para que se observe la pragmática de matrimonios, April 19, 1788, *Colección de documentos para la historia de la formación social de Hispanoamérica, 1493–1810,* ed. Richard Konetzke, 3 vols. (Madrid, 1958–62), 3:625–26.

14. Such changes were also made, although less frequently, in the notarial records. In one very rare notation, John Lynd, himself a notary, requested that Benjamin van Pradelles change the description of his slave Cecile from "negro" to "mulatto." Cecile, whom he had manumitted one week earlier, was the mother of Lynd's probable quarteron son, Robert, whom he had freed the previous year (manumission of Cecile, October 14, 1808, Pradelles, NONA, 2:428; registration of liberty by Sieur John Lynd, October 2, 1807, N. Broutin, NONA, 17:150).

15. Baptism of María Cruzat, September 25, 1793, SLC, B13, 84. María de la Paz may have been María Page who had successfully sued for freedom on the basis of Indian ancestry just a few months earlier. The baptism entry describes her as a native of Illinois and her daughter is given the surname Cruzat, the same as Page's former owner. See discussion in the text.

16. See, for instance, baptism of María Adelaida Cheval, July 20, 1777, SLC, B8, 21; baptism of María Francisca Foucher y Bernoudy, November 8, 1781, SLC, B8, 238; baptism of Arieta, February 25, 1782, SLC, B8, 253; baptism of María Amada Durel, May 20, 1784, SLC, B10, 53.

17. See, for instance, baptism of María Anna Dragon, May 2, 1777, SLC, B8, 13; baptism of Paul Hazeur, December 27, 1790, SLC, B12, 195; baptism of Josef María Meyeur, August

7, 1791, SLC, B12, 260; baptism of María Rochon, July 1, 1797, SLC, B13, 393; baptism of Luis Josef de Morant, July 3, 1797, SLC, B13, 395.

18. See, for example, the entries in the registry for baptisms of negros esclavos and mulatos, 1777–83, SLC, B8, 21, 247–49, 285, 300.

19. Baptism of Rosa, October 13, 1792, SLC, B13, 3; baptism of Joseph Boisdore, November 4, 1792, SLC, B13, 7; baptism of Carlos Josef, November 4, 1792, SLC, B13, 9; baptism of Manuel, May 5, 1793, SLC, B13, 51; baptism of Felicitas, August 11, 1793, SLC, B13, 75.

20. Baptism of María Forastal, April 23, 1788, SLC, B12, 57; baptism of María Rosa Favrot, January 11, 1793, SLC, B13, 19; baptism of María Ramona Castelan, August 31, 1793, SLC, B13, 79; baptism of Miguel Matheo Celestine, January 20, 1795, SLC, B13, 177; baptism of Franc[isc]o Forstall, May 12, 1796, SLC, B13, 283; baptism of Luis Fernandes-Tejeiro, March 31, 1798, SLC, B13, 456. "Tierceron" does appear, although rarely, in records after 1803. See, for instance, baptism of Marie Françoise and Jean Pierre Cuillon, September 23, 1810, SLC, B23, 48–49; St. Louis Cathedral, marriages of negros and mulatos, 1777–1830, SLC, M3, 53v, 91.

21. Baptism of Claudio Chaler, August 15, 1779, SLC, B8, 130.

22. Baptism of Francisco Facinte, September 12, 1791, SLC, B12, 262; baptism of Anastasia Glod, May 1, 1797, SLC, B13, 368. See also baptism of María Josefa Favrot, January 30, 1791, SLC, B12, 203, and baptism of Francisco Fortier, November 25, 1797, SLC, B13, 430.

23. See, for instance, sale of property, February 3, 1784, Perdomo, NONA, 5:101; marriage of Francisco Durand and Luisson Manbille, September 27, 1785, SLC, M3, 5; baptism of Sofia Lesassier, July 13, 1789, SLC, B12, 110; sale of slaves, January 18, 1791, Pedesclaux, NONA, 12:37–38; Luison (Duran) Brouner, will, January 27, 1794, Ximénez, NONA, 6:27; sale of slaves, July 13, 1796, Pedesclaux, NONA, 27:321–22; funeral of Francisco Declouet, July 21, 1800, SLC, F4, 90v; donation of property, July 14, 1802, Pedesclaux, NONA, 41:500. Clara's half sister was also sometimes unmarked by race (*Sofi Brunet v. Marmillon and Mercier,* August 9, 1783, SJR).

24. As Kimberly Hanger notes, "A person's racial designation depended on who recorded it, what purpose it served, when it was recorded, and what physical characteristics were considered most relevant" (*Bounded Lives, Bounded Places: Free Black Society in Colonial New Orleans, 1769–1803* [Durham, N.C., 1997], 15). Cf. Thomas N. Ingersoll, *Mammon and Manon in Early New Orleans: The First Slave Society in the Deep South, 1718–1819* (Knoxville, Tenn., 1999), 216, who reaches conclusions based on the assumption that racial ancestry was accurately recorded.

25. In Spanish America, where officials attempted to rule through segregated republics of Spaniards and Indians, census takers ignored the presence of Indians among Spaniards because, as Patricia Seed notes, "from their viewpoint Indians did not rightly belong there" ("Social Dimensions of Race," 576). Helen C. Rountree argues that in late eighteenth- and early nineteenth-century Virginia, Indians "were occasionally overlooked by [census] enumerators (or they avoided the enumerators)" (*Pocahontas's People,* 189–90).

26. Baptism of María Francisca Foucher y Bernoudy, November 8, 1781, SLC, B8, 238. María Francisca's father was Don Jose Foucher, the treasurer of the royal household, and

her mother, Francisca Bernoudy, was granted the title "demoiselle," a very unusual occurrence for a woman of color.

27. Baptism of Marie, July 6, 1733, SLC, B1, 40; baptism of Charlotte, April 13, 1748, SLC, B2, 122; baptism of Antonia, July 20, 1782, SLC, B8, 291.

28. Stephen Webre, "The Problem of Indian Slavery in Spanish Louisiana, 1769–1803," *LH* 25 (1984): 124; Usner, "American Indians in Colonial New Orleans," 109; Usner, *Indians, Settlers, and Slaves,* 55, 132–33; Hanger, *Bounded Lives, Bounded Places,* 15. People of Indian ancestry were also raced as mulatto in the English North American colonies in a process that Herndon and Sekatau call "documentary genocide" ("The Right to a Name"). Political circumstances also caused Indian slaves to have their identities changed. In early eighteenth-century New France, enslaved Fox Indians were increasingly described as "panis" after French officials signed a treaty with the Fox Indians obliging them to return Fox captives in 1716. See Brett Rushforth, "Slavery, the Fox Wars, and the Limits of Alliance," *WMQ,* 3rd ser., 63 (2006): 64–65, 70.

29. Peter H. Wood, "Indian Servitude in the Southeast," in *Handbook of North American Indians,* ed. William C. Sturtevant and et al. (Washington, D.C., 1978–90), 4:407.

30. *General Census of All Inhabitants of New Orleans and Environs, as Reported by Le Sieur Diron,* November 24, 1721, *Census Tables,* 17–22; *General Census of Inhabitants in the Area of Biloxi and Mobile, as Reported by Le Sieur Diron, Habitants of Fort Louis de la Mobile,* June 26, 1721, *Census Tables,* 23–27; *Census of Louisiana,* September 2, 1771, *SMV,* 1:196.

31. Claiborne to James Madison, June 21, 1808, *Letter Books,* 4:180.

32. In Virginia, Kathleen Brown found a similar situation in that "free Indians may have enjoyed some slight advantage over their free African counterparts" (*Good Wives, Nasty Wenches, and Anxious Patriarchs: Gender, Race, and Power in Colonial Virginia* [Chapel Hill, N.C., 1996], 242).

33. O'Reilly, Proclamation, December 7, 1769, *SMV,* 1:125–26. O'Reilly also ordered the commandants to make a census of all Indian slaves in their posts, calling for a list of their names, ages, sex, descent, names of their masters, and their estimated prices. At least two posts complied ("Indian slaves at Ste. Geneviève," May 28, 1770, *SMV,* 1:167–70; "Declarations Received by Pedro Piernas Concerning Indian Slaves at St. Louis," July 12, 1770, *SMV,* 1:172–79; Webre, "Problem of Indian Slavery," 122–23). Louisianans would later recollect O'Reilly's decree and at least some remembered it as immediately freeing all Indian slaves. See testimonies of Jean B. Reviere and Marguerite Reviere, *Marguerite v. Chouteau,* 2 Mo. 71 (1828), 72–73.

34. Emancipation [of Luison], April 30, 1770, SJR, *LHQ* 6 (1923): 330.

35. Manumission of Henrieta, María, Suzana, María Luiza, Hasty, and Henrieta la mayor, November 29, 1773, Garic, NONA, 4:333.

36. Manumission of Marie Anne and son, May 11, 1770, indexed in Gwendolyn Midlo Hall, "Louisiana Free Database, 1719–1820," in *Databases for the Study of Afro-Louisiana History and Genealogy, 1699–1860: Computerized Information from Original Manuscript Sources,* ed. Gwendolyn Midlo Hall (Baton Rouge, La., 2000).

37. Manumission of Juan, April 2, 1783, Perdomo, NONA, 97; *Juaneta v. Mr. Moroteau,* August 21, 1783, SJR; manumission of Juanita, September 6, 1783, Rodríguez, NONA, 794.

38. Stephen Webre found a total of thirteen cases ("Problem of Indian Slavery," 127). Several other claims, however, are referred to in other sources. For instance, in May 1793, mulata libre María Josefa Lalande granted power of attorney to mulato libre Juan Baudoire in order to prosecute her suit against Don Bartolomé Lebreton for the freedom of her nephews, Jose and Noel, described as indios mestizos (power of attorney, May 10, 1793, Ximénez, NONA, 4:248–49v). One witness in an 1817 case claimed that a sauvagesse named Isabelle approached Carondelet requesting freedom for herself, her several children, and at least one grandchild, while, in the same case, the Louisiana Supreme Court mentioned two Indians, Alexis and David, whom Carondelet ordered back to their owners (*Seville v. Chretien,* 5 Mart. [O.S.] 275 [1817], docket no. 184, SCLHA, UNO, quotations from witness testimony and published report, 289–90).

39. Miró to Cruzat, April 10, 1786, AGI, PC, leg. 4, 366–66v.

40. *Pierre v. Cruzat Heirs,* May 4, 1790, SJR; manumission of Pedro Morau, May 10, 1790, Perdomo, NONA, 15:254–55; manumission of María Page, May 6, 1790, Perdomo, NONA, 15:243–44; *Baptiste v. Bourgignon,* January 23, 1790, SJR, doc. 2. Having access to New Orleans' courts certainly helped, for in Spanish Illinois, Pedro and María would have had very limited access to the courts authorized to hear these cases; Baptiste's suit includes a petition to the court for protection in order to prevent Bourgignon from removing him from the city, which would have interfered with his ability to press the suit. See also Gilbert C. Din, "Carondelet, the Cabildo, and Slaves: Louisiana in 1795," *LH* 38 (1997): fn16, and Webre, "Problem of Indian Slavery," 127.

41. *Bourgignon v. Lalumendière Heirs,* January 21, 1791, SJR.

42. *Marianne v. Pomet,* January 13, 1791, SJR; *Juan Bautista v. Morel,* January 13, 1791, SJR; Manumission of Therese, May 23, 1791, Attakapas County Records, indexed in Hall, "Louisiana Free Database"; *Thérèse v. Veuve Bienvenu,* April 27 1791, SJR; *Julien v. Fallon,* July 12, 1791, SJR; *Joseph v. St. Cyr,* July 12, 1791, SJR; Webre, "Problem of Indian Slavery," 127n30.

43. *María Theresa v. Josef Verloin DeGroy,* July 19, 1793, SJR; *Cécile v. Tounoir,* August 7, 1793, SJR; *María Juana v. Manuel Monsanto,* September 4, 1793, F. Broutin, NONA Court Proceedings, 22:302–87.

44. *María Theresa v. Josef Verloin DeGroy,* July 19, 1793, SJR.

45. *Cécile v. Tounoir,* August 7, 1793, SJR.

46. *Cecilia v. Émond,* October 17, 1793, F. Broutin Court Proceedings, NONA, 24:21–81.

47. Webre also points to a change in the locations from which slaves were petitioning. The earliest successful suits came from slaves in Spanish Illinois or New Orleans whose Indian ancestries were, he states, easier to demonstrate. The later unsuccessful ones came from those in Pointe Coupée and the German Coast. Webre argues that the latter "were not generally reputed, at least by the whites in their communities, to be Indians" ("Problem of Indian Slavery," 127).

48. *Cecilia v. Émond,* October 17, 1793, F. Broutin, NONA, 24:21–81.

49. María Juana's children were Antonio Sarazin, identified as a mestizo, and María, labeled a grifa, a term in New Orleans usually applied to the child of a negro and a mulato but perhaps here referring to the child of a mestiza and a negro.

50. J. Poydras et al. to Carondelet, February 28, 1794, AGI, SD, leg. 2563, 968–69; "Representación de varios habitantes sobre esclavos indios Natchez," 1794–95, AGI, SD, leg. 2532, 607, 609–10.

51. See, for instance, *Cécile v. Tounoir*, August 7, 1793, SJR, 2; *María Juana v. Manuel Monsanto*, September 4, 1793, F. Broutin, NONA, 22:303; *Cecilia v. Émond*, October 17, 1793, F. Broutin, NONA, 22v.

52. *Cécile v. Tounoir*, August 7, 1793, SJR; *Cecilia v. Émond*, October 17, 1793, F. Broutin, NONA, 24:21–81.

53. The 1771 census enumerated seventy-one Indian female and forty-three Indian male slaves (*Census of Louisiana*, September 2, 1771, *SMV*, 1:196).

54. "Representación de varios habitantes sobre esclavos indios Natchez," 607–607v. In one of the nineteenth-century cases I discuss in this chapter witnesses referred to the slave petitioners as "mulâtres and mulâtresses descended from Sauvages" and "Métis noir" (*Seville v. Chretien*, 5 Mart. [O.S.] 275 [1817], docket no. 184, testimony of Antoine Blanc, SCLHA, UNO).

55. *María Juana v. Manuel Monsanto*, September 4, 1793, F. Broutin, NONA, 22:303v; *Antonio, mulatto, v. Deshotels succession*, March 7, 1774, SJR, *LHQ* 10 (1927): 300–301.

56. Baptisms of negros and mulatos, 1792–98, SLC, B13, passim. Dismissing claims to Indian ancestry of those perceived to be of African ancestry perpetuates the colonial legacies of Indian erasure and has made it difficult for some self-defined native groups to gain federal and state recognition. See Brian Klopotek, "The Long Outwaiting: Federal Recognition Policy in Three Louisiana Indian Communities" (PhD diss., University of Minnesota, 2004).

57. *Ignacio v. Estate of Juan Soubie*, November 8, 1793, F. Broutin Court Proceedings, NONA, 24:136v, 141.

58. "Representación de varios habitantes sobre esclavos indios Natchez," 610v–12v.

59. Webre, "Problem of Indian Slavery," 132.

60. A search in 1816 of the notarial archives found evidence that a suit was filed in the 1790s, but there were no records detailing its conclusion.

61. *Agnes v. Judice* 3 Mart (O.S.) 171, 182 (1813), docket no. 1, SCLHA, UNO; *Seville v. Chretien*, 5 Mart. (O.S.) 275 (1817), docket no. 184.

62. *Seville v. Chretien*, 5 Mart. (O.S.) 275 (1817), docket no. 184, quotations from published report, 283–84, and certifications by Pierre Pedesclaux and Christoval de Armas.

63. *Seville v. Chretien*, 5 Mart. (O.S.) 275 (1817), docket no. 184, SCLHA, UNO, quotations from published report, 275, 289–90, and witness testimony.

64. *Ulzere v. Poeyfarré*, 8 Mart. (O.S.), 155 (1820), docket no. 468, SCLHA, UNO, quotations from Ulzere's petition and published decision, 156.

65. *Ulzere v. Poeyfarré*, 8 Mart. (O.S.), 155 (1820), docket no. 468, SCLHA, UNO, 156; *Ulzere v. Poeyfarré*, 2 Mart. (N. S.) 504 (1824), docket no. 989, SCLHA, UNO. The 1824 decision was also based on a presumption "in favour of the freedom of the plaintiffs arising from their colour," a presumption that had been established in an 1810 case discussed in chapter 7, as well as on the fact that they "had enjoyed their freedom for 5 or 6 years without [their owner] objecting."

66. *Marguerite v. Chouteau*, 2 Mo. 71 (1828), 71–74. Although lower Louisianans might have been underemphasizing the presence Indians in their communities, those of upper

Louisiana were un-remembering black slaves who, in the mid-eighteenth century, outnumbered Indian slaves about three to one (Carl J. Ekberg, *French Roots in the Illinois Country: The Mississippi Frontier in Colonial Times* (Urbana, Ill., 1998), 152; Cécile Vidal, "Africains et Européens au Pays des Illinois durant la Période Française (1699–1765)," *French Colonial History* 3 [2003]: 52).

67. *Marguerite v. Chouteau*, 2 Mo. 71 (1828), 71, 76–77, 80–82.

68. *Marguerite v. Chouteau*, 3 Mo. 540 (1834), 540, 542.

69. *Seville v. Chretien*, 5 Mart. (O.S.) 275 (1817), docket no. 184, testimonies of Antoine Blanc and Louis Charles de Blanc, SCLHA, UNO.

70. [Louis Narcisse] Baudry des Lozières, *Second voyage à la Louisiane, faisant suite au premier de l'auteur de 1794 à 1798*, 2 vols. (Paris, 1803), 1:209–10.

71. Berquin-Duvallon, *Vue de la colonie espagnole du Mississipi*, 255–56. Berquin-Duvallon went on to argue that Spanish and Portuguese bans on Indian slavery had nothing to do with "the so-called maxims of justice and humanity" but rather came about because colonizers had quickly discovered Indians "have always preferred death to servitude" (259–60). The French Crown had earlier articulated a similarly "essential difference between Indians and Negroes." Indians, it declared in 1767, were "born free and have always preserved the advantage of liberty," while nègres, having been brought to the Caribbean as slaves, had a "stain that spreads on all their descendants and the gift of liberty cannot delete it." It granted Indians and their descendants the capacity to be "assimilated as Subjects of the King," thus able to "claim all the Offices and Dignities of the Colonies" and to register their titles of nobility; Africans and their descendants could not (Lettre du ministre aux administrateurs, concernant une décision sur trois points relatifs aux Races Noires et Indiennes, January 7, 1767, *Loix et constitutions*, 5:80–82).

72. "Representación de varios habitantes sobre esclavos indios Natchez," 607–607v. On ideas about the relative strengths of Indian, African, and European blood, see Circe Sturm, *Blood Politics: Race, Politics, and Identity in the Cherokee Nation of Oklahoma* (Berkeley, Calif., 2002).

73. Baptism of María, May 12, 1796, SLC, B13, 283; baptism of María Francisca Foucher y Bernoudy, November 8, 1781, SLC, B8, 238; baptism of Babe, March 31, 1800, SLC, B14, 114; baptism of Jose, March 31, 1800, SLC, B14, 114; baptism of Eugenio, March 31, 1800, SLC, B14, 114; baptism of Silvano, March 31, 1800, SLC, B14, 114. The use of "mestizo" to refer to children who had one Indian parent (almost always their mother) regardless of the racial category of their other parent raises the interesting question of why priests, notaries, or census takers did not use two words. Elsewhere in the Americas, but only occasionally in New Orleans, "griffe" or "grifo" was used to denote the child of an Indian and an African.

74. Baptismal ceremonies provided for Luisa Declouet, January 25, 1795, SLC, B13, 177.

75. Baptism of Clara Lopez de la Peña, April 4, 1778, SLC, B9, 19.

76. [Diligencias promovidar por Clara Lopez de (la) Peña para justificar su descendencia de India y que la partida de su hija Luisa se traslade del libro de negros al de blancos], September 14, 1799, Records of the Diocese 8:677–78. Luison was also deemed a doña in the record for Clara and Louis' marriage (marriage of Luis Declouet and Clara [Lopez] de la Peña recorded November 20, 1801, SLC, M5, 156).

77. Emancipation [of Luison], May 9, 1770, SJR, *LHQ* 6 (1923): 331.

78. Sofi's father is not named until the 1800 baptism of her own son (baptism of Luis Azael Latill, May 8, 1800, SLC, B14, 121). My calculation of Sofia's birth date is based on the assumption that she must have been at least fifteen in 1789 when her first child was born (baptism of Sofi Lesassier, July 13, 1789, SLC, B12, 110).

79. *Census of New Orleans,* June 1778, *Louisiana Census and Militia Lists, 1770–1789,* ed. Albert J. Robichaux, 2 vols. (Harvey, La., 1973–74), 1:23–68; Luison Brouner (Duran), last will and testament, January 27, 1794, Ximénez, NONA, 6:26–30.

80. Marriage of Francisco Durand and Luisson Manbille, September 27, 1785, SLC, M3, 5; marriage of Josef de la Peña and Rosalia Viera, February 22, 1786, *SR,* 4:82. De la Peña's first wife was Michaela Perez, a native of Havana, suggesting that he lived in Cuba before his arrival in New Orleans. He and Perez had three children baptized in New Orleans between 1770 and 1776. Clara's birth date of April 1778 suggests that Perez died after April 1776 but before October 1777 (baptism of María Josefa de Belen, September 9, 1770, *SR,* 2:223; baptism of Joseph María Le Peigna, September 19, 1772, *SR,* 3:179; baptism of Antonio Rafael de Jesus de la Peña, April 11, 1776, *SR,* 3:80).

81. Luison Brouner (Duran), last will and testament, January 27, 1794, Ximénez, NONA, 6:26–30; [diligencias promovidar por Clara Lopez de (la) Peña para justificar su descendencia de India y que la partida de su hija Luisa se traslade del libro de negros al de blancos], September 14, 1799, Records of the Diocese 8:677–78.

82. Based on references to Luison and Clara as "mulata," "parda," or "quaterona," Hanger argues that María Juana was in fact a negra rather than mestiza or india, although she does acknowledge that the title "doña" was rarely granted to those of either African or Indian ancestry. It is certainly possible that Luison and Clara created María Juana's ethnicity as part of their efforts to reposition their descendants within New Orleans' racial hierarchy. However, given the presence of Indian slaves in early Louisiana, it is equally possible that Luison and Clara were telling the truth (Hanger, *Bounded Lives, Bounded Places,* 93–94).

83. Marriage of Etienne Teyssier and Madeline Renée de Mandeville, September 18, 1725, *Love's Legacy: The Mobile Marriages Recorded in French, Transcribed, with Annotated Abstracts in English, 1724–1786,* ed. Jacqueline Olivier Vidrine (Lafayette, La., 1985), 20–21; funeral of François De Mandeville, October 25, 1728, *SR,* 1:74; baptism, March 10, 1729, Mobile, parish register, cited in Marcel Giraud, *Histoire de la Louisiane française,* vol. 4, *La Louisiane après le système de law (1721–1723)* (Paris, 1974), 431–32; Marcel Giraud, *A History of French Louisiana,* vol. 5, *The Company of the Indies, 1723–1731,* trans. Brian Pearce (Baton Rouge, La., 1991), 351–52. Naming Mandeville as the father, after his death, might have been the priest's attempt to "out" Mandeville's extramarital relationship.

84. Luison's pattern of first having a relationship with a white man that resulted in children and sometimes property and then marrying a man of color was not infrequent in late colonial New Orleans.

85. Luison had at least three daughters, whom she mentions in her will: Clara, Sofi, and Henrieta. Hanger also found reference to an additional daughter and one son (Luison Brouner [Duran], last will and testament, January 27, 1794, Ximénez, NONA, 6:26–30; Hanger, *Bounded Lives, Bounded Places,* 85). For more on Sofi's relationships with white men—one extramarital, the other eventually marital—see chapter 7.

86. Of Alexandre Declouet and Louisa Favrot's seven sons born between 1761 and 1779, Louis, unfortunately, is the only one for whom no extant baptism record exists. Given the spacing between his siblings' births and his entrance into the military as an "aspirant" in 1777, he was probably born in 1766 or 1767, making him eleven to twelve years older than Clara.

87. Baptism of María del Carmen Declouet, January 21, 1797, SLC, B14, 22; baptism of María Clara Declouet, January 24, 1799, SLC, B14, 79.

88. Baptismal ceremonies provided for Luisa Declouet, January 25, 1795, SLC, B14, 99v, emphasis mine. This entry appears between two dated September 1799.

During her term as supervisor and deputy registrar of vital statistics at the Louisiana Bureau of Vital Statistics in the mid-twentieth century, Naomi Drake similarly changed vital records when ordered to by the courts. For instance, in 1962, when Larry Lille Toledano won the right to have his birth certificate changed, Drake "cross[ed] out the word colored and [wrote] over it in red ink the word white. She also inserted 'altered 6/14/62 by court order.'" Toledano was not satisfied and sued again to force Drake "to erase and completely obliterate the word *colored* from the face of the records" (Virginia R. Dominguez, *White by Definition: Social Classification in Creole Louisiana* [1986; rpt., New Brunswick, N.J., 1994], 39–40).

89. See, for example, baptism of Luis Declouet, August 29, 1801, SLC, B14, 171.

90. In the decade following the Louisiana Purchase, Declouet twice sought permission from Spain to emigrate to Mexico, and in 1814 he penned a memorial suggesting how Spain could reconquer Louisiana. Whether or not his personal experience—marriage to a woman of color, the successful whitening of his eldest daughter, and his service as commander of the battalion of free mulatos and negros in 1800—predisposed him to Spanish rule, especially after a decade of Anglo-American governance, is difficult to determine but he eventually received a commission from the Spanish government and migrated to Cuba, where, in 1819, he founded the town of Cienfuegos (Stanley Faye, ed., "Louis Declouet's Memorial to the Spanish Government (Conditions in Luisiana and Proposed Plan for Spanish Reconquest)," [1814], *LHQ* 22 [1939]: 795–818; Charles Gayarré, *History of Louisiana,* vol. 3, *The Spanish Domination* [New York, 1854–66], 626).

91. Baptism of Francisco Declouet, July 20, 1800, SLC, B14, 128; baptism of Luis Declouet, July 20, 1800, SLC, B14, 128v; funeral of Francisco Declouet, July 21, 1800, SLC, F4, 90v; marriage of Luis Declouet and Clara [Lopez] de la Peña recorded November 20, 1801, SLC, M5, 156.

92. Baptism of François Joubert, March 25, 1819, SLC, B30, 98; baptism of Rose Joubert, March 25, 1819, SLC, B30, 98–99. For other cases in twentieth-century Louisiana that involved claims of Indian ancestry and denials of African ancestry, see *Lee v. New Orleans Great Northern Railroad Co.,* 125 La. 236, 51 So. 182 (1910), docket no. 17,590, and *Sunseri v. Cassagne,* 191 La. 209 (1938), docket no. 34,572.

Chapter 7. Codification of a Tripartite Racial System in Anglo-Louisiana

1. *Macarty v. Mandeville,* no. 626, 3 La. Ann. 239 (1848), 240. See also Shirley Thompson, "The Passing of a People: Creoles of Color in Mid-Nineteenth Century New Orleans" (PhD diss., Harvard University, 2001), 108–29.

2. On the legal and political incorporation of Louisiana into the United States, see George Dargo, *Jefferson's Louisiana: Politics and the Clash of Legal Traditions* (Cambridge, Mass., 1975), and Peter J. Kastor, *The Nation's Crucible: The Louisiana Purchase and the Creation of America* (New Haven, Conn., 2004).

3. John G. Clark, *New Orleans, 1718–1812: An Economic History* (Baton Rouge, La., 1970), 304–5; Thomas N. Ingersoll, *Mammon and Manon in Early New Orleans: The First Slave Society in the Deep South, 1718–1819* (Knoxville, Tenn., 1999), 283–314; Ira Berlin, *Many Thousands Gone: The First Two Centuries of Slavery in North America* (Cambridge, Mass., 1998), 325–57; Paul F. Lachance, "The Politics of Fear: French Louisianians and the Slave Trade, 1786–1809," *Plantation Societies in the Americas* 1 (1979): 162–97.

4. Mrs. B. H. B. Latrobe to Mrs. Catherine Smith, April 18, 1820, in Benjamin Henry Latrobe *Impressions Respecting New Orleans: Diary and Sketches, 1818–1820*, ed. Samuel Wilson Jr. (New York, 1951), 180.

5. Latrobe, *Impressions Respecting New Orleans*, 18–22.

6. John H. B. Latrobe, *Southern Travels: Journal of John H. B. Latrobe 1834,* ed. Samuel Wilson Jr. (New Orleans, 1986), 43.

7. Frederick Law Olmsted, *A Journey in the Seaboard Slave States, with Remarks on their Economy* (New York, 1856), 594, 583–84.

8. Médéric-Louis Élie Moreau de Saint-Méry, *Description topographique, physique, civile, politique et historique de la partie française de l'isle Saint Domingue,* 3 vols. (Paris, 1958), 1:86–89.

9. *State v. Harrison, a Slave,* 11 La. Ann. 722 (1856), docket no. 4464. Despite ruling that the 1855 Act was indeed unconstitutional, the Louisiana Supreme Court affirmed Harrison's conviction under earlier legislation.

10. Ingersoll, *Mammon and Manon*.

11. *Census of the City of New Orleans, Exclusive of Seamen and the Garrison,* 1803, *American State Papers: Miscellaneous* (Washington, D.C., 1832–34), 10:384. "By some unaccountable mistake," the census omitted gens de couleur libre in the city's second quarter and thus "the population is thought to be underrated."

12. Gabriel Debien and René La Gardeur, "The Saint-Domingue Refugees in Louisiana, 1792–1804," in *The Road to Louisiana: The Saint-Domingue Refugees, 1792–1809,* ed. Carl A. Brasseaux and Glenn R. Conrad (Lafayette, La., 1992), 113–243; Lachance, "Politics of Fear," 186–87; Paul F. Lachance, "The 1809 Immigration of Saint-Domingue Refugees to New Orleans: Reception, Integration and Impact," *LH* 29 (1988): 109–41; Paul F. Lachance, "The Foreign French," in *Creole New Orleans: Race and Americanization,* ed. Arnold R. Hirsch and Joseph Logsdon (Baton Rouge, La., 1992), 101–30.

13. Leonard P. Curry, *The Free Black in Urban America, 1800–1850: The Shadow of the Dream* (Chicago, 1981), 251; Paul Lachance, "The Limits of Privilege: Where Free Persons of Colour Stood in the Hierarchy of Wealth in Antebellum New Orleans," *Slavery and Abolition* 17 (1996): 68. Of the fifteen cities whose populations Curry tracked, New Orleans had the largest percentage of free blacks from 1810 to 1830, significantly more than Charleston's 5–8 percent. By 1840, Washington, D.C., had surpassed New Orleans' 17.95 percent with 20 percent and Baltimore was just behind at 17.56 percent. Even with the dramatic decline of

the city's free black population by 1850, it still ranked fourth, behind Washington, Baltimore, and Philadelphia.

14. Treaty between the French Republic and the United States, Concerning the Cession of Louisiana, Signed at Paris, April 30, 1803, *Constitutions of the State of Louisiana and Selected Federal Laws,* ed. Benjamin Wall Dart (Indianapolis, Ind., 1932), 410.

15. Claiborne to James Madison, July 3, 1804, *Letter Books,* 2:234–35.

16. Benjamin Morgan to Chandler Price, August 7, 1803, *The Territorial Papers of the United States,* vol. 9, *The Territory of Orleans, 1803–1812,* ed. Clarence Edwin Carter (Washington, D.C., 1940), 9:7. Claiborne and other Anglo-American officials believed that neither gens de couleur libre nor white Francophone Louisianans were ready for the American system of government (Claiborne to Madison, July 3, 1804, *Letter Books,* 2:234–35).

17. An Act, Erecting Louisiana into Two Territories, and Providing for the Temporary Government Thereof, March 26, 1804, *Public Statutes at Large of the United States of America,* ed. Richard Peters (Boston, 1845), 2:286, §9; *An Act to Incorporate the City of New Orleans,* February 17, 1805 ([New Orleans], 1805), §§1, 9; An Act Regulating the Practice of the Superior Court, in Civil Causes, 1805, *Louisiana Acts,* §5; Constitution of Louisiana, January 22, 1812, *Constitutions of the State of Louisiana,* article 2, § 8. Property requirements limited the granting of suffrage to only about one third of the state's adult free men until 1845. Even after that, however, race and residency requirements continued to exclude about three-fifths of them (Constitution of Louisiana, 1845, *Constitutions of the State of Louisiana,* title 2, § 10; Constitution of Louisiana, 1852, *Constitutions of the State of Louisiana,* title 2, § 10; Warren M. Billings, "From This Seed: The Constitution of 1812," in *In Search of Fundamental Law: Louisiana's Constitutions, 1812–1974,* ed. Warren M. Billings and Edward F. Haas [Lafayette, La., 1993], 10).

18. Conseil de ville, minutes, March 1, 1805, CVOP, 1:250. Free men of color could vote in one Louisiana parish between 1838 and 1860 as well as in some North Carolina and Tennessee counties before 1835 (Roger Wallace Shugg, "Negro Voting in the Ante-Bellum South," *Journal of Negro History* 21 [1936]: 357–64).

19. James Wilkinson to Secretary of War, December 21, 1803, *Territorial Papers,* 9:139.

20. Claiborne to James Madison, December 27, 1803, *Letter Books,* 1:313–14. Daniel Clark put the number of militiamen at three hundred, organized into two companies of mulattoes and one of negroes (Daniel Clark to James Madison, September 3, 1803, *Territorial Papers,* 9:33).

21. "Address from the Free People of Color," January 1804, *Territorial Papers,* 9:174–75.

22. Claiborne to James Madison, January 17, 1804, *Letter Books,* 1:339–40.

23. Henry Dearborn to Claiborne, February 20, 1804, *Letter Books,* 2:54.

24. Claiborne to Henry Dearborn, June 9, 1804, *Letter Books,* 2:199–200; Claiborne to Henry Dearborn, June 22, 1804, *Letter Books,* 2:217–18; Claiborne to Major Fortier, June 22, 1804, *Letter Books,* 2:216.

25. Claiborne to secretary of state, January 8, 1806, *Territorial Papers,* 9:561. During the War of 1812, Andrew Jackson made a similar argument, telling Claiborne "distrust them, and you make them your enemies, place confidence in them, and you engage them by Every dear and honorable tie to the interest of the country who extends to them equal rights and

privileges with white men" (Andrew Jackson to Claiborne, September 21, 1814, *The Papers of Andrew Jackson*, ed. Sam B. Smith and Harriet Chappell Owsley [Knoxville, Tenn., 1980–], 3:144). For Jackson's praise of "every noble hearted generous brave freeman of color" who volunteered for service during the War of 1812, see Andrew Jackson, "To the Free Coloured Inhabitants of Louisiana," September 21, 1814, *Correspondence of Andrew Jackson*, ed. John Spencer Bassett (Washington, D.C., 1926–35), 2:58–59.

26. An Act to Organize a Corps of Militia for the Service of the State of Louisiana, as Well as for Its Defense as for Its Police, a Certain Portion of Chosen Men from among the Free Men of Colour, September 6, 1812, *Louisiana Acts*, 72; An Act for Regulating and Governing the Militia of the State of Louisiana, February 12, 1812, *Louisiana Acts*, 40; Roland C. McConnell, "Louisiana's Black Military History, 1729–1865," in *Louisiana's Black Heritage*, ed. Robert R. Macdonald, John R. Kemp, and Edward F. Haas (New Orleans, 1979), 40. For more on these conflicts, see Donald Everett, "Emigrés and Militiamen: Free Persons of Color in New Orleans 1803–1815," *Journal of Negro History* 38 (1953): 377–402; Ira Berlin, *Slaves Without Masters: The Free Negro in the Antebellum South* (New York, 1974), 118–128; and Kastor, *Nation's Crucible*, 91, 164–67.

27. Treaty between the French Republic and the United States, April 30, 1803, 408–11; An Act Prescribing the Rules and Conduct to Be Observed with Respect to Negroes and Other Slaves of This Territory, June 7, 1806, *General Digest*, Crimes and Offenses, §6.

28. Edward Livingstone, Louis Moreau-Lislet, and Pierre Derbigny, *Civil Code of the State of Louisiana* (New Orleans, 1825), 12, book 1, title 1, articles 35 and 38; *General Digest*, §§10, 15–16, Crimes and Offenses, §§1–3; *State v. Harrison, a Slave*, 11 La. Ann. 722 (1856), docket no. 4464, 724.

29. *State v. Henry Levy and Jacob Dreyfous*, 5 La. Ann. 64 (1850), SCLHA, UNO, quotations from both the published decision and the original trial transcripts. The Louisiana Supreme Court upheld the right to jury trials in *Augustin Borie, f.m.c., v. Ruben Bush and Guillaume Danos* (1826), docket no. 579, SCLHA, UNO; *Bore v. Bush*, 6 Mart. (N.S.) 1 (1827).

30. On the "quasi citizenship" of free people of color in New Orleans in contrast to those elsewhere in the South, see H. E. Sterkx, *The Free Negro in Ante-Bellum Louisiana* (Rutherford, N.J., 1972), 160–99. Paul Lachance cautions that "discriminatory as these measures undoubtedly were, the degree to which legal discrimination increased in the American period should not be exaggerated" ("The Formation of a Three-Caste Society: Evidence from Wills in Antebellum New Orleans," *Social Science History* 18 [1994]: 229).

31. An Act Prescribing the Rules and Conduct to Be Observed with Respect to Negroes and Other Slaves of This Territory, June 7, 1806, *General Digest*, 100–119; An Act Relative to Slaves and Free Colored Persons, March 15, 1855, *Louisiana Acts*, 377–91. It was this latter act that was ruled unconstitutional in *State v. Harrison*. On the Black Code as demonstrating a commitment to white supremacy shared by white creoles and Anglo-Americans, see Ingersoll, *Mammon and Manon*, 321–23, and Kastor, *Nation's Crucible*, 77, 81–86. Kastor does acknowledge that the Black Code reflected the "goals of white policymakers" and "was limited by the willingness of people to observe those rules and the government's capacity to enforce them" (86).

32. An Act for the Punishment of Crimes and Misdemeanors, May 4, 1805, *General Digest*, §§4–10, 16; An Act Prescribing the Rules and Conduct to be Observed with Respect

to Negroes and Other Slaves of This Territory, June 7, 1806, *General Digest,* Crimes and Offenses, §7; An Act to Amend the Act Entitled "An Act for the Punishment of Crimes and Misdemeanors," June 7, 1806, *General Digest,* §1; An Act to Amend the Penal Laws of This State, March 1, 1827, *Louisiana Acts,* 44; An Act to Prevent Free Persons of Colour from Entering into This State, and for Other Purposes, March 16, 1830, *Louisiana Acts,* 92. See also An Ordinance for the Police of the Streets, Public Places, Court Yards, and Lots, October 8, 1807, *Police Code, or Collection of the Ordinances of Police Made by the City Council of New-Orleans* (New Orleans, 1808), 78, 80, and Ordinances of Police: An Ordinance Concerning the General Police, March 14, 1808, *Police Code,* 44–55.

33. *Stachlin v. Destrehan,* 2 La. Ann. 1019 (1847), docket no. 539.

34. *John Gardiner v. Benjamin Cross,* 6 Rob. 454 (1844), docket no. 5425; *Stachlin v. Destrehan,* 2 La. Ann. 1019 (1847), docket no. 539. On the racing of corporal punishment in colonial North Carolina, see Kirsten Fischer, *Suspect Relations: Sex, Race, and Resistance in Colonial North Carolina* (Ithaca, N.Y., 2002), 159–90.

35. An Act Prescribing the Rules and Conduct to Be Observed with Respect to Negroes and Other Slaves of this Territory, June 7, 1806, *General Digest,* Crimes and Offenses, §§9–10, 15–16, 33, 35. An 1814 act extended capital punishment to include slave assaults against white, but not gen de couleur libre, overseers (An Act Supplementary to the Act Entitled "An Act to Repeal all Laws or Provisions of Laws Prescribing the Manner of Remunerating the Owners of Slaves Sentenced to Death or Killed whilst Running Away," February 22, 1814, *General Digest,* §2.

36. An Act Prescribing the Rules and Conduct to Be Observed with Respect to Negroes and Other Slaves of This Territory, June 7, 1806, *General Digest,* §18, 40; conseil de ville, minutes, May 18, 1808, CVOP, 2:190. In 1818, the legislature discovered that some gens de couleur libre had been engaging white redemptioners as servants "contrary to the true intent and meaning" of the 1806 Black Code and banned them from doing so in the future (An Act for the Relief and Protection of Persons Brought into this State as Redemptioners, March 20, 1818, *Louisiana Acts,* 186).

37. An Act to Prevent Free Persons of Colour from Entering into this State, and for Other Purposes, March 16, 1830, *Louisiana Acts,* §9.

38. An Act Prescribing the Rules and Conduct to Be Observed with Respect to Negroes and Other Slaves of This Territory, June 7, 1806, *General Digest,* §21; An Ordinance Concerning Negroes and Mulattoes Navigating to the Lake Pontchartrain, May 18, 1808, *Police Code,* 256; An Ordinance Concerning Slaves Employed as Hirelings by the Day, May 12, 1808, *Police Code,* 248–50, article 1. On the lack of enforcement, see Richard Tansey, "Out-of-State Free Blacks in Late Antebellum New Orleans," *LH* 22 (1981): 369–86.

39. An Act to Provide for the Recording of Births and Deaths, April 10, 1811, *General Digest,* 97–98; An Act Supplementary to an Act Entitled "An Act to Provide for the Recording of Births and Deaths,["] Passed on the 10th April, 1811, March 6, 1819, *General Digest,* 99; An Act to Prescribe Certain Formalities Respecting Free Persons of Colour, March 31, 1808, *General Digest,* 499–500; An Act to Provide for the Registry of Births and Deaths, March 9, 1855, *Louisiana Acts,* 41.

In Virginia, the phrase "person of color" did not become common until after 1815 (Eva Sheppard Wolf, *Race and Liberty in the New Nation: Emancipation in Virginia from the*

Revolution to Nat Turner's Rebellion [Baton Rouge, La., 2006], 157–60). It is possible that Louisiana's racial terminology spread northward after the Louisiana Purchase, as Claiborne and other Anglo-American politicians, including Jefferson in correspondence with Claiborne, were using the phrase consistently from 1803. See, for instance, Claiborne to Madison, December 27, 1803, *Letter Books,* 1:314, and Thomas Jefferson, [notes on a cabinet meeting], October 4, 1803, Thomas Jefferson Papers.

40. Latrobe, *Southern Travels,* 80.

41. *Adéle Auger v. Frederick Beaurocher, Joseph L. Carpentier, C. L. Blach* (1810), docket no. 2634, Records of the Superior Court, NOPL; *Adéle v. Beauregard,* 1 Mart. (O.S.) 183 (1810). My thanks to Ken Aslakson for finding the original city and superior court transcripts and discovering that François Xavier Martin's published report mislabeled the case *Adéle v. Beauregard.*

42. Ariela J. Gross, "Litigating Whiteness: Trials of Racial Determination in the Nineteenth-Century South," *Yale Law Journal* 108 (1998): 129. Most states followed the burden of proof established in *Hudgins,* but North Carolina also established a presumption of freedom for those of mixed ancestry in an 1802 case cited by Moreau-Lislet in his *Adéle* decision (*Gobu v. E. Gobu,* 1 N.C. 188 [1802]; see also *Samuel Scott v. Joseph Williams,* 12 N.C. 376 [1828], and Thomas Morris, *Southern Slavery and the Law, 1619–1860* [Chapel Hill, N.C., 1996], 25–26).

43. *Hudgins v. Wrights,* 11 Va. 134 (1806), 135, 139–42. Despite concurring with the lower court's decision to free the plaintiffs, the five Virginia Supreme Court judges in *Hudgins* were all explicit in denying the lower court's reasoning, which had relied "on the ground that freedom is the birthright of every human being" (135).

44. *State v. Cecil,* 2 Mart. (O.S.) 208 (1812); *Forsyth v. Nash,* 4 Mart. (O.S.) 385 (1816), docket no. 150, SCLHA, UNO, 388; An Act to Emancipate Cynthia, a Slave Illegally Introduced in the State of Louisiana, March 13, 1827, *Louisiana Acts,* 74. Other cases that favorably cite *Adéle* include *Ulzere v. Poeyfarré,* 2 Mart. (N. S.) 504 (1824), docket no. 989, SCLHA, UNO, and *Sally Miller v. Louis Belmonti,* 11 Rob. 339 (1845). In *Beard v. Poydras* (4 Mart. [O.S.] 348 [1816], docket no. 72, SCLHA, UNO), mulatto Venus Beard tried to argue she had been "born, reputed, and acknowledged as free" but "the presumption of her free-birth" was destroyed by her owner's will that included a clause manumitting her. An 1857 bill that would have defined a " 'person of color' as anyone with a 'taint of African blood,' " specifically to prevent whites from marrying those who looked white but had some limited African ancestry, failed to become law (cited in Virginia R. Dominguez, *White by Definition: Social Classification in Creole Louisiana* [1986; rpt., New Brunswick, N.J., 1994], 26).

45. *Census of New Orleans,* November 6, 1791, NOPL.

46. Conseil de ville, minutes, December 2, 1803, CVOP, 1:4.

47. Conseil de ville, minutes, April 25, 1804, CVOP, 1:82–83; conseil de ville, minutes, December 12, 1803, CVOP, 1:14–15; conseil de ville, minutes, August 25, 1804, CVOP, 1:165–66; conseil de ville, minutes, January 14, 1806, CVOP, 1:171; conseil de ville, minutes, February 15, 1806, CVOP, 1:6; conseil de ville, minutes of the extraordinary session, December 12, 1807, CVOP, 2:88–89; conseil de ville, minutes, April 19, 1809, CVOP, 2:50.

48. An Act to Prevent the Introduction of Free People of Colour, from Hispaniola and

the Other French Islands of America, into the Territory of Orleans, June 7, 1806, *General Digest,* §2; An Act to Prevent the Emigration of Free Negroes and Mulattoes into the Territory of Orleans, April 14, 1807, *General Digest,* §1 (§2 of the 1807 act specifically repealed the relevant sections of the earlier act, making immigrants from the French islands subject to the ban); *State v. Vincent Lewis* (1823), Office of the Mayor, Decisions of the Mayor in Criminal Cases, 1823–32, NOPL; An Act to Prevent Free Persons of Colour from Entering into this State, and for Other Purposes, March 16, 1830, *Louisiana Acts,* 90–94; An Act to Amend an Act Entitled "An Act to Prevent Free Persons of Colour from Entering into This State, and for Other Purposes," Approved March 16th, 1830, March 25, 1831, *Louisiana Acts,* 98; An Act More Effectively to Prevent Free Persons of Color from Entering into This State, March 16, 1842, *Louisiana Acts,* 314. The 1842 act was amended the following year to permit "free blacks, who have resided since 1838, to remain, on giving evidence of good character, with bonds to obey the laws, and being registered" (An Act to Amend An Act Approved March 16, 1842 Entitled "An Act More Effectively to Prevent Free Persons of Color from Entering into This State,["] and for Other Purposes, 1843, *Louisiana Acts,* 133).

In 1796, when Virginian George St. Tucker pondered where to send ex-slaves in a proposal for gradual emancipation, he suggested Spanish Louisiana, perceiving the colony to be a place where free African Americans and Euro-Americans could peacefully coexist, despite his doubts to the contrary (Sheppard Wolf, *Race and Liberty in the New Nation,* 106). That free African Americans from elsewhere in the United States continued migrating into Louisiana, at least through the 1830s, suggests that they too believed life would be relatively better in New Orleans.

49. Louis Sala-Molins, *Le code noir; ou, Le calvaire de Canaan* (Paris, 1987), 647; Real cédula sobre la educación, trato y occupaciones de los esclavos, May 31, 1789, *Colección de documentos para la historia de la formación social de Hispanoamérica, 1493–1810,* ed. Richard Konetzke, 3 vols. (Madrid, 1958–62), 3:647, article 6. For a case in which a slave was deemed to be ineligible for emancipation because of her "bad reputation" and her "thievish" and "insolent" behavior, see *Nole v. Charles De St. Romes and Wife,* 3 Rob. 484 (1843), 484.

50. An Act to Regulate the Conditions and Forms of the Emancipation of Slaves, March 9, 1807, *General Digest,* 454–56. The only exception was when the legislature itself ordered the emancipation for a slave's service to the state (An Act Prescribing the Rules and Conduct to Be Observed with Respect to Negroes and Other Slaves of This Territory, *General Digest,* Crimes and Offenses, §19). For a typical manumission following the new procedures, see manumission of Guillaume Flavy and Elizabeth Honorine, November 9, 1820, Lavergne, NONA, 284.

51. An Act to Determine the Mode of Emancipating Slaves Who Have Not Attained the Age Required by the Civil Code for Their Emancipation, January 31, 1827, *Louisiana Acts,* 12–14; An Act to Prevent Free Persons of Colour from Entering into This State, and for Other Purposes, March 16, 1830, *Louisiana Acts,* 92–94; An Act Concerning the Emancipation of Slaves in This State, March 18, 1852, *Louisiana Acts,* 214–15; An Act to Prohibit the Emancipation of Slaves, March 6, 1857, *Louisiana Acts,* 55. On manumissions during the late antebellum era, see Judith Kelleher Schafer, *Becoming Free, Remaining Free: Manumission and Enslavement in New Orleans, 1846–1862* (Baton Rouge, La., 2003).

52. An Act to Amend an Act Entitled "An Act to Prevent Free Persons of Colour from

Entering into This State, and for Other Purposes," Approved March 16th, 1830, March 25, 1831, *Louisiana Acts,* 98–100.

53. An Act Relative to Slaves and Free Colored Persons, March 15, 1855, *Louisiana Acts,* 377–91, §§72–73.

54. Joe Gray Taylor, *Negro Slavery in Louisiana* (Baton Rouge, La., 1963), 154. The nine acts were An Act for the Relief of Hal Frazier, a Mulatto Man, Suing for His Freedom in the District Court of the Parish of Claiborne, March 31, 1853, *Louisiana Acts,* 51–52; An Act to Emancipate Jane Mary, the Slave and Daughter of Patsy, f.w.c., April 28, 1853, *Louisiana Acts,* 162; An Act to Enable Baptist Dupreyre, or His Legal Representatives, to Emancipate the Slave Zoe, without Removing Her Out of the State, April 28, 1853, *Louisiana Acts,* 163–64; An Act to Emancipate George, William, Desdemona and Elizabeth Robertson, Children of George Robertson, f.m.c., of the Parish of East Baton Rouge, April 28, 1853, *Louisiana Acts,* 177; An Act to Emancipate the Slave Eulalie, Belonging to Amadeo Landry, of the City of New Orleans, April 30, 1853, *Louisiana Acts,* 272; An Act to Emancipate the Slaves John, Rosie and Henry, Belonging to the Estate of the Late Jehu Wilkinson, Deceased, April 30, 1853, *Louisiana Acts,* 272; An Act to Emancipate the Slaves Belonging to the Estate of the Late J. B. Cajus, of the Parish of Orleans, April 30, 1853, *Louisiana Acts,* 273–74; An Act to Manumit or Emancipate Marie Melandy, Slave of Moise Hebert, of the Parish of St. Landry, April 30, 1853, *Louisiana Acts,* 276; An Act to Emancipate Henrietta, Slave of Rebecca Coleman, of the Parish of East Baton Rouge, April 30, 1853, *Louisiana Acts,* 276–78.

Virginia required freed slaves to leave the state as early as 1806 but the requirement was "more often ignored than enforced" (Sheppard Wolf, *Race and Liberty in the New Nation,* 138; see also Sumner E. Matison, "Manumission by Purchase," *Journal of Negro History* 33 [1948]: 151–53, and Marvin Patrick Ely, *Israel on the Appomattox: A Southern Experiment in Black Freedom from the 1790s through the Civil War* [New York, 2004]).

55. Laurence J. Kotlikoff and Anton J. Rupert, "The Manumission of Slaves in New Orleans, 1827–1846," *Southern Studies* 19 (1980): 172–81; Judith Kelleher Schafer, *Slavery, the Civil Law, and the Supreme Court of Louisiana* (Baton Rouge, La., 1994), 183. Kotlikoff and Rupert examined all 1,166 petitions filed with the New Orleans Police Jury between 1827 and 1846; only 7 were denied. Every request to remain in the state after passage of the 1830 law was granted. As in the eighteenth century, women and "light colored children" were overrepresented among the manumitted.

56. All calculations in this and the following paragraphs are based on Gwendolyn Midlo Hall, "Louisiana Free Database, 1719–1820," *Databases for the Study of Afro-Louisiana History and Genealogy, 1699–1860: Computerized Information from Original Manuscript Sources,* ed. Gwendolyn Midlo Hall (Baton Rouge, La., 2000).

57. Registration of liberty by Sieur John Lynd, October 2, 1807, N. Broutin, NONA, 17:150. Lynd purchased and manumitted Robert's mother a year later. Sale of slave, September 1, 1808, N. Broutin, NONA, 339; manumission of Cecile, October 14, 1808, Pradelles, NONA, 2:428. According to Roulhac Toledano and Mary Louis Christovich, Broutin himself had a free woman of color for a consort, another factor that may have influenced his decision to abet Lynd's illegal manumission ("The Role of Free People of Color in Tremé," in *New Orleans Architecture,* vol. 6, *Faubourg Tremé and the Bayou Road,* ed. Roulhac Toledano and Mary Louise Christovich, [Gretna, La., 1980], 92).

58. Manumission of Louise, May 16, 1808, Pradelles, NONA, 2:309–9v. Marie Louise had purchased her own freedom, with the help of mulatto libre Pedro Langliche, from William fourteen years earlier (manumission of Carlota and María Luisa, May 6, 1794, Ximénez, NONA, 6:179–81v). Three months after recording Louise's emancipation despite her underage status, notary Benjamin van Pradelles recorded another for four-year-old négresse Marguerite, freed by négresse libre Helene (manumission of Marguerite, September 3, 1808, Pradelles, NONA, 2:398v–99).

59. Sebastian Ferrer, will, November 15, 1817, Philippe Pedesclaux, NONA, 3:787–88; manumission of Catherine, September 28, 1818, Philippe Pedesclaux, NONA, 6:786–86v.

60. Declaration of Francisco Delille Dupard, August 24, 1808, Quiñones Court Proceedings, NONA, 644–45; manumission of Nard María, August 24, 1808, Quiñones Court Proceedings, NONA, 645v–46v.

61. Baptism of Manuel, October 28, 1808, SLC, B21, 145; baptism of Luis, June 15, 1809, SLC, B21, 233; baptism of Eugenia Virginia [Ferrand], June 12, 1809, SLC, B21, 232; baptism of Domingo Salvador Recio, September 27, 1809, SLC, B23, 6; baptism of María Magdalena, May 14, 1810, SLC, B23, 31; baptism of Louis Manville, November 18, 1810, SLC, B23, 166.

62. Sale of slave, June 30, 1814, Pedesclaux, NONA, 68:266v–67; [registration of freedom], July 22, 1814, Pedesclaux, NONA, 69:302v–3Bv.

63. Sale of slave, December 26, 1816, M. de Armas, NONA, 11, act 810.

64. Sale of slave, May 16, 1820, Lafitte, NONA, 17:213–13v.

65. Sale of slaves, October 25, 1820, Lafitte, NONA, 17:383–84; sale of slave, October 14, 1820, Lafitte, NONA, 17:373v–74. See also sale of slaves, September 4, 1817, Philippe Pedesclaux, NONA, 3:645–45v; sale of slaves, June 20, 1820, Lafitte, NONA, 17:274v–75v; sale of slave, June 21, 1820, Lafitte, NONA, 17:275v–76v.

66. *Henry Hardesty, Sen., v. Sukey Wormley,* 10 La. Ann. 239 (1855), docket no. 3056, SCLHA, UNO.

67. An Act for the Relief of Catherine Moreau, March 18, 1820, *Louisiana Acts,* 106–8; An Act Supplementary to the Act Entitled "An Act for the Relief of Catherine Moreau," Approved March 18, 1820, March 14, 1826, *Louisiana Acts,* 64–66.

68. An Act to Authorize the Emancipation of Certain Slaves, February 14, 1826, *Louisiana Acts,* 32; An Act to Dispense Certain Slaves Therein Mentioned with the Age Required by Law for the Emancipation of Slaves, February 22, 1826, *Louisiana Acts,* 40; An Act to Authorize the Emancipation of Certain Slaves Therein Mentioned, March 22, 1826, *Louisiana Acts,* 106–10.

69. The provision of the act banning forced coartacións actually went into effect immediately on passage in March (An Act to Regulate the Conditions and Forms of the Emancipation of Slaves, March 9, 1807, *General Digest,* 456).

70. Manumission of Foinette and her two sons, May 15, 1807, Pedesclaux, NONA, 54:307v–8; manumission of Anne Elizabeth, May 27, 1807, N. Broutin, NONA, 16:43; manumission of Jean, March 17, 1807, Pedesclaux, NONA, 54:113–13v; manumission of Pognon, May 23, 1807, Lynd, NONA, 3[.2]:98–99; manumission of Laurent, January 16, 1807, Pedesclaux, NONA, 54:23; manumission of Constance and her three daughters, May 5, 1807, Pedesclaux, NONA, 58:240v–41; manumission of Genevieve, August 31, 1807, Pedesclaux, NONA, 55:540–40v. It is possible that as coartacións declined as a percentage of

all manumissions, those of children and/or consorts increased (Lachance, "Formation of a Three-Caste Society," 230).

71. Manumission of Paul, March 22, 1806, N. Broutin, NONA, 12:122v–23v.

72. *Prince Mathews v. Michael Boland and Another,* 5 Rob. 200 (1843).

73. *Victoire v. Dussuau,* 4 Mart. (O.S.) 212 (1816), docket no. 103, 212–14, emphasis added. In an 1848 case, however, the Louisiana Supreme Court upheld the use of oral testimony to prove the existence and fulfillment of a manumission agreement (*Gaudet v. Gourdain,* 3 La. Ann. 136 [1848]). Delaware in 1797 and Tennessee in 1833 also recognized slaves' right to contract for their own freedom (Matison, "Manumission by Purchase," 154–55).

74. Manumission of Coffy, December 24, 1785, Rodríguez, NONA, 1144; internment of Andres Almonester y Roxas, April 26, 1798, *SR, 6:5; Marie Cuffy v. Widow Madame Castillon,* no. 255, 5 Mart. (O.S.) 494 (1818).

75. *Betsy Seves v. Marianne Delogny and Jean Mayat* (1812), docket no. 3383, Records of the Superior Court, NOPL.

76. *Pierre Meteye v. Adelaide* (1818), docket no. 1589, SCLHA, UNO; *Adelaide Meteye (f.w.c.) v. Noret,* no. 1035 (1818); *Adelaide Metayer v. Louis Noret,* 5 Mart. (O.S.) 566 (1818), docket no. 288; *Pierre Metayer v. Adelaide Metayer,* 6 Mart. (O.S.) 16 (1819), docket no. 318.

77. A survey of the legislative journals revealed that only a handful of emancipation bills presented to the legislature were rejected.

78. Louis Moreau-Lislet and James Brown, *A Digest of the Civil Laws Now in Force in the Territory of Orleans (1808): Containing Manuscript References to Its Sources and Other Civil Laws on the Same Subjects (The de la Vergne Volume)* (Baton Rouge, La., 1968), book 1, title 4, article 8.

79. I discuss a number of documented marriages in the text; in addition Diana Williams has found compelling evidence that Catholic priests performed "marriages of conscience" for interracial couples in the antebellum era, many of which were registered after Louisiana repealed its interracial marriage ban ("'They Call It Marriage': The Interracial Louisiana Family and the Making of American Legitimacy" [PhD diss., Harvard University, 2007], especially 141–50; see also Virginia Meacham Gould, *Chained to the Rock of Adversity: To Be Free, Black, and Female in the Old South* [Athens, Ga., 1998], 7–8).

80. Baptism of Sofi Lesassier, July 13, 1789, SLC, B12, 110; baptism of María Francisca Hanrrieta Le Sassier, October 3, 1792, SLC, B11, 222; baptism of Carlos Latill, September 22, 1793, SLC, B11, 278; baptism of Josef Latill, July 7, 1796, SLC, B14, 8; baptism of Luis Azael Latill, May 8, 1800, SLC, B14, 121; baptism of Luisa Virginia Latill, August 30, 1800, SLC, B14, 131; funeral of Luisa Virginea Brunet, August 31, 1800, *SR,* 7:41; marriage of Alexo Dupres and Sophia Le Sassier, July 10, 1811, *SR,* 10:163, 284; marriage of Pablo Michel Fauconnet Decalogne and María Francisca Hanrrieta Lesassier, November 26, 1815, *SR,* 11:169, 274; marriage of Joseph Timecour Latil and María de la Merced Clermont, July 21, 1816, *SR,* 12:81, 226–27; marriage of Luis Azael Latil and María Carmelita Ruiz, March 20, 1824, *SR,* 16:230, 354. Esteves's daughters married men who were born in Paris and Saint-Domingue; her sons' brides were native New Orleanians.

81. Marriage of Gabriel Girodeau and Félicité Pomet, July 3, 1817, SLC, M6, 195; note regarding marriage of Gabriel Girodeau and Félicité Pomet, SLC, M3, 54. It is clear that

Sedella was not operating under the assumption that a preponderance of European ancestry made one white, because Girodeau, whose lineage is very well recorded in the sacramental records, had, at best one great-grandparent who was identified as negra; the rest were blancos.

82. Marriage of Juan Pedro Cazelar and María Ygnacia Odil Fernandes de Velasco, June 9, 1823, SLC, M7, 33; note regarding marriage of Jean Pierre Cazelar and Marie Ygance Odille Fernandez de Velarco, SLC, M3, 73; marriage of Francisco Estevan Dalcour and Margarita Docmint de Morant, May 22, 1823, SLC, M7, 32; marriage of Joseph María Bayset and Ana María Michel Desban, December 7, 1825, SLC, M7, 74; note regarding marriage of Joseph Baysett and Anne Marie Michel Desban, SLC, M3, 81; marriage of Juan Clay and María Antonia Eufemia Moor, November 17, 1825, SLC, M7, 73; note regarding marriage of Jean Clay and Marie Antoinette Moor, SLC, M3, 81; marriage of Pedro Dupre and María Theresa Journe, August 28, 1826, SLC, M7, 88; note regarding marriage of Pierre Dupré and Marie Thereze Journé, SLC, M3, 82; baptism of Pedro Dupre, August 4, 1811, SLC, B24, 78. Sedella also rectified baptism records entered in error. See, for instance, baptism of Francisco Felix Perriat, August 1, 1818, SLC, B31, 21; baptism of François Felix Perriat et Yamora, 1818, SLC, B30, 36; baptism of Francisca María Carlota Callico, February 5, 1823, SLC, B33, 157; baptism of Ysavel Estelle Thiac y Goy, February 5, 1823, SLC, B33, 157; and baptism of Elizabeth Estelle Thiac et Goy, February 5, 1823, SLC, B33, 1.

83. By the early nineteenth century, according to Earl C. Woods and Charles E. Nolan, the editors of the *Sacramental Records,* Sedella frequently "corrected mistakes or, less frequently, omissions, by his colleagues," whether of place names, transliteration of non-Spanish names, or racial labels (*Sacramental Records of the Roman Catholic Church of the Archdiocese of New Orleans* [New Orleans, 1987–92], 7:xvii, 8:xvii).

84. Marriage of George Heno and Marie Louise Rufignay, October 20, 1768, *SR,* 2:148, 246; baptism of Pierre George Heno, December 4, 1770, *SR,* 2:148; marriage of [Pedro?] Heno and Margarita Tonnelier, June 20, 1789, *SR,* 4:161, 298; baptism of Juan Bautista Heno, September 29, 1796, *SR,* 6:149; baptism of Nicolas Ursino Heno, May 22, 1799, *SR,* 6:149; baptism of Celeste Solidele Heno, April 24, 1804, *SR,* 8:174; *Census of New Orleans,* November 6, 1791, NOPL.

85. Baptism of Margarita Solidel Heno, April 27, 1818, *SR,* 13:210; baptism of Pedro Fanchon, March 26, 1808, *SR,* 9:140; baptism of Juan Bautista Fanchon, April 22, 1811, *SR,* 10:175; baptism of Juan Andres Heno, June 10, 1813, *SR,* 11:216; baptism of Amelie Heno, January 27, 1817, *SR,* 12:194; baptism of Agathe Heno, June 26, 1820, *SR,* 14:199; internment of Catiche Heno, March 7, 1823, *SR,* 15:198.

86. *George Heno, Solidelle Heno, and Marguerite Heno v. Pierre Heno,* 9 Mart. (O.S.) 643 (1821), docket no. 510, SCLHA, UNO. See also Mary Williams, "Private Lives, Public Orders: The Heno Family and the Legal Regulation of Sexuality in Early National Louisiana" (paper presented at the Berkshire Conference on the History of Women, University of Connecticut, June 2002). For a case in which the court ruled a husband did not have to support his white wife and children, despite having abandoned them for "a woman who had been his mother's slave," see *Alphonse Dorwin v. Aimee Wiltz,* 11 La. Ann. 514 (1856).

87. Baptism of Agathe Heno, June 26, 1820, *SR,* 14:199.

88. *J. M. Dupré v. the Executor of Boulard, f.w.c.,* 10 La. Ann. 411 (1855), docket no. 3743.

89. *Raimond Domec v. S. Barjac and Coral Lalande* (1859), docket no. 14851, SCLHA, UNO; *Succession of Jean Michel Minvielle,* 15 La. Ann. 34 (1860), docket no. 6447, SCLHA, UNO.

90. *Jung v. Doriocourt,* 4 La. 175 (1832). Jung's mother was Rosette, one of the children André Jung had acknowledged in his will in 1784 (succession of André Juen, inventory and appraisement of his estate, September 14, 1784, SJR, *LHQ* 24 [1941]: 1258–74).

91. This was not the first time that Françoise Bernoudy was taken to court by a free woman of color. In 1819, Bernoudy was sued by Genevieve, who claimed that Bernoudy had imprisoned her for three days and had her "tied with a rope and cruelly flogged." Bernoudy's son and cousin were found guilty of abuse, but Genevieve also sought 1,500 dollars in damages (*Genevieve v. Doriocourt, Widow* [1819], docket no. 2096, Orleans Parish Court Records, NOPL).

92. Williams, " 'They Call It Marriage,' " 250–61.

93. Livingstone, Lislet, and Derbigny, *Civil Code,* 294, article 914, 68, article 226.

94. For technical reasons, the court actually ruled that three of Jung's children were entitled to just over 200 dollars each, far less than the 1,000 dollars their grandfather had sought to leave them.

95. Marriage of Joseph Le Blanc de Villanueva and Adelaida Jung, April 1, 1816, *SR,* 12:208, 233. The baptisms of the two oldest children were recorded in the book for "negros and mulatos"; the third child had his baptism recorded in both the white and nonwhite registries; and the fourth's was recorded in the white registry (baptism of Josephina Adelayda Le Blanc, November 11, 1794, *SR,* 5:236; baptism of Luis Jose Neree Le Blanc de Villanueva, March 19, 1798, *SR,* 6:172; baptism of Jose Terencio Albino Le Blanc, March 19, 1803, *SR,* 7:194; baptism of Josefa Rosa Le Blanc, March 19, 1803, *SR,* 7:194).

96. *Jung v. Doriocourt,* 4 La. 175 (1832), 177, 180, 181; marriage of Augusto Passage and Josephina Adelaida Leblanc de Villanueva, June 7, 1817, *SR,* 7:233, 294.

97. Livingstone, Lislet, and Derbigny, *Civil Code,* 473, article 1468.

98. Moreau-Lislet and Brown, *Digest of 1808,* book 1, title 1, article 4, and title 7, articles 4–6, 21, 25, 30; Dominguez, *White by Definition,* 62–79; Judith K. Schafer, " 'Open and Notorious Concubinage': The Emancipation of Slave Mistresses by Will and the Supreme Court of Antebellum Louisiana," *LH* 28 (1987): 165–82.

99. *Philippe Pijeaux v. Francis Duvernay* (Parish Court of New Orleans, 1815), SCLHA, UNO.

100. *Philippe Pijeaux v. Francis Duvernay,* 4 Mart. (O.S.) 265 (1816), docket no. 147, SCLHA, UNO; Livingstone, Lislet, and Derbigny, *Civil Code,* 66, article 221. Pijeaux, a native of France, recognized several children of color with two different women, both before and after an apparently short-lived marriage to a third, probably white, woman (baptism of María Francisca Pijeaux, September 28, 1799, *SR,* 6:223; baptism of Josephina Celestina Piegon, March 23, 1804, *SR,* 8:262; marriage of Philippe Pijeaux and Julie Senet, April 27, 1807, *SR,* 9:293, 337; baptism of Francisca Pijeaux, March 23, 1811, *SR,* 10:351; baptism of Marie Anne Pijeaux, October 7, 1811, *SR,* 10:351; baptism of Juan Pijeaux, November 10, 1814, *SR,* 11:349; baptism of Therencio Pijeaux, November 10, 1814, *SR,* 11:349; baptism of Josephine Pijeau, March 23, 1820, *SR,* 14:319).

101. *John Compton and Others, Heirs of Leonard B. Compton, Deceased, v. Aaron Prescott*

and Another, Executors of Said Leonard B. Compton, and Others, 12 Rob. 56 (1845), 56; *Marie L. Badillo v. Francisco Tio,* 6 La. Ann. 129 (1851), 138; *Turner v. Smith,* no. 5076, 12 La. Ann. 417 (1857), 418.

102. Livingstone, Lislet, and Derbigny, *Civil Code,* 282, article 883.

103. Livingstone, Lislet, and Derbigny, *Civil Code,* 473–76, 294, articles 1470–73, 914.

104. Most appellate cases regarding interracial sex, at least through the 1930s, involved contestations over property (Peggy Pascoe, "Race, Gender, and the Privileges of Property: On the Significance of Miscegenation Law in the U.S. West," in *Over the Edge: Remapping the American West,* ed. Valerie J. Matsumoto and Blake Allmendinger (Berkeley, Calif., 1999), 217. Based on southern appellate decisions involving interracial inheritance disputes between 1868 and 1900, Mary Frances Berry argues that white men's testamentary wishes were most often upheld and that judges "expressed neither pleasure nor displeasure with the reality of interracial concubinage" ("Judging Morality: Sexual Behavior and Legal Consequences in the Late Nineteenth-Century South," *JAH* 78 [1991]: 854). For a detailed analysis of one woman of color's successful legal battles against her white father's legitimate relatives, see Virginia Kent Anderson Leslie, *Woman of Color, Daughter of Privilege: Amanda America Dickson, 1849–1893* (Athens, Ga., 1995).

105. *Wm. Reed v. H. H. Crocker,* 12 La. Ann. 436 (1857). The court did acknowledge that once they had inherited Crocker's estate, his white relatives were free to dispose of the property as they saw fit, including donating it to Crocker's children.

106. *Margaret Bush, f.w.c., v. Margaret Décuir and Her Husband,* 11 La. Ann. 503 (1856), docket no. 4339. In 1814, the Louisiana Supreme Court reduced the inheritances of J. B. Senet's four natural children to the legal limit but the published opinion makes no reference to whether the children were white or not, and the originals have not been located (*Sennet v. Sennet's Legatees,* 3 Mart. [O.S.] 411 [1814]).

107. Joseph Carrel, will, September 25, 1806, Lynd, NONA, 3:126–27; *Carrel's Heirs v. Cabaret,* 7 Mart. (O.S.) 375 (1820), docket no. 391, SCLHA.

108. *Jacques L. Prévost and Another, Heirs of Maurice Prevost, Deceased, v. Pierre Martel, Testamentary Executor of the Deceased, and Others,* 10 Rob. 512 (1845).

109. *Robinett v. Verdun's Vendees,* 14 La. 542 (1840). See also *Marie L. Badillo v. Francisco Tio,* 6 La. Ann. 129 (1851), 138–39, 141.

110. For the story of one legitimate son who abided his father's wishes regarding his mulatto half siblings, see Ann Patton Malone, *Sweet Chariot: Slave Family and Household Structure in Nineteenth-Century Louisiana* (Chapel Hill, N.C., 1992), 223.

111. Jean-Baptiste Macarty, will, November 21, 1808, N. Broutin, NONA, 18:491v–92; baptism of Theophilo De Macarty, July 21, 1799, *SR,* 6:85. Beaulieu was to enjoy only usufruct rights to the 2,000 piastres; the actual sum would go to her son on her death. Macarty did allow his legitimate children to revoke the additional 2,000 piastres if they thought it was too much, but he insisted that Theophile get his 4,000 piastres.

112. Joseph Dauphin, will, November 2, 1809, Pedesclaux, NONA, 59:499v–501; interment of Joseph Dauphin, January 6, 1810, *SR,* 10:115.

113. Jean Dubreuil, will, April 25, 1811, N. Broutin, NONA, 24:271v–74.

114. Jean Baptiste Picou, will, October 12, 1812, Pedesclaux, NONA, 65:436–37.

115. Marie Perou, will, March 20, 1810, N. Broutin, NONA, 245v–46.

116. Based on his analysis of antebellum wills, Lachance argues that racially exogamous relationships that led to bequests declined between 1800 and 1860 in part because of the formation of a self-defined gens de couleur libre community that began practicing marital endogamy ("Formation of a Three-Caste Society," 211–42; cf. Williams, "'They Call It Marriage,'" 202, 256–57, who argues that interracial relationships "went underground" as it became increasingly difficult for white men to transfer property to their nonwhite families after 1825).

117. Pierre-Clément de Laussat, *Memoirs of My Life to My Son during the Years 1803 and After, Which I spent in Public Service in Louisiana as Commissioner of the French Government for the Retrocession to France of That Colony and for Its Transfer to the United States,* ed. Robert D. Bush, trans. Agnes-Josephine Pastwa (Baton Rouge, La., 1978), 16, 52–53, 72; baptism of Helena Hazeur, October 25, 1792, SLC, B13, 5; baptism of Antonita Hazeur, December 2, 1796, SLC, B13, 333; baptism of Luisa Hazeur, July 16, 1798, SLC, B15, 23; baptism of Susana Hazeur, March 10, 1803, SLC, B16, 112; baptism of Adelaide, October 26, 1786, SLC, B8, 208; baptism of María de Vost, March 20, 1789, SLC, B12, 96; manumission of Feliciana, January 31, 1793, Pedesclaux, NONA, 16:77v–78; baptism of Paul Hazeur, December 27, 1790, SLC, B12, 161; baptism of Subsana Hazeur, April 26, 1794, *SR,* 5:202; Louis François Xavier Hazeur Delorme, will, December 16, 1816, Will Books, NOPL, 3:126–27. Louis François Xavier's same-day purchase and manumission of mulatica Victoria in 1782 suggests his paternity of her as well (sale and manumission of Victoria, March 6, 1782, Almonester, NONA, 129v–32). On the prevalence of interracial relationships on rural plantations and their disruptive impact on the slave community, see Malone, *Sweet Chariot,* 218–24.

118. Latrobe, *Impressions Respecting New Orleans,* 131; Latrobe, *Southern Travels,* 56, 80. See also Alexis de Tocqueville, *Journey to America,* trans. George Lawrence (London, 1959), 71–72, 105–6; Paul Alliot, "Historical and Political Reflections on Louisiana," July 1, 1803–April 13, 1804, *Louisiana Under the Rule of Spain, France and the United States, 1785–1807: Social, Economic, and Political Conditions of the Territory Represented in the Louisiana Purchase, as Portrayed in Hitherto Unpublished Contemporary Accounts by Paul Alliot and Various Spanish, French, English, and American Officials,* ed. James Alexander Robertson, 2 vols. (Cleveland, 1911), 1:71; C. C. Robin, *Voyage to Louisiana, 1803–1805: An Abridged Translation from the Original French,* trans. Stuart Landry Jr. (New Orleans, 1966), 56; Frances Trollope, *Domestic Manners of the Americans* (New York, 1949), 14; and just about any other travel account of early nineteenth-century New Orleans.

119. Caryn Cossé Bell, *Revolution, Romanticism, and the Afro-Creole Protest Tradition in Louisiana, 1718–1868* (Baton Rouge, La., 1997), 77–78; Monique Guillory, "Under One Roof: The Sins and Sanctity of the New Orleans Quadroon Balls," in *Race Consciousness: African-American Studies for the New Century,* ed. Judith Jackson Fossett and Jeffrey A. Tucker (New York, 1997), 67–92. Diana Williams argues that the quadroon balls were not "a vestige of a more racially fluid, seigniorial culture" but rather were "commercial innovations" in the post–Louisiana Purchase era ("'They Call It Marriage,'" 163–88, quotation on 170).

120. Loren Schweninger, "Property-Owning Free African-American Women in the South, 1800–70," *Journal of Women's History* 1 (1990): 19, appendix 1. These figures included only women identified as heads of households, therefore omitting those who resided in

white male-headed households. According to Leonard P. Curry, whose numbers differ slightly from Schweninger's, almost 60 percent of New Orleans' free population of color were women but were just under half the free people of color property owners (*The Free Black in Urban America,* tables C-1 and C-4).

121. For a critique of depicting New Orleans' gens de couleur libre as privileged, see Lachance, "The Limits of Privilege," 65–84.

122. In the registry for marriages of negros and mulatos, priests continued using the labels "negro," "mulato," and "quateron" up through July 1818. After that, "femme de couleur libre" and "homme de couleur libre," which had only occasionally appeared previously, became the dominant labels and almost fully supplanted the other labels by 1821 (marriages of negros and mulatos, 1777–1830, SLC, M3). The baptism registries, however, continued to a variety of labels.

Epilogue

1. Alexis de Tocqueville, *Journey to America,* trans. George Lawrence (London, 1959), 378, 164–65, 28, 181, 222. Very little of what he observed in New Orleans made it into his *Democracy in America,* 4th rev. and corr. ed., 2 vols. (New York, 1841).

2. For those emphasizing culture, see Gilberto Freyre, *The Masters and the Slaves: A Study in the Development of Brazilian Civilization,* trans. Samuel Putnam, 2nd rev. ed. (1956; rpt., Berkeley, Calif., 1986); Magnus Mörner, *Race Mixture in the History of Latin America* (Boston, 1967); Carl N. Degler, *Neither Black Nor White: Slavery and Race Relations in Brazil and the United States* (Madison, Wisc., 1971); David D. Smits, "'Abominable Mixture': The Repudiation of Anglo-Indian Intermarriage in Seventeenth-Century Virginia," *Virginia Magazine of History and Biography* 95 (1987): 157–92. For materialist explanations, see B. W. Higman, *Slave Population and Economy in Jamaica, 1807–1834* (Cambridge, England, 1976); Philip D. Morgan, "British Encounters with Africans and African-Americans, circa 1600–1780," in *Strangers Within the Realm: Cultural Margins of the First British Empire,* ed. Bernard Bailyn and Morgan (Chapel Hill, N.C., 1991), 157–219; Gary B. Nash, "The Hidden History of Mestizo America," *JAH* 82 (1995): 941–62; and Cornelius J. Jaenen, "Interracial Societies: The French Colonies, Canada," in *Encyclopedia of the North American Colonies,* ed. Jacob Ernest Cooke (New York, 1993), 2:169–76.

3. *General Census of All Inhabitants of New Orleans and Environs, as Reported by Le Sieur Diron,* November 24, 1721, *Census Tables,* 17–22; *Census of the Colony of Louisiana,* September 1763, *Some Late Eighteenth-Century Louisianians: Census Records 1758–1796,* comp. and trans Jacqueline K. Voorhies (Lafayette, La., 1973), 4–13; Kimberly S. Hanger, *Bounded Lives, Bounded Places: Free Black Society in Colonial New Orleans, 1769–1803* (Durham, N.C., 1997), 22.

4. Gwendolyn Midlo Hall convincingly argues that Louisiana's slave culture was one of the most Africanized in North America because of the heavy importation of slaves from concentrated regions of West Africa in the 1710s and 1720s and then again in the 1780s and 1790s with virtually no slaves from anywhere arriving in the intervening decades (*Africans in Colonial Louisiana: The Development of Afro-Creole Culture in the Eighteenth Century* [Baton Rouge, La., 1992]). While this was most assuredly true for the plantation districts

throughout the lower Mississippi River Valley, in New Orleans itself, French culture, language, and religion exerted a greater influence on those generations of Afro-Louisianans born between the 1720s and 1780s. As Emily Clark notes, "By the end of the eighteenth century, women of color constituted the majority of regular worshippers in the Catholic churches of New Orleans" ("A New World Community: The New Orleans Ursulines and Colonial Society, 1727–1803" [PhD diss., Tulane University, 1998], 286).

5. One group of white immigrants was more likely than the others to participate in interracial unions: those from Saint-Domingue who arrived in great numbers around 1810. In his analysis of antebellum wills, Paul Lachance found that the percentage of white male testators who mentioned interracial unions declined from almost 15 percent in the two decades after the Louisiana Purchase to under 2 percent by 1860 ("The Formation of a Three-Caste Society: Evidence from Wills in Antebellum New Orleans," *Social Science History* 18 [1994]: 211–42).

6. Louis Moreau-Lislet and James Brown, *A Digest of the Civil Laws Now in Force in the Territory of Orleans (1808): Containing Manuscript References to Its Sources and Other Civil Laws on the Same Subjects (The de la Vergne Volume)* (Baton Rouge, La., 1968), book 1, title 4, article 8.

7. On "racial variability," see Patricia Seed, "Social Dimensions of Race: Mexico City, 1753," *Hispanic American Historical Review* 62 (1982): 569–606.

8. This criticism is made forcefully by Stephen Small, "Racial Group Boundaries and Identities: People of 'Mixed Race' in Slavery across the Americas," *Slavery and Abolition* 15 (1994): 29–31.

9. Philip D. Morgan, "Interracial Sex in the Chesapeake and the British Atlantic World, 1700–1820," in *Sally Hemings and Thomas Jefferson: History, Memory, and Civil Culture,* ed. Jan Lewis and Peter Onuf (Charlottesville, Va., 1999), 52–84, quotation on 56; Joshua D. Rothman, *Notorious in the Neighborhood: Sex and Families across the Color Line in Virginia, 1787–1861* (Chapel Hill, N.C., 2003); Martha Hodes, *White Women, Black Men: Illicit Sex in the Nineteenth-Century South* (New York, 1997). See also Thomas E. Buckley, "Unfixing Race: Class, Power, and Identity in an Interracial Family," *Virginia Magazine of History and Biography* 102 (1994): 349–80; Cynthia Kennedy-Haflett, "'Moral Marriage': A Mixed-Race Relationship in Nineteenth-Century Charleston, South Carolina," *South Carolina Historical Magazine* 97 (1996): 206–26; Timothy J. Lockley, "Crossing the Race Divide: Interracial Sex in Antebellum Savannah," *Slavery and Abolition* 18 (1997): 170; Peter W. Bardaglio, "'Shamefull Matches': The Regulation of Interracial Sex and Marriage in the South before 1900," in *Sex, Love, Race: Crossing Boundaries in North American History,* ed. Martha Hodes (New York, 1999), 112–38; Kirsten Fischer, *Suspect Relations: Sex, Race, and Resistance in Colonial North Carolina* (Ithaca, N.Y., 2001). For flexibility in interracial interactions more generally, see, for instance, R. Douglas Cope, *The Limits of Racial Domination: Plebeian Society in Colonial Mexico City, 1660–1720* (Madison, Wisc., 1994); Philip D. Morgan, *Slave Counterpoint: Black Culture in the Eighteenth-Century Chesapeake and Lowcountry* (Chapel Hill, N.C., 1998), especially chapters 5–7; Timothy J. Lockley, *Lines in the Sand: Race and Class in Lowcountry Georgia, 1750–1860* (Athens, Ga., 2000); John Wood Sweet, *Bodies Politic: Negotiating Race in the American North, 1730–1830* (Baltimore, Md., 2003); Suzanne Lebsock, *A Murder in Virginia: Southern Justice on Trial* (New York, 2003); and Marvin

Patrick Ely, *Israel on the Appomattox: A Southern Experiment in Black Freedom from the 1790s through the Civil War* (New York, 2004). For a noteworthy fictionalized effort to capture the complexity of interracial interactions in antebellum Virginia, see Edward P. Jones, *The Known World* (New York, 2003).

10. Jack P. Greene, *Pursuits of Happiness: The Social Development of Early Modern British Colonies and the Formation of American Culture* (Chapel Hill, N.C., 1988).

11. Nash, "Hidden History of Mestizo America," 954.

12. For this argument, see Thomas N. Ingersoll, *Mammon and Manon in Early New Orleans: The First Slave Society in the Deep South, 1718–1819* (Knoxville, Tenn., 1999).

Terms used to describe an individual's calidad

FRENCH	SPANISH	ENGLISH
affranchi		manumitted or freed
blanc/blanche	*blanco/-a*	white
	bozal	African-born slave, recently arrived
concessionaire		owner of a concession
engagé		indentured servant
esclave	*esclavo/-a*	slave
gens de couleur libre	*gente de color libre*	free people of color
griffe	*grifo/-a*	griff (in New Orleans, commonly used for the child of a *negro/-a* and *mulata/-o* and occasionally for Afro-Indians)
habitant		member of the permanent, settled population of the colony (as opposed to soldiers, coureurs de bois, etc.)
homme/femme de couleur libre		free man/woman of color (often abbreviated f.m.c./f.w.c.)
libre	*libre*	free person
métis	*mestizo/-a*	Afro-Indian or Euro-Indian
	moreno/-a	dark-skinned person of African descent
mulâtre/sse	*mulato/-a*	mulatto
	mulatico/-a	young mulatto
née libre		born free
nègre/négresse; noir	*negro/-a*	negro, black

FRENCH	SPANISH	ENGLISH
	pardo/-a	light-skinned person of African descent
régnicole		natural inhabitant of a state (used to distinguish French citizens from foreigners)
quarteron/né	*cuarterón/a*	quadroon
sang-mêlé		mixed blood
sauvage/sse	*indio/-a, salvaje*	Indian
sieur	*don/doña*	title of respect
	vecino/-a	resident, citizen of a town

French

autres personnes libres	other free persons
commandeur	overseer
commissaire ordonnateur	fiscal officer, second in command after the governor
concession	large land grant, plantation
coureurs des bois	fur traders
dit(e)	known as, nicknamed
épouseuse	a woman sent to the colonies to be married
habitation	small land grant
petites nations	small Indian nations
personnes nées libre	persons born free
pièce d'Inde	prime slave
procureur général	attorney general
veuve	widow
voyageur	French trader

Spanish

alcalde	judge and member of the cabildo
bando	decree, edict
cabildo	town council
calidad	quality

carta de libertad	act or certificate of manumission ("carta" for short)
casta	*lineage, race*
cédula	decree
coartación	self-purchase
compadrazgo	godparentage
escribano	court scribe, notary
graciosa/graciosamente	(manumitted) freely, without conditions
letrado	legal adviser
libro de blancos, negros, etc.	sacramental registries for whites, negros, etc.
limpieza de sangre	purity of blood
madrina	godmother
padrino	godfather
regidor	officer of the cabildo
viuda	widow

Units of Money and Measurement

arpent	French measure of both length (between 180 and 190 feet) and area (0.84 acres)
league	French measure of length (between 2½ and 2¾ miles)
peso	basic Spanish monetary unit, equivalent to 1 dollar
livre	basic French monetary unit during the eighteenth century (replaced by the franc in 1795); its value fluctuated greatly during the early eighteenth-century
piastre	French name for Spanish coin; usually worth about 5 to 8 livres; by the beginning of the nineteenth century it was interchangeable with "peso" and "dollar"
real	Spanish coin equivalent to 8 pesos
sol	French coin equivalent to 1 livre

Writing about sex and race in early America is difficult. Much of the historical evidence consists of moralistic diatribes (which do not tell us whether the acts being railed against were in fact taking place nor, even if they were, with what frequency nor whether the speaker's horror was representative of the few or the many) and court records (which might represent persistent persecution of most relationships or the exceptions that, for whatever reason, were not tolerated or ignored). For New Orleans, these diatribes most often came from nineteenth-century visitors, particularly Anglo-Americans. Anyone interested in these relationships in early New Orleans has to begin with the plethora accounts by travelers who were nothing if not obsessed with describing what they saw as a unique aspect of New Orleans life. Some of the richest descriptions of racially exogamous relationships can be found in Berquin-Duvallon, *Vue de la colonie espagnole du Mississippi ou des provinces de la Louisiane et Floride Occidentale, en l'année 1802* (Paris, 1803); [Louis Narcisse] Baudry des Lozières, *Second voyage à la Louisiane, faisant suite au premier de l'auteur de 1794 à 1798,* 2 vols. (Paris, 1803); C. C. Robin, *Voyage to Louisiana, 1803–1805: An Abridged Translation from the Original French,* trans. Stuart Landry Jr. (New Orleans, 1966); Timothy Flint, *Recollections of the Last Ten Years, Passed in Occasional Residences and Journeyings in the Valley of the Mississippi from Pittsburg and the Missouri to the Gulf of Mexico, and from Florida to the Spanish Frontier* (Boston, 1826); Alexis de Tocqueville, *Journey to America,* ed. J. P. Mayer, trans. George Lawrence (London, 1959); John H. B. Latrobe, *Southern Travels: Journal of John H. B. Latrobe 1834,* ed. Samuel Wilson Jr. (New Orleans, 1986); and Frederick Law Olmsted, *A Journey in the Seaboard Slave States in the Years 1853–1854 with Remarks on Their Economy,* 2 vols. (New York, 1904). Although not all travelers' accounts were critical of public displays of racial exogamy, even those whose descriptions were favorable tended to see what they had come to expect to see. It is, therefore, necessary to go beyond travelers' accounts and delve into the rich sources produced by New Orleanians themselves.

It is the contention of this book that the workings of race can only be fully understood through a two-pronged analysis that examines how officials codified racial ideas into the laws of a given society and how the members of that society operated within and around that racialized social order. Such an analysis requires that attention be paid to two very different sets of sources: one that reveals how those with political power encoded race into the social order and one that shows how all New Orleanians, of all ancestries and qualities, responded to these elite efforts. For overviews of both types of sources, see: Jack D. L. Holmes, *A Guide to Spanish Louisiana, 1762–1806* (New Orleans, 1970); Carl A. Brasseaux, "French Louisiana," in *A Guide to the History of Louisiana,* ed. Light Townsend Cummins and Glen Jeansonne (Westport, Conn., 1982); and Henry Putney Beers, *French and Spanish Records of Louisiana: A Bibliographical Guide to Archive and Manuscript Sources* (Baton Rouge, La., 1989).

Ideas about race promulgated by the elite and their efforts to codify those ideas into the social order are revealed in official correspondence and reports as well as legislation and other official orders. The correspondence between officials, both secular and religious, in Louisiana with their counterparts and superiors in the metropole illuminate the officials' views and their attempts at creating order out of the colony's diverse population. In their letters and reports, officials complained about their circumstances and offered solutions that they thought would best enable the colony's establishment and development.

For official correspondence during the French era, see several of the series of the Archives des Colonies, Archives nationales de France, currently archived at the Centre des archives d'outre-mer, Aix-en-Provence, France. The most important series for Louisiana are Correspondance à l'arrivee en provenance de la Louisiane, series C13, 1678–1819 (indexed in Marie-Antoinette Menier et al., *Archives nationales: Inventaire des Archives coloniales: Correspondance a l'arrivée en provence de la Louisiana,* 2 vols. [Paris, 1984]), and Recensements, series G1, vol. 464 (microfilm copies of both of these are held by the Historic New Orleans Collection). Additional relevant series include Actes du pouvoir soverain, series A, 1712–68; Correspondence envoyée, Ordres du roi, series B, 1698–1801; Correspondence générale, Canada, series C11, 1540–1800; and Collection Moreau de Saint-Méry, series F3, 1674–1806. Transcriptions of selected documents from these series are held in the Manuscript Division of the Library of Congress (for a description, see James E. O'Neill, "Copies of French Manuscripts for American History in the Library of Congress," *JAH* 51 [1965]: 674–91). Transcripts and translations of selected documents from these collections can also be found at the Mississippi Department of Archives and History (under the title French Provincial Records, 1678–1762), which also published translations in the five-volume set entitled *Mississippi Provincial Archives: French Dominion,* vols. 1–3, ed. Dunbar Rowland and A. G. Sanders (Jackson, Miss., 1927–32), vols. 4–5, ed. Dunbar Rowland and A. G. Sanders, rev. and ed. Patricia Galloway (Baton Rouge, La., 1984).

Other collections of official French-era correspondence include Paul Du Ru, *Journal of Paul du Ru (February 1 to May 8, 1700), Missionary Priest to Louisiana,* trans. Ruth Lapham Butler (Chicago, 1934); *The Jesuits Relations and Allied Documents: Travels and Explorations of the Jesuit Missionaries in New France, 1610–1719,* ed. Reuben Gold Thwaites, vol. 67 (Cleveland, 1900); "Cadillac Papers [1669–1723]," *Michigan Historical Collections* 33 (1903): 36–715, and 34 (1904): 11–214; Vaudreuil Letterbooks, 1743–47, Manuscripts Department, Huntington Library; and Vaudreuil Papers, French Colonial Manuscripts, 1743–53, Manuscripts Department, Huntington Library (for a guide to these last two collections, see *The Vaudreuil Papers: A Calendar and Index of the Personal and Private Records of Pierre de Rigaud de Vaudreuil, Royal Governor of the French Province of Louisiana, 1743–1753,* ed. Bill Barron [New Orleans, 1975]).

Spanish-era correspondence is contained in three separate collections. Two are archived in the Archivo General de Indias, Seville, Spain: AGI, Santo Domingo, 1757–1810 (described in José María de la Peña y Cámara et al., *Catálogo de documentos del Archivo General de Seville, sección V, gobierno, audiencia de Santo Domingo, sobre le época española de Luisiana* [Madrid and New Orleans, 1968]), and AGI, Papeles Procedentes de Cuba, 1766–1803 (described in *Descriptive Catalog of the Documents Relating to the History of the United States in the Papeles Procedentes de Cuba Deposited in the Archivo General de Indias at Seville* [New York, 1965]). The third, Records of the Diocese of Louisiana and the Floridas, 1576–1803, is housed at the University of Notre Dame Archives, South Bend, Indiana (see *Guide to the Microfilm Edition of the Records of the Diocese of Louisiana and the Floridas, 1576–1803* [Notre Dame, Ind., 1967]). Microfilm copies of all three of these collections are held by HNOC. In addition, the Special Collections in the Manuscripts Department at Howard Tilton Memorial Library, Tulane University, possess translations undertaken by the Works Progress Administration of many Spanish documents, including Spanish Governors of Louisiana Dispatches, 1766–91; Confidential Despatches of Don Bernardo de Gálvez, Fourth Spanish Governor of Louisiana, Sent to his Uncle, Don José de Gálvez, Secretary of State and Ranking Official of the Council of the Indies, 1770–82; and Spanish Governors of Louisiana Dispatches, El Baron de Carondelet, 1789–97. The Bancroft Library, Berkeley, California, holds a selection of documents from the Archive General de Indias (Louisiana Papers, BANC MSS M-M 508, 1767–1816), many of which have been translated and published in *Spain in the Mississippi Valley, 1765–1794: Translations of Materials from the Spanish Archives in the Bancroft Library (Annual Report of the American Historical Association for the Year 1945 in Four Volumes),* ed. Lawrence Kinnaird, 3 vols. (Washington, D.C., 1945).

For an official memoir describing the brief French interregnum in 1803, see Pierre-Clément de Laussat, *Memoirs of My Life to My Son during the Years 1803 and after, Which I spent in Public Service in Louisiana as Commissioner of the French Government for the Retrocession to France of That Colony and for Its Transfer to the United States,* ed. Robert D. Bush, trans. Agnes-Josephine Pastwa (Baton Rouge, La., 1978).

For Anglo-Louisianan correspondence, see William C. C. Claiborne, *Official Letter Books of W. C. C. Claiborne,* ed. Dunbar Rowland, 6 vols. (Jackson, Miss., 1917); Claiborne, *Interim Appointment: W. C. C. Claiborne Letter Books, 1804–1805,* ed. Jared William Bradley (Baton Rouge, La., 2001); and *The Territorial Papers of the United States,* vol. 9, *The Territory of Orleans, 1803–1812,* ed. Clarence Edwin Carter (Washington, D.C., 1940).

Other sources that can help one understand official ideas about how race should work include laws, enacted both locally and abroad, that illuminate how officials imagined an ideal social order and local governmental records that reflect their struggles to create such an order and broaden the focus somewhat to address the concerns of local elites in addition to official authorities. Numerous compilations of French and Spanish colonial laws have been published. See, for instance, *Recueils de règlemens, édits, déclarations et arrests, concernant le commerce, l'administration de la justice, et la police des colonies françaises de l'Amérique, et les engagés: Avec le code noir et l'addition audit code* (Paris, 1765); Médéric Louis Élie Moreau de Saint-Méry, *Loix et constitutions des colonies françaises de l'Amérique sous le Vent,* 6 vols. (Paris, 1784–89); Richard Konetzke, ed., *Colección de documentos para la historia de la formación social de Hispanoamérica, 1493–1810,* 3 vols. (Madrid, 1958–1962); and *The Laws of Las Siete Partidas, Which Are Still in Force in Louisiana,* trans. Louis Moreau-Lislet and Henry Carleton, 2 vols. (New Orleans, 1820). Many of the French laws enumerated in Lawrence C. Wroth and Gertrude L. Annan's *Acts of French Royal Administration Concerning Canada, Guiana, the West Indies and Louisiana, Prior to 1791* (New York, 1930) can be found at the John Carter Brown Library, Providence, Rhode Island.

Territorial and state laws have been compiled in the annually published *Acts of the Legislature* (various volume titles and imprints, 1812–57); François-Xavier Martin, *A General Digest of the Acts of the Legislature of the Late Territory of Orleans and of the State of Louisiana, and the Ordinances of the Governor under the Territorial Government: Preceded by the Treaty of Cession, the Constitution of the United States, and of the State, with the Acts of Congress, Relating to the Government of the Country and the Land Claims Therein* (New Orleans, 1816); Edward Livingstone, Louis Moreau-Lislet, and P. Derbigny, *Civil Code of the State of Louisiana* (New Orleans, 1825); Louis Moreau-Lislet, *A General Digest of the Acts of the Legislature of Louisiana, Passed from the Year 1804, to 1827 Inclusive, and in Force at This Last Period with an Appendix and General Index* (New Orleans, 1828); and *Constitutions of the State of Louisiana and Selected Federal Laws,* ed. Benjamin Wall Dart (Indianapolis, Ind., 1932).

The local governmental records include the Records of the Superior Council, 1714–69, Louisiana State Museum (microfilm copies at repositories throughout New Orleans, including the Tulane University Law Library; for an index, see "Index to the Records of the Superior Council of Louisiana," *LHQ* 1–26 [1917–43]); the Acts and Deliberations of the Cabildo, 1769–1803, NOPL (selected documents transcribed and translated in "The Cabildo Archives," ed. Henry P. Dart, trans. Heloise H. Cruzat, *LHQ* 3–5 [1920–22]); Conseil de Ville, Official Proceedings, 1803–1829, NOPL; and Conseil de Ville, Ordinances and Resolutions, 1803–1836, NOPL. For a guide to, and selected translations of, the Cabildo Records, see Ronald R. Morazán, "A Translation of the Letters, Petitions, and Decrees of the Cabildo of New Orleans for the Year 1800" (MA thesis, Louisiana State University, 1967), and Ronald R. Morazán, "Letters, Petitions, and Decrees of the Cabildo of New Orleans, 1800–1803: Edited and Translated" (PhD diss., Louisiana State University, 1972).

In contrast to officials, who produced voluminous amounts of documentation, few nonofficial eighteenth-century Louisianans recorded their thoughts for us to peruse, in great part because few could read or write beyond their signature. Further, there were no local newspapers until the 1790s. There are a few extant collections of letters and other personal documents of prominent Euro-Louisianan families. These include the Rosemonde E. and Emile Kuntz Collection, 1655–1878, HT (indexed in *The Rosemonde E. and Emile Kuntz Collection, Donated by Felix H. Kuntz, Collector: A Catalogue of the Manuscripts and Printed Ephemera,* ed. Guillermo Náñez Falcón [New Orleans, 1981]); Favrot Family Papers, 1695–1937, HT (published as *The Favrot Family Papers: A Documentary Chronicle of Early Louisiana,* ed. Guillermo Náñez Falcón, 5 vols. [(New Orleans), 1988–2001]); *Le Chevalier de Pradel: Vie d'un colo français en Louisiane au XVIII° siècle d'après sa correspondance et celle de sa famille,* ed. A. Baillardel and A. Prioult (Paris, 1928); and Letters of Baron Joseph X. Pontalba to His Wife, 1796, HT. There are also four early memoirs written by Europeans who resided in the colony for a substantial length of time during the French era (one of which was written by a carpenter and thus offers rare access to one working Euro-Louisianan's thoughts): Jean François Benjamin Dumont de Montigny, *Mémoires historiques sur la Louisiane, contenant ce qui y est arrivé de plus mémorable depuis l'année 1687 jusqu'à present,* ed. Jean Baptiste Le Mascrier, 2 vols. (Paris, 1753); Antoine Simon Le Page du Pratz, *Histoire de Louisiane, contenant la découverte de ce vaste pays,* 3 vols. (Paris, 1758) (for a translation, see Antoine Simon Le Page du Pratz, *The History of Louisiana: Translated from the French of M. Le Page du Pratz,* ed. Joseph G. Tregle Jr. [1774; rpt., Baton Rouge, La., 1975]); Jean Bernard Bossu, *Nouveaux voyages aux Indes Occidentales, contenant une relation des différens peuples qui habitent les environs du grand fleuve Saint-Louis appelé vulgairement le Mississipi,* 2 vols. (Paris, 1768) (for a translation, see M. [Jean Bernard] Bossu, *Travels through That Part of North America Formerly Called Louisiana,* trans. John Reinhold Forster, 2 vols. [London, 1771]); and André Pénicaut, *Fleur de Lys and Calumet: Being the Pénicaut Narrative of French Adventure in Louisiana,* ed. and trans. Richebourg Gaillard McWilliams (Tuscaloosa, Ala., 1988).

Although official reports and memoirs written by prominent planters can be usefully probed for an expression of their hopes and fears, a second set of sources allows the diligent researcher to begin to uncover how ordinary New Orleanians behaved, which, in turn, can be used to analyze how successful elite efforts were. Among these are court records, censuses, sacramental registries, and notarial acts. No where in the evidentiary base for New Orleans can the voices of elites and ordinary New Orleanians be found together as clearly as in court records. Despite some restrictions, slaves, soldiers, free people of color, petty merchants, small farmers, and great planters, as well as judges, scribes, and governmental officials might, in any given case, be allowed to speak. Two sets of cases were especially important to the research for this book. The first were contested manumissions, especially from the Spanish and post–Louisiana Purchase eras; the second were probate hearings and suits involving contested wills, which were almost nonexistent in the eighteenth century, that are especially revealing of racially exogamous families and the struggles they endured after the Louisiana Purchase. The French-era court records are contained in the already cited Records of the Superior Council. For the Spanish era, see Spanish Judicial Records, 1769–1803, Louisiana State Museum (microfilm copies at most New Orleans repositories, including the Tulane University Law Library; for indexes and abstracts, see "Index to the Spanish Judicial Records of Louisiana," *LHQ* 6–31 [1923–48]; for an index of criminal cases, see Derek Noel Kerr, *Petty Felony, Slave Defiance and Frontier Villainy: Crime and Criminal Justice in Spanish Louisiana, 1770–1803* [New York, 1993]). The Louisiana Division of the New Orleans Public Libraries is the repository for the city and parish court records from the first half of the nineteenth century including: First Judicial District Court (Orleans Parish), Suit Records, 1813–46; Office of the Mayor, Decisions of the Mayor in Criminal Cases, 1823–32; Orleans Parish, Court of Probates, Suit Records, 1805–1846, and Will Books, 1805–1846; Orleans Parish Court, Suit Records, 1813–46, and Petitions for the Emancipation of Slaves, 1814–1843; and Territory of Orleans, Superior Court, Suit Records, 1804–1813. The Supreme Court of Louisiana Historical Archives, 1813–1920, are housed at the Earl K. Long Library, Special Collections, University of New Orleans.

Richly detailed testimony in many other cases was also useful, as witnesses often offhandedly described social conditions in the fledgling city. In addition to the secular courts, New Orleans had an ecclesiastical court that oversaw religious matters, including marriage, and the proceedings of these courts include limpieza de sangre suits and parental opposition to children's spousal choices. For these cases, see Court Proceedings of Esteban de Quiñones, 1778–1802; Court Proceedings of Francisco Broutin, 1790–99; and Court Proceedings of Narcisse Broutin, 1795–1802, all housed at NONA.

Censuses can be read for the information they contain about the numbers of free persons of color and racially exogamous families, although they cannot generate precise numbers because of the problems of labeling and undercounting examined in chapter 2. As importantly, they can be analyzed for the ways in which censuses takers organized New Orleanians into different categories, using gender, age, status, and in addition to, and sometimes instead of, ancestry. Original French- and Spanish-era censuses and other population enumerations can be found in the collections of official correspondence cited above. French-era censuses are also contained in Archives de Colonies, Archives nationales de France, section Outre-Mer, état civil recensements, 1706–41 (microfilm copy at HNOC), and Passagers, series F5b, 1717–65; transcriptions of selected originals can be found at the Manuscripts Division, Library of Congress. The original *Census of New Orleans,* November 6, 1791, is held in the Louisiana Division of the New Orleans Public Library. Many censuses have been compiled and translated for easier access. See, for example, *The Census Tables for the French Colony of Louisiana from 1699 through 1732,* ed. Charles R. Maduell Jr. (Baltimore, Md., 1972); *The First Families of Louisiana,* comp. and trans. Glenn R. Conrad, 2 vols. (Baton Rouge, La., 1970); *Louisiana Census and Militia Lists, 1770–1789,* ed. Albert J. Robichaux (Harvey, La., 1973–74); and *Some Late Eighteenth-Century Louisianians: Census Records 1758–1796,* comp. and trans. Jacqueline K. Voorhies (Lafayette, La., 1973).

The richest sources for examining everyday practices and creating a depiction that is more than just numbers are the Catholic Church's sacramental registries and the city's notarial archives, in which every sale, commercial transaction, manumission, and will were recorded. Sacramental registries for St. Louis Cathedral and surrounding parishes, in which priests recorded all baptisms, marriages, and funerals that they performed, are rich sources for examining the development of racial categories, the incidences of racial exogamy and the changing perceptions of it, and the connections or ruptures among New Orleans' families of all ancestries. French priests usually kept three books—one for each type of sacrament— but Spanish priests instituted the practice of keeping two sets of parallel books: one for blancos, the other for all others. This practice generally began when the registries started during the late French era had been filled and lasted long after the Spanish had left. The St. Louis Cathedral registries include baptisms, marriages, and funerals, 1731–33; baptisms, 1744–59 (2 vols.); baptisms and marriages, 1759–66 (2 vols.); baptisms, 1767–76 (2 vols.); baptisms of negros and mulatos, 1777–1820 (12 vols., various titles); baptisms [of blancos], 1777–1825 (7 vols.); funerals, 1772–90; funerals of negros and mulatos, 1793–1803 (2 vols., various titles); funerals [of blancos], 1784–1815 (6 vols.); marriages, 1720–30, 1764–74 (2 vols.); marriages of negros and mulatos, 1777–1830 (1 vol.); and marriages [of blancos], 1777–1830 (4 vols.). I also used the St. Charles Borromeo registry of baptisms, marriages, and funerals, 1739–55. All of these registries are housed at Archives of the Archdiocese of New Orleans.

Beginning in 1987, the Archives of the Archdiocese began publishing translations of the sacramental records (*Sacramental Records of the Roman Catholic Church of the Archdiocese of*

New Orleans, vols. 1–7, ed. Earl C. Woods and Charles E. Nolan [New Orleans, 1987–92]; vols. 8–18, ed. Charles E. Nolan and Dorenda Dupont, trans. J. Edgar Burns [New Orleans, 1993–2003]). In addition to making some of the information contained in the registries more widely accessible, these volumes serve as an excellent index, but, unfortunately, only for those to whom the priests gave surnames. In addition, the published volumes have omitted any references to racial labels or to birth status, making it necessary to consult the original registers. Published translations of sacramental records of Mobile, Natchitoches, and Opelousas also exist: see *Love's Legacy: The Mobile Marriages Recorded in French, Transcribed, with Annotated Abstracts in English, 1724–1786,* ed. Jacqueline Olivier Vidrine (Lafayette, La., 1985); *Sacramental Records of the Roman Catholic Church of the Archdiocese of Mobile,* ed. Michael L. Farmer (Mobile, Ala., 2002); *Natchitoches, 1729–1803: Abstracts of the Catholic Church Registers of the French and Spanish Post of St. Jean Baptiste des Natchitoches in Louisiana,* comp. Elizabeth Shown Mills (New Orleans, 1977); and *Marriage Contracts of the Opelousas Post, 1766–1803,* trans. and abstr. Jacqueline Olivier Vidrine and Winston De Ville (Ville Platte, La., 1960).

If the sacramental registries reveal the intimate connections among New Orleanians, the notarial archives reveal their everyday, often prosaic but sometimes momentous, interactions. Governed by civil law that required all economic transactions and contracts to be recorded by a notary, New Orleanians of the eighteenth and early nineteenth century left behind an enormously rich source documenting of their day-to-day activities, comprising more than 350 bound volumes, containing tens of thousand of individual acts. Notaries preserved records of sales and donations of slaves and property, financial agreements, powers of attorney, and, most importantly for this project, manumissions and wills. The notarial acts consulted for this book were those of Juan Bautista Garic (1771–79), Andrés Almonester y Roxas (1771–82), Leonardo Mazange (1779–83), Rafael Perdomo (1782–90), Fernando Rodríguez (1783–88), Pierre Pedesclaux (1788–1814), Francisco Broutin (1790–99), Carlos Ximénez (1790–1803), Narcisse Broutin (1799–1811; to distinguish between Francisco and Narcisse Broutin's records, citations to their court proceedings, as well as their notarial acts, include their first initials), Hugues Lavergne (1803–13), John Lynd (1805–20), Benjamin van Pradelles (1806–8), Michel de Armas (1809–23), Marc Lafitte (1810–26), and Philippe Pedesclaux (1816–26; to distinguish between Pierre and Philippe Pedesclaux in the notes, references to the latter include his full name), all housed at NONA. At least some of Estevan Quiñones' acts have been compiled and translated in *Love, Honor and Betrayal: The Notarial Acts of Estevan de Quiñones, 1778–1784,* trans. and abstr. Elizabeth Becker Gianelloni (Baton Rouge, La., 1964), and *The Notarial Acts of Estevan de Quiñones, 1785–1786,* trans. Elizabeth Becker Gianelloni (1964). For studies of manumissions, Gwendolyn Midlo Hall has provided an invaluable resource in the form of a CD-ROM (*Databases for the Study of Afro-Louisiana History and Genealogy, 1699–1860: Computerized Information from Original Manuscript Sources,* ed. Gwendolyn Midlo, Hall, CD-ROM ed. [Baton Rouge, La., 2000]) containing information on almost every manumission and slave sale in Louisiana through the long eighteenth century, many of which are originally notarial acts and can be found in the volumes cited above. The CD-ROM also includes censuses, maps, and images. The New Orleans Notarial Archives is moving toward creating electronically searchable indexes that will greatly facilitate future research, enabling even richer stories to be retold (NONA, *Guide to the French Colonial Records (1733–1767)* [New Orleans, 2007], www.notarialarchives.org/research.htm [accessed June 9, 2008]).

HISTORIANS HAVE LONG been interested in the intersection of race and sex in the early Americas. Until recently, the driving question was why it happened more in some colonies and less in others. One answer, the cultural argument, focused on the sociohistorical and cultural aspects of the colonizing nation. Spanish and Portuguese colonizers, these historians argued, had a long history of interactions, including sexual relations, with people of different cultures, and more importantly, with those of a darker color, namely Moors and other northern Africans. In contrast, most northern Europeans, especially the British, lacked this experience of culture interactions and thus they were more suspicious of interracial contacts. Among those who take this position are Gilberto Freyre, *The Masters and the Slaves: A Study in the Development of Brazilian Civilization,* trans. Samuel Putnam, 2nd rev. ed. (1956; rpt., Berkeley, Calif., 1986), 4, 84; Magnus Mörner, *Race Mixture in the History of Latin America* (Boston, 1967); Carl N. Degler, *Neither Black Nor White: Slavery and Race Relations in Brazil and the United States* (Madison, Wisc., 1971); Joel Williamson, *New People: Miscegenation and Mulattoes in the United States* (New York, 1980); David D. Smits, "'Abominable Mixture': The Repudiation of Anglo-Indian Intermarriage in Seventeenth-Century Virginia," *Virginia Magazine of History and Biography* 95 (1987): 157–92; and David D. Smits, "'We Are Not to Grow Wild': Seventeenth-Century New England's Repudiation of Anglo-Indian Intermarriage," *American Indian Culture and Research Journal* 11 (1987): 1–32.

The argument that the cultural attitudes of the colonizing nation explained the presence or absence of racially exogamous sex was seriously challenged by historians who noted that colonies governed and peopled by the same European nation, such as British Barbados and New England, had very different histories. Instead, these scholars pointed to demography, particularly sex ratios among the European population and the ratios of Africans, Indians, and Europeans in any specific place. A scarcity of European women, they argued, in conjunction with a preponderance of Indians and/or Africans, led European men to find sexual and domestic partners among local non-European populations. Historians who emphasize demography over culture include Winthrop Jordan, *White Over Black: American Attitudes Toward the Negro, 1550–1812* (Chapel Hill, N.C., 1968); Gary B. Nash, "The Hidden History of Mestizo America," *JAH* 82 (1995): 941–62; and Philip D. Morgan, "British Encounters with Africans and African-Americans, circa 1600–1780," in *Strangers Within the Realm: Cultural Margins of the First British Empire,* ed. Bernard Bailyn and Morgan (Chapel Hill, N.C., 1991), 157–219.

The demographic explanation does adequately account for general patterns of differences and similarities among disparate colonies, but most historians who argue this perspective assume a kind of demographic determinism—European men sought sex with whatever partners were available—that takes into account neither the social construction of sexuality nor women's agency, however slight and constrained by gender, race, and class (for demographic interpretations that do take women's choices into account, see B. W. Higman, *Slave Population and Economy in Jamaica, 1807–1834* [Cambridge, England, 1976], 143–46, and Kimberly S. Hanger, *Bounded Lives, Bounded Places: Free Black Society in Co-*

lonial New Orleans, 1769–1803 [Durham, N.C., 1997]). Neither interpretation comfortably explains the presence of racial exogamy where the basis of interaction between groups is trade rather than slavery. Here, the tendency is to focus on the pragmatic needs of both Europeans, on the one hand, and Indians or Africans, on the other. See, for example, George E. Brooks Jr., "The *Signares* of Saint-Louis and Gorée: Women Entrepreneurs in Eighteenth-Century Senegal," in *Women in Africa: Studies in Social and Economic Change,* ed. Nancy J. Hafkin and Edna G. Bay (Stanford, Calif., 1976); William B. Cohen, *The French Encounter with Africans: White Response to Blacks, 1530–1880* (Bloomington, Ind., 1980); Sylvia Van Kirk, *Many Tender Ties: Women in Fur-Trade Society, 1670–1870* (Norman, Okla., 1983); and Tanis C. Thorne, *The Many Hands of My Relations: French and Indians on the Lower Missouri* (Columbia, Mo., 1996).

Given that is unlikely that the frequency of these relationships will ever be accurately pinned down, due to the nature of the evidence, recent scholarship has wisely moved away from the question of how much, where, and why. Rather, this literature has focused on the role that sex (and gender) played in constructing race. Investigating locations as far flung as seventeenth-century Anglo-Virginia and twentieth-century Dutch Indonesia, historians and anthropologists have examined how tropes of race, gender, and sexuality informed and justified imperialism. This body of work includes Ann L. Stoler, *Carnal Knowledge and Imperial Power: Race and the Intimate in Colonial Rule* (Berkeley, Calif., 2002); Robyn Wiegman, "The Anatomy of Lynching," *Journal of the History of Sexuality* 3 (1993): 467; Anne McClintock, *Imperial Leather: Race, Gender and Sexuality in the Colonial Contest* (New York, 1995); Robert J. C. Young, *Colonial Desire: Hybridity in Theory, Culture and Race* (New York, 1995); Kathleen M. Brown, *Good Wives, Nasty Wenches, and Anxious Patriarchs: Gender, Race, and Power in Colonial Virginia* (Chapel Hill, N.C., 1996); Kirsten Fischer, *Suspect Relations: Sex, Race, and Resistance in Colonial North Carolina* (Ithaca, N.Y., 2001); Jennifer L. Morgan, *Laboring Women: Reproduction and Gender in New World Slavery* (Philadelphia, 2004); and Sharon Block, *Rape and Sexual Power in Early America* (Chapel Hill, N.C., 2006). Such work has demonstrated that the regulation of sex was one of the pivotal axes around which categories of difference were constructed in colonial societies.

Italic page numbers refer to illustrations. Individuals who are discussed on only a single page are not included in this index.